GOVERNANCE, INDUSTRY AND LABOUR MARKETS IN BRITAIN AND FRANCE

This volume brings together well-known scholars from a wide range of disciplines to provide a meticulous analytical and historical overview of how state policy has affected established economic and labour market systems in Britain and France.

While economic growth and stable employment have been major objectives of government policy in both nations, contrasting political conventions have shaped the nature and extent of state intervention in economic affairs. The contributors to this book explore some of the crucial questions: How 'dirigiste' was the French state in reality? Why was state intervention less acceptable in Britain than in France? How do differences in state intervention help explain the respective economic performance of the two countries since the second world war?

This book illuminates the distinctive frameworks of governance within which issues of industrial relations, technical training, economic policy, social security and social justice have been constructed in Britain and France. These frameworks have evolved from differences in expectations of state action, in the conventions governing co-ordination between economic agents, and in the state's role in fostering effective performance.

The book draws on hitherto unpublished primary research by scholars in economic and social history, industrial relations, economics, law, political science, sociology and social policy. It provides a welcome and timely intervention into debate on the politics of modern labour markets specifically, and the role of the state in economic modernisation generally. The book will appeal to researchers and students in several disciplines, and to public servants in many countries.

Noel Whiteside is Reader in Public Policy at Bristol University, **Robert Salais** is Director of the CNRS Research Centre 'Institutions, Emploie et Politique Economique' (IEPE) in Paris.

ROUTLEDGE STUDIES IN THE EUROPEAN ECONOMY

GOVERNANCE, INDUSTRY AND LABOUR MARKETS IN BRITAIN AND FRANCE

The modernising state in the mid-twentieth century

Edited by
Noel Whiteside and Robert Salais

London and New York

First published 1998
by Routledge
11 New Fetter Lane, London EC4P 4EE

Simultaneously published in the USA and Canada
by Routledge
29 West 35th Street, New York, NY 10001

© 1998 Noel Whiteside and Robert Salais

Typeset in Garamond by Keystroke, Jacaranda Lodge, Wolverhampton
Printed and bound in Great Britain by Biddles Ltd, Guildford and King's Lyn

British Library Cataloguing in Publication Data
A catalogue record for this book is available from the British Library

Library of Congress Cataloging in Publication Data
A catalogue record for this book has been requested.

ISBN 0–415–15733–1

CONTENTS

CONTENTS

FIGURES AND TABLES

Figures

Table

CONTRIBUTORS

BRITISH CONTRIBUTORS

Keith Burgess is Reader in History at the Roehampton Institute, London. He is author of *The Challenge of Labour* (Croom Helm, London, 1979) and of several articles in academic journals on the history of industrial training.

Simon Deakin is a lecturer in law and Fellow of Peterhouse at the University of Cambridge. He is Assistant Director of the ESRC Centre for Business Research at Cambridge. His interests lie principally in labour and security law and in the economic theory and analysis of law. He has published in a variety of academic journals on these subjects in both France and Britain.

James Gillespie is head of Politics at the University of Macquarie, Sydney, Australia. He is author of *The Price of Health* (Cambridge University Press, Cambridge, 1991) and co-editor of *Developments in Australian Politics* (Macmillan, London, 1994). He has also published a number of articles on the London labour market in academic journals and books.

Roy Mankelow's thesis *The Effects of Modernisation and Change in the London Docks* was awarded a DPhil by Cambridge University in 1994.

Nick Tiratsoo is Senior Research Fellow at the University of Luton and Research Fellow at the Business History Unit at the London School of Economics. He has edited books on the Attlee and Wilson governments; he authored *Reconstruction, Affluence and Labour Politics: Coventry 1945–60* (Routledge, London, 1992) and co-authored *Industrial Efficiency and State Intervention* (Routledge, London, 1993) with Jim Tomlinson. He has recently published *England Arise* (Manchester University Press, Manchester, 1994) with Steven Fielding and Peter Thompson and is currently working on a history of British management in the postwar period.

Noel Whiteside is Reader in Public Policy at Bristol University. She co-edited *Aux sources de chômage* (Editions Belin, Paris, 1994) with Robert Salais.

She is author of *Bad Times* (Faber & Faber, London, 1991) and co-author of *Casual Labour* (Oxford University Press, London, 1986) with Gordon Phillips, as well as numerous articles in academic journals and books addressing state policy and labour market issues. She is currently completing a book, *Wages and Welfare*, for Macmillan.

Frank Willkinson heads the Department of Applied Economics at Cambridge University and is Director of the ESRC Centre for Business Research. In the course of a long and distinguished career, he has published extensively in the field of industrial relations and employment change in the twentieth century, most recently co-editing *Employers Strategies and the Labour Market* (Oxford University Press, London, 1994) with Jill Rubery.

Jonathan Zeitlin is Professor of History, Sociology and Industrial Relations at the University of Wisconsin-Madison. He has written widely on British and comparative industrial and labour history; his publications include *Shop Floor Bargaining and the State* (Cambridge University Press, Cambridge, 1986) and *The Power to Manage? Employers and Industrial Relations in Comparative-Historical Perspective* (Routledge, London, 1991) – both co-edited with Steven Tolliday; *World of Possibilities: Flexibility and Mass Production in Western Industrialisation,* co-edited with Charles Sabel (Cambridge University Press, Cambridge, 1996). He is currently completing *Between Flexibility and Mass Production: Strategic Debate and Industrial Organisation, 1830–1990* for Oxford University Press.

FRENCH CONTRIBUTORS

Françoise Birck is a historian and a researcher at ARESSLI (Association de recherches et d'études en sciences sociales sur la Lorraine industrielle). She is the author of numerous articles in academic journals and is currently editing a book on the history of training in twentieth-century France.

Claude Didry is a sociologist; he is employed on permanent research at two CNRS-funded Centres: CIRCID (Centre de recherches critiques sur le droit – Saint-Etienne) and IEPE (Institutions, emploie et politique economique – Paris). He is the author of a number of articles in academic journals on the development of legal judgments in the field of employment law and work contracts and is currently writing a book on this subject.

Philippe-Jean Hesse is Professor of History at the Université de Nantes and researcher at the research centre (Droit et changement sociale) co-funded by the CNRS there. He specialises in the history of social security and is currently preparing a book on this subject.

Michel Margairaz is Professor of Economic History at the Université de Paris VIII and also works at the Banque de France. He is author of *L'Etat, l'économie et les finances*, 2 vols (Imprimerie Nationale, Paris, 1991) as well as numerous articles in academic journals on economic change and its relationship with public policy in this period.

Robert Salais, Director of the CNRS research centre 'Institutions, emploie et politique économique' (IEPE), is an economist who specialises in the history of industry and work. His extensive publications include *L'invention du chômage* (PUF, Paris, 1986) with Nicolas Bavarez and Benedicte Reynaud; *Aux sources du chômage* (Editions Belin, Paris, 1994) co-edited with Malcolm Mansfield and Noel Whiteside; *Les mondes de production. Enquête sur l'identité économique de la France* (Editions de l'EHESS, Paris, 1993), published in English as *Worlds of Production: The Action Frameworks of the Economy* (Harvard University Press, 1997) co-authored by Michael Storper.

Michelle Zancarini-Fournel works at the Université de Paris VIII, where she is Maître de conferences in contemporary social history at the Jean Bouvier Centre. She co-edits *CLIO: histoire, femmes et sociétés* is co-author of *Parscours de femmes: realités et représentations* (PUL, Lyon, 1993) with Mathilde Dubesset, and co-edited *Differences des sexes et protection sociale, XIXe–XXe siècles* (PUV, Paris, 1995) with Leora Auslander.

ACKNOWLEDGEMENTS

The editors wish to thank the following organisations for their financial support for seminar meetings of contributors and for research for this book: the Economic and Social Research Council (ESRC), the British Council (Paris), the MIRE (Ministère des Affaires Sociales), le Centre Jean Bouvier (Université de Paris VIII) and the Centre nationale de la recherche scientifique (CNRS). We should also like to thank the Leverhulme Trust for providing the funds for translating French contributions into English.

We also wish to acknowledge the work of our translators:

S. Taponier: Chapter 1: Introduction and Chapter 4 (Robert Salais);
L. Parrott and F. Brunet: Chapter 2 (Michel Margairaz) and Chapter 9 (Michelle Zancarini-Fournel);
M. Mansfield and J. Wood: Chapter 6 (Françoise Birck) and Chapter 8 (Claude Didry);
E. Boccaletti: Chapter 10 (Philippe-Jean Hesse).

1

INTRODUCTION

Political economy and modernisation[1]

Noel Whiteside and Robert Salais

The modernisation that took place in Britain and France in the mid-twentieth century was driven by new forms of state intervention and labour market regulation. These developed from the promotion of industrial modernisation and the growth of public sector employment, particularly the expansion of nationalisation and state welfare. After the second world war, new products to meet new needs and new markets appeared, realising the technological potential of the interwar years. This involved change – in specific industrial sectors, in the organisation of work, in the construction of skill, in the nature of industrial bargaining. Changed modes of economic thought fostered novel assumptions about the powers of the state as an agency for social and economic amelioration. The success of state action in promoting new economic and social systems, however, demanded the acceptance by established interests (employers, workers, financial institutions) of the terms within which policy was now being discussed, the internalisation of new macro-economic modes of labour market analysis and co-operation with new official agencies created to co-ordinate and implement policy. For this to happen (and both countries experienced resistance to this extension of state powers), existing diversities in labour management, in economic co-ordination, in working conventions and agreements had to conform to new political and economic orthodoxies. In general terms, established forms of collective co-ordination, which shaped economic activity among entrepreneurs, workers and public authorities at local and national level, had to readjust continuously to accommodate changing conditions. Such adjustments, the different ways actors adapted according to product, branch, region and scope for collective action, created new typologies of state intervention.

These developments depended fundamentally on changing established expectations about the role the state should play in the economy. There is a complex interaction between the nature of products in which an economy specialises internationally – in terms of their diversity, their markets, their responsiveness to changing demand, their production systems, their working conventions – and the types of government intervention that may prove acceptable. When seeking to modernise industry, Britain's postwar leaders confronted a variety of barriers: the duty to protect sterling, the variance of product standards found in international markets for British exports, the diversity of production systems and – partly following from this – the orientation of both sides of industry towards *laissez-faire* government. Over and above this last factor, but partly rooted in it, the view that it was best to let industry manage its own affairs translated into weak state training and manpower policies. State-sponsored rationalisation, standardisation or modernisation was thereby rendered extremely difficult. Sectors of the ruling elite – including some industrialists and trade union leaders – might be convinced of the merits of state direction and planning, but the conversion of employers, workers and financial interests to this new perspective was much more problematic. By contrast, the assumption that it was the state's duty to protect the national general interest endowed the French government with responsibility for the rational organisation of industrial infrastructure, the basic industries and, with trade union consent, standardised work practices – developments which all reflected confidence in the benefits of state action. This helped sustain political consensus for a model of economic growth which gave priority to internal markets and the satisfaction of national requirements, a strategy which, initially at least, was to prove highly successful.

CONVENTIONS, GOVERNANCE AND THE POLITICS OF STATE INTERVENTION

In short, to explore the successful establishment of full employment, state welfare and economic policy, it is necessary to understand the political context within which policy was developed, the ways in which it influenced established ways of thinking – as well as the means used to secure change. This book does not analyse policy from the perspective of the state machine itself. Rather, it reveals the limits of official intervention by examining its outcomes in specific locations and industrial contexts. Different social and economic interests expected state intervention to secure different objectives. As the heterogeneity of expectations did not diminish in this period (there was no reason why it should), and as established systems of co-ordination were so diverse, sources of conflict between ostensibly legitimate demands for state action were numerous – and differed between Britain and France. State intervention had to be responsive if it was to be effective; if extensively contested, official intervention could prove counterproductive. So government had to create compromise, both pragmatic and political. State intervention, in short, was shaped collectively by all agents, including the bureaucracy, within specified contexts. In this respect, our analysis modifies the arguments of public choice theory by exposing the socio-political factors defining the spheres of effective state action.

The problem was further complicated by diverse conceptions of what the legitimate – and thus acceptable – principles governing state intervention ought to be. Four broad conventions for the proper role of government in regulating economic affairs can be determined from the contributions to this book. These are present in both countries in varying degrees and help explain the different types of governance established in France and Britain during the twentieth century.

The first assumes that all official intervention is not only pointless, but also counterproductive. In Britain, the experience of slump and war converted many on the political left to the merits of direct state planning. Yet no political framework existed within which state corporatist structures with executive powers might legitimately be introduced, unless this involved direct nationalisation. Even after the war, most employers and many trade unionists anticipated the adaptation of voluntary association and collective bargaining to the promotion of industrial policies and employment reform in the private sector. Conventions of industrial self-governance helped stimulate the adoption of consensual tripartism as the main mechanism for industrial modernisation. The postwar creation of representative advisory committees and development councils, devoid of all executive authority, typified this approach. State intervention to promote collective association and agreement through the creation of joint industrial councils and wages councils was welcomed; permanent official interference in the operation of these bodies was not. Established expectations concerning proper decision-making processes based on voluntary association proved hard to shift; efforts to superimpose state authority tended to stimulate criticism, particularly from employers, that such extensions of official powers represented an improper invasion of the rights of private property.

Such suspicion of government finds its roots in the ideas of economic liberalism. Yet the political conventions manifest here do not align well with arguments supporting a free market based on individual self-interest. To secure such conditions (our second framework for state action), government must intervene to outlaw the creation of associations, monopolies or barriers to entry formed by specified competences – not to promote them. As market co-ordination is founded on individual freedom, paradoxically this 'free market' state comes to violate it own principles. The state does intervene, often in an authoritarian fashion. Any reader of the minutes of the postwar Anglo-American Council on Productivity (created in 1948 following the introduction of the US Marshall Plan) will note the very different expectations of state obligations towards trade associations displayed by American and British employers. The latter assumed that such organisations were ideal vehicles through which government should promote industrial policy: the former that the state should outlaw their very existence. In both cases, government's duty was associated with the promotion of free markets. In both cases, government was expected to 'regulate in' the conditions for this to happen, an expectation which extended from national to international policy (and the restoration of free trade), as Barry Eichengreen has recently demonstrated.[2] However, Britain's postwar attempts to regulate against monopoly (introduced in response to American pressure) remained weak and confused. In the late 1940s, competition on the domestic market was absent, thanks to the persistence of foreign exchange and trade controls. Government proved reluctant to eliminate business cartels, which had been positively encouraged in the 1930s as a means to protect British trade interests during the slump years. The voluntarist conventions underpinning British governance cannot be readily equated with forms of economic liberalism found in the United States.

Within both these systems, however, there is no 'common good' other than that which is engendered through the promotion of private goods. The other two conventions look to the state to define and achieve a common good which, if not transcending private interests, requires their conformity. The third framework for state activity involves official participation determining the forms and nature of collective action, which the French call *l'Etat subsidiaire*.[3] The actors themselves define autonomously a common good suited to their situation, their problems and their perceptions of both, with official encouragement. The state initiates this defining process, guarantees that fundamental criteria are respected, makes resources available to help achieve the common goal. The nationalisations of the French Third Republic typify this approach. In the transport industries and general public utilities, operational decisions concerning appropriate technologies and financial systems were left to the most qualified and capable; industrialists defined the most appropriate techniques, local authorities determined definitions of need. Official financial assistance was conditional on conformity to agreed principles governing public services (open access and common charges in line with the republican virtues of equality and liberty).

The fourth principle for state intervention, as clearly visible then as now, is that of the external dirigiste state. As interventionist as the free market state, although from the opposite direction, this enforces global policies – macro-economic or macro-social – to secure a common good which it has a duty to define and impose. The French state of the postwar years was master of the general interest. As our contributors show, the state engineer corps (*corps d'ingénieurs*) and senior civil servants (*hauts fonctionnaires*) were professionally charged with defining the general interest in their own specific areas of expertise. While British governments remained largely orientated towards varying conceptions of the free market, the postwar French state promoted the organised market as the surest way to achieve the supreme common good:

full employment. When efforts were made to adapt French methods to solve Britain's industrial problems following the London Conference of 1961 (which produced the National Economic Development Council, among other bodies), the strategy failed – not because the concept was flawed, but because the necessary socio-political substructure (a technologically informed bureaucracy, collective faith in the merits of state action) was not strong enough to sustain its effective operation.

These various conventions of governance are less real, sociologically observable principles than possible frameworks legitimating state action, allowing agents (firms, workers) to act on the basis of *expectations* of plausible policy interventions which would offer them the means to secure their own future. The efficacy of collective action is directly dependent on whether these collective expectations can form a coherent whole. In the conception of governance we promote, it is the convergence of actors' objectives and anticipations in one form or another which creates the corresponding form of government, not the official institutions by themselves. There is every chance that there is not one state, but many possible 'states' in both France and Britain, whose principles of action vary by area and over different periods of time. Even as we note the dominance of one form of governance in a specific period, the plurality of possible forms of governance[4] shapes conflict between groups and contributes to the dynamic history of economies analysed in this book; because the actual state, which economic agents face and which shapes their choices, continues to evolve, in response to pressures towards alternative possibilities.

The consequences of these differences in spheres of state intervention and frameworks of policy form the comparative theme of this book; the 'modernisation' of employment and labour markets is the focus for our attention. This perspective allows economic and social policy initiatives to be explored from an angle different from that usually used in historical discussions to explain the state's 'presence' in this area. This, we argue, allows a better and more comprehensive appreciation of the comparative development of 'institutional effects' resulting from official intervention in our economies than explanations which focus simply on comparative expenditure, on structural historical determinants or on empirical features of public institutions.

MODERNISATION AND THE SPHERE OF INDUSTRIAL POLITICS

The slump years set the agenda for labour market reform, although this agenda was focused on the issue of full employment in Britain and on economic recovery in France. In the mid-1940s, such issues became inextricably entangled with reconstruction, industrial modernisation and productivity, all central to the establishment of postwar economic growth. This is the area covered by the first six contributions.

In much Anglo-Saxon historiography, the United States – implicitly or explicitly – appears as a model of economic modernity which other nations have sought to emulate. The largest and most powerful economy in the world offered a paradigm to other western democracies in terms of industrial standardisation and systems of mass production, technological innovation, high productivity, professional costing systems and labour management. Under the Marshall Plan and the subsequent technical assistance programmes, the adaptation of American methods and know-how to aid European recovery became one of the main objectives of American foreign policy. It is true that French and British managers and trade unionists visited America to explore American best practice. It is also true that postwar governments on both sides of the Channel issued reports on the advantages of American production systems and provided a variety of incentives to industry to adopt them.

Nevertheless, as the chapters of Jonathan Zeitlin and Robert Salais on the engineering industries in Britain and France both suggest, American influence was heavily filtered and re-interpreted within the context of national working conventions and entrepreneurial traditions. Those study trips to the United States repeated well-established prewar practice among industrialists from both countries. Of the two principles of mass production (standardisation and the creation of large-scale markets), André Citroën and Louis Renault aimed chiefly at the first, which both adopted and adapted. The application was only partial; both preserved their large pool of craftsmen to serve varied, specialised markets – notably the profitable armaments market. Prewar French engineering and electrical industries drew their strength from the concentration around Paris of a skilled labour force and a variety of highly specialised products. These advantages continued after the war and the reorientation of the industry towards mass production was compromised with production methods reliant on worker know-how. This was achieved because the industry benefited from a favourable macro-economic environment (lower input prices, rising public procurement) generated for it by public modernisation programmes involving both infrastructure and the basic industries.

Similarly, American methods and their applicability to domestic conditions had long been studied in Britain. While appreciating advantages of cost reduction and economies of scale, critics noted the inflexibility of equipment dedicated to mass production, the additional cost of organisation and the risks to future innovation of standardisation. British engineering required flexible production methods to maintain competitive advantage in diversified, international markets. Economies of scale – competing on price rather than product variety or quality – made sense in the context of a large, homogeneous domestic market, but exporters needed to adapt manufacturing plant to short-run orders, while chronic steel shortages constrained extensive re-equipment. This did not prevent some firms selectively appropriating innovations likely to improve products without impairing flexibility. However, employers remained dependent on worker and trade union control over labour organisation, which might obstruct modernisation, unless changes in work practices could be agreed. Further, higher productivity through standardisation and rationalisation was more easily introduced alongside new investment; the product, the way of producing it and the product market all had to change together, requiring the renegotiation of working conditions and wages. Such conditions, available in France thanks to public investment, were not present in Britain. Labour shortages, the urgency of the export drive (and the defence of sterling) meant that higher productivity had to be achieved in the absence of additional resources. Under such circumstances, new systems might appear to be a direct attack on mutually acceptable working arrangements already taken for granted or whose postwar restoration was eagerly anticipated.

State-directed industrial modernisation thus remained highly controversial and problematic in Britain during the immediate postwar reconstruction period, when conflicts within the government between the promoters of central planning and the defenders of economic voluntarism were most marked. In contrast, macro-economic policies to secure the stability of sterling were commonly anticipated. These translated into the promotion of the common good by securing the pound as a world trading currency and by promoting the security of Empire. In the long run, policy failed to secure both objectives, since they were at odds with each other. By the late 1950s, British industry was losing world market share in its traditional specialisms. The French experience was different; the German occupation had forced French heavy industry to supply the Nazi war machine. While the taint of collaboration discredited industrial opposition to any extension of government regulation following the Liberation, industry was widely exposed to centralised co-ordination (and nationalisation) between 1936 and 1950. During the war, the Vichy government created corporative organisations (Comités d'organisation) in each industrial sector, a marked extension of state direction and control. The wartime Conseil National de la Résistance, which embraced all political forces including the Communist Party, had achieved a political compromise in favour of a planned economy and the nationalisation of basic industries. But the objective was not a centrally planned, controlled economy. On the contrary, economic rationalisation was encouraged in order to regenerate a regulated, efficient market for the private sector while also stimulating conditions for growth. This outcome provoked open conflict after the war among political forces previously united under the Resistance, some of whom had anticipated – through central direct planning – the creation of a socialist state.

The application of Marshall Plan finance reflects differences between the two countries. Chronic dollar shortages in postwar Europe delayed industrial re-equipment and threatened economic reconstruction, a deadlock resolved by American aid. While all dedicated a proportion of aid to food imports, France, Germany and Austria used the greater part of these funds to promote industrial modernisation. In France, American aid formed 93 per cent of public investment in 1948, the funds being isolated in an account for modernisation and equipment (FME) which was concentrated on four major, largely nationalised sectors: electricity and gas, coal, railways, iron and steel. The focus on large enterprises was marked; iron and steel, for example, absorbed between one-third and one-fifth of public investment in 1949–50, nearly all of which went into the construction of two large strip steel mills using capital equipment imported from the USA. Public sector investment was to provide enterprise with efficient power and communication systems. By the mid-1950s, central direction shifted from indicative planning to financial inducements. The application of public loans through state-owned banks and investment agencies helped stimulate the modernisation of smaller businesses from the late 1950s; this became the principle avenue through which industrial policy was subsequently implemented. In the immediate postwar years, French strategies stimulated inflation and generated opposition within the United States administration, the source of the required finance. In Britain, by contrast, American pressure, the sterling balances and the determination to protect confidence in the pound discouraged any automatic conversion of Marshall Aid into imported American technologies and equipment. In conditions of strong export demand and constrained supply, the government used dollars to import essential raw materials (notably steel), and counterpart funds to retire debt. Scarce supplies of steel were dedicated principally to the manufacture of capital goods for export, not to domestic reconstruction.[5]

These differences, however, cannot be interpreted solely in terms of Britain's postwar financial position and its effect on industrial investment. If the French experience illustrates the fragility of collective faith in the merits of free market economics, that of Britain demonstrates the exact opposite. In Britain, the convention of keeping government out of industrial affairs survived the slump; the acceptance of wartime controls remained conditional on their removal once hostilities ceased. Unlike France, where industrial opinion was discredited, British industrialists emerged triumphant from a war which – to them and others – had demonstrated the superiority of the British form of economic voluntarism over the state-directed economies of the fascist dictators. This faith in the freedom of both sides of industry to order their affairs as they saw fit was also reflected within sectors of the industrial labour movement. Some British trade union leaders were willing to trade official controls over wages and employment policy in exchange for full-blown state planning, involving central direction over prices, profits and investment. As Labour abandoned dirigisme, so trade unionists reverted to traditional strategies to protect their members – a tendency strengthened during the Cold War.

It would be a mistake to contrast the two countries, as happens too frequently, by labelling one 'interventionist' and the other 'economically liberal'. The contribution of Michel Margairaz explores the nature of the French state's involvement in the economy. He shows how the 'republican compromise' underpinning the foundations of the Third Republic following the Commune (1870–1) sustained government-controlled firms up to the second world war. This compromise was the opposite of state dirigisme. Although direct public management in the tradition of the *Ancien Régime* was not excluded, the state commonly entrusted private actors, professional associations or local and regional authorities with the organisation of economic activities serving the general interest (manufacturing monopolies, national defence, energy, transport and communication networks, public facilities, public utilities). Nationalisation was the political province of neither the left nor the right. The state was neither manager nor financier, but played a moral-political role, using financial and statutory leverage to guarantee the founding principles of the Republic (liberty and equal access to individual rights). This alchemy of political economy and moral philosophy, combining collective autonomy and central co-ordination, explains (even today), French 'exceptionalism' in the technical and economic efficiency of the public sector. However, 1945 marked a turning-point. The three possible readings of the post-1945 nationalisation programme (as government economic planning, state provision of social security, rationalisation of the national market for basic products) all confer technical legitimacy on state intervention. From 1945, this technical legitimacy fostered the convention that the state was omniscient, or even omnipotent, encouraging the development of the interventionist state in France today.

In Britain, while the war witnessed the extension of state controls on an emergency basis, the new Labour government remained committed to four basic tenets of policy (the 'iron quadrilateral', according to Jim Tomlinson[6]): the sovereignty of Parliament, economic management through consensual tripartite negotiation, the promotion of industrial efficiency through the reform of corporate structures (more technocratic management in larger industrial units), and the continuation of voluntarism in industrial relations. Dollar shortages, the dirth of raw materials, the opposition of industry and Whitehall all combined to defeat the 'planners' in the Labour party; the post-war government eventually resorted to a series of pragmatic policy responses, reliant on indirect incentives rather than state direction. Nick Tiratsoo's contribution shows how political opposition ultimately undermined the postwar Labour government's efforts to promote higher productivity and to modernise industry. Most employers opposed such official initiatives, regarding them as an initial step on the road to nationalisation. Their hostility undermined Labour's attempts to introduce modern methods by voluntary tripartite consensus and helped discredit policies which, as the Cold War deepened, became associated with communist-inspired collectivism and the demise of democratic freedoms. Paradoxically, Labour's initiatives were much more ambitious than those of the French government. The public sector apart, the latter avoided intervening directly in the private affairs of firms, considering them strictly their owners' responsibility. In contrast, the Labour government tried to change prevailing manufacturing methods by educating company directors. No route existed through which the British state might influence working conventions or industrial co-ordination. Lacking any technical legitimacy (and for good reason), Labour's policies could easily appear interventionist and partisan.

The issue of technical legitimacy exemplifies possibly the most significant policy difference between the two countries. Adapting state-of-the-art technologies to industrial purposes requires an extensive comprehension of their application and possibilities. Such comprehension is rooted in education and training. As the contributions of Keith Burgess and Françoise Birck show, the successful promotion of industrial modernisation in France owed much to the promotion of technical training and know-how – and to a general willingness to invest in an approach which allowed new technologies to be judged on their own merits. In Britain, industrial training remained largely outside the purview of state education. Although the interwar Board of Education sought to extend state-sponsored systems of national certification, Burgess's paper shows how administrative structures and employer indifference combined to undermine the purpose of state policy, which was regarded as an intrusive and unnecessary encroachment on the rights of business management. The consequences of such attitudes were reflected in the proliferation of dubious investment decisions and poor co-ordination, notably in the public sector, and in a general mistrust of imported technologies. Public and private bureaucratic structures kept technological expertise 'on tap, but not on top'.

In France, by contrast, the Grandes Ecoles in Paris provided a technologically trained bureaucracy which headed industry and worked (as *grands ingenieurs de l'état*) on a range of public projects. Technological and intellectual expertise was rewarded with the highest positions – thus forming an arguably over-centralised meritocratic elite, ultimately a source of political tension. In the course of the twentieth century, industry and local and central government co-operated to fund training programmes pertinent to specific sectors. Françoise Birck's contribution traces how such programmes were applied in the industrial area around Nancy, where training was strongly influenced by the proximity of Germany. Here we witness growing state involvement in vocational training, which extended to skilled manual workers in the 1940s and 1950s, certificated to uniform national standards. These differences in training provision had repercussions for investment and for the credibility of the public sector. In France, university-trained engineers adapted the latest American technology to install electrical power-generating plant with both higher output and lower labour costs than their British equivalents. British design was developed independently by engineers trained through traditional apprenticeship plus a certificate from a technical training college. By the mid-1950s, having started from a much lower base, electricity generated in France provided more reliable supply at lower cost than its British equivalent.[7]

LABOUR MARKETS AND THE POLITICS OF FULL EMPLOYMENT

Both French and British postwar governments were formally committed to full employment, but there similarity ends. In France, unemployment never attained the political significance it acquired in Britain; the object of policy was to raise the attractions of formal employment and to align working practices with new industrial requirements while sustaining social justice and industrial peace. This last was to be secured through official ratification of newly established collective industrial agreements (*conventions collectives*), involving a legal minimum wage and, after the second world war, collective systems of social security. The state was expected to guarantee workers' representation, both in formulating agreed systems and in their administration. In Britain, full employment policy found its reality in budgetary policies regulating levels of demand. Direct state intervention to determine working practices was unacceptable; official efforts to raise productivity were confined to voluntary exhortation. The introduction of universal social insurance was intended to reduce fears of redundancy to allow greater rationalisation of work. Hence we find that official attempts in France and Britain to secure social objectives used contrasting policy pathways to attain these ends: these form the focus of the remaining contributions. The nature of employment in British and French economies presented quite different structural features, hence any programme of modernisation of employment and regularisation of work practices had to be inscribed on very widely varying conditions. For this reason alone, we might expect similar programmes to have stimulated diverse outcomes. We present an overview of the main features of employment in Britain and France, before going on to examine how variance in industrial relations, state policies to rationalise labour markets and the preference of workers and employers for autonomous collective bargaining interacted in each country.

The nature of employment in France and Britain

Craft modes of production – of textiles, leather goods, clothing, foodstuffs and various consumer goods – formed an important part of the French economy. The Paris Basin and the north-east of the country were extensively industrialised; outside heavy industry, much manufacture was still small-scale and concentrated on luxury products, which, like agriculture, were subject to marked seasonal variation. More generally, skilled workers provided the labour resources required for the development of engineering industries, characterised by widespread networks of small and medium-sized firms. Heavy industry was dominated by paternalistic employers and tight labour management. Laws governing employment (rooted in the *droit du travail*) which stipulated the rights and duties of employers and employed,[8] were effective only in unionised sectors and in firms that held state contracts. Government employment was widespread, although these jobs varied in nature and status. The rural economy – which dominated employment to the south and west of the country – remained highly significant. In 1938, 87 per cent of French farms were under 20 hectares and 86 per cent of the active agricultural population were unwaged peasant owners. Traditional rural industries were mostly small family concerns, sometimes workshop-based, sometimes utilising *travail a domicile* – and largely reliant on female workers. Less than 50 per cent of the working population was salaried in the 1930s and 30 per cent of the salaried sector worked in enterprises employing fewer than ten people.[9] In general, employment practices and traditions varied widely, according to region, product, market and branch of industry, and were regulated according to local tradition. Household income depended less on a single male breadwinner than in Britain; married women's work was more common. Even workers ostensibly employed full time in heavy industry might retain a financial interest in family-owned land. The extent of seasonal employment allowed family members to follow different occupations at different times of the year: sometimes as self-employed subcontractors, some- times as salaried workers. This wide variance in the nature of employment makes the impact of the 1930s slump hard to assess, especially since, unlike Britain, France had never before known widespread unemployment.

In Britain, the mid-twentieth century witnessed greater continuity of employment – with less mobility of workers between different firms and its concentration in larger units.[10] Even so, compared with those in Germany and the USA, British manufacturing units were small, under-capitalised and reliant on a skilled workforce to produce high-quality goods for export. Interwar growth in firm size signified the acquisition of financial control over small concerns, with relatively little rationalisation or modernisation of long-established systems of production. The nature of employment varied according to the nature of the product, regional tradition, forms of labour management. Short-time working was used extensively in the production of footwear, pottery, hosiery, and in coal-mining, textile manufacture and textile engineering during periods of slack demand. In the manufacture of bicycles, automobiles, furniture, clothing, extensive systems of subcontracting allowed firms to externalise risk during the slack season, forcing outsiders to absorb part of the cost of recession. Such structures continued to foster irregular employment, particularly as unemployment levels remained high throughout the interwar years.[11] Falling labour mobility between firms did not translate into greater regularity of work – or greater job security – as employers reverted to traditional strategies designed to shed surplus unskilled labour at the earliest opportunity (on the grounds that it would always be available if needed). The services of experienced or skilled employees, vital for business revival, were retained by sharing any available work as widely as possible. Here, the unemployment insurance scheme – extended to all manual workers in 1920 – could permit skilled trade unionists to supplement reduced earnings with state benefits if they could negotiate an appropriate distribution of work. In the 1930s, as the slump bit, benefit-supplemented short-time working virtually disappeared, but the principle of work-sharing remained. Trade associations in coal, textiles, iron and steel and other export sectors extended mutual protection by apportioning output, sharing markets and fixing prices among member firms: strategies which, in the case of the first two sectors at least, were reinforced by the introduction of tariff protection, part of an unsuccessful government initiative to promote rationalisation in the industries concerned. State policy during the interwar recession reinforced traditional diversities in labour management and perpetuated employment variation between different sectors and in different regions.

France: wages, welfare and collective agreements

In France, the employment contract – defining mutual obligations between employer and employed in major establishments – had long been subject to legal regulation. The extension of this rule of law to the general adjudication of disputes had been rendered compulsory during the first world war in armaments and defence industries. In 1919, new legislation extended this arrangement to cover peacetime conditions, although without the legal sanctions to make implementation effective. This system of wage determination was revived in the 1930s when, in response to a mass strike by two million workers in the Paris region in June 1936, the Popular Front government made collective industrial agreements (*conventions collectives*) legally enforceable in large firms, offered official recognition to workers' elected delegates, and reinforced industrial arbitration, while introducing statutory paid holidays and a forty-hour week. Collectively negotiated and legally ratified agreements could be extended by statutory fiat to other firms in the same industrial sector or within the same region. During subsequent years, local and regional systems for determining wages and working conditions began to cohere, eventually to produce a grid of remunerative scales based on certificated skills, productivity, seniority. These developments stimulated conflict: first, between different conceptions of the state's role in mediating industrial bargaining; second, over how this might contribute to a politics of full employment; finally, over the connection between the two. As the contributions of Claude Didry, Michelle Zancarini-Fournel and Philippe

Hesse show, the way this conflict was resolved and the compromises that were achieved varied widely by place and time.

Claude Didry's analysis of specific examples of state intervention in social conflict, as the new system became established (1936–9), reveals the nature of the problem. Two different conceptions of state intervention underlay the drafting of collective agreements and the arbitration of disputes, conceptions which combined in varied practical compromises. On the one hand, the state official might focus on established industrial structures and working practices, reinforcing existing conventions by authenticating agreements between employers and workers and thereby preserving the specific human capital requirements of the industry. Endogenous local economic development was thus encouraged (traces of which are still visible today in the light metalwork industries of the Arve Valley in the alpine Haute Savoie). Alternatively, the arbitrator might give priority to the macro-economic imperative of fighting inflation in settling the conflict, and press to have salaries adjusted according to rising prices. The arbitrator imposed a strictly 'industrial' conception of productivity, pushing the industry towards rationalisation of the labour process and product standardisation. In such cases, compulsory arbitration supported a minimum wage, squeezing differentials to compensate employers and fostering the use of other benefits – long-service bonuses and family allowances (*allocations familiales*) – to supplement the incomes of specific groups meriting extra protection. In this way, official surveillance of collective agreements sought to reconcile economic necessity with social justice. Generally, state intervention was popular among industrial workers because it strengthened trade union organisation and enforced recognition of workers' rights to representation in negotiations. Two different principles of state action emerge: either state officials underwrote an agreed 'common good' defined by local representatives, or they acted as agents for an externally defined common good by imposing centrally defined, macro-economic objectives.

Until 1939, as the contribution of Michelle Zancarini-Fournel suggests, this system of dispensing justice seemed to have reinforced variation in working practices, systems of production and regional economies – generating highly contextualised legal precedent which permitted political tactics to influence the adjudication of disputes. The process of grading and classifying particular types of employment within associated enterprises helped standardise remuneration and relativities in pay. But, in so doing, it tended to reinforce the peculiarities of the trades involved in each firm. Thus, the Manufacture des Armes et Cycles in Saint-Etienne involved three worlds of production, each with its own collective agreement: steelworkers, workers in wood and book manufacture (both craft based) and shop employees. Such complexity was not necessarily conducive to greater efficiency. Negotiations between male trade unionists, employers and official representatives promoted the gendering of work, grading male work on a higher scale than female and reserving specific (commonly lower-graded) jobs for women workers. Arguably, therefore, attempts to rationalise the labour process and to promote more systematic wages and conditions also consolidated the structure of women's work and differentiated it from male employment, even in small establishments.

The long march towards compulsory unemployment insurance, only established in France in 1958 by national collective agreement, also illustrates the continuing conflict between two modes of state intervention in employment. This national collective agreement was independent of French laws on social security, whereas in Great Britain unemployment insurance had existed since 1911 under the aegis of the state. The French system, when finally introduced, recognised the links between industrial bargaining, working practices and unemployment. The British system did not. Philippe Hesse indicates that, until the 1960s, both workers and employers expected the state to ratify collective bargaining in industrial relations, to sustain the diversity of its results and not to impose any *a priori* objectives upon it. A gradual shift in the other direction was taking shape, from the Vichy government's *Charte du Travail* to the laws on collective labour agreements (1946, 1951) – all reflecting a centralising, homogenising type of state intervention that failed to take root at that time. The incipient conflict between these two major paradigms of state intervention underpins our explanation for the strikes that recurred from the mid-1950s.

The notion of unemployment thus remained highly idiosyncratic in France, at least until the later 1950s. Even at the height of the 1930s' slump, sources of relief remained geographically dispersed, with local practice identifying the 'unemployed' and the extent to which they might be helped. Recession was not automatically converted into redundancy among workers in every enterprise, particularly in those small concerns where mutuality of interest between employer (*patron*) and worker fostered systems of labour management very different from those found in large firms, or in industrial networks of mobile skilled workers:

> in France during the 1930s, fluctuations in the amount of work presented a different meaning and reality in different places (particularly industrial cities and the countryside) because of the dominant conventions. . . . There is no more unemployment in the modern sense, for example, if companies do not make the dismissal of redundant workers a principle of efficient economic management.[12]

Hence, while 864,000 were registered as 'unemployed' in 1936 (the height of the crisis), the proportion of the working population recorded as economically active had fallen by 1,423 million over the previous five years. In many sectors, distinctions between employer and employed – essential for

15

the collection of contributions and the establishment of benefit rights – remained incapable of effective application, thanks to the prevalence of family enterprise, the impact of seasonality and the problems of distinguishing the self-employed, sub-contractors and wage-labourers in different parts of the economy and at different times of the year.[13]

Such diversity makes it easier to understand why the introduction of unemployment insurance posed as many problems as it solved. Most evident is continuing political confidence in the ability of the actors themselves to handle these problems; the state's role was to encourage this process, restricting itself for most of this period to subsidising voluntary local unemployment funds (the Ghent system). Quantitative strategies derived from employment macro-economics (sharing the volume of work, hindering entrance to the job market and speeding up departures) enjoyed little success, aside from the determination to protect national employment. In 1945, the will to set up a social security system that would preserve 'the earning capacity'[14] of workers against risk did not extend to unemployment insurance. And social security was administered through a complex of mutual societies, firm-based or trade-based funds, managed democratically until 1967, with workers electing 75 per cent of the administrators of the funds and employers the remaining 25 per cent.

Britain: modernisation and the voluntarist tradition

While in France official regulation of collective bargaining was actively promoted (if only to enforce and extend its results), in Britain any permanent official intervention was effectively outlawed. As Simon Deakin's contribution suggests, employment existed in two separate legal spheres: the first encompassed skilled or quasi-professional labour and the second stipulated employment relations between blue-collar workers and their employers – which derived directly from the law on masters and servants. The latter excluded independent contractors and wage-earners with higher social status. 'Modern' concepts of the employment relationship were the product of social legislation, particularly the social insurance acts of 1911 and 1946, both inspired to some extent by Beveridge. The 1911 Act set up a limited scheme of national insurance confined to workers earning below a stipulated annual income, which required legally defined responsibilities from an employer, who controlled the way in which work was performed. The second Act, following the Beveridge Report of 1942, assumed full employment as the foundation for universal insurance against all social risks, and extended protection to all wage-earners regardless of status. In this way, social legislation redefined employment relations through the extension of social duties (occupational health and safety, employment protection and social insurance), establishing legal obligations between employer and employed. This attempt at institution-building was similar to the legal handling of the relationship between labour contracts and social security in France.[15] But it did not achieve the same economic success. In Britain, industrial agreements remained outside the purview of state influence. As the state was excluded from collective bargaining, laws governing employment relations could not be linked to efficient labour deployment, to the reform of working conventions, to the issue of productivity.

In France, a centralised project of modernisation was gradually captured by collective bargaining because the ruling elite was 'able' (or rather, was forced) to allow such bargaining to develop. By underwriting resulting agreements, this elite could bring a project into the bargaining process. Due to the particular political circumstances of the Liberation, structured employment developed rapidly in the postwar period, creating the conditions for economic growth while making room for other forms of modernisation. It earned a technical legitimacy which it was unable to achieve in Britain. Beveridge's conception of a full employment strategy involved the same two elements, making use of the first (stabilising employment and job security through social protection) to succeed in the second (improving productivity).[16] But, as government had no place in the negotiation of industrial agreements, Beveridge's project remained an instrumental, political project. Isolated, it failed.

The tradition of voluntarism in British industrial relations proved unbreachable. Frank Wilkinson and Roy Mankelow show that, in older industrial sectors such as steel and shipbuilding, both structures of collective bargaining and systems of arbitration dated back to the nineteenth century, reflecting traditional, strongly defended forms of work organisation which determined pay, seniority and job security. Here and on the docks, established labour hierarchies and working practices proved hard to shift. Unprofessional management exacerbated divisions between owners and shop floor, manifest in poor industrial relations. Postwar full employment witnessed the reconstruction of traditional defences against the re-emergence of unemployment, and the introduction of new technologies and new processes tended to stimulate demarcation disputes which impeded job rationalisation. Official efforts to restructure industry, raise productivity or regulate employment met with little success. Although the Trades Union Congress (TUC) and its member unions strongly supported the productivity drive and the extension of collective bargaining (fifty-six more joint industrial councils were created or re-established during the 1940s), traditional working practices were still used to underwrite job security. Hence a 'second-best' equilibrium was perpetuated. Employers were incapable of securing new conventions to create compromise between the need to rationalise the labour process while accommodating worker independence. The work ethic and the spirit of responsibility characteristic of old skilled unionism was replaced by opportunistic behaviour, using union power for short-term objectives with little regard for the consequences.

The newly revitalised wages councils failed to rationalise the workshop trades – as promoted by official policy. Jim Gillespie shows in his contribution how institutions created to impose a minimum wage (which aimed to foster rationalisation) were adapted by the industries concerned to protect existing structures, not transform them. Here, product markets (such as fashions in clothing) were seasonal and unpredictable. Sub-contracting and the maintainance of small, innovative firms were in this case economically rational. Trade boards and wages councils were adapted to prevent unfair competition from entrepreneurs using sweated labour. Higher wages did not, however, provide the incentive to rationalise established industrial structures. In this way, state institutions preserved the principles of manufacturing and innovation required for market success while at the same time ensuring a minimum of social protection. Here we have a paradoxical example of potentially successful failure: employees in firms serving markets resistant to product standardisation required protection, which in this case could not be secured through industrial concentration or mass production. As Gillespie notes – and this approach underpins our book – the analysis of public policy does not lie in a comparison between objectives and results, but in the ways new forms of state intervention become appropriated by existing employment and production systems within specific circumstances.

Noel Whiteside emphasises that, even in the newly extended public sector, the drive to rationalise employment proved uneven. On the one hand, in an expanded civil service, reforms in the mid-1940s generated uniform grading, formalised incremental scales and extended job protection across central government departments. The structure of local government was overhauled; uniform administrative systems aimed to raise efficiency in central–local relations. Both war emergency and postwar export drive fed common concerns to promote economies of scale, particularly in non-productive employment (such as public administration) where rationalisation could release manpower for vital jobs in manufacturing. Outside the immediate purview of government, however, state initiatives met limited success. In the newly created National Health Service, financial crises, varied managerial structures and labour shortages combined to generate a new diversity of employment systems. While governmental authority was welcome in establishing mechanisms of collective bargaining in public sector employment, it proved impossible to use these new structures to co-ordinate wage rates and differentials, which proved as vulnerable to wage drift as their private counterparts. In coal-mining as on the docks, many workers continued to put in irregular hours. For face-workers, this was an active way of denying that full employment necessarily meant transformations in established work systems – thereby introducing higher productivity norms by covert means. The emergence of a new language of 'restrictive practices' and 'absenteeism' signified changed expectations about the world of work – at least among the 'modernisers', who used these terms to describe working conventions which, to the external eye, appeared to impede production unnecessarily.

CONCLUSION

All the essays point to a final, provocative question: At root, what exactly was the 'modernisation' that was pursued during this period? Marked by efforts to standardise products and rationalise the labour process, seeking to increase price competitiveness and capture shares of supposedly mass markets, modernisation appears to have aimed at implementing a specific world of production, the industrial world. It would appear in retrospect that this industrial paradigm does not have, and never did have, any claim to universality. It was suited only to certain configurations of products, markets and demand, not others (such as luxury products and capital goods intended for diversified, rapidly changing markets). This explains resistance by both workers and industrialists to policies aimed at disseminating this prototype at the expense of other production systems offering speciality, flexibility and variety. Moreover, has there ever been a genuine model of modernisation, a coherent national project? This appears to be an illusion. Of course, projects did arise, but they were incompletely formulated, contradicted each other and, above all, were based on hypotheses and expectations of state action that varied between social groups in each country and within those social groups. They contained within themselves several possible constructions of 'the state'. Hence, the desire to restore prewar working conventions and forms of bargaining can under no circumstances be assumed to be a proof of backwardness and inefficiency, nor can rationalisation be viewed as systematic progress. We can ascribe no substantial rationality to these attempts that would enable us to evaluate their efficiency *a posteriori* by simply comparing their objectives to their results.

The forms of governance that have come into being in both countries reflect a series of compromises that varied according to the area of state activity. Dominant characteristics are most evident, but changes in orientation can also be detected. For the essential point is that agents incorporated a political, economic or social measure – or a state institution – into established conventions of co-ordination in specific markets, production relations, systems of employment. How do agents accommodate new policy initiatives? The state is not aloof and out of the fray, but is immersed in it. The sphere of governance is defined by its viability in specific contexts, which is shaped by a complex outcome of expectations towards it and the way new initiatives are appropriated. These are all of far greater significance than the actual 'text' of official proposals or the motives behind them.

Within our analysis, it is the acceptance – even the expectation – of official involvement in economic affairs that permits the successful integration of public policy into the realm of private business. The issue of state 'intervention' – as the word implies – signals an unexpected, and possibly unwelcome intrusion by public authorities into a private world to secure policy objectives (which may or may not be commonly valued), possibly at the expense of established systems of governance and authority. Seen from this angle, the postwar British state appears as 'interventionist' as its French counterpart in its attempts to restructure production systems, employment and the outcomes of collective bargaining. By contrast, the French state, although usually seen as infinitely more dirigiste, sought to use state power to co-ordinate the results of decentralised collective bargaining as the means to secure new working conventions: to establish a 'market' of corporatist dimensions.

To say that the British government was more interventionist would be paradoxical only to those who consider the state opposed to the market. Within such accounts, state intervention is perceived as a drag on economic performance, as undermining growth through the diversion of funding for private industrial investment to other, less profitable ends.[17] We beg to differ; such a juxtaposition of the state and the market takes a restricted view of social and economic relations and the role of government in regulating them. First, much analysis of market mechanisms assumes uniformity in market operation which, on closer inspection, is hard to sustain. All markets operate within complex systems of social convention and expectation, some of which are reinforced by law. These define acceptable forms of behaviour, the construction of fraud, how agreements should be reached or payments made, whether a gift to a potential buyer – or a subsidy to an agent – should be considered a bribe, and so on. Conventions differ according to the nature of the product, the type of transaction, established precedent, regional or national tradition, as well as over time.[18] Their roots are commonly buried in custom and common practice. Every market is socially constructed and politically regulated – even those which profess to operate outside the remit of state intervention. States generate markets which are acceptable because they promote and sustain prevailing concepts of fair exchange in the distribution of goods and services.

In our period, we observe how the French state created the market through the intervention of nationalised industries, investment by publicly owned banks, the legal regulation of industrial agreements and the promotion of social insurance – all of which became integrated into a form of planning which sought to employ market incentives to reconcile economic prosperity and social justice. Postwar French governments aimed to reinforce public expectation about the performance of the economy, to draw an increasing proportion of the population into salaried employment through the extension of social protection, to reward skill and to establish the security of the Republic from its enemies, external and internal. This particular mode of governance was not universally acceptable. Its objectives were contested by both unions and the political left. However, the performance of the French economy by the late 1950s indicates that the greater involvement of the state improved 'market' performance.[19] Here, a reasonably peaceful transformation of work into salaried employment relied strongly on the rule of law through the close integration of industrial bargaining, economic planning and social welfare.

These contrasts illustrate the difficulties involved in making direct comparisons between the effects of state action on economic performance in different countries. The conventions determining the spheres open to state influence do not allow similar significance to be attached to specific areas of policy. Although our account reinforces notions of 'path dependency' in policy development, it also demonstrates the particularity of these pathways, how deviations are established and new paths form. In making our comparisons, our analysis cannot be interpreted as a blanket criticism of British policies; the avenues for shaping or influencing economic and social outcomes differed radically in these two countries. The richness of comparative studies does not lie in measures of performance as such, but elsewhere. It lies in re-establishing the fundamental link between economic efficiency and politics, in understanding how different political expectations and conventions for the role of the state influence economic outcomes. It also lies in the way comparisons allow us to explore sources of diversity – a more fruitful objective than a search for elusive points of similarity on which to base conclusions about comparative developments in state policies.

NOTES

1 The authors would like to acknowledge the comments of Jonathan Zeitlin and Jim Tomlinson on an earlier draft of this introduction; the usual reservations apply.

2 B. Eichengreen, *Europe's Postwar Recovery*, Cambridge University Press, Cambridge, 1995, Introduction.

3 C. Millon Delsol, *L'Etat subsidiaire*, PUF, Paris, 1992.

4 M. Storper and R. Salais, *Worlds of Production: The Action Frameworks of the Economy*, Harvard University Press, Cambridge, MA, 1997. For a focus on the French case, see R. Salais and M. Storper, *Les mondes de production. Enquête sur l'identité économique de la France*, Editions de l'EHESS, Paris, 1993.

5 A. Milward, *The Reconstruction of Western Europe*, Methuen, London, 1984, esp. pp. 101–8. For France, see M. Margairaz , *L'Etat, les finances et l'economie: histoire d'une conversion 1932–52*, PUF, Paris, 1990, vol. 1 chs XXIX and XXX; W.J. Adams, *Restructuring the French Economy*, Brookings Institution, Washington, DC, 1989; essay by Esposito in Eichengreen, *Europe's Postwar Recovery*. The British postwar economic situation has stimulated an extensive literature. For the impact of dollar shortages on British industrial re-equipment, see J. Tomlinson, 'Another Lost Opportunity? Marshall Aid and the British Economy in the 1940s', *Economic History Review* (forthcoming).

6 J. Tomlinson, 'A missed opportunity? Labour and the productivity problem', in G. Jones and M.W. Kirby (eds), *Competitiveness and the State*, Manchester University Press, Manchester, 1991. Also his *Democratic Socialism and Economic Policy*, Cambridge University Press, Cambridge 1996, concluding chapter.

7 L. Hannah, *Engineers, Managers and Politicians: The First Fifteen Years of Nationalised Electricity Supply in Britain*, Macmillan, London, 1982, ch. 8.

8 C. Didry, 'Le chômage entre conciliation et contrat de travail', in M. Mansfield, R. Salais, and N. Whiteside (eds), *Aux sources du chômage, 1880–1914*, Editions Belin, Paris, 1994.

9 R. Castels, *La metamorphose de la question sociale*, Fayard, Paris, 1995, ch. 7.

10 Howard Gospel, *Markets, Firms and the Management of Labour in Modern Britain*, Cambridge University Press, Cambridge, 1992.

11 N. Whiteside and J. Gillespie, 'Deconstructing unemployment', *Economic History Review*, vol. XLIV, November 1991, pp. 665–82.

12 R. Salais, 'Labour markets, industrial relations and social welfare: introduction', *Comparing Social Welfare Systems in Europe* Vol. 1, MIRE Rencontres et Recherches, Paris, 1994, pp. 491–2.

13 R. Salais, N. Baverez, and B. Reynaud, *L'invention du chômage*, PUF, Paris, 1984, ch. 3 (whence much of the information in this section is derived); D. Renard, 'Assistance et assurance dans la constitution du système de protection sociale français', *Genèses*, vol. 18, 1995, pp. 30–47.

14 Under the terms of the first article of the ordinance of 4 October 1945.

15 A. Supiot, *Critique du droit du travail*, PUF, Paris, 1994, and 'L'avenir d'un vieux couple: travail et sécurité sociale', *Droit social*, 9–10, Septembre–Octobre 1995, pp. 823–31.

16 See Nick Tiratsoo's contribution. Although separated by thirty years, this project retained nearly identical objectives to those found in the pre-1914 labour market reforms, particularly the object of labour exchanges to secure more regular forms of employment and to raise the efficiency of labour. Cf. M. Mansfield, 'Naissance d'une définition institutionnelle du chômage en Grande-Bretagne (1890–1914)', in M. Mansfield, R. Salais, and N. Whiteside (eds), *Aux sources du chômages*, pp. 295–324.

17 For example, C. Barnett, *The Audit of War*, Macmillan, London, 1986, and *The Lost Victory*, Macmillan, London, 1995.

18 R. Salais, 'Les institutions de marché: le regard d'un economiste', *Revue du Nord*, vol. LXXVI, no. 307, 1994, pp. 701–10.

19 Here we strongly contest the analysis made by P. Sicsic and C. Wyplosz in N. Crafts and G. Toniolo (eds), *Economic Growth in Europe since 1945*, Cambridge University Press, Cambridge, 1996, pp. 210–40.

Part I

MODERNISATION AND THE SPHERE OF INDUSTRIAL POLITICS

2

COMPANIES UNDER PUBLIC CONTROL IN FRANCE, 1900–1950

Michel Margairaz

State intervention in the French economy grew in the first part of the twentieth century. This extension of controls under public authority – the state or local bodies – can be interpreted as a sign of increasing official ascendancy. The 'turning point of 1945' has been frequently emphasised, where plans for nationalisation, economic planning and, more generally, the 'modernising Keynesian state',[1] embodying a Keynesian convention of full employment,[2] all converged.

The notion of regular progress, from a liberal economic order in 1900 – opposed to state regulation of enterprise – to the establishment of a sizeable public sector by the end of the 1940s, is nevertheless highly unsatisfactory. This evolution was discontinuous and chaotic, complicated by the inter-twining of multiple factors.[3] We must also question the historical rupture in 1945: did government create rationalised, 'modern' forms of employment through schemes of public financing and social regulation? Can such developments be identified specifically with a public sector composed of companies under state control?

Although state intervention is often constrained by limited resources, Jean Bouvier reminded us at the time of the 1986 privatisations: 'the state then has never been *light* in relation to the economy and society. It has always been *heavy*.'[4] This is also true for the *Belle Epoque*. However, understanding this half-century is rendered complex by the existence of contradictory factors. A three fold clarification is required. First, blatant distortions appear between the principles of economic liberalism, as articulated by the masters of fiscal probity and their disciples in government, and the actions of state administrators. From Paul LeRoy-Beaulieu (1843–1916), who denounced the incurable incompetence of government in economic affairs, to Clément Colson (1853–1939), economic liberals have combined a radical critique of state control of private enterprise with a mistrust of parliamentary intervention. The civil service, by contrast, has long relied on established practices of regulation, extending to state takeover of companies. The foundations of these practices go back to the *Ancien Régime*. In spite of the liberal discourse surrounding the Revolution, companies that were already under state authority – such as the Gobelins or Sèvres manufacturers – remained there. Before 1986, there was hardly a single example of a company formerly owned by the state being returned to private ownership. Whatever the debates at the time, the nineteenth century added to the total rather than subtracted from it. In addition, the state trained a competent workforce to run these companies: in particular, engineering graduates from the *Grandes Ecoles* (elite national schools) created in the eighteenth century, such as the Ponts-et-Chaussées (School of Bridges and Highways) in 1747, the Mines (Mining School) in 1783, complemented by the Ecole Polytechnique (Polytechnic School) in 1794. Senior civil servants, starting with Necker and Roland, argued that in economic matters public authority existed as guardian of the general interest, that it could even play an innovatory role – a tendency reinforced by French administrative law.[5]

Second, it is not easy to distinguish state intervention designed to accelerate economic and technical modernisation from that promoted to protect existing activities, to reinforce social stability. Because historians are as subject to fluctuating ideological preferences as anyone else, such distinctions tend to be ignored. Instead, we should heed Jean Bouvier's last piece of advice:

> Over the centuries the state has always been a focal point for impassioned discussion; sometimes it is decried as the supreme obstacle, and sometimes it is called upon as the supreme resource. ... The role of the state ... deserves neither excessive vilification nor excessive praise.[6]

The issue must be approached on a case-by-case basis. Public policy commonly involves multiple strategies and justifications; in some cases, public decisions have been simply the transferred suggestions made by private businessmen.

Companies under public control can be analysed in terms of their stated *motives*, the *institutions* and *practices* they use, and the *products* or *services* they offer. Since Colbert, three sectors have been subject to public supervision: monopolies instituted for fiscal reasons; companies linked to national defence and armaments, such as arsenals and shipyards; and finally, activities connected with the extension or modernisation of communication systems. In these three cases, public control has differed in form and degree, depending partly on whether the firms in question were in competition with other companies in the private sector. The study of the early twentieth century allows us to distinguish three interconnected histories. The first concerns the regulation by the state or public bodies of the three traditional sectors mentioned above. A second history, that of the economic situation, disturbs the long-term trends of the former. Difficult times, such as the two world wars and the depression of the 1930s, have multiplied opportunities to extend state controls in response to growing weakness. In the third, public control over important companies may have interfered with the social, political, ideological or even symbolic preoccupations of social and political forces at specific times. With its climaxes (1936 or 1944–5 in one direction, 1940 in another), this history also combines with the two preceding ones.

THE *BELLE EPOQUE*: TRADITIONAL REALMS OF INTERVENTION

From the turn of the century to the Great Depression (1930s), the direct takeover of industrial companies by public bodies was limited and frequently rooted in the remote past, sometimes going back to Colbertism. Aside from state manufactures, arsenals and shipyards, the government retained the monopoly of the postal service, which became an independent administration in 1878, and of telecommunications, as well as of the production, sale and international marketing of tobacco (dating back to the seventeenth century), to which it added the monopoly of matches in 1899.

In the case of tobacco products, public control appears to have been total. The Nantes 'Manu', the history of which over the half-century preceding the first world war has been studied, was a state-run company managed by Polytechnique graduates, state engineers whose main concern was rationalised production serving the general interest. The state guaranteed both the market, which was planned a year in advance, and the funding, which was registered as a budgetary expense. A bureaucratic world ruled by norms and controls, the tobacco administration anticipated 'by almost half a century the process of rationalisation of production', as well as professional management of the workforce, which was protected and endowed with extensive rights.[7]

The defence industries: direct controls

Here, the state was simultaneously consumer, producer and protector, depending on the products. Public controls over armament companies varied. In cases such as artillery and shipbuilding, armament production was largely confined to state firms or major private firms in the metallurgical industry, such as Schneider or Firminy, and in the shipyards. Control was exercised through technical pre-eminence; state engineers designed the equipment, leaving private sector firms to compete with state-run companies by ensuring lower prices and investment costs. In aeronautics, still in its infancy, technical innovation lay largely outside the sphere of the military, which did not have its own specialist arsenal. The Chiefs of Staff were reluctant to place all aircraft design and manufacture with one company, preferring to divide orders between several small suppliers. Some see this form of control as the reason why companies experienced difficulties in securing continuous growth. Excessive sub-division of military orders meant that production schedules were stretched, causing the failure of the 1912 rearmament programme.[8] However, this also reflected a lack of maturity within the industry.

The state protected both civil and military shipbuilding, passing a series of laws between 1881 and 1906 which secured 60 per cent of the domestic market for French industry (as opposed to only 27 per cent in 1880). Initially, subsidies for arming ships encouraged the construction of sailing boats! After 1906, however, funding distinguished between construction and outfitting. The state fostered the creation and modernisation of a dozen large private shipyards through its orders for battleships, although extra costs were incurred by insufficient concentration within the industry.

Railways and urban transport: compromise between public and private

Transport remained a traditional area of state intervention; it made up almost 10 per cent of state expenditure by 1914, although this refers only to the quasi-total of expenditure labelled 'economic' (amounting to less than 12 per cent of the whole).[9]

Following the Railway Charter of 1842, the relationship of the private railway company with the government was characterised by heated argument punctuated by successive agreements. The agreement of 1883 confirmed the monopoly of the six great networks – Nord, PLM (Paris–Lyon–Marseille), PO (Paris–Orléans), Ouest, Est, Midi – reflecting official desire to confirm the central position of Paris. It also extended the system of guaranteed interest through repayable state loans, in compensation for the earlier construction of unprofitable lines. This compromise allowed the funding of such expenses, which exceeded the state's resources (government share in initial expenditure was about a third of the total), as well as those of the companies themselves. The financial problems of the Compagnie de l'Ouest led the state to buy it out in 1908; this was the consequence of unforeseen circumstances, not an initial step in a pre-established plan. In exchange for a varying degree of public funding (higher for the Est and Paris–Orléans networks, lower for the PLM and the Nord), the companies had to tolerate increased administrative intervention in their operation; in particular, they deplored official controls over fares. By 1914, under state pressure, the system could offer an extensive network, egalitarian low fares and parsimonious company management, which still, nevertheless, suffered from financial difficulties.[10]

Urban transport companies were also under public control; from the 1890s they were affected by the rise of tramways. In Paris, public supervision systems overlapped and sometimes clashed. The Compagnie Générale des

Omnibus (CGO) clung to its monopoly in the capital, a monopoly which had been granted by the City in 1855; at the end of the century it fell to the state to grant concessions to tramway companies in order to serve growing suburbs. In 1898, the concession of an underground network in Paris was the product of a twenty-year struggle between two rival projects. On the one hand, the Ministère des Travaux Publique, backed by the Ponts-et-Chaussées engineers, the Paris Chamber of Commerce and the Conseil d'Etat, envisaged a network in Paris connecting the lines of the railway companies, which would construct the underground system. This option offered technical rationalisation, by connecting city and suburban traffic, and shifted the financial burden on to the railway companies. This plan, however, did not appeal to the elected officials of the City of Paris, or to the engineers of the municipal transport services, anxious to preserve their sovereignty by creating a dense local network limited to the inner city and not connected with the railway lines. Municipal selfishness triumphed in 1898 when the City granted a concession to the Compagnie du Chemin de Fer Métropolitain de Paris (CMP).[11] The municipal council of Paris has been charged with narrow-mindedness for confining the underground in a Haussmanian iron collar.[12] Such restricted vision, however, did not prevent it from entrusting its operation to a technically advanced company, an offshoot of the Belgian conglomerate EMPAIN. Further, it also introduced a very modern network for its time: reliable, profitable for both the CMP and the city, whose coverage to this day has remained substantial for traffic within Paris. In France more generally, cities had their local networks built by powerful industrial conglomerates or by railway companies which won concessions for these operations.

From the 1880s, in both railways and urban transport companies, a republican or near-radical compromise was formed. This compromise combined public service requirements laid down by public authorities – such as the geographical extension of lines beyond the profitable areas, and the maintainance low-fare systems – with those technical and financial commitments necessary to private companies. Further, the specific features of mechanised transport, notably safety requirements, called for new methods of labour management, even prior to the introduction of public controls which later reinforced such schemes. The companies drew on old regulations governing dangerous trades – such as those covering mining or the *Ancien Régime* navy – and formulated guarantees of job stability and indirect benefits (health care and pension funds) for their personnel to compensate for the risks incurred in their work, to promote safety and thus an uninterrupted service for travellers.[13]

Energy

In contrast, in electricity supply, cities such as Paris (1888) or Lyon (1897) initially extended concessions to several companies, threatening the formation of efficient, co-ordinated networks. The 1906 law established the system of concessions for the next forty years, dividing them between a multitude of distributors. However, this probably reflects the fragmentation of the industry itself, particularly in the hydroelectric power sector where numerous small firms emerged. In 1907, a Paris agreement promoted a merger of the six initial concession holders into one firm, the Compagnie Parisienne de Distribution d'Electricité (CPDE) by 1914.

From April 1810, the state played a decisive role in the partition of coal mine concessions, aiming to avoid monopoly and thereby securing low prices. In the Nord–Pas-de-Calais area, concessions appear to have been large enough to keep costs relatively low without creating a monopoly.[14] The combination of state supervision with company strategies to stabilise the workforce fostered a specific type of personnel management: job guarantees and work status were granted in compensation for the constraints and risks resulting from dangerous conditions. In addition, the engineers from the Corps des Mines were charged with enforcing the law, limiting the rights of the state to fiscal demands and the supervision of safety rules. Nevertheless, because of the chronic underproduction of coal, which covered only two-thirds of the country's needs, state officials paid close attention to the proper functioning of the companies.

Aside from the traditional areas of transport and energy, public intervention was minimal, thanks partly to a lack of resources. By 1914, public control over companies varied according to the kind of products, markets or agents involved. In the armaments industry, official controls could slow down or speed up concentration and rationalisation, varying between specific cases and over periods of time. Such controls did not, however, undermine the continued existence of older, small companies, which were little mechanised and employed a workforce that was skilled but out of step with recent innovations.

In energy and transport, public intervention was most often designed to extend access to the greatest number of people. According to an ideology derived from Radicalism, control did not primarily reflect a preoccupation with economic rationalisation, but a republican compromise between private interests and public authority over the provision of public services, guaranteeing users general and egalitarian access. This compromise, however, translated into different forms of organisation in different sectors. In both coal-mining and railways, large companies divided up the national market; meanwhile, in electricity and urban transport, concessions granted by local bodies profited a number of firms scattered over the entire country. In addition, while public officials did not want to upset the balance between small and big companies through overselective intervention, public transport subsidies contributed to cost-cutting and service extensions. They also had a domino effect on the metallurgical and electrical construction industries and even fostered the modernisation of financial markets. In that sense, it accompanied the growth movement of the *Belle Epoque*.

FROM THE FIRST WORLD WAR
TO THE DEPRESSION:
THE MIXED-ECONOMY FIRM

The first world war: an interlude?

Economic mobilisation for war purposes brought private companies under greater state control. This was legitimized by the climate of *union sacrée* (united front) that prevailed until September 1917. Its significance, however, must be mediated on three counts.

First, state intervention was only introduced gradually. The first controls, which affected imports, were partial and disorderly. They did not prevent speculation by importers who took advantage of rising prices. The government did not introduce consistent controls until 1916 – even March 1917 – in response to the impact of the war at sea and British entreaties to co-ordinate allied purchases. Second, the birth of this wartime economy did not mean that existing administrative structures were strengthened. For want of an alternative, the state endowed the Comité des Forges (Ironworks Committee) with responsibility for the allocation of manufacturing in 1916, the centralisation of purchases and, from August 1917, the exclusive acquisition of steel and iron products. Finally, intervention did not translate into the growth of the public sector at the expense of private companies, especially since it was clear, particularly to businessmen, that these arrangements were only for the duration of hostilities.

As early as August 1914, the Ministre de Guerre, Alexandre Millerand, recognised that armament requirements exceeded the capacity of the state arsenals. He initiated a policy, continued by the Socialist Albert Thomas (Ministre de l'Armement from December 1916), granting contracts to large private metallurgical and engineering companies under the technical control of artillery engineers. In addition, the state requisitioned shipyards and factories, such as Michelin, for conversion to war production. Albert Thomas started the construction of a huge arsenal at Roanne. This public company was intended to be exemplary, both as an experiment in organisational productivity and as a show-case of industrial harmony between management and workers. The project, however, turned into an 'administrative and legislative nightmare', according to Kuisel, and was abandoned under pressure from parliamentary opposition. In early 1917, Thomas introduced joint arbitration committees and workshop delegates in all the state factories.[15]

Chronic shortages in maritime transport led Etienne Clementel (Ministre du Commerce, 1915–19) to requisition the merchant marine; from March 1917, imports were supposedly co-ordinated, subject to authorisation, by consortia – groups of businesses manufacturing the same products. Advisory committees of high-ranking civil servants and manufacturers, interministerial committees and finally inter-Allied offices – where Jean Monnet first became known – negotiated the planning of imports. These committees numbered almost 300 by the end of the war. In early 1918, most basic products were controlled by consortia. Simultaneously, the ministry tried to control certain prices, but without much success.

Due to deficient information, state representatives often found themselves dependent on professional organisations or large companies within the consortia. Although disparities existed, excessive profiteering was not controlled, nor did the consortia manage to promote modernisation and more intensive industrialisation. Clementel wanted to use these structures after the war by subordinating them to a Ministère de l'Economie Nationale: a balance between etatism and corporatism would have ensured a 'mixed economy' and provided French industry with secure access to raw materials, better export capacity and increased productivity. Following the Armistice, however, private businessmen proved anxious to abolish public controls; this, together with the Anglo-Saxon drive to close the inter-Allied offices and restore free trade, dashed the hopes of the minister, who resigned from office after his defeat in the November 1919 elections. In the spring of 1919, Louis Loucheur, a Polytechnique graduate and civil engineering contractor in charge of the Ministère de la Reconstruction Industrielle since the Armistice, announced a decision to 'return industry to normal competition' by eliminating controls and consortia and by converting state arsenals to the manufacture of civil industrial equipment for reconstruction purposes.[16]

Industrial controls only lasted as long as the two-year crisis in supply. Was the war then a mere interlude? The demands of total war gave substance to the notion of a 'general interest' and strengthened the idea of public service for those activities (transport, energy) over which the state or local bodies exerted some control. This was increasingly relevant as the economic and financial consequences of the war affected their profitability. Significantly, in 1920 the Confédération Générale du Travail (CGT), which had supported state intervention during the war, advocated nationalisation of these sectors shortly after Albert Thomas's (unsuccessful) proposal to nationalise the railways.[17]

The consequences of the war: increased control?

After the war, the traditional realms of public control – transport and energy – experienced a strengthening of regulation from two directions. First, deteriorating profitability required a redefinition of the relationship between public and private sectors. Second, the tensions born of industrial mobilisation drew to public attention the close links between these activities and the national interest and, consequently, how such controls could help define a national economic policy.

Total railway company defecits reached FF 5,000 million in the period 1914–20; this ushered in new levels of public control. The Le Troquer agreement (1921) redefined the compromise between the state and the networks at a time when, following the rejection of Thomas's nationalisation scheme, public officials could not ignore the technical expertise of the companies. The state took charge of existing deficits and the reconstruction of the network and guaranteed a subsidy. While the system of guaranteed interest disappeared, it was retained in the form of Treasury advances. The cornerstone of the new arrangement was a common fund 'to allow the profits of prosperous networks' (the Nord and the PLM) 'to be allocated to the poorer ones'. This reform reflected a concern for fare unification, demanded by members of parliament since the beginning of the Third Republic. A Conseil Supérieur d'Administration – representing the networks, management, personnel, the state and customers – was to subordinate private to public interest. According to one historian, state regulation of the railway increased: an 'advance nationalisation' which swept away the companies' profit-sharing scheme.[18] The introduction of public service criteria in railway management led to a minimum level of train service on all lines and an egalitarian fare structure which was unrelated to real costs. Others emphasise the fact that the networks still profited from this arrangement, for instance when the Compagnie du Nord enabled other companies in the conglomerate to benefit from orders and advantageous rates.[19] However, companies from then on were managed more as administrative departments than as commercial ventures. In 1920, the situation of railway workers was brought in line with those of state employees by extending guarantees and benefits as well as integrating the unions.

Similarly, after 1914 urban transport suffered from growing deficits linked to a freeze in fares introduced at a time when inflation was rising. In the Paris area, the various companies of the surface rail network were unified in 1921 by the Seine *département*, which entrusted the operation as a public service concession to the Société des Transports en Commun de la Région Parisienne (STCRP). Again, compensation for increased control over transport meant public absorption of the operating deficit, which had become chronic as the networks expanded to serve the growing urban area. Last, in 1920 government took control of the Compagnie des Messageries Maritimes (CMM) to ensure the survival of shipping lines serving the 'imperial interest'.

In the energy sector as well, public intervention increased after 1918; the war had raised official awareness of the constraints arising from deficient coal supplies. Hence the interest shown in hydroelectric power, leading to the landmark law of 16 October 1919, which gave to the state the ownership of energy from tides, lakes and waterways, making it possible to override the interests of private dam constructers and to grant concessions. A commentator of the time spoke of a 'nationalisation' of hydraulic energy. In July 1922, the state was empowered to construct high-voltage networks, foreshadowing the integration and regulation of the electricity industry. To achieve the interconnection of existing networks, senior technical administrators infiltrated the sector to impose official views on a profession whose approach had been anarchic and individualistic.[20]

By contrast, the policy of reduced electricity tariffs, imposed by public regulation until 1927, was widely criticised by firms and contributed to disorganisation. Local authorities experimented with the 'mixed-economy' firm in this area; such firms had operated in Belgium, Sweden and Germany since the turn of the century. The amount of investment required to harness the Rhône and the project's dubious profitability led to the creation of the Compagnie Nationale du Rhône in 1921 (combining the Seine *département*, public bodies, the PLM and private interests), which undertook research on the Génissiat dam. Similar associations were established for the Haute Dordogne (1921) and the Moyenne Dordogne (1928). Finally, in 1925 a 'mixed-economy' status was adapted for electricity distribution purposes.[21]

In 1917–18 as well, public officials became dramatically aware of France's utter dependency on external oil supplies. Strategic and patriotic concerns led to the development of national sources of crude oil and to the promotion of refining on French soil. For this purpose authorities combined the creation of public institutions with collaboration between the state and private capital. In 1924 the Compagnie Française des Pétroles (CFP) was created to manage the share (23.75 per cent) in the Iraq Petroleum Company allocated to France. The state took control of 35 per cent of the CFP, thereby proving its 'willingness to create an instrument capable of introducing a national petroleum policy' (R. Poincaré). Prospecting, however, did not yield significant results. It was not until 1939 that the Saint-Marcet oil field was discovered by the Centre de Recherche du Pétrole du Midi, soon to become the Régie Autonome des Pétroles (RAP). The objective was to control the oil market. The 1928 law promoted this by limiting imports, protecting France's share of oil refining (the CFP controlled the Compagnie Française de Raffinage), and by forcing Anglo-Saxon subsidiaries to create a refining industry in France. Quotas, which were enforced from 1931 to 1950, ensured that over 58 per cent of refinery production was carried out by French conglomerates, and only 41 per cent by international companies. This is a fine example of dividing the spoils between the state and private firms, both French and foreign, which were thus bound by a marriage of convenience.

Reconstruction and prosperity: state sponsored growth

Because of its inflationary and geopolitical consequences, the first world war increased the public hold over the traditional sectors mentioned above through the extension of concessions or mixed-economy firms. Further, the state was able to capitalise on the victory and create new national companies. The German defeat led to the Alsatian potash mines being placed under a provisional authority before being transferred to state control in 1924, thereby depriving the large chemical firms (Saint-Gobain, Kuhlmann, Péchiney) of a much-coveted area for future development. After complex negotiations with private conglomerates had collapsed, the state also secured German patents on synthetic ammonia by creating the Office National Interprofessionnel de l'Azote (ONIA). Although Saint-Gobain directors claimed that this was an etatist plot inspired by the military and senior civil servants, it is not clear that public officials meant to establish the foundations for a coherent state-owned industrial sector.[22]

In other areas of business, state intervention was often limited by weak financial resources, which, despite the extension of taxation, were burdened at least until 1926 by the costs of the war and reconstruction.[23] Under the law of 17 April 1919, industrial damages, estimated at roughly FF8,000 million (1914 values), were eligible for full compensation. Procedure was cumbersome and state use of compensation proved to be minimal, except in a few cases.[24] In sum, the state cannot always be blamed for letting many companies rebuild using outdated equipment, because the legislature wanted to give free rein to private initiative.

New financial institutions were indeed created under indirect state control: the Banques Populaires (1917), Crédit National Hôtelier (1924), Crédit National (1919), with the aim of providing financial support to small and mid-sized companies. The role of the Crédit National was limited, however, by the paucity of the means allocated to it and its obligation to reserve 80 per cent of advances for the reconstruction of disaster areas. In housing, state intervention presented contradictory features. For social reasons, rent controls – initially introduced in 1914 – were maintained until after the second world war, except for rents over FF9,000 after 1929. This helped to jeopardise the profitability of the sector, feeding a crisis of housing investment and, more particularly, slowing down the construction of low-rent dwellings for the working class.[25]

Recently, the later years of the 1920s have been reappraised. Thanks to the stabilisation of the currency, the restoration of finances and the appearance of a budget surplus for the first time since the war, the Poincaré government initiated a policy of public investment and subsidies which, in the context of the 1927 recession, seem like the 'ingredients of a Keynesian recipe'.[26] Aside from armament firms and the traditional civil areas (transport, communications), companies involved in social housing, urban planning or rural equipment also benefited from this state-induced boom. In addition, the Loucheur law of 1928 created publicly financed housing, whose main beneficiaries in the early 1930s were the fast-growing residential suburbs. At that time public officials promoted policies fostering concentration and rationalisation among companies in strategic sectors. This can be seen in the iron and steel industry, a target for European integration plans.[27] The same attitudes prevailed in mechanical construction, long the beneficiary of public sector orders. In aeronautics, under the leadership of Pierre-Etienne Flandin until 1928, state policy revived the tradition of spreading orders, reinforcing the proliferation of companies and workshops. Later, however, engineer Albert Caquot of the Corps des Ponts-et-Chaussées and director at the Ministère de l'Air, promoted the modernisation and concentration of firms by reserving large orders for 'rationalised firms', which would be able to fulfil them 'thanks to the regrouping of existing manufacturers'.[28] The same strategy was also applied to shipbuilding.

Thus, during the 1920s, government strengthened its direct and indirect controls in the traditional areas, often promoting concentration or industrial rationalisation, while similar efforts were also being made by private companies in mechanical and electrical construction. The stormy years of the 1930s, however, were to interrupt these trends.

THE CRISIS OF THE 1930s: THE WAR AND INITIAL DESIGNS FOR A STATE INDUSTRIAL SECTOR

The difficulties arising from the crisis were underestimated by public officials, thanks to continuing monetary stability and relatively low levels of unemployment. They none the less led to tentative state intervention which was torn between widespread liberal sympathies and the need to reinforce protection of activities long supervised by the state.

The crisis, the Popular Front and the mixed economy.

Successive 'plans' for major public works (Tardieu plan of 1929, Steeg and Laval plans of 1931, Marquet plan of 1934) are somewhat deceptive; they involved very limited sums of money and were only partly implemented. Their impact on the economic situation was slight, and they did not involve increased public control over private companies.[29] The state, however, had to rescue companies threatened by the crisis, but this cannot be interpreted as a global plan. Again, the domain of mixed-economy firms expanded in an unpremeditated fashion.

Transport companies, subject to dwindling traffic, became the main targets for intervention. In 1931, confronted by its severe financial difficulties, the state became the major shareholder of the Compagnie Internationale des Wagons-lits, through a capital increase subscribed by the Caisse des Dépôts. The state was represented in the company by Raoul Dautry and René Mayer, two outstanding figures straddling the divide between public and private interests in transport. The latter, the main negotiator of the transaction, became chairman of the board of the company in 1932. In that capacity, he became the executive officer of Air-Union (Bréguet).

Air transport companies, cut from eleven to five by mergers, were hit by the crisis in late 1932. As on the railways, the state had multiplied premiums and subsidies to these companies on condition that they continued to run unprofitable services. Over a period of fifteen years, government devoted FF2,000 million francs (including FF1,400 million in subsidies) to air transport. The Aéropostale scandal and a report from the Conseil économique hastened the passing of a law in December 1932 that introduced mixed-economy status. Pierre Cot, Ministre de l'Air in January 1933, called upon René Mayer to negotiate with the companies and pronounced himself in favour of a single concern. The result was the creation of the limited company Air-France in August 1933, in whose capital the state held a 25 per cent interest. The same year, the state saved the Compagnie Générale Trans-atlantique by acquiring an 83 per cent interest in its capital. In response to the crisis, the state thus increased the number of mixed-economy firms, this time without shying away from acquiring a majority interest.

The policies adopted in the wake of the Popular Front victory in 1936–7 continued those of 1931–3, rather than abandoning them. This *Rassemble-ment populaire* political platform, made public in January 1936, included very few nationalisations, relying more on boosting consumption.[30] Hostile to nationalisation, the radicals preferred the established system of mixed-economy firms. The Communists, anxious to secure a political alliance between working and middle classes, also rejected nationalisation. Even the Socialists, who supported CGT plans for 'industrialised nationalisation', sympathised with the old Guesdist dislike of the state boss and with Communist criticisms of economic planning, which – embodying managerial revisionism – stood accused of abandoning revolutionary principles. In the industrial sector, only the armament companies were mentioned. They featured in the chapter on 'political demands', concerned to improve the ethics of the 'cannon merchants'. The law was passed by a majority exceeding the supporters of the ruling coalition: 484 in favour and 45 against in the Chamber, voted by a show of hands in the Senate on 7 August 1936. After the enforcement orders, one firm that worked for the navy and eight that worked for the Ministère de Guerre were transformed into state arsenals. The most obvious change concerned aeronautics. Here Pierre Cot, who resumed office as Ministre de l'Air in June 1936, won acceptance of his proposal for national companies to operate under private law. The radical minister wanted to establish state control over production while preserving, in the absence of state engineers, the initiative and competence of the manufacturers in innovation and design. Twenty-two factories were regrouped into six national aeronautical construction firms, in which the state's interest stood at 67 per cent. These firms were still managed by their former directors, such as Potez, Dassault and Dewoitine, whose research offices remained private and whose salaries were unchanged: 'I don't want men with a 500,000-franc lifestyle to feel cramped,' Pierre Cot announced in the Senate.

In contrast, engine manufacturers (Gnome et Rhône, Hispano-Suiza) kept state involvement to a minority interest. The nationalisation of the sector, initially intended to improve its ethics, was to contribute to its rationalisation in the context of rearmament. These effects, however, only began at the end of 1938, although historical analyses diverge on the relative efficiency of state-sponsored reorganisation.[31]

The SNCF, a nationalisation alien to Popular Front ideology?

Already threatened by growing competition from cars, the crisis increased the railway companies' financial problems. In 1934, the state initiated an illusory policy of 'transport co-ordination'.[32] Earlier negotiations between the state and the companies in 1931 sought to revise the 1921 agreement, which was by now unenforceable. No solution was forthcoming and Léon Blum's downfall in June 1937 saved the companies from expropriation, as proposed by Jules Moch of the Section Française de l'Internationale Ouvrière (SFIO). The subsequent presence of moderate radicals in the government (Chautemps as Prime Minister, Bonnet at Finance and Queuille at Travaux Publics) together with the Senate's vigilance, induced Edouard de Rothschild, president of the Compagnie du Nord, and René Mayer, his chief aide, to seize the opportunity to avoid nationalisation pure and simple. This time, Mayer negotiated as the companies' sole representative. A pragmatic compromise was agreed and signed on 31 August 1937. The new Société Nationale des Chemins de fer Français (SNCF) took over all the networks on 1 January 1938. After heated discussions, the state allowed the companies' 'private domain' to be preserved and agreed to pay roughly FF700 million in forty-five annual instalments in compensation; the final payment was made on 31 December 1982! The state obtained a 51 per cent interest in the capital and secured majority representation on the board (seventeen out of thirty-three). This arrangement warrants the use of the term 'nationalisation', although it embodied the tradition of the earlier mixed firms, combining state control with the operators' technical expertise. Continuity in management, personnel and operation bears witness to this 'subtle compromise'.[33] François Caron has emphasised that this nationalisation was hardly 'revolutionary'. The former railway directors were anxious to rid themselves of the responsibility for such an unprofitable system; they had no authority to solve the financial position but debt still threatened to compromise management itself. Nationalisation only speeded up a process which, since the late nineteenth century, had restricted the powers of company officials, especially over rates and line operation. After 1937, the withdrawal into the private domain, and particularly the conversion of the Nord, PO and PLM into holding companies of the Rothschild group, indicated an irreversible disengagement.[34]

This redistribution of powers resembled more a state take-over (*étatisation*) than nationalisation, which should have involved tripartite management (state, users, personnel) according to the plans of the CGT Federation des Cheminots, whose chief secretary voiced his disappointment in May 1939 by translating the SNCF acronym as *'Sabotage de la Nationalisation par le Capitalisme Ferroviaire'* (sabotage of nationalisation by railway capitalism). Rather than a 'socialist' measure won in the 'upturn' of 1936, this was a compromise worked out between private interests and the politically moderate fraction of the Popular Front, by then on its last legs. All these reorganisations of transport companies were 'nationalisations' – in the sense that the state gained authority – in transition, mirroring the politics of the radicals (Cot, Queuille, Mayer) who negotiated them. They embodied a compromise between public control and private interest, while signalling a new stage in state control and the technical unification of the network.

State surveillance of energy

At the same time, the state strengthened controls over energy, although it did not call company ownership into question. The law passed on 18 August 1936 on the organisation of the coal market fulfilled the aim of Sous-secretaire d'Etat aux Mines Paul Ramadier to abolish business controls over price-setting. In an inflationary period, the state acquired powers to authorise higher prices on request. Subsequently, government permitted increases provided that the company observed social laws governing paid vacations and the forty-hour week and set aside a portion for new works (later condemned as insufficient) to be conducted under the technical and financial control of the Administration des Mines. In return, the French market was strongly protected against foreign imports and the state helped mines with 'difficult conditions'. Again, we find compromise between private profitability and public interest, which from 1936 to 1944 continued to require modernisation to raise production and cut imports, damaging the balance of trade. Various investigations by engineers showed the technical necessity of concentrating management, whatever the terms of the public–private compromise.

Similarly, public control over the electricity industry was increased and the co-ordination of firms was extended, again a technical necessity from a professional point of view. In 1935, a statutory order introduced public control over thermal production; other statutory orders regulated tariffs, which had been untouched by the crisis, even imposing a 10 per cent cut, to the dismay of management. By 1936, however, a national grid was in prospect and the CGT was discussing nationalisation. Financial problems caused the owners to turn to the state to adjust tariff policy and to facilitate financing in order to restore investment, in view of the stagnation of financial markets. In 1938, Pierre Simon, directeur de l'Electricité au Ministère des Travaux Publics, urged the two heads of the main private conglomerates, Durand and Mercier, to harmonise hydraulic and thermal interests and to come up with an equipment programme: 'I give you a month to bring it to me. If in a month you haven't done anything, I will do it myself . . . ' Thus was born the 1938 plan, known as the 'three thousand million plan': a vast programme of dam-building over five years (Génissiat, l'Aigle), to be carried out by mixed-economy firms and financed by loans issued by a debenture group under state control, in which most companies participated. As a result, this 'osmosis between public and private' contributed to the creation of a national private management, a crucial factor in the rationalisation of the industry.[35] Both state engineers and private managers belonged to the *Corps des Ponts*, facilitating co-operation between industrial capital and the spirit of public service.

At the end of 1937, the government commissioned a production enquiry, promoting dialogue between unions and employers. While this investigation did not lead to agreement, it revealed the main obstacles to economic recovery (specifically, insufficient coal production) and formulated investment plans capable of removing them: plans for hydraulic plant construction, for the electrification of railways, for the modernisation of coal mines, coke works and iron and steel factories, all of which aimed to cut coal consumption.[36] This macro-economic diagnosis was to serve largely as a guide for state technicians and private businessmen in the following years.

The second world war: the genesis of dirigisme

Because of the war, then defeat and the Occupation, the French state was weakened while – in contrast – its grip over numerous companies was strengthened. Private managers acknowledged that circumstances imposed a controlled economy. State authorities extended the controls established in September 1939 – of prices, salaries and foreign trade – by setting up an extended apparatus of price regulation and of raw material allocation. Comités d'Organisation (CO) regrouped companies by sector, headed by employers' representatives; these were officially empowered to co-ordinate production and allocate raw materials.[37] Advocates of corporatism were soon disillusioned, however, for at the top the Ministère de la Production Industrielle and the Office Central de Répartition des Produits Industriels (OCRPI), under the surveillance of the occupying powers, arbitrated in matters of allocation and strengthened their hold when shortages became worse in 1941. In effect, CO efficiency was uneven. In industrial sectors which were already concentrated before the war (coal mines, electricity, the iron and steel industry, the chemical industry), the COs – dominated by major employers – had to handle shortages exacerbated by German levies. However, the CO also served as a forum within which employers and the state – in sectors where a prewar dialogue had been established – could explore ideas on future objectives, whatever the immediate difficulties.[38]

Likewise, in the traditional areas of state intervention – energy, transport – official controls extended to new frontiers. In the oil industry, collaboration between state and private companies in oil prospecting increased; after the Saint-Marcet discovery, several national firms were created between 1941 and 1944, including the Société Nationale des Pétroles d'Aquitaine (SNPA) in 1942.[39] In the Parisian transport system, the state prompted a merger between the underground and the surface network in 1942. From a legal and financial standpoint, private interests were safeguarded by the continued existence of the CMP, which took over the STCRP.

In less organised sectors, such as consumer goods (textiles, leather and so on), COs were often headed by smaller employers, whose activities were impeded by bureaucracy and the complexity of the task involved. Further, company activity could be affected by the policy of state collaboration with German authorities in 1941; from the spring of 1942, it was further disrupted by German pressures on labour resources. Although their influence was limited, the COs' influence appeared negative to small or medium-size companies and their spokesmen, like Léon Gingembre, who were highly critical of the 'trusts', echoing a type of anti-capitalism manifest during the Vichy period.

Although weakened by 1944 by multiple shortages, the transport crisis and growing unpopularity, central controls and the CO structure were maintained by the governments which emerged after the Liberation.

FROM LIBERATION TO THE 1950s: A DOMINANT PUBLIC SECTOR?

Following the Liberation in 1944, the state's hold over companies was subjected to two contradictory pressures: shortages, which called for a reinforcement of control structures, and the disrepute of these structures, which public opinion identified with the Occupation.

Nationalisation in three stages

Under the Occupation, *France libre* (Free France) plans promoted the development of nationalised companies. While still underground, the Conseil National de la Résistance produced an agreement to 'return the great monopolies in the means of production to the nation', which appeared in its programme of 15 March 1944.[40] At that time, economic preoccupations were focused on how a reconstruction programme could be implemented which would not be undermined by short-term investment. Further, there was a desire to punish employers suspected of collaboration and to secure social peace in companies where tensions and resentment ran high. This combination of motives varied over a relatively short period which can be divided into three stages.

The first period, from the Liberation to the summer of 1945 – called a 'post-insurrectional, both Jacobin and anti-capitalist phase' – seems paradoxical.[41] On the one hand, in a hundred or so companies in southern France (Toulouse, Lyon and Marseille), the local workforce sought to sack their former employers and to establish workers' control. This led to the creation of worker management committees and to measures involving requisitioning or impounding (Berliet) of a strictly temporary nature. The few opinion polls taken at that time showed widespread popular support for nationalisation. However, this reflected the heat of the moment and was not echoed politically at national level, although it partly explains the ordinance of 22 February 1945, which introduced works councils. These councils had no authority over management; their power was limited to the provision of social benefits. After an official investigation and the intervention of the Conseil d'Etat, most expropriated companies were restored to their former owners in 1948. In a few isolated examples the movement did promote nationalisation. Such was the case for the Nord-Pas-de-Calais coal mines, where tension between miners, employers and lower management threatened the production which was crucial for economic recovery. After the mines were requisitioned (27 September 1944) and former employers were suspended, the Houillères nationales were created on 13 December 1944; ownership of the mines, however, remained untouched. In two other cases, patriotic motives led to the dismissal of managers charged with collaboration with the enemy. Renault (nationalised on 16 January 1945) and Gnome-et-Rhône (29 May 1945) constitute typical examples; both, however, had been dependent on public policy contacts and contracts since before the war. To these can be added the CMP, which was first placed under a temporary authority upon Liberation; its case was definitively settled in 1948. Likewise, the ordinance of 26 June 1945 transferred to the state a minimum interest of 60 per cent in the capital of Air France, Air Bleu and Air Transatlantique, but did not make a permanent settlement. This relative timidity must be interpreted as the result of various delaying strategies on the part of the political parties, the senior civil servants and General de Gaulle himself, who was careful to retain provisional settlements until public opinion had been ascertained.

The second phase was the winter of 1945–6, by which time nationalisations could be decided calmly by a constituent Assembly, where the majority was held by the PC (Communist Party) and the SFIO (Socialist

Party), which had published a nationalisation programme in March 1945. Now nationalisation meant total state ownership. In industry, with the creation of EDF–GDF (Electricite de France–Gaz de France) on 8 April 1946 – merging over a thousand private firms dealing in generation, manufacture and distribution – and of the Charbonnages de France on 17 May 1946, the major part of the energy sector was affected. The motives for these two nationalisations, articulated by Communist Minister Marcel Paul, highlighted 'the current facilities of the country', 'rational management' and a 'very significant increase in production'. In both cases, full nationalisation was the conclusion of a long history of growing public control, now vitally necessary since it was portrayed as the lever for rationalising industries destined to form the foundations for economic recovery. These nationalisations were not vindictive; with hindsight, compensation appears quite generous, combining a fixed minimum interest rate of 3 per cent and a variable interest rate amounting to 1 per cent (EDF) or 0.25 per cent (Charbonnages) of turnover. In the case of the coal mines, pressure from the CGT union underscored the significance of social objectives. In the case of electricity, the transformation received full support from the parliamentary political majority, the workforce and management (owners excepted), for whom nationalisation meant a concentration and unification of the network, in keeping with previous work by the state engineers.[42]

Parallel to this, the state reinforced the oil policies defined before the war: prospecting for crude and co-operating with large international firms for refining. The Bureau des Recherches Pétrolières (BRP), created in 1945, dominated the SNPA, supervised the Régie Autonome des Pétroles and founded two new overseas firms (the SNRepal in Algeria in 1946; the SPAE in the Congo in 1949). Thus strengthened, the public oil sector scored a further success with the discovery of Lacq gas in 1951. As early as 1944, the Centre National d'Etudes des Télécommunications (CNET) was launched. In October 1945, de Gaulle created the Commissariat à l'Energie Atomique (CEA), which was to organise French atomic interests in the face of Anglo-Saxon dominance.

After the first constitutional reform was rejected in the summer of 1946, a swing to the right occurred; public opinion proved receptive to criticisms levelled against the management of nationalised companies. The three-party ruling coalition broke up in 1947 and the SFIO moved closer to the moderates; residual nationalisations more closely resembled the measures of the 1930s. In February of 1948, the Compagnie Générale Transatlantique and the Compagnie des Messageries Maritimes were retained as mixed-economy firms, the state holding 64 per cent and 69 per cent of the capital respectively. In June 1948, after three years of debate, Edgar Faure placed Air France under mixed-economy status, with 30 per cent of the capital to be held by persons other than the state. Finally, in the case of the RATP, nationalisation was ruled out in March 1948; instead an authority was instituted under the control of an Office Régional des Transports Parisiens, in keeping with control over public services.[43]

Macroeconomic coherence and adverse effects

At this point, we would like to modify in two ways the notion of a public sector coinciding with a vast domain of modern employment, rationalised according to the industrial model: first, by re-examining the diverse expectations of political and social forces in 1945, which reveal numerous competing possibilities; second, by distinguishing particular time perspectives which, coming together at the Liberation, display the specifically French configuration of the state's role in the economy behind the deceptive veil of homogeneity.

Roughly speaking, three interpretations may be given of the 1944–6 nationalisations, corresponding to three socio-political or professional groups. We can discern the concept of 'industrialised nationalisation' (1919) of the old CGT confederations, as articulated in the CGT's 1935 Plan and defended in 1944–6 by socialist ministers who supported economic planning, such as André Philip or Jules Moch. In their vision, the public sector would fit into a mixed economy and be subjected to a plan, which would be managed by representatives of the state, the unions and consumers, alongside centrally administered institutions designed to secure social compromise (such as collective industrial agreements, subjected to state control).[44]

The communists and the CGT's former unitarians were late converts to nationalisation, thanks both to circumstances and their general political strategies. Nationalised industries indeed served the purpose of the 'Production Battle', declared in November 1944; they gave the CGT new leverage to influence industrial affairs through the powers its representatives acquired in the nationalised companies. On 15 June 1946, Maurice Thorez stated in a (confidential) communication to the Communist Party Central Committee: 'as to nationalisations . . . we support them at the given moment, as they constitute . . . a means of curbing the domination of capital, so as to be able to mobilise the masses'.[45]

Finally, a number of high-ranking engineers connected to the Ministère de l'Industrie, as well as to the companies concerned, welcomed nationalisation as a convenient framework for the national unification of the market for specific products or services, as well as for a rationalisation that promoted the general interest – following a pattern already explored before the war and during the Occupation.

The 1945–6 legislation was originally inspired by the prewar principles of 'industrialised nationalisation'; it created tripartite management (personnel, state, consumers), in order to avoid state takeover, pure and simple. During the first few months of implementation, however, the weight of state representation increased. The Charbonnages served as a testing ground. As a result of the policies of the (communist) Sous-secretaire d'Etat, Auguste Lecoeur, the CGT had a majority on the board in 1946 through its representation of workers, consumers and even the ministry. The following year, this prompted the ruling coalition to push aside consumer interests and to increase the state's weight at the expense of the board. At EDF, Marcel Paul used a different approach, bypassing union officials in favour of senior technicians, who supported nationalisation. Further, a class of managers with much technical expertise had emerged from among their number. Some – especially at EDF – were to launch theoretical studies of management, resulting in innovative rules for tariff calculations (as illustrated by M. Boiteux's works) and for investment. Thus, the state engineers' version triumphed at an early stage, though some elements of the alternative inter-pretations were retained. Even though public companies did not turn into the perfect employers some had anticipated, salaried workers often enjoyed a more advantageous status in them than in common law, greater job stability, extensive systems of company benefits, personnel committees and guarantees of union freedom. These companies did little or nothing to involve their workers in strategic policy; they did, however, contribute to the evolution of good industrial relations. The unions affiliated with the then still unified CGT were able to raise employee status to the highest standard within the large national companies, extending or amplifying benefits that had long been granted to compensate for constraints connected with job risk (mines, railways) and/or the requirements of public service.

At the end of the 1940s, national industrial and commercial companies (including the SNCF and the PTT) employed nearly 1.3 million salaried employees, or 10 per cent of the non-agricultural working population. At the end of the 1950s, the public sector supplied over 13 per cent of national pro-duction. Beyond this global assessment, however, the key role of companies under public control was rooted in their economic and technical coherence, despite their great diversity in status.

In several of these companies (SNCF, Charbonnages, EDF), public control corresponded to regrouping, rationalisation and a measure of technical harmonisation, which underscored the state's clear preference for large com-panies and economies of scale. 'Public companies were able to think big.'[46] The greater part of the newly nationalised sector was made up of large, capital-intensive companies, financing heavy investments well suited to new structures of central public funding, and implementing programmes formally worked out by engineers from both state departments and the industries concerned. The products and services were standardised, sensitive to economies of scale, submitted to largely protected or monopolised markets, and situated in the upstream sectors of the economy (energy, transport), whose recovery was central for a return to growth. Further, these companies typically maintained rates or prices below the average and received subsidies for a large part of their operating budgets in compensation.[47] Contemporary witnesses, notably officials in charge of national accounting, were aware of this. As early as 1952 they observed that, by compelling national companies to sell at below operating costs, the state exempted client companies – especially major consumers of energy or transport – from paying their share of these investments. On this count, the French proceeded differently from officials in the British Labour government, who raised prices in the basic sectors so as to facilitate self-financing.

Rather than being won over to an explicitly Keynesian policy – Keynes really only became known to national accounting experts in 1948–50 – state officials were converted to a dual production policy, involving massive public financing of investments in the basic industries that privileged the nationalised sector. By a double multiplier effect, public investment supported growth – not only through the operation of (both national and private) companies in these industries, but also through the windfall of orders for the re-equipment of nationalised companies: great EDF dams, the modernisation of the coal mines, especially those in the east, electrification of the SNCF's Paris–Lyon line. Reports by the Commissariat Général au Plan (CGP) or the Commission des Investissements repeatedly pointed to the 'chain reactions' induced by the funds made available to the nationalised sector, which served to funnel funds towards the private equipment industries through orders for tools or works (to construction and civil engineering, electrical, mechanical, railway or naval construction, and, secondly, to the iron and steel industry and manufacturers of construction materials).[48] Calculations by the CGP show that in 1949 public investment generated half the production value of equipment goods and one-third of total industrial production.[49] Thus, the state provided private companies with the prospect of continuous growth. This followed the suggestions of Auguste Detoeuf, a major business leader in electrical construction, who had advocated in June 1936 'a ten year plan for regulating the economy', under which the state, faced with the 'refusal to invest', could change 'the general psychosis' by funding a programme 'of at least one hundred thousand million [francs]', which would 'be considered bottomless by everyone'.[50] In summary, by its etatist methods of funding as well as through its orders, the nationalised sector created the prospect of strong and lasting demand.

The focal position of the public sector was not derived so much from partial or total state ownership as from its centrality in relation to the priorities defined for the 'basic sectors' in the first Plans. State-controlled planning and financing proved one of the most efficient levers for turning these priorities into reality, at a time when the financial market still seemed depressed. Thus, national energy (CDF, EDF–GDF, CNR) and transport companies (SNCF, Air France) benefited from powerful public financing, through the agency of the Fonds de Modernisation et d'Equipement (FME), which became the Fonds de Développement Economique et Social (FDES) in 1955; until 1951, the largest part of Marshall aid was channelled through the FME. These five companies reaped between 40 per cent (in 1951) and 90 per cent (in 1948) of FME funds. The iron and steel companies, however, though they remained private, were also well endowed, whereas the RATP, though public, was sacrificed as not being a priority.

None the less, from 1947–8 economists, business leaders and politicians expressed criticism of companies under public control, simultaneously denouncing mismanagement, the demagogic status of the personnel, politicisation and even deadlocks in their development.[51] It is sometimes difficult to distinguish between economic or technical arguments and a more general ideological denunciation of state tyranny. Questioning certain goals ultimately addressed the rulers' economic choices. Does this mean that public choices in technological or economic matters bore down heavily on growth as a whole? We should distinguish, among companies under public control, those which enjoyed a growing, protected market. The priority given to the basic sectors sacrificed mechanical engineering, housing, telecommunications and urban transport at the beginning of the 1950s. In these sectors there were also public companies which sometimes successfully overcame this handicap: here, Renault's dynamism contrasts with the RATP's apathy. Maintaining certain policy preferences – the predominance of coal, the support for an iron and steel industry that was not properly restructured, the problems of aeronautics – also paved the way for future disappointments. Does this, however, reflect simply the choices of public decision-makers, or is it a consequence of professional preference, according to the tendencies of a 'corporatist–etatist management' (Pierre Rosanvallon)? In addition, as was recently emphasised by François Bloch-Laine (Directeur du Tresor, 1947–52), state financial officials ceaselessly attempted to make way for market mechanisms, as evidenced by an early 'debudgetisation'.[52]

Some of the priorities were redefined with the Second Plan, especially through aid to construction. And as compensation, the windfall to other companies appears to have been undeniable: in public works, business relied largely on public investment programmes (by EDF and the SNCF especially) and low-price policies benefited numerous companies downstream, stimulating remarks about 'transfers from the state to industry'.[53]

Three time-sequences and three interpretations

Nationalisation mainly affected the traditional areas of intervention by state engineers (transport, energy) and signalled a further step in public control, building on the granting of concessions and the creation of mixed-economy firms. It revived a long history of public service policy, favoured by the state's technical and political leaders who exerted pressure towards unified, low and egalitarian prices and towards benefits granted to employees to compensate for particular constraints. Thus, the engineers were able once again to employ their experience and competence in the service of a compromise between economic policy and business management.

This history, rooted in the long term, became doubly articulated within a medium-sized time-sequence embracing the Depression years 1930–44. Faced with a double collapse (economic and financial after 1931, political in 1940–4), state financial leaders engineered a 'conversion' towards productive expenditure. New institutions (FME, Commission des Investissements, national accounting) were grafted on to the traditional apparatus of the state, especially the Directeur du Tresor in the Ministère de Finance, in combination with a newcomer, the CGP, headed by Jean Monnet. Heavy investment in the basic industries could thus benefit from public resources, fortunately increased by Marshall Aid from 1948 to 1952, that had been so deficient since the beginning of the crisis.

This made possible the great investment programmes that had been worked out in the preceding fifteen years – through the dialogue between engineers of (the then private) companies and those of the state: from the diagnosis of the production enquiry (1937), to the 'three thousand million' electrical programme (1938), to the modernisation programmes (coal mines, hydroelectric energy, SNCF, coke works and steel works) conceived by the Comités d'Organization during the Occupation – down to the programmes attached to the Monnet Plan in 1946. This medium-term history deals with state elites, both financial (with the innovators at the Inspection des Finances, such as François Bloch Laine or Claude Gruson) and techno-economic (engineers from the Corps des Mines and the Corps des Ponts), who harmonised their views with the productivist social consensus created by the Commissions de Modernisation of the CGP.

Last, this history would not have unfolded had it not combined with a third, based on the short term: the socio-political situation at the Liberation. The stronger elements of the workers' movement (the CGT and the PCF) were converted to nationalisation and, from 1944 to 1947, to the cause of national recovery. As a result of the Occupation, several private leaders of large companies, strategic for reconstruction, were discredited. Various components of the Resistance supported these developments, well beyond the traditional left, as illustrated by the programme of the Conseil National de la Résistance and by the attitude of General de Gaulle himself. This helped to legitimise a new role for the state and confirmed the authority of its economic and financial leaders. While the latter regarded their responsi-bilities as ephemeral at the time, their actions were decisive at the specific moment when the investment effort reached its climax. By the dawn of the 1960s, when public companies made up less than a quarter of total investment, as opposed to over a third a decade earlier, they still reaped more than half of long-term credits and more than two-thirds of issued bonds.

These three histories, with their distinct time-sequences, also reflect the three types of nationalisation discussed above. The dominant interpretation, that of the professional engineers, has its roots in the long term. It contributed to the modernisation of energy and transport, rationalised according to the industrial model. In spite of adverse effects, the nationalised sector's dynamism was doubtless due to the fact that the state was no outsider to these companies, even before it became a shareholder. Things were different for the nationalised companies in competitive industries which did not have the character of a public service. In the banking sector, the 1945 nationalisation changed neither the management nor a number of former practices.[54] In mechanical engineering (Renault, aeronautical industry), finally, public control did not entail a different evolution from the private sector.

But the 'socialist' interpretation – central planning combined with a powerful nationalised sector – left its mark, even though former supporters of planning such as André Philip and Jules Moch resigned as early as 1948. Later illustrations might be found in the Services d'Etudes Economique et Financières of the Ministère de l'Economie et Finances (around Claude Grusson in Pierre Mendes France's cabinet in 1954–5), in the aborted attempts at an incomes policy, or even in discussions and conferences on democratic planning in the 1960s. National accounting and planning circles have been culturally marked by these events.

Finally, the interpretation favoured by the CGT's former unitarians survived through the rights, guarantees and benefits granted to workers in nationalised companies as well as in strong union representation in parallel institutions created in 1945–6 (especially the works councils). Even after the break of 1947–8, the CGT still recognised the nationalised companies as some of the 'gains' of the Liberation. All these specifically French configurations strongly coloured the years of growth, the *Trente Glorieuses*. Though it was no longer adequate by 1970, they continued to shape economic perspectives during the subsequent slump.

(Translated by L. Parrott and F. Brunet)

NOTES

1 P. Rosanvallon, *L'Etat en France de 1789 à nos jours*, Le Seuil, Paris, 1989, p. 243.
2 R. Salais *et al.*, *L'invention du chômage*, PUF, Paris, 1986, pp. 140ff.
3 R. Kuisel *L'Etat et capitalisme en France: modernisation et dirigisme au XX siècle* (French translation), Gallimard, Paris, 1984.
4 J. Bouvier, 'Le capitalisme et l'Etat en France', *Recherches et travaux*, Institut d'Histoire économique et sociale, Université de Paris 1, Bulletin no. 15, December 1986, p. 6.
5 A. Plessis (ed.), *Naissance des libertés économiques*, IHI, Paris, 1993.
6 J. Bouvier, 'Libres propos d'une démarche revisionniste', in P. Fridenson and A. Straus (eds), *Le capitalisme français XIX–XX*, Fayard, Paris, 1986, p. 24.

7 J.N. Retiere, 'Une entreprise d'Etat seculaire: les Tabacs', *Entreprises et histoire*, no. 6, 1994, p. 127.

8 E. Chadeau, *L'industrie aeronautique en France, 1900–1950. De Bleriot à Dassault*, Fayard, Paris, 1987, pp. 49ff.

9 C. André and R. Delorme, *L'Etat et l'économie*, Seuil, Paris, 1983, p. 55.

10 F. Caron, 'L'évolution du régime français des chemins de fer: aux origines de l'économie mixte', *Revue d'histoire des chemins de fer*, hors serie, no. 1, 1989, pp. 142ff.

11 D. Larroque, 'Les transports en commun de la Région parisienne. Enjeux politiques et financiers, 1855–1939', Thèse de IIIième cycle, EHESS, 1980, pp. 91ff.

12 M. Roncayolo, 'La ville industrielle', in *Histoire de la France urbaine*, vol. 4, Le Seuil, Paris, 1983.

13 G. Ribeill, *La revolution ferroviaire. La formation des compagnies de chemins de fer, 1823–70*, Editions Belin, Paris, 1993, p. 326,

14 M. Gillet, *Les charbonnages du Nord de la France au XIXième siècle*, Mouton, Paris, 1973, pp. 52ff.

15 P. Fridenson (ed.), *1914–1918: L'autre front*, Cahier du mouvement sociale, Paris, 1977, pp. 111ff.

16 Kuisel, *L'Etat et capitalisme en France*, pp.107ff.

17 J.L. Robert, in C. Andrieu *et al.*, *Les nationalisations de la Liberation*, Presses de la FNSP, Paris, 1987, p. 21.

18 F. Caron, 'L'évolution du régime français', p. 448.

19 G. Ribeill, *Les cheminots*, La Decouverte, Paris, 1990, p. 25.

20 H. Morsel, in Fridenson and Straus, *Le capitalisme français*, p. 387.

21 H. Morsel (ed.), *Histoire de l'électricité en France*, vol. 2, Fayard, Paris, 1994, pp. 30ff.

22 J.P. Daviet, *Un destin internationale: la Compagnie de Saint-Gobainde, 1830–1939*, Editions des archives contemporaines, Paris, 1988, p. 190.

23 M. Lescure, *Les banques, l'Etat et le marche immobilier en France a l'époque contemporaine, 1820–1940*, Editions de l'EHESS, Paris, 1991, pp. 256–73.

24 O. Hardy-Hemery, *De la croissance à la desindustrialisation. Un siècle dans le Valenciennois*, Presses de la FNSP, Paris, 1981, p. 95.

25 Lescure, *Les banques*.

26 P. Saly, 'Poincaré keynesien?', in Fridenson and Straus, *Le capitalisme français*, p. 44.

27 E. Bussière, *La France, le Belgique et l'organisation economique de l'Europe*, Imprimerie Nationale, Paris, 1992.

28 Chadeau, *L'industrie aeronautique*, p. 159.

29 Saly, 'Poincaré keynesien'.

30 M. Margairaz, *L'Etat, l'économie, les finances, 1932–52*, Imprimerie Nationale, Paris, 1991, vol. 1, ch. V.

31 Chadeau, *L'industrie aeronautique*.

32 N. Neiertz, 'La co-ordination des transports en France de 1918 à nos jours', Thèse pour le doctorat en histoire, Université de Paris IV, 1995.

33 Ribeill, *La révolution ferroviaire*, p. 25.

34 Caron, 'L'évolution du régime français', pp. 559ff.

35 Morsel, in Fridenson and Straus, *Le capitalisme française*, p. 389.

36 Margairaz, *L'Etat, l'économie, les finances*, pp. 394ff.
37 M. Margairaz and H. Rousso, 'Vichy, la guerre et les entreprises', *Histoire, économie et société*, 1992–3, pp. 337–68.
38 Ibid.
39 M. L'Huillier, 'La strategie de la CFP durant la Seconde mondiale', *Histoire, économie et société*, 1992–3, pp. 463–78.
40 Andrieu *et al.*, *Les nationalisations de la libération*.
41 Ibid., pp. 236ff.
42 Morsel, *Histoire de l'électricité en France*, p. 1334.
43 G. Ribeill in Andrieu *et al.*, *Les nationalisations de la libération*, pp. 40ff.
44 Margairaz, *L'Etat, l'économie, les finances*, vol. 2, ch. XXI.
45 M. Margairaz, 'Le précipité d'une double histoire', in Association pour l'Histoire d'Electricité en France, *La nationalisation de l'électricité en France*, PUF, Paris, 1996, p. 121.
46 M. Maillet-Chassagne, *Influence de la nationalisation sur la gestion des entreprises publiques*, SEDES, Paris, 1956, p. 32.
47 M. Dolle, 'Forces et faiblesses des entreprises nationales', *Economie et statistique*, no. 103, 1978, pp. 3–22.
48 Commission des Investissements, *Troisième Rapport*, 1950.
49 Cf. Margairaz, *L'Etat, l'économie, les finances*, pp. 1240ff.
50 AN. F60 423, Auguste Detoeuf, 'Essai d'un plan décennal pour la régulation de l'économie', 19 June 1936, published in *Etudes et Documents*, vol. II, 1990, pp. 525–38.
51 Margairaz, *L'Etat, l'économie, les finances*, vol. 2, pp. 1240ff; Fridenson and Straus, *Le capitalisme français*, pp. 175ff.
52 F. Bloch-Laine and J. Bouvier, *La France restaurée, 1945–54*, Fayard, Paris, 1986, pp. 121ff.
53 A. Le Pors, *Les bequilles du capital*, Le Seuil, Paris, 1976, p. 29.
54 J. Bouvier, *Un siècle de banque français*, Hachette, Paris, 1973, pp. 154ff.

3

THE GOVERNMENT, FULL EMPLOYMENT AND THE POLITICS OF INDUSTRIAL EFFICIENCY IN BRITAIN, 1945–1951

Nick Tiratsoo

INTRODUCTION

The Labour administration which won the 1945 election believed that full employment was an absolutely central objective. The electorate had voted decisively against a return to the deprivations of the 1930s and it was now the government's responsibility to turn popular aspirations into reality. The new Cabinet accepted that one of the major weapons in this battle would be a macro-economic strategy aimed at regulating both investment and demand. However, ministers were also agreed about the need for more precise intervention. Viable and secure jobs would only be guaranteed if firms continued to be fully competitive as trade revived in the postwar world. The government, therefore, must promote efficiency wherever it could, especially at the level of individual businesses. In this sense, improved productivity came to be viewed as one of the most important bridges to a full-employment society.

This chapter examines these 'micro' aspects of the official stance.[1] The discussion begins with a consideration of Labour policy, looking at how it developed and what it actually entailed in the years to 1951. The conclusion from this survey is that Labour did not achieve all that was desired, and this obviously raises questions about why change continued to be inhibited. It is argued here that the government's problems were largely political – it had too many enemies and not enough friends – and the chapter ends with an examination of two case studies which illustrate this theme.

LABOUR POLICY

Formation

In the interwar years, Labour developed a fairly straightforward analysis of employment issues. Capitalism, it was argued, inevitably produced structural and cyclical unemployment and so any reforming administration would have to deliberately encourage countervailing tendencies. Various policy options appeared appropriate. It might be necessary to raise wages or investment, and thus boost total demand. Some measure of nationalisation, too, was seen as inevitable. Industries like fuel and transport were so strategically crucial that they could not be left in private hands. The only question that excited and divided was whether the government should create an even bigger public sector.

During the second world war, as part of a wider commitment to reconstruction planning Labour decided to look again at these nostrums. Many in the party were quite happy with the traditional approach, but there was also a growing feeling that modifications might be necessary. The existing view tended to see unemployment as being caused by insufficient demand. In other words, it was generally assumed that most firms would respond effectively once orders were placed. However, there was increasing evidence to suggest that the supply-side could not be relied upon to work in this way. Labour ministers in the Coalition knew, for example, of a Board of Trade review, conducted during 1944, which was highly pessimistic about British industry's prospects in postwar export markets, suggesting bluntly that many companies would not even be able to regain their pre-1939 trade shares. Given this situation, it was concluded, there were good reasons for insisting that Labour's thinking about employment needed to be extended, so as to encompass what occurred inside, as well as outside, firms. Indeed, some went so far as to argue that achieving improved efficiency across industry was the key to constructing socialism. Herbert Morrison, in charge of Labour's electoral strategy, made this point during the 1945 party conference:

> Permanent social reform and security cannot be built on rotten economic foundations, and if we try to build large and expensive social reforms and big schemes of social security on bad capitalistic foundations we shall experience from time to time Geddes' axes and financial crises. Social security, social reform, a permanent advance in the economic standard and life of our people can only proceed side by side with greater efficiency in industry, greater production, and a greater national drive in industry to meet national economic needs.[2]

Turning this perception into policy was not easy, but, in the final year of the war, there were a number of suggestions about what it might entail.

Stafford Cripps, the socialist Minister of Aircraft Production, was a particularly vocal contributor to the debate. He proposed that efficiency could be generated in three main ways. First, it would be necessary to ensure that much of industry re-equipped itself and adopted modern practices, since there were too many factories which were completely out of date and too many employers who remained constrained by their conservatism. British manufacturing had long suffered 'the drawbacks of the pioneer' and now needed to catch up with the techniques that were normal in, for example, America.[3] Second, Cripps argued, there must be profound changes in the way labour was treated within companies. It was no longer good enough to shut the shopfloor out of decision-making. Treating workers as human beings would unlock capabilities and potentials. 'You could not have an efficient shop unless it was a happy shop', Cripps emphasised, adding that 'where there was good personnel management, a smoothly working production committee, and a well-recognised trade union organisation, there you would always find efficiency'.[4] All of this directed attention, finally, to the problem of management. Cripps had run one factory during the first world war and visited several hundred others a quarter of a century later in his capacity as minister, and he was struck by how poor some managers were at their jobs. What industry needed, he concluded, was better-qualified leaders and more systematic mechanisms governing promotion. The point was made forcefully in a speech to the Institute of Industrial Administration during January 1945:

> There is really no justification for handing over the fortunes and future of a factory and all the employees in it to an unqualified individual because he happens to be the chief shareholder's niece's husband. Managers should be chosen for their qualifications, and professional standards should be just as much insisted upon as in the case of a doctor or a solicitor.[5]

By the end of the war, therefore, Labour had generated a far broader approach to the employment issue. It stuck by its commitments to increase demand and directly control some sectors, but was also emphatic on the importance of efficiency. As the party's general election manifesto, *Let Us Face the Future*, underlined, full employment was an absolutely central Labour objective. However, 'a policy of Jobs for All' in the end depended on 'a policy of general economic expansion and efficiency'. Indeed, the document continued, there was no point in pursuing the former without the latter: 'If the standard of life is to be high – as it should be – the standard of production must be high. This means that industry must be thoroughly efficient if the needs of the nation are to be met.'[6]

Implementation

After winning the election of 1945, Labour attempted to develop policies which reflected these insights. About one-fifth of the economy was nationalised, and developments here are examined by Whiteside in Chapter 14 of this volume. What follows focuses on that part of industry which remained in private hands. How did the government attempt to raise efficiency in these sectors?

There was three types of initiative. First, ministers were keen to spread know-how, particularly about the most modern methods, in whatever way they could. Very shortly after Labour's victory, Cripps, now at the Board of Trade, created working parties – composed of employers, trade unionists and outside experts – to review methods in seventeen consumer goods industries and to make recommendations about how each could be brought up to the maximum pitch of efficiency. A few years later, a similar exercise was instigated under the auspices of the Anglo-American Productivity Council (AACP). Washington had become worried by Britain's continuing economic problems and suggested that British industry should be shown what was best practice across the Atlantic. Cripps agreed, and the two governments then created a programme which took sixty-six British teams, composed of 956 employers, managers and workers, on study tours of the USA. The impact of this exercise was magnified by the fact that the teams were expected to produce reports of their findings and publicise them as widely as possible.

Second, the government tried to change attitudes about the way labour was treated in the enterprise. Key figures in the Cabinet were broadly sympathetic to a 'human relations' approach and so backed schemes which conformed to this perspective. The Ministry of Labour used its Personnel Management Advisory Service to persuade firms that trained specialists should be appointed in this field. Furthermore, there was a substantial, if diffuse, campaign to encourage a rapprochement between the two sides of industry. Joint production committees had proved effective in wartime, and so Labour was enthusiastic when the Trades Union Congress (TUC) and the Federation of British Industries (FBI) agreed to call for their re-establishment in 1948. Within a year or so, these committees were operating across much of the country, an outcome that will be examined in greater detail below (pp. 67–9).

Alongside all of this, finally, were various initiatives aimed at improving management standards. During 1946 the government established a committee to examine management education and accepted its subsequent recommendation for a new, integrated qualification system. In the same spirit, Labour was also behind the creation of the British Institute of Management (BIM), a body that was launched with £150,000 of public money in 1948. The idea here was to create the 'organiser and spearhead' of a 'national drive for better management', which would be responsible for 'the compilation of knowledge about management', the 'promotion of education and training facilities' and 'the propagation of knowledge about management, and the stimulation of interest in the subject'.[7]

Success or failure?

This was a formidable raft of reforms, far more substantial than anything that had been attempted by any previous peacetime UK administration. Labour was in effect trying to transform several different aspects of industry and hoped to gain results in the short term. To what extent was it successful in achieving tangible change?

Contemporary observers differed in their assessments of the programme. Harold Wilson, following Cripps at the Board of Trade, reviewed the way in which the working parties had operated, and catalogued some useful results. On the other hand, he was doubtful that they had provoked many real breakthroughs, remarking: 'the fundamental problem which led to the setting up of the Working Parties has still not yet been solved, that is the problem of getting some new initiative into private industry'.[8] A few years later, an official audit of the AACP's activities was more upbeat. It judged that the Council had been 'a most effective instrument for collecting and disseminating information about American industrial practice, and for stimulating thought on productivity problems at all levels of UK industry'.[9] However, others were less certain about such claims. Individual teams had certainly performed differently and some appeared to have been partial failures. The British Productivity Council, the successor of the AACP, launched sector enquiries to measure progress at the beginning of the 1950s, and produced a very uneven picture. The AACP team for the bronze and brass casting industry, for example, had really only invigorated a small number of firms, leaving the majority unaffected. It was gloomily reported: 'Many bronze and brass foundries have not only ignored the advances referred to ... but have failed to adopt such desirable techniques as job simplification ... mechanisation ... an adequate costing system, or work study.'[10] Such evidence convinced many that the sum total of progress had been small. A *Statist* editorial of 1952, looking back over the previous year's efforts, repeated a fairly common refrain:

> There is now a wealth of examples of what can be done if the job is tackled along the right lines. But for every enterprise which has taken some trouble to improve the quality of its management – and through that, its productivity – there are probably a score which have been content to carry on in the traditional way.[11]

One way of judging between these various claims is to adopt a tighter focus and to examine how specific techniques and objectives, which were at the heart of Labour's programme, fared on the ground in British industry during these years. The examples chosen here relate to management. The government, as has been shown, wanted managers to be more professional. Is there any evidence that they were responding?

Progress with popularising the idea of management education was certainly not impressive. An FBI inquiry in 1953 remarked candidly:

> Most industrialists are not easily convinced of the value of formal instruction in learning the task of management, and when it is suggested to them that at least it can be used to learn about the techniques of management, they are inclined to take the view that knowledge of the techniques can be gained well enough by having to apply them.[12]

Two years later, a survey by the *Economist* came to similar conclusions: 'The majority of British top executives are not convinced that the results to date have shown that managers can be made or that management is a science which can be swotted out of books and attested in examinations.'[13] Given such attitudes, few showed much interest in the new qualification system. Between seventy and eighty colleges offered relevant courses in the middle of the 1950s, but only between one and two thousand students had bothered to enrol. Indeed, one estimate was that only 3,000 of the estimated 250,000 managers in Britain at this time were involved in any kind of vocational education.

Nor did it seem that managers and employers were any more impressed with other parts of the 'professionalisation' package. British companies were reportedly cautious about internal management development schemes and unwilling to adopt formalised procedures. A study of 112 enterprises in the north-western industrial area found that only about one-third took this issue seriously. Symptomatically, the whole personnel function was rarely much cultivated outside a minority of big firms. The Institute of Personnel Management was growing at this time – it had 2,881 members in 1945 and 3,434 six years later – but many in industry remained sceptical about its objectives. One enquiry in the Bolton area at the beginning of the 1950s examined why personnel managers were not being appointed, and identified five main reasons:

1   lack of interest on the part of management;
2   fusing of the job of personnel manager with that of general manager, or in some cases that of a director;
3   appointment of 'welfare officers' who do First Aid and sick visiting only;
4   lack of information on personnel management combined with indifference, and in some cases antagonism;
5   lack of interest in training for management generally.[14]

This hardly suggested that employers were weighing the different possibilities with any great care.

In fact, many companies continued to run on what were effectively the antithesis of 'human relations' principles. Managing directors tended to dominate and exercise power almost unilaterally. The ranks of middle and junior management were usually subdivided, with a hierarchy of grades and a proliferation of status symbols. Some companies operated six or seven management restaurants, while more or less luxurious executive lavatories were also used to distinguish rank. Inevitably, too, little thought was given to relationships with the shopfloor. Writing in 1960, the ex-personnel manager turned social scientist Nancy Seear noted that few managements took 'the initiative in approaching worker representatives with a statement of problems and a proposed solution for them'. She continued:

> Management, accustomed to consider the initiation of new schemes an essential part, indeed the very core of its job, in all other aspects of industrial life, has been curiously slow to innovate in the field of labour relations. Traditionally, managements have waited for an approach to be taken up by the unions rather than themselves assuming the lead.[15]

The conclusion which emerges from these examples, therefore, does not support the idea that Labour was able to generate important changes. Much of British industry seems to have continued relatively undisturbed, evolving on its own terms rather than being shaped by the government. If this is correct, it is obviously necessary to ask why the official programme had so little impact. The following sections look at various possible explanations, beginning with those that stress the financial implications of innovation.

ENTERPRISE CALCULATION AND THE WIDER ECONOMIC CONTEXT

Broadberry and Crafts, influenced by Olson, have recently argued that British businesses had little incentive in the late 1940s to modernise.[16] They suggest that a cosy system of encompassing cartels and restrictive labour practices had formed during the 1930s and remained unaltered after the war. This might have been good for political stability, but it was certainly not beneficial for economic restructuring. Feather-bedded in a sellers' market by collusive agreements and hedged in by trade unions, industrialists simply lacked the will or outside stimuli to change their methods. However, this thesis is not in the end a convincing explanation of why Labour struggled.

The first point to make is that, though there was something of a sellers' market after 1945, its impact and longevity can easily be exaggerated. Many

British companies were successful at exporting in the immediate postwar years but by no means all established strong overseas roots. Trade journals constantly warned that problems were likely unless exporters made more of an effort on price and quality. In fact, the honeymoon period ended quicker than almost anyone had predicted. During 1949, the Engineering Advisory Council petitioned the Board of Trade about growing German competition, and thereafter this theme became a commonplace in business and government interactions. By 1952, the *Iron and Coal Trades Review* was arguing that a clear watershed had been reached:

> Every year since the war we have been warned by one Minister after another about the growing threat to our overseas markets from Germany and Japan . . . but so far the markets have been able to absorb the growing output from all of them. There are now signs that the whole picture is changing. In one trade after another the sellers' market has gone, or is about to go.[17]

A similar observation can be made about the extent of collusion. Evidence unearthed by the Monopolies Commission shows that some industrialists were engaged in restrictive agreements. Nevertheless, the charge that competition was widely absent is untenable. Some industries were oligopolies, but as Mercer has recently underlined, this does not mean that they were necessarily uncompetitive.[18] In fact, contemporary studies demonstrated that high levels of concentration and intense rivalry could easily occur together, particularly when foreign-owned companies were present. Nor were trade associations as influential as Broadberry and Crafts imply. The number of such bodies certainly grew after the war, but it is clear that many essentially existed for political purposes – the representation of a trade's interests – rather than to enforce any restraints.

The emphasis on the union straitjacket is also misleading. Few at the time believed that British industry was riddled with restrictive practices, though one or two sectors (shipbuilding, the docks and printing) did have their difficulties. Conversely, it is quite clear that most unions did what they could to help the productivity drive. The most positive part of the union movement was undoubtedly the TUC. Its members made many speeches in favour of what the government was trying to achieve and were capable of being remarkably forthright about the need for greater efficiency on the shopfloor. Indeed, the TUC eventually organised its own productivity mission to the USA and this made a series of recommendations which echoed those in the AACP reports. It was stated quite categorically, for example, that unions should co-operate in the application of 'scientific management' ('not an exact science' but, nevertheless, certainly one capable of making 'a valuable contribution to increasing productivity') and be positive about new machinery and job redeployment. The TUC's one condition in advancing this advice was that unions should at least be consulted before changes were made.[19]

Outside the TUC the position was more complex. A few union executives remained doubtful about aspects of the government's programme and argued that too much power was being ceded to management. Furthermore, ordinary workers were not always enthusiastic. A Washington staffer who interviewed the TUC productivity team after it had returned home was told that long-standing prejudices about American industrial relations still coloured attitudes amongst workers in Britain. He reported:

> the team members ... encountered the paradox that most trade unionists welcomed American machines and gadgets but resented suggestions of American methods of working. In a few cases, this sprang from an anti-American political bias, but in general it was the result of historical industrial attitudes in the UK and a slow-dying belief that American trade union leaders worked hand in hand with management.[20]

Nevertheless, there was little evidence to suggest that grumbling of this type ever turned into outright opposition. Indeed, what impressed American observers above all was the fact that the TUC's wishes were so generally respected. Overall, they noted, the position in Britain was very different from that pertaining in France and Italy, where communist-backed unions were doggedly fighting all productivity-enhancing measures. In general, therefore, it is hardly plausible to argue that the unions played any major part in Labour's difficulties.

Finally, it is worth pointing out that Broadberry and Crafts's emphasis on financial incentive structures is misleading in a more general way. Their focus suggests that firms were being exhorted to make major expenditure decisions by Labour. However, this simply misunderstands what was being attempted in the productivity drive. The whole idea of the government's programme was to spread know-how, new techniques and methods which cost very little but could transform the way a business worked. The emphasis was on analysis and incremental change, not sweeping innovation. Much of what Labour proposed could be (and, on occasion, was) introduced by any type of enterprise, regardless of size or financial strength.

THE EMPLOYERS AND THE PRODUCTIVITY DRIVE

In fact, the reasons why the Attlee government had such difficulty in fostering modernisation during this period were primarily political rather than economic. The basic fact was that most British employers continued to be jaundiced about any degree of state-sponsored activity, and some were persuaded to join campaigns of outright opposition. Attitudes here were fuelled by the common perception in boardrooms that Labour was a party of wholesale nationalisation. The basis for this uncompromising stance had been laid during the course of the war. British industry had entered the war with great confidence, but it soon found itself publicly criticised from all sides as the country plunged into the production crisis of 1940–2. Meanwhile, other spectres were beginning to appear on the horizon. The state was in control of the economy and had legislated so that labour played a much bigger role in decision-making within enterprises. What was going to happen, it was asked in many boardrooms, when the conflict ended? Given these anxieties, employers began to plan their own strategy. The FBI announced itself in favour of industrial self-government. However, behind closed doors, it was generally agreed that the key objective must be the full restoration of a private enterprise system. An ex-official of the Economic League, seeing at first hand what battle was like after being called up, circulated a confidential memorandum denouncing this hidden agenda:

> The statement that 'we are all fighting to create a better Britain' is not, unfortunately, wholly true. We must face the fact that there are individuals, and groups . . . , some holding positions of power and authority, who are watching other people fight to save for them and their friends the particular kind of Britain they desire to see . . . They want to see the restoration of a Britain that would be a comfortable and profitable place for themselves. They are not concerned as to whether it would be comfortable or uncomfortable for the majority of the people.[21]

The last few months of the war were extremely tense in industry, as employers waited to see who would gain the upper hand once the Churchill Coalition left office. As the *Economist* noted in February 1945, the 'problem of industrial relations' cast 'a shadow of doubt over every aspect of production'.[22] When elections were finally called, employers were surprised and dismayed at the scale of Labour's triumph. For a time, some seemed to be on the verge of panic. However, the steadying hands of realists like Norman Kipping at the FBI had a calming effect, and it was recognised that employers would simply have to become more aggressive and vigorously defend their own interests. Few shared Labour's enthusiasm for a 'human relations' approach, and many feared that, whatever the party said, it was intent on creating a massive public sector. On the other hand, there was general agreement that employers needed to do more than just oppose. Pro-business and anti-Labour sentiment would have to be maximised if the Conservatives were ever to regain office. The strategy which emerged, therefore, involved twin emphases: intense manoeuvring behind the scenes, aimed at frustrating government schemes as they were prepared, together with a public campaign to win hearts and minds.

The weapons used in dealing with Whitehall included non-co-operation, obstruction and delay. The problems which enveloped the BIM are a good example of what could be achieved. Cripps's first move to establish this organisation was the appointment of a committee under Sir Clive Ballieu (President of the FBI) charged with making recommendations about how it should be run. Thereafter, however, the minister found further progress extremely hard to attain. A report in *Tribune* at the beginning of 1948 catalogued a saga of delay and confusion:

July 1945	Cripps became President of the Board of Trade
November 1945	Ballieu Committee set up . . .
14 March 1946	Cripps announced findings of Ballieu Committee
12 December 1946	Cripps named Chairman of the First Council of British Institute of Management. (Nine months to find a chairman!)
December 1946/early 1947	Remaining members of Council appointed
August 1947	Director of the Institute appointed. (Seven months to find a director!)
August 1947–January 1948	Institute's affairs shrouded in impenetrable mystery.[23]

The problem was that some powerful figures amongst the employers were doing everything possible to dissuade their colleagues from any involvement. Moreover, action aimed at undermining the BIM continued even after it had finally begun functioning. The *Sunday Express* reported in 1952, for example, that prominent industrialists were receiving an anonymous letter attacking the organisation and alleging that it was squandering public money.

The public campaign, meanwhile, developed the theme that unfettered capitalism could best deliver the goods – a potent message given the widespread shortages and continuation of rationing. Use was made of nominally independent bodies like the Economic League and Aims of Industry, and propaganda was distributed at the factory gate as well as to journalists. Activity reached a peak during 1950 and 1951, around the two general elections. Aims of Industry was estimated to be spending £75,000 per annum at this time, a figure that was 50 per cent more than Labour's press and publicity budget. The Economic League, too, was very energetic: in one month of 1951 alone it distributed 1.6 million leaflets and organised 5,000 meetings.

LABOUR AND THE EMPLOYERS' OPPOSITION

Labour responded to this onslaught by continually stressing its own moderation and wish to proceed through co-operation. Ministers emphasised that they did not intend to pursue wholesale nationalisation, whatever Opposition politicians alleged. At the same time, they also launched several publicity campaigns of their own, aimed at explaining the need for increased production and productivity. Between March 1946 and March 1947, for example, Cabinet members addressed some twenty-six conferences, composed of 28,000 delegates, on aspects of the efficiency question. Nevertheless, many in Labour's ranks concluded in the end that they had been beaten. The employers were simply too astute in their campaigning. Any future Labour government would have to consider enacting new legislation to gain greater control over private industry.

This outcome proved disappointing at the time and provoked some mild grumbling on the left of the party. However, a later generation of historians has tended to be rather more critical, several suggesting that Labour's failure was both symbolic and in part self-inflicted. Barnett and Mercer, writing from very different premises, agree that the government was ill-prepared to deal with private industry, lacked strategic objectives when engaged in reform, and remained over-inclined to compromise. Hinton argues that Labour was held back by its statist traditions. The problem, he concludes, boiled down to the fact that the Attlee Cabinet would not ally itself with the one group that had shown itself in favour of change: a radicalised stratum of shopfloor activists.[24]

Was Labour really as culpable as these accounts allege? There is certainly something in the critics case. It is quite clear, for example, that the efficiency drive was often insufficiently harmonised with other government policies (particularly the export drive), which blunted its overall effectiveness. Moreover, ministerial resolution to pursue goals seems to have declined quite sharply after the devaluation crisis of 1947. A profile in *Business* during 1945 painted Cripps as 'a fanatic for business efficiency'. At around the same time, *Industry Illustrated* commented: 'There can be no question of the present government's serious determination to make British industry the most efficient instrument possible for restoring this country to an early condition of solvency.'[25] By contrast, journalistic comment at the end of the 1940s rarely mentioned these themes. Finally, there can be no doubt that Labour's policies were sometimes put into practice with insufficient care. An amusing example concerns the publicity campaign for productivity. Speakers were sent into industrial districts to explain Labour's case but they did not always have the desired impact. In the Blackburn area, the audience was alienated for a rather unexpected reason, as a trade union official complained: 'Married women form the majority of the staff of the mills and when they observe young females driving these speakers around they think it the limit and do not hesitate to show . . . and declare their attitude.'[26]

While accepting all this, however, it is difficult to accept that the critics are right when they assert that Labour should have pushed the employers harder. For, as ministers recognised, there were good reasons for thinking that this would have been politically unfeasible. Vigorous and punitive action was only possible given a strong popular mandate. Some trade unionists and left-wingers were in favour of more interventionist measures. However, the majority of ordinary workers did not share these views. In fact, as the following brief review will establish, most were not particularly interested in productivity and related issues at all.

It is worth noting, to begin with, that the popular mood in general after 1945 was hardly radical. Writing in 1947, Tom Harrisson of Mass Observation emphasised that politics came low down on many people's list of priorities:

> In the crucial 1945 election, people had to decide – for the first time in ten years – who should run the country. Over a third failed to spare a few minutes during the day to make a cross on a piece of paper against the candidate of their choice. They can be even more negligent; some County councils are elected by under 10 per cent. Yet most of these people spend quite a while every week marking a complex system of crosses and numbers on football pool coupons.[27]

What the majority wanted, opinion polls showed, was a house and a job, and then some peace and quiet. Ideological dogma – more or less national-isation, more or less control of industry – elicited relatively little interest.

Turning to economic issues, the first point to make is that most workers were broadly satisfied with the private enterprise system. There was unease about aspects of business behaviour (for example, high profits) but no general feeling that capitalism itself was wrong. Typically, when a sample of trade unionists was asked in 1950 if their bosses were 'good chaps', 67 per cent replied in the affirmative. One year later, a wider enquiry came to similar conclusions. The British Institute of Public Opinion asked 2,000 people what they felt about 'free enterprise' and found that 65 per cent of the total sample and 60 per cent of working-class respondents believed it to be 'on the whole a good thing'.[28]

What about the efficiency issue itself? Opinions here are not easy to summarise. First, it is quite evident that many understood little of the public debate about productivity. Independent advertising and public relations executives who were called in to advise the government concluded that rank and file workers had 'neither the desire nor the ability to follow a reasoned economic argument' and this was very evident in relation to the more specific question of efficiency. Only a small minority could define the word 'productivity' with any exactitude: unsurprising, given that it was a term which rarely featured in popular discourse.[29] Moreover, confusion and incomprehension increased down the class structure. An official Social Survey report which examined the various phases of public campaigning about efficiency made the following observations:

> Nearly a quarter of unskilled labourers and nearly one fifth of operatives did not know that the government wished to increase production; amongst those who did know, in these two grades, only about one in ten were sufficiently familiar with the phrase 'increasing productivity' to be able to explain clearly what it meant.[30]

In fact, working-class views on this subject tended to be guided by long-standing assumptions about the way labour markets and employers operated. There was little unemployment in the immediate postwar years, but most workers believed that slump conditions were very likely to reappear at any time. Some accepted the argument that increased productivity would boost the chances of sustained growth, but many others wanted only to make the best of what they saw as temporarily favourable conditions. Ferdynand Zweig, a social investigator who interviewed many shopfloor workers, noted the prevalence of instrumental attitudes:

> I must say that the labour market idea is still deeply ingrained in the workmen's own minds and in my conversation with them it has often been referred to. The sellers' market of labour, or the effects of full employment on productivity, are not the illusions of professional economists, but a reality widely known among the workers ... Many workers would say: 'My boss tries to get as much as he can for as little as he can, so why shouldn't I do the same. Business is business.'[31]

In these circumstances, it is not surprising to find that opinions about productivity as such tended to be nebulous and lightly held. When asked directly about how efficiency might be increased, many gave highly conventional answers – everybody should 'work harder' – while far fewer opted for novel or controversial alternatives. Moreover, only a small minority minded strongly about the options. Workers accepted that they had to work but most felt little sense of responsibility for what went on within factories. A report by the Institute of Personnel Management in 1949 captured the popular mood:

> It is unfortunately true to say that a workplace is still a place to which many do not want to come and from which many want

to escape; that many people do not genuinely believe that their work has value; that work-people only vaguely understand the problems and responsibilities of management; that the nature of our economic crisis in spite of all propaganda efforts is not understood and certainly not the part which each individual can play in helping the country to its feet.[32]

In the light of this evidence, therefore, it is hard to agree with the critics' contention that the government should have been more aggressive in enforcing objectives. Labour could have chosen a more radical path, of course, but there is little reason to think that this would have been popular with working-class voters. Indeed, firmer action might easily have led to political isolation, especially since the Conservative party had quickly recovered from its 1945 defeat and was again ready to challenge for power.

THE MECHANICS OF OPPOSITION

(1) BETRO

The previous sections have advanced the argument that Labour's efficiency drive failed because it became entangled in a wider field of industrial politics. The government faced tenacious opposition from employers but found that its room for manoeuvre was strictly limited. Crucially, there appeared to be little chance that the public would back it in any test of strength. The way in which all this worked itself out in practice can be illustrated by examining two specific examples. The first of these concerns an initiative to improve marketing.

In 1945, many British companies were not unnaturally apprehensive about their future overseas prospects. Accordingly, about sixty big firms (including Dunlop, General Electric, Pressed Steel, Reckitt & Coleman, Spillers and Lever Bros) came together and formed the British Export Trade Research Organisation (BETRO) to provide fresh information on foreign markets. They wanted the organisation to be self-supporting, financed by subscribers who would pay an annual fee for whatever help they needed.

At first, BETRO prospered, but by 1947 it was experiencing difficulties, hit by rising costs and a slower than expected build-up of membership. Cripps was alerted and he agreed to help, pledging £150,000 of government money over the next five years – an almost unprecedented subsidy. In defending this move, the minister emphasised that BETRO's aims fitted in well with Labour's overall productivity programme. The sellers' market would not last forever, he noted, and so firms would have to become more market conscious. Responding to the customers' needs was very much integral to efficient production.

The injection of funds stabilised BETRO in the short term, but by the end of the decade it was again struggling. Relatively few firms were apparently convinced about the merits of market research, many continuing to rely upon the 'feel' of the chief executive when it came to assessing commercial possibilities. To make matters worse, BETRO had also gained an unfortunate reputation because of its official connections: as the *Economist* explained, the fact that the organisation was receiving government money 'hampered it in gaining the confidence of industry'.[33]

At this point, the FBI began to play a much greater part in BETRO affairs. It had always wanted to keep the new organisation in 'the family circle' and now saw an opportunity of attaining this end. After bilateral talks, it was agreed that BETRO should hand back what remained of the government subsidy and henceforth depend on the FBI to supply commissions. The two bodies would, in future, operate as allies, with BETRO firmly removed from the clutches of the state.

It is unclear how sincere the FBI was in brokering this deal, but the new arrangement did not, at any rate, generate much extra business for BETRO. Accordingly, both organisations soon found themselves back in discussions, this time to determine whether BETRO had any future at all. FBI officials recognised that they had some degree of moral responsibility to keep their junior partner functioning. An internal memorandum recorded: 'the FBI having persuaded BETRO to abandon its subvention from HMG [Her Majesty's Government] and having entered into a Concordat with BETRO is under some obligation to keep it alive'. On the other hand, all sides frankly accepted that much of industry had not yet 'generally accepted the value of market research'. In the end, commercial considerations proved decisive, and the FBI decided that the current arrangement should be terminated. BETRO, in the words of its chief executive, had been condemned 'to die a fairly ignominious death'.[34] He might have added: 'at the hands of the FBI'.

(2) *Joint production committees*

The second example concerns joint production committees (JPCs). Labour was attracted to this type of plant-based, employer–employee representative body for several reasons. JPCs had been widely used in the war and were generally felt to have been successful at involving the worker and stimulating production. More fundamentally, the idea of joint consultation was at the very heart of Labour's socialism: the worker had a right to be heard in the factory and not just at election times. Thus, when the trades unions mooted the idea of re-establishing JPCs during 1947, government ministers were quick to respond with some enthusiasm.

However, it was soon clear that establishing a common form acceptable to both sides of industry would not prove easy. The trade unions wanted to keep existing collective bargaining machinery intact and so insisted that questions relating to wages and hours must not be part of the JPC purview. Employers' bodies were uneasy about the whole idea of joint consultation, and certainly did not want it to be imposed. Accordingly, the agreement eventually hammered out contained several limitations. All the parties underlined that they were in favour of JPCs, provided it was 'clearly understood' that the committees should be 'voluntary and advisory', not concerned with 'the terms and conditions of employment', and constructed as individual industries saw fit.[35]

During the following few years, JPCs were established across much of British industry. Progress was particularly noticeable in engineering, where 63 per cent of employees in federated firms had access to such committees by 1950. Nevertheless, though proponents of JPCs were gratified by this geographical spread, they did not feel that the initiative as a whole was living up to expectations. The problem, in their view, was that JPCs were tending to become mere talking-shops, endlessly discussing 'tea and toilets' but miserably failing to extend industrial democracy.

What had gone wrong? It seems clear that Labour was genuine in its support for JPCs. Some ministers were worried about the possibility of communist infiltration, but this did not dim their overall enthusiasm for the committees. However, employers once again took a very different line. The FBI was, it is true, formally favourable, but elsewhere scepticism and hostility lurked just beneath the surface. Sir Robert Sinclair, a leading industrialist, won applause at a conference in 1951 for his blunt assertion 'that the line of authority must be kept clear and that "you can't have class representation at any stage in the chain of management"'.[36] At a private meeting organised by Management Research Group One during the previous year, several participants had gone a good deal further. The views of a Dunlop director were by no means untypical:

> There was much loose talk of joint management . . . [He] did not believe that workers wanted to manage . . . Workers needed confidence. We talked of joint consultation, but for us to have confidence in our politicians, such as Churchill, we did not wish to sit in his inner Cabinet. We did not want to know all the facts, when we had confidence in those who managed our national affairs.[37]

If managers accepted JPCs, therefore, it was usually because they allowed a more efficient means of communicating information downwards. Few believed that the new bodies should be allowed to modify traditional management prerogatives.

The final ingredient in this situation was provided by the trade unions. As has already been suggested, most union leaders were in favour of JPCs, provided they did not interfere with collective bargaining. However, union support was perhaps less significant than at first sight seems likely. For it was quite obvious that the rank and file felt very much less strongly about this issue than the leadership did. An investigation by Helen Baker from Princeton during 1951 reported: 'The apathy of the mass of workers to joint consultation was pointed out by almost everyone who had observed or worked with joint consultation.' One year later, the National Institute of Industrial Psychology surveyed how JPCs worked at 700 firms, and made similar observations. The 'clear' conclusion was that 'large numbers of . . . workers knew little about joint consultation, and tended to be apathetic about it unless it happened to be dealing with something of immediate concern to themselves'. Only a 'small group' in each location were really interested.[38] Thus, while union officials could enthuse about JPCs in theory, they also had to recognise that their real powers of influence over this issue were strictly limited.

The disappointing outcome in relation to JPCs, therefore, reflected a particular balance of power. Labour had a clear picture of what it wanted to achieve but was baulked by the employers. Breaking out of this stranglehold proved virtually impossible because – like productivity issues in general – JPCs did not arouse public interest. The result was an impetus to reform which struggled for real substance.

SOME CONCLUSIONS

Placed in a longer-term perspective, Labour policies to improve productivity in the 1940s appear both innovative and far-sighted. The party's approach to employment issues had been traditionally dominated by rather vague and general formulations, pitched at a macro-economic level. Attlee's ministers moved beyond this inheritance and focused on the axiom that security and prosperity for workers could only be established with any certainty if industry worked efficiently. As Jim Tomlinson has pointed out, they had, in effect, been converted to a 'supply-side socialism'.[39]

Once in power, however, Labour found its problems multiplying. Most of the government's policies were both well constructed and appropriate. British industry *was* in need of 'modern' know-how and *did* need to improve its shopfloor relations. Significantly, many big progressive firms were already moving down the road that Labour was signposting. On the other hand, convincing the balance of employers to change proved far from easy. British business had emerged from the war in offensive mood and meant to re-create a 'free' private enterprise system at all costs. The public remained uninterested. Labour could, therefore, only persuade and exhort. The end product was a set of policies which achieved much less than had originally been hoped for.

Of course, at the time little of this seemed to matter much to those who were not directly involved. The predicted postwar slump failed to occur, the result of favourable trading conditions and the government's battery of macro-policies. Nevertheless, more far-sighted observers like Cripps and Wilson were right to warn that Britain was living in a 'fools' paradise'. When competition increased, from the mid-1950s, their prognostication that inefficient industry could not provide secure jobs began to ring all too true.

NOTES

1 The argument presented here builds on themes first presented in N. Tiratsoo and J. Tomlinson, *Industrial Efficiency and State Intervention: Labour 1939–51*, Routledge, London, 1993, and Steven Fielding, Peter Thompson and Nick Tiratsoo, *'England Arise!': The Labour Party and Popular Politics in 1940s Britain*, Manchester University Press, Manchester, 1995. I am grateful to Noel Whiteside for stimulating observations on an earlier draft.

2 *Report of the Forty-fourth Annual Conference of the Labour Party, 1945*, Labour Party, London, 1945, pp. 89–90.

3 *Engineer*, 14 September 1945.

4 *Engineer*, 25 August 1944.

5 S. Cripps, 'Management's contribution to post-war prosperity', *Industrial Administration*, vol. 6, 1945, p. 5.

6 Labour Party, *Let Us Face the Future*, Labour Party, London, 1945, p. 5.

7 Anon, 'British Institute of Management', *Industry*, vol. 16, 1948, p. 17.

8 R.D. 214/November 1948, H. Wilson, 'Progress report of Working Party Recommendations', p. 2, Labour Party Archive, National Museum of Labour History, Manchester.

9 Quoted in N. Tiratsoo and J. Tomlinson, 'Exporting the "Gospel of Productivity": United States Technical Assistance and British Industry, 1945–60', *Business History Review*, Spring 1997 (forthcoming).

10 British Productivity Council, *A Review of Productivity in the Bronze and Brass Casting Industry*, British Productivity Council, London, 1955, p. 1.

11 *Statist*, 28 June 1952.

12 Federation of British Industry, *Education and Training for Management*, FBI, London, 1953, p. 12.

13 *Economist*, 17 December 1955.

14 20 January 1951, Institute of British Management, Bolton Survey, MSS 97/3/SUR/1, Modern Records Centre, University of Warwick (hereafter, MRC)

15 N. Seear, 'Relationships at factory level', in B.C. Roberts (ed.), *Industrial Relations: Contemporary Problems and Perspectives*, Methuen, London, 1962, pp. 164–5.

16 See, for example, S. Broadberry, 'Employment and unemployment', in R. Floud and D. McCloskey (eds), *The Economic History of Britain since 1700*, vol. 3: *1939–1992*, 2nd edn, Cambridge University Press, Cambridge, 1994, pp. 211–13; and N.F.R. Crafts, 'The assessment: British economic growth over the long run', *Oxford Review of Economic Policy*, vol. 4, 1988, p. x.

17 *Iron and Coal Trades Review*, 9 May 1952.

18 H. Mercer, *Constructing a Competitive Order*, Cambridge University Press, Cambridge, 1995.

19 Trades Union Congress, *Trade Unions and Productivity*, TUC, London, 1950, p. 60.

20 Undated memorandum of 1952, 'Survey of United Kingdom trade union productivity team follow-up activities', File 10, Box 10, subject files of G. Atkinson, Labour Division, Office of Economic Policy and Planning, Mission to the UK, R.G. 469, National Archives, Washington, DC.

21 31 August 1942, unsigned memo, enclosed with letter J.G. Gribble to J. Forbes Watson, MSS 200/B/3/2/C940 Pt. 1, MRC.

22 *Economist*, 17 February 1945.

23 *Tribune*, 23 January 1948.

24 J. Hinton, *Shop Floor Citizens: Engineering Democracy in 1940s Britain*, Edward Elgar, Aldershot, Hants., 1994.

25 C. Chisholm, 'Elbow room for free enterprise', *Business*, vol. 75, 1945, p. 43; and 'Editorial', *Industry Illustrated*, vol. 13, 1945, p. 11.

26 28 August 1947, Letter T. Seed to Central Office of Information, INF 12/220, Public Records Office, London (hereafter PRO).

27 T. Harrison, 'The public's progress', in A.G. Weidenfeld (ed.), *The Public's Progress*, Contact Publications, London, 1947, p. xii.

28 Anon., 'Does Britain Believe in Business?', *Future*, vol. 5, 1950, pp. 16–17; Anon., 'What Do Workers Think?', *Future*, vol. 5, 1950, p. 18; Anon., 'What the Public Thinks about Free Enterprise', *Director*, vol. 3, 1951, pp. 45–8.

29 12 November 1948, Memorandum from S.H. Benson Ltd, p. 1, INF 12/245, PRO; and February 1951, H.D. Willcock, 'Survey', RG 23/115, PRO.

30 H.D. Willcock, *Ignorance*, Methodological Series no. 72, London, Social Survey, 1951, p. 9.

31 F. Zweig, *The British Worker*, Penguin, Harmondsworth, Middx, 1952, p. 118.

32 Report of the Institute of Personnel Management for the year 1948–49, p. 16, MSS 200/97/4/1/24, MRC.

33 *Economist*, 22 April 1950.

34 Undated memorandum, 'British Export Trade Research Organisation', p. 1, MSS 200/3/F/S1/43/1, MRC; and 20 December 1951, Letter R. Falk to D. Walker, MSS 200/3/F/S1/43/1, MRC.

35 Tiratsoo and Tomlinson, *Industrial Efficiency*, p. 94.

36 Quoted in 'Special Correspondent', 'Harrogate and Man Management', *Times Review of Industry*, December 1950, p. 14.

37 4 May 1950, 'Report of Directors' Dinner Discussion', Box 6, MRG Papers, British Library of Political and Economic Science, London.

38 H. Baker, 'Joint consultation in England: an American's comments', *Journal of the Institute of Personnel Management*, vol. 33, 1951, p. 60; National Institute of Industrial Psychology, *Joint Consultation in British Industry*, Staples, London, 1952, pp. 85, 87 and 211.

39 J. Tomlinson, 'Mr. Attlee's supply-side socialism', *Economic History Review*, vol. 46, 1993, pp. 1–22.

4

THE 'REAL' WORLD OF THE ENGINEERING AND ELECTRICAL INDUSTRIES IN THE PARISIAN BASIN

The development of state intervention, 1925–1955

Robert Salais

Paris is the centre of political and economic power in France. During the period 1925–55, not a single institutional innovation or change in state policy could have developed without first being the subject of conflict, experiment and political compromise between members of the ruling elite and the population of the Seine. The engineering and electrical industries of the Seine *département* (Paris and its bordering suburbs) became a laboratory for official economic and social policy development. Here, these policies took shape, emerged and ultimately acquired their independence.

The engineering and electrical industries, including the defence industries, experienced major product innovations in transport (automobiles, lorries, aircraft), in the use of electricity and in communications (telecommunications and broadcasting) that are still of major social importance. In France, these innovations were all developed in the Paris area. The industrial sector was closely tied to the state through its development of transport infrastructure and public utilities and through the Ministère de la Défense. Major firms, such as Citroën, Renault, Thomson-Houston and Hotchkiss, were established in the Seine. The area was the heart of the metalworking industry. With 14,000 firms (only 84 of which employed more than 500 people) and more than 300,000 factory and office workers,[1] this was one of the major centres of French economic development. The working class in the industry was large, concentrated, politically organised and well-trained. Technical skills had emerged from craft traditions, also the foundation of the many small firms specialising in highly diversified products. While such skills were

72

an essential resource, they also impeded the introduction of mass production and the scientific management of labour, notably in automobiles. In 1936, this industry served as a model for collective bargaining agreements that later spread to every other sector across the nation. The metalworking industry was the birthplace of the 1936 strikes, and provided the context in which the subsequent Matignon Accord was composed.

For these economic, social and political reasons, the decisive factors and aims underlying the growth of state intervention between the 1930s and 1960 can be understood only in the context of the economic dynamics of the diverse engineering and electrical industries of the Seine and their changes over time. This chapter forms an initial contribution to continuing research.

THE PROBLEM

The diversity of enterprises which we consider here is reflected in the plurality of their products. These products did not correspond to goods defined in mainstream economic theory. Instead, they were the result of *co-ordination* among economic actors. This co-ordination had a number of dimensions, and took place among firms using skills and various specialised technologies to achieve a complex final product (such as an aeroplane). It also involved workers co-operating and combining their know-how within a system of production based on regulations as well as on work and wage conventions. As manufacturers anticipated and customers required specific uses for marketed products, the market could not function without agreement on product 'quality'. Tensions, breakdown and conflicts between agents – as well as innovation – were evidence of the overall dynamics of the sector.

The state was centrally involved in the process of co-ordination. On the one hand, the state was a principal agent in various ways: through public services and public procurement; by initiating legislation, providing finance, establishing norms; and through its economic, social and tax policies. On the other hand, the legitimacy of state action was much disputed in this period. The business of the state was conventionally accepted as compensating for inadequate co-ordination, for market failure.[2] The state was the focal point of expectations: expectations that had to cohere in political agreement on the nature of the common good and the appropriate policy options this involved. Our hypothesis here is that the pace of product development and multiple breakdowns in co-ordination during the 1930s forced the French government to accept responsibility for a global mission to secure economic recovery, a mission that was to become a macroeconomic growth policy after the war.

We will be discussing the various facets of this process, ranging from products to the state itself. For each product and for the economy as a whole, distinct periods mark the evolution of the process. To demonstrate the variety of change over time, we resort to several types of empirical studies. First, we exploit two very different focuses on the macro-economic dynamics in the period between the wars: the estimates of a vectorial auto-regressive (VAR) model based on monthly series of economic figures from 1928 to 1939,[3] and the results of a neo-Keynesian model based on annual series of economic figures from 1919 to 1939.[4] Second, we have made two analyses of firm production. Both exercises used a sample of fifty-three manufacturing firms having at least one production unit in the Seine, tracked annually from 1925 to 1955 through management reports to their boards of directors. The use of accounting data from the balance sheets over four sub-periods (1925–9; 1930–9; 1940–4; 1945–55) reveals the underlying diversity of these firms and their evolution. Textual analysis of the annual reports of nine firms over twenty-five years[5] revealed the thinking behind their strategic expectations. The division into sub-periods is based on the type of expectations uncovered by this analysis. Finally, we have started to make use of available sector and firm publications (Appendices 1 and 2 provide technical details).

PRODUCT VARIETY AND BALANCE-SHEET STRUCTURES OF ENGINEERING AND ELECTRICAL FIRMS IN THE SEINE: THE GOLDEN AGE OF THE 1920s

In general, product variety was structured throughout the period according to two fundamental principles: first, the nature of demand, and second, the mode of organisation. Both influenced the system of production within the industrial fabric of the sector.

Products

Product diversity stemmed from the type of demand firms were trying to meet. Dedicated products tailored to specialised demand (e.g. brakes or railway signals or weapons) can be contrasted to generic products for new, growing markets (such as automobiles and, later, consumer-oriented tele-communications products). This contrast appears in the firms' balance sheets and annual reports. Firms making dedicated products had few inputs, low stocks and offered little customer credit while enjoying good profit margins. In contrast, firms making generic products mobilised proportionately more circulating capital, obliged as they were to produce in large batches and to attract customers through the extension of credit. These factors were accentuated for major automobile manufacturers, such as Citroën and Renault, which adopted a vertical integration policy. Starting from raw materials, they made (in the Seine) almost all of the automobile components they assembled. The same contrast can be observed in the degree to which their management fostered liquidity and profit. The more firms moved toward generic products, the less liquid their assets became. This is a general observation for the period, as is the continuing presence of firms making dedicated products, even during the phase of industrial rationalisation advocated after the second world war.

The second fundamental difference emerges from the mode of organisation prevailing in these firms. Highly capitalised firms, oriented towards economies of scale, strove to rationalise work and standardise products. The situation was very different in organisations whose products still depended on manual craft skill. This polarity was especially apparent in the automobile industry, distinguishing firms that continued to produce limited numbers of quality cars using traditional components produced by external suppliers from the 'big three' mass production firms (Citroën, Peugeot, Renault) which began investing heavily in rationalising and extending production in the 1920s. Yet the vertical integration policy followed by these three until the late 1930s did not prevent them retaining numbers of specialist craftsmen to meet orders for military weapons and to sustain diversification. An important point is that the translation of this distinction in the balance sheets was to change from one sub-period to the next.

Shattering the coherence of the real world of production

The second distinction operates through the capital-intensity variable (Figure 4.1) during the second half of the 1920s.[6] At the time, the system of production in the engineering and electrical industries of the Seine *département* was a 'real world of production'.[7] The material expectations of firms gradually shifted from the short to the long term. Firms focused on expectations for growth based on the development of technologically new products.[8] The division of labour between firms in the Seine deepened, allowing the development of a variety of activities and products covering a range of possibilities, without the growth of rationalisation and mass production jeopardising the coherence of the whole. Co-operation and complementarity went hand in hand with expansion. The conventions of co-ordination remained unchanged. The role of the financial market grew in importance in the 1920s, though it was to disappear completely in 1930.[9] The expectations and interests of investors, bankers and firms converged in the financial potential of shareholding. For partly contingent reasons (the franc was devalued by two-thirds in 1920), 'safe' long-term investment no longer took the form of fixed-income assets, but of shares.

The main strength of this industrial sector lay in its co-ordination, evident in all its many specialised, technologically advanced products. This allowed the sector to take advantage of a strongly concentrated labour force, economies of proximity and close links to departments of state with their

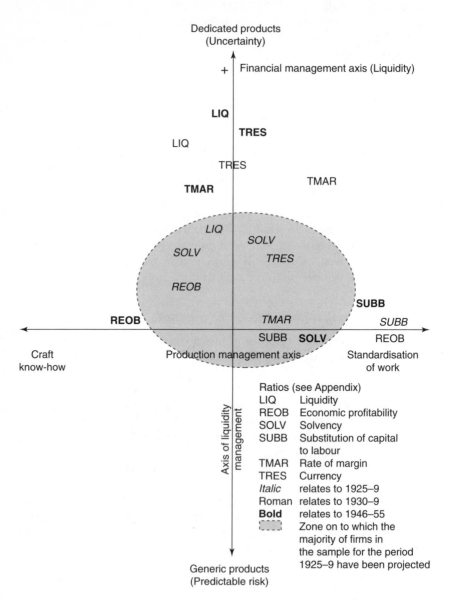

Figure 4.1 Product variety and balance-sheet structure of firms, 1925–55

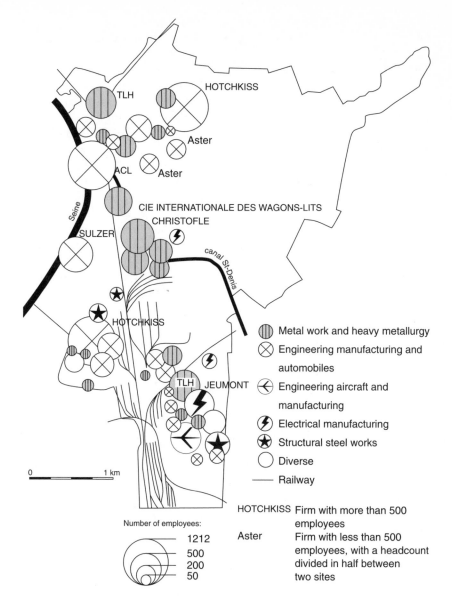

Legend contained in figure:

- Metal work and heavy metallurgy
- Engineering manufacturing and automobiles
- Engineering aircraft and manufacturing
- Electrical manufacturing
- Structural steel works
- Diverse
- Railway

HOTCHKISS Firm with more than 500 employees
Aster Firm with less than 500 employees, with a headcount divided in half between two sites

Number of employees:
1212
500
200
50

Figure 4.2 Metallurgy firms and companies in Saint-Denis in 1939
Source: D Rousselier-Fraboulet, *Enterprises et occupation. La métallurgie dyonisienne 1937–1947*, PhD thesis, Ecole des Hautes Etudes en Sciences Sociales, 1995

Notes:
1 The total headcount for Tréfileries et Laminoirs du Havre and the Hotchkiss and Aster firms, which had two sites in the district, has been halved.
2 TLH = Tréfileries et Laminoirs du Havre; ACL = Ateliers et Chantiers de la Loire.

investments in civil infrastructure and military procurement. The map of the Saint-Denis industrial sites (Figure 4.2) illustrates this geographical proximity.[10]

This coherence was to be shattered in the following years, and a new path for development would not emerge until after 1945, this time organised under a profoundly different system. On the whole, the management of systems of production in the 1930s was structured not by progress in rationalisation, but by concern about returns on investment. Economic yield and profit margins were the discriminating variables of balance-sheet structures. Until 1938, strategic expectations of firms were primarily financial and short-term. Dividends were the major concern. The prevailing attitude was one of every man for himself. The cartels of the period were the exact opposite of the sort of efficient co-ordination required. However, from 1944 there was new interest in the long term, through concerns about financing growth and investment. Production management was again structured along capital-intensive lines, in contrast to the earlier drive for instant profit. With declining interest in profitability, the balance-sheet solvency that was needed to repay medium- and long-term loans emerged as a relevant management factor.

YEARS OF TENSION 1930–9: 'BEHIND' THE PRODUCTS, A MACROECONOMY IN DISEQUILIBRIUM

The 1930s in France are central to historiographical controversies over the origins of the economic crisis, the failure of the economy to recover after 1935, the forty-hour work week, the availability of skilled labour, and the contradictions of economic and monetary policy. Without going into detail, we shall explore these factors from our sources and the questions they raise concerning the economic dynamics of the engineering and electrical industries of the Seine, their structural maladjustment and the attempts to reorganise the system.

Time perspectives and expectations of firms

The textual analysis of annual reports drawn up by managing directors for their boards of directors offers insights into the way their economic expectations were formed. These senior managers presented analyses of the firms' economic and financial situation. Thus, we are given access to their cognitive and pragmatic intentions for future action. Figure 4.3 shows the internal structure of their reports according to the statistical correlation appearing among the eight 'analytic registers' revealed in the textual analysis.[11] The analysis of each report differs from the others according to the way it breaks down into these eight registers. By grouping them together, we projected on to the figure the years showing differences according to the weight given to the registers in each year. Figure 4.4 performs the same operation for the firms studied, taking all the years together. On the whole, the registers can be grouped into quadrants. The horizontal axis contrasts the financial dimension with the material dimension[12] of action, whereas the vertical axis contrasts the long term with the short term. Four types of strategic perspective can be distinguished, defining specific temporal perspectives.

First, the 'dividend distribution' register defines, when it is dominant, short-term financial expectations. The economic analysis and action of the firm were determined by problems concerning dividend payments. This expectation characterises the period from 1930 to 1938. It also dominated Saurer, Ducellier, Salmson and Westinghouse for the whole period (although each company may have experienced minor changes from one year to the next). These were primarily manufacturers of specialised, dedicated products (brakes, beams, industrial vehicles, luxury cars).

Second, the 'operating problems' register and, to a large extent, the 'overall economic situation' register characterise short-term, material expectations. The firm focused on what it considered to be an unexpected short-term shock affecting its turnover and upsetting its operating cycle (costs, prices, supply, sales). The years 1931 (the beginning of the depression), 1936 (the Matignon Accord and Popular Front measures[13]) and 1953 (reversal of the economic situation) are typical. SAGEM (various electrical products) and the Compagnie d'Application Mécaniques (ballbearings) in particular used the outside register of the overall situation to explain why they were in trouble.

Third, the 'product development' and 'factories' registers characterise long-term, material expectations[14] based on prospects opened up by techno-logical innovation and new products. Hence, we regularly find Citroën, Thomson and Hotchkiss in these registers with, in each case, a twofold dimension of civil and military production. This corresponds to long-term expectations (as opposed to speculation) of the sort discussed by Keynes in chapter XII of the *General Theory*.

Fourth, the 'financing growth' register defines long-term financial expec-tations in which, once the scope of the business has been defined, action is directed towards funding investment. This type of strategic expectation characterised the period from 1944 to 1955, a period of reconstruction and modernisation. It is not specific to any firm in particular, but was shared by all during this period.

Trajectories within time periods are also quite instructive. For example, we can observe the reversal of long-term material expectations as early as 1929 from a peak in 1928. The low point of the depression was reached in 1932. New expectations of growth began in 1933, 1934 and, above all, in 1935. Momentarily shattered in 1936, they reappeared in 1937 but never became dominant. Without the war, would the phase of 'postwar' expansion

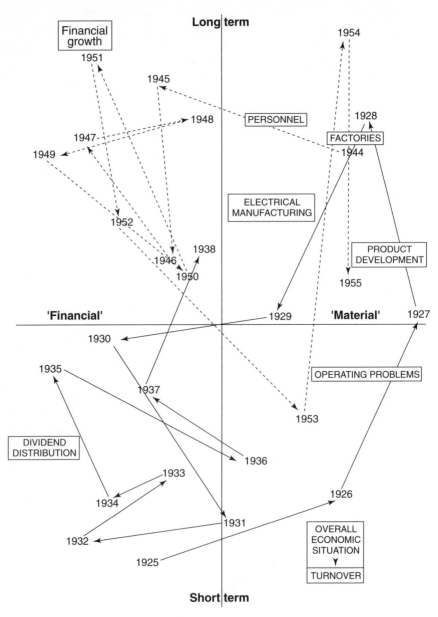

Figure 4.3 Expectations: textual analysis of reports to boards of directors – the years

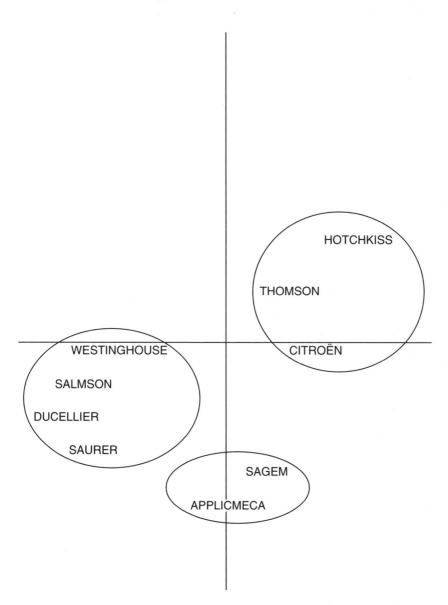

Figure 4.4 Expectations: textual analysis of reports to boards of directors – the firms

have begun in 1939? An affirmative answer would mean that we think the material, conventional and political framework required for postwar growth was established by the end of the 1930s. In other words, that changes corresponding to products – in terms of new demands, new markets, new technologies and collective bargaining agreements as well as firm organisation and strategic principles – were already taking place in a co-ordinated way and that economic policies already met the expectations of economic agents (firms, employees and trade unions).

In one sense, this was indeed the way economic actors in the 1930s gradually understood the problems, but failed to resolve them. According to a survey on production made in 1937 to analyse the reasons for the absence of economic recovery, the industrial production index was 25 per cent below that of 1929, whereas the 1929 level had been exceeded elsewhere (by 19 per cent in Germany and 25 per cent in Great Britain).[15] The strength of long-term material expectations was such – and here the shareholders' reports are enlightening – that no one seriously doubted the potential for economic development and the emergence of new demand from innovations developed during the previous decade. The issue was one of recovery, formulated (in contradictory terms) through a process of politicising economic issues. This process culminated in 1936 with the victory of the left in the 1936 elections and the attempt of the new Popular Front government to implement its programme. For the first time in peacetime, the state was asked to find an answer to the problem of economic recovery.

During this period, political (but not yet technical) macro-economics emerged as an area of controversy about which economic policy the state should promote. We will not analyse this process,[16] but will show what current modelling techniques can teach us in retrospect about the economic dynamics of the 1930s. First, we will identify the macro-economic factors, inaccessible to contemporary actors, that prevented a lasting economic recovery. Then, placing ourselves at the decisive level of productive co-ordination (in our view, economic policy authorises but does not explain), we shall link the macro factors to the failures of co-ordination that remained insurmountable during the period.

Retrospective lessons from a macroeconomic analysis[17]

Figure 4.5 below reproduces the dynamic causality at work among nine macroeconomic variables (monthly series from January 1928 to May 1939), estimated by adjusting a vectorial auto-regressive (VAR) model. The advantage of the VAR model is that it is not dependent either on a particular theory or on *a priori* exogenous variables. The nine variables create a world representing an economic dynamic, inspired by national income accounting, a world congruent with Keynesian macroeconomic policy, as recommended after the war. In technical terms, a variable x is said to cause a variable y

within this world if, and only if, the best possible forecast for *y* can be improved by the added knowledge of *x*. Figure 4.5, therefore, shows the structure of dynamic dependence internal to the economy, the lines along which shock waves were propagated on this or that economic dimension. What is revealed is a structure which was very specific to the French economy.

A group of three 'real' variables (industrial production, exports, labour productivity) is the overall cause of the six others. These six are either variables of price or relative cost: real interest rates, real wages, relative prices in France and Britain (the latter chosen as an indicator of competitiveness); or variables of balance between supply and demand: share issues taken as an indicator of investment spending, payroll purchasing power and imports. This means that a shock affecting the second group of variables had no delayed effect on the first group. Price and relative cost do not 'cause' the real variables, particularly production or export performance, contrary to the causal explanations put forward, above all, by supporters of deflation and critics of the Popular Front. On the other hand, the domestic demand group appears to have required impetus from the first group, especially demand resulting from exports.

Under the influence of Alfred Sauvy, existing research has emphasised the destabilising effects of social and economic policies pursued by the Popular

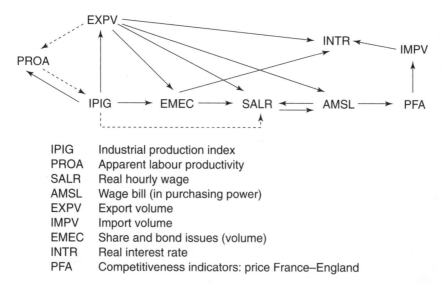

IPIG	Industrial production index
PROA	Apparent labour productivity
SALR	Real hourly wage
AMSL	Wage bill (in purchasing power)
EXPV	Export volume
IMPV	Import volume
EMEC	Share and bond issues (volume)
INTR	Real interest rate
PFA	Competitiveness indicators: price France–England

Figure 4.5 Dynamic causal relations among macro-economic indicators (monthly data, 1928–39)

Note: The dotted arrows indicate relations of lowest intensity (significant between 5 per cent and 10 per cent only).

Front: the wage rise resulting from the Matignon Accord and the law proclaiming the forty-hour working week, increased costs (balanced by the devaluation of the franc in September 1936), scarcity of supply and disruption within production systems. A macroeconomic perspective offers a different view: no shock appeared in the VAR model resulting from these unexpected policies. According to Villa (see note 4), 90 per cent of lost working hours were offset by increased work intensity and reorganisation, the remainder by additional hiring.

The main macroeconomic effect of Popular Front policy seems paradoxical and anti-Keynesian. Demand was restricted by limiting and stabilising the total wage bill, the effects of reduced work time being offset by increasing hourly wages. A negative spiral of restrictions on demand and supply would explain the non-recovery. Only accelerated growth in state defence expenditure stimulated demand in the public sector, beginning in 1937 and expanding in 1938. When war was declared, armaments composed 34 per cent of industrial production in metalworking industries in France. In Saint-Denis, for example, every firm benefited from defence expenditure.[18] Elsewhere, the prolonged absence – or extremely low rates – of investment and the consequent ageing of plant limited productive capacity. The sharp upturn in economic profitability in 1935[19] did not restore pre-1930 levels, and there was consequently insufficient reinvestment for recovery. The financial market was depressed, state share issues competed with rare private issues and, after 1929, investors returned to a preference for annuities and sources of fixed income. Savings banks experienced their best years in the 1930s.

Stimulating supply and product variety: an unsolved problem

The internal causes of the real blockage revealed by the VAR model indicates a deeper problem than 'error' in government economic policy. Production appears here as a 'cause' of exports, and not a consequence, as would be expected by Keynesian theory. Increased production leads to an improvement in exports. Production and exports taken together are the cause of labour productivity. But the problem is not only quantitative. The conclusion that emerges is that the underlying structural problem in the 1930s was one of supply. Production structures were oriented, in terms of both products and targeted markets, towards exports more than towards domestic demand. What is more, they were unspecialised and reacted only mildly to variation in foreign demand.[20] They also appear to have faced competition from imports on the domestic market (cf. the influence of price competition on imports in Figure 4.5). Finally, in the same way, Villa shows the far-reaching negative influence of limited productive capacity. The simulation of shocks by the VAR model shows that a positive shock on the industrial production index (an increase in independent production) produces a durable, pronounced and delayed effect that is often positive on the other variables. It lowers real interest rates, for example.

Thus, the recovery of product supply appears retrospectively as 'the solution' to the crisis once the nadir of the depression in 1932 had passed, especially as prices stabilised rather quickly. This supply would have to involve qualitatively new products, stimulating a distribution of revenues, wages and profits adequate to support sufficient demand. Can the major breakdowns in co-ordination that prevented the implementation of this 'virtuous' macro-economic process, be identified? A detailed examination of the historiography and the development of specific research on the products would be required to go further than the responses presented below.

Three examples of co-ordination failure

The available literature on the engineering and electrical industries of the Seine allows us to identify at least three breakdowns in product co-ordination that deserve further research. First, the emerging political consensus on the necessity for rearmament cannot hide serious co-ordination failures surrounding product specification.[21] Contrary to the assumption that armaments were being adapted to the coming war, military strategies detailing potential uses for aircraft, tanks and artillery on the battlefield remained unclear.[22] Product quality conventions sufficiently detailed to permit efficient co-ordination were not forthcoming. For example, aircraft construction firms remained small, poorly rationalised (still working on limited series without standardised parts) and unco-ordinated.[23] The nationalisation of war industries generated conflicts over the division of productive capacity between public and private sectors. A policy of official advance payments guaranteed by a specialist institution (la Caisse Nationale des Marchés de l'Etat) was yet to be established and banks were reluctant to accept bills of exchange from firms working for national defence; this led to financial problems. Alongside the engineers, highly skilled craft workers occupied key positions in these industries. The CGTU[24] strongholds were there; from 1935, the union organised strikes and drew up lists of claims that served as a basis for the later Matignon Accord and for the collective agreement of the Parisian metallurgy industry in June 1936, itself the paradigm for hundreds of collective bargaining agreements concluded in 1936 and 1937.[25]

Second, the automobile industry dropped from second to fifth position worldwide during these years and this stagnation persisted. In spite of constant references to the American model, the three largest firms agreed to abandon the market for mass-produced inexpensive cars, although each had a project ready.[26] Their reservations focused on the capacities of the sales network and the low prices in the second-hand car market. Attempts to co-ordinate the activities of small producers – to promote product rational- isation and to reduce prices through the mass production of common components – came to nothing and the average number of models per manufacturer increased once again before 1939.

André Citröen[27] and Louis Renault both remained politically determined to build their respective industrial empires under their own dominion. They had no interest in utilising the skills and competencies found in the surrounding industrial fabric by co-ordinating with the activities of outsiders. On the contrary, both sought to integrate as fully as possible, producing in their own factories everything required for an automobile except energy and raw materials, while also controlling marketing and sales. Renault owned sand quarries in the Paris region and had even considered the possibility of becoming a glass-maker to avoid dependence on Saint-Gobain and also acquired upstream holdings in equipment manufacturing companies.[28] Ford inspired both entrepreneurs more than General Motors. Starting later than Ford, General Motors took advantage of the dissemination of mass-production industry skills in the network of sub-contractors and equipment manufacturers that Ford had fostered in Detroit.[29] Did Citroën and Renault managers do anything more than implement a strategy based on the power of standardised techniques discovered on their trips (and those of their collaborators) to the United States? In 1928, Allyn Young[30] demonstrated the dynamics that linked the expansion of a sector to product and process innovation deepening internal divisions of labour, which pushed firms into responding to requirements from other companies in the sector, thereby stimulating a virtuous circle of growth in which demand and supply responded to each other. This rested on the interaction of two factors, productivity gains and market expansion. Before 1939, only the first of these seems to have attracted the attention of French industrialists. This was because short-term financial considerations, namely the value of the dividend, underlay strategic thinking.

Third, in addition to the equipment lags and factory bottlenecks that impeded recovery, a systematic defect held back the development of rationalisation – it was not designed to co-ordinate business activity between firms, but focused solely on worker activity within firms. The general report of the 1937 production enquiry identified 'the need to organise production in a rational way with the view to lowering cost prices and improving quality (rational organisation of labour, standardisation of products, close co-operation of industry with research)' for the metallurgy industries, steel-making (particularly the speciality steels required for armaments) and automobiles.[31] Louis Renault, for example, complained about the quality of his sheet metal supply (the quality specifications he required and which had evolved with product innovation were not produced by the steel makers). In 1931, he established a subsidiary in Lorraine,[32] the Société des Aciers Fins de l'Est. There was increasing standardisation, but on a small scale, each major manufacturer and a few professional partnerships developing their own standards.

Industrial accounting based on measuring costs (standard cost and direct costing), although already widespread in the United States, was little known despite the efforts of a few pioneers.[33] It remained incomprehensible until the 1950s, possibly later, in spite of productivity missions in 1948 and 1951. The report of the French mission of certified public accountants[34] which uncovered American techniques in 1951 emphasised that accounting in France had developed historically to provide legal and financial information, whereas in the United States it was a tool of management, serving pragmatic purposes: 'In Europe, it is used to justify a firm's commercial operations, to determine its results and its financial situation', a principle extending to industrial accounting. In the United States, 'standard accounting consists of deciding on the future cost price of a product through in-depth study and taking economic circumstances into account. This pre-determined price is used in registering accounts. Real manufacturing expenses are then recorded and compared with the expenses pre-determined by the standard.'[35] The establishment of such reference points, of strategic thinking external to contingencies, the analysis of accounts as a means of raising productivity – allowing the introduction of productivity bargaining – remained unknown to French industrialists.[36]

Complaints about skilled labour shortages indicate something different: the inability to move a labour force endowed with skills and know-how into mass production. Mass production did not de-skill; it created a new specialist hierarchy: regulators, fitters, machine maintenance personnel, prototype innovators, methods engineers, technicians. Upgrading and innovation continued to require initiative. This shift required collective apprenticeship in new working conventions. Several factors prevented this happening. Conflicts emerged between piecework wages, which workers appreciated, and efficiency wages (i.e. bonuses dependent on time saved), which they detested because of the uncertainty and because of the downward pressure exerted on wages.[37] The authoritarianism which underpinned the hierarchies of large firms clashed with the traditions of collective autonomy, basic to the work practices of skilled craftsmen. Demands for free time and a share in the increasing amount of wealth produced, made by populist movements in 1936, continued to be rejected and did not elicit any response from the established economic order.

1944 AND AFTER: EXPECTATIONS OF LONG-TERM GROWTH

Figure 4.3 traces the different orientations of firms. The year 1944 stands alongside the year 1928, as if the trajectory of the sector had returned to the point at which it had broken off in that year, on track for long-term growth and with the necessary investment, as if nothing had happened during the

1930s or the years of war and Occupation. From 1944, a growth strategy continued (although a decline appeared between 1953 and 1955). How should the link between this strategy and the events of the preceding years be assessed? We will try to formulate a few hypotheses.

The ambition of those wielding economic and political power in the aftermath of the war was, according to the Secrétaire de l'Etat à l'Economie Nationale, 'to prepare a marriage of reason, and if possible of love, between freedom and organisation'.[38] That was how the link between the future and the past was perceived. The phrase remains ambiguous: the various inter-pretations of freedom (which kind and for whom?) and organisation (by whom and for what?) could be contradictory.

After the war, the firms in the sample which chose the route of capital intensity and mass production accepted a lower return on capital (a lower return encouraged by the predictable character of their markets) and entered, in a moderate way, into medium- and long-term debt (cf. Figure 4.1). How were their investments funded? Only a small part came from the Marshall Plan, the major portion of which was reserved from 1948 to 1950 for industrial re-equipment in the four nationalised firms (CDF, EDF, GDF, SNCF[39]) and the steel industry. Private investment was precocious and began as early as 1943 and 1944. It came from several sources. Internal financing was available from resources accumulated during the Vichy period by allocating profits to reserves. These firms had been profitable during the war, possibly as a result of German orders, wage freezes and so on. The revaluation of balance sheets, authorised by the decrees of 15 April 1945, 5 and 28 February 1946 gave firms additional room to manoeuvre. Long-term share issues were made from 1943. Capital increases (from issuing shares, or incorporating revalued reserves, or increasing share par values) and medium-term loans followed soon afterwards in 1945. For instance, long-term bonds were issued by Thomson in 1941 (for FF75 million), by the Compagnie d'Applications Mécaniques in 1942 (FF50 million), and by Westinghouse in 1942 (FF35 million). The Compagnie d'Applications Mécaniques created new issues for larger amounts in 1944, 1945 and 1946, as did Thomson in 1945, 1946 and 1948.

There were few direct references to the state and its policies in reports to the boards of directors of firms in the engineering and electrical industries in the Seine, either after the war or before it. Apart from public procurement (armaments and infrastructure – in the 'product development' register) or the shock brought about by the rise in wages and the forty-hour week in June 1936 (in the 'operating problems' register), such references were limited to mentioning national policy measures (in the 'overall situation' register), taxes (in the 'dividend distribution' register), or alluding to specific laws and decrees governing capital increases. These firms operated autonomously and determined their strategies by themselves. Was their interpretation of freedom any different from that of economic liberalism?

After the war, the state was omnipresent but remained an external force, operating either upstream or downstream from these firms. In a sense, government opened the way to capital accumulation by removing any quantitative obstacles that might have obstructed progress. This seems to us to be the organisational component of the 'marriage' mentioned above. Upstream, public funding of investments in basic industries (coal, electricity, gas, railways, iron and steel), and coal and oil imports paid for by dollars under the Marshall Plan helped to clear quickly the bottlenecks caused by scarcity of raw materials and energy. Downstream, re-equipping basic industries generated demand that benefited firms in the engineering and electrical industries. The reports of the Commissariat au Plan forcefully emphasised this 'chain reaction'. The money made available to nationalised industries was then redistributed by them within the private sector through orders for tools, machines and construction equipment. Basic industries represented only 10 per cent of total investment, but the 10 per cent vital to the other 90 per cent. Organisation thus assumed the features of centralised, semi-'socialist' planning, but restricted to the government's economic sphere of action – the basic industries. Thus free space was made available for private enterprise.

The state pursued a production policy rather than a Keynesian policy. This policy concentrated on products that could directly and immediately support the flow of money transfer and create a predictable environment for private firms. If indeed 'Keynes was National-Income Accounting',[40] then Leontieff was his prophet for French planners. The policy followed was based on a system for propagating dynamic effects, through a TEI (table of inter-sector trade), which charted the expenditure of public investment. This ensured demand for downstream industries, which were thereby freed from uncertainty and able to plan their business. Productivity gains were thought to propagate themselves through the TEI, freeing resources for future investment. This reflex naturally culminates in rationalisation as the products at the heart of this policy, that shape it, are basic products for which only volume and price matter.

Raising productivity first emerged as a problem of efficiency wages. At the end of 1946, the Commission de la Main d'Ouevre du Plan Monnet recommended that productivity be stepped up, provided that 'any increase in productivity translates into a real increase in the standard of living'. This framework, less a social compromise than a set of productivity conventions on a national, economic and political scale (which would have revived the democratic processes embodied in the collective labour agreements of 1936), was rapidly replaced by a campaign for rationalisation, proposed as the route to higher productivity. On this point, a number of elements of continuity – as well as a renewal of ideas, projects and approaches explored before the war – are significant. The productivity missions revived the pre-war tradition of trips to the United States for progressive managers. The Ministère de l'Economie Nationale took up the work and contacts that Jean Coutrot had established in the 1930s (at COST[41]) with professional organisations interested in standardisation. Four objectives were defined here: standardisation, rationalisation of industries, organisation of markets under a system of competitive economy, and new relations in the labour market. Innovation appears to have been limited. The second objective conveys the desire for major companies to supervise small and medium-sized firms whose activities required co-ordination 'without trying to make them disappear' (because they were considered a 'factor of social cohesion'), 'by leading them to specialise and to integrate into chains of production, as in the United States'. This aimed to put productivity at the service of social convergence. Despite the events of 1936, this was again presented as a way to avoid antagonism within the economy and to reorientate trade unions towards consultation, bucking the trend towards efficiency wage[42] agreements likely to provide a foundation for endogenous, decentralised growth.

Although the 'virtuous' marriage between (economic) freedom and (state) organisation was inspired by a quantitative and accounting approach, it helped to preserve long-term expectations within the engineering and electrical industry firms of the Seine after the war. Public sector contracts remained very important. Major production projects had either been ready before the war (such as projects for popular inexpensive cars like the Citroën 2CV[43]), or developed during the war (for innovation went on behind the scenes).[44] All they needed was to be launched and financed since the volume of expected demand reduced uncertainty. The pace at which public infrastructure and utilities programmes were carried out rapidly increased, because of the intervention of the state's engineers as well as the standardisation of products (whose future development bore the stamp of their origin).

Was there a 'real', lasting solution to the co-ordination breakdowns left unresolved at the end of 1938? Just how far did the long-term expectations of firms, which seem to revive independently, converge with macro-economic intervention by the state? Was it not paradoxical that the room for maneouvre given to the state by political consensus on the need for reconstruction and modernisation actually authorised an 'external' process of economic growth that was largely dependent on the state? And if so, until when? And in what way? What price would be paid for the shared belief in the ability of an 'external' state to repair, through centralised macro-economic policy, earlier breakdowns of co-ordination at the level of products, sectors and territories? Although our research on the engineering and electrical industries in the Paris region after the war is still in an embryonic stage, it has encouraged us, at the very least, to address these questions.

CONCLUSION

This chapter explores the dynamics of an economy through its diverse products and its specific time periods. The case study offers a new approach, modifying the commonly accepted interpretation which explains postwar growth in France as the positive effects of a macro-economic model for growth set up by the state after the war, together with the successful negotiation of a national social compromise.

Returning to material foundations – products, firms, innovations, the industrial fabric, manpower capabilities, conventions – inclines us to be more modest and to avoid jumping to such conclusions. Neither the temptation to adopt an evolutionary view nor teleological explanation nor the omnipotence of the state can withstand this test. Certain directions appear to be priorities for the next stage of research into the period from the 1920s to the 1950s: to explore further the variety of products and trajectories of innovation in various sub-periods; to examine other socio-economic areas equally strategic for the understanding of overall dynamics; to study labour agreements in their relationship to products as well as to the nature of political compromises on how the problem of collective breakdowns (unemployment, inflation, living standards, etc.) was formulated and handled by the state.

APPENDIX 1:
TWO ANALYSES OF MACRO-ECONOMIC DYNAMICS IN THE 1930s

1 Estimates of a vectorial auto-regressive model based on monthly data from January 1928 to May 1939

The value of a vectorial auto-regressive model is that it is not biased either towards a particular theory or towards an external cause or on exogenous variables. It seeks to establish every statistical correlation in a series, both current and with various delays within a world of representation. In technical terms, each variable of this world is explained by its own past and by the past of the other variables, allowing only for random disturbance (called 'innovation'). An innovation may be defined as an unpredictable shock impacting variable x. A variable x is said to cause the variable y within this world if and only if the best possible prediction of y can be improved by the added knowledge of x.

The nine variables selected (Figure 4.5) create a world of representation portraying the economic dynamics inspired by national accounting, in other words a world congruent with a macro-economic policy inspired by Keynes. First, we find the final demand in its various component parts and the division between domestic production and imports; we also find the evolution of productivity and the factor costs, traditional variables of demand functions and assessment of competitiveness. The series was established from seventy-one monthly returns gathered from the directories of the General Statistics of France. The monthly index of hourly wages was taken from A. Sauvy, *Histoire économique de la France entre les deux guerres*, 4 vols (Fayard, 1965, 1967, 1972, 1975, Paris). It would have been possible to add the money supply, public spending or a certain disintegration by sector. However, it is difficult to multiply the number of variables without making their interpretation excessively complicated (see F. Maurel and R. Salais, 'La conjoncture économique des années 1930 en France: une exploration par l'économétrie des modèles multivariés', Internal Memorandum GdR IEPE, no. 67/87, June 1987) The estimate shows that a delay on the order of 1, representing one month, is sufficient to represent the overall dynamics. Figure 4.5 retains only the statistically significant relations (coefficient superior in absolute value to 2 or 1 standard errors).

2 A neo-Keynesian model of interwar macro-economic dynamics

Starting from available statistical data and an initial account established by the statistician L.A. Vincent for the year 1938, Villa reconstructed annual national accounts for the French economy comprising four agents (firms, households, administrations, foreign countries) with complete TEI (sectoral trade tables) from 1919 to 1938. He then estimated the equations for a neo-Keynesian model of an open economy with no differentiation among goods (*Une analyse macroéconomique de la France au XXème siècle*, CNRS Editions (Monographies économétriques), Paris, 1993).

The model introduces a supply effect into the export function (dependent upon foreign production, export profitability and tensions relating to production capacities) and has a 'real' explanation of inflation, which results from tensions over the division between wages and profits, tensions relating to demand and imported inflation. Investment is increasingly dependent upon expected demand and profit rate with short reaction times (non-existent for demand, one year for profit rate). Imports are linked to domestic production and to import price relative to domestic production, with flexibility of close to 1, as well as to taxes on imports (protection). The use of the model provides a description of macro-economic dynamics by time period (e.g. stabilisation under Poincaré, 1923–6) and makes it possible to simulate the effects of policies followed by governments (e.g. the impact of the devaluation of the franc in September 1936). The author notes two restrictions on his work: the triggering of the 1929 crisis is referred to exogenous variables and expectations are not dealt with.

APPENDIX 2:
THE STATISTICAL ANALYSIS OF BALANCE SHEETS AND REPORTS TO THE BOARD OF DIRECTORS OF FIFTY-THREE FIRMS IN ENGINEERING AND ELECTRICAL INDUSTRY IN THE SEINE, 1925–55

The sample is from a file containing all the firms of the manufacturing sector quoted on the Paris Stock Exchange in 1936, as recorded by the Crédit Lyonnais, one of the largest French banks; this represents 330 firms tracked annually (with some gaps) from 1925 to 1955. Firms that folded before 1936 or were created after 1936 are not included; the focus on large firms limits this defect. The fifty-three engineering and electrical firms selected had at least one production unit in the Seine *département*.

1 The statistical analysis of balance sheets and profit and loss accounts

These balance sheets were harmonised as far as possible for key items: depreciation, gross and net assets, operating cash flow (retracing the economic profitability of invested capital) and net income or net loss (retracing the financial profitability of shareholders' equity). The absence of operating income statements rarely makes it possible to know the turnover, the total wage bill, the number of employees or value added. The data are in current French francs.

The object of the analysis is to detect, in the variety of firm accounting structures, the underlying diversity of products along two lines: the type of market and the mode of organisation. The assumption (verified for this period in M. Storper and R. Salais, *Les mondes de production*, EHESS, Paris, 1993), is that the type of market and mode of organisation exert 'real' constraints on firm management, especially those contributing to its economic profitability. Here it was necessary to estimate the missing data.

On the market axis, *generic* products intended to meet general public demand and relying on predictable markets are opposed to *dedicated* products intended to satisfy individual orders generated in markets that are uncertain by nature. In the first case, the firm can plan its production and accept the lower liquidity of its assets and, in particular, commit relatively large amounts of circulating capital (for example, to sell its product, it will offer credit to customers and accept high inventories). In the second case, faced with uncertainty, the firm tends to promote flexibility and short-term adaptability, which translates into greater asset liquidity. Generally speaking, to offset the absence of some data while estimating average rates per subperiod, we have hypothesised the positive correlation between circulating assets, turnover and the volume of labour hours. This hypothesis is justified by the high degree of short-term flexibility of production and its low average capital-intensive nature during the period studied. It appeared to be admissible, lacking a better solution, for the few firms and years for which we had data to verify it.

The preceding distinction was roughly approached using three ratios. A margin rate (TMAR) was estimated by taking the ratio between the operating cash flow and circulating assets. The percentage of circulating assets (TVRC) was measured in relation to gross fixed assets. Liquidity (LIQ) was measured as the ratio between the amount of money available in the short term and indebtedness of one year maximum. Theoretically, the more dedicated the firm's products, the higher the TMAR and LIQ ratios and the lower the TVRC ratio.

On the mode of organisation axis, *specialised* products manufactured using specific, idiosyncratic know-how (craft and specialist team skills) are contrasted to *standard* products manufactured using common technology and scientific organisation of labour. In the second case, firms sought to implement economies of scale based on investments in standardisation aimed at reducing unit costs. The first case relied on the individual skills and production in small, less-mechanised series. These contrasts have been expressed in two ratios, both roughly estimated. An indicator of the rate of substituting capital for labour (SUBB) was constructed as the ratio between gross production assets on the balance sheet and circulating assets. A solvency ratio (SOLV) was taken as equal to the ratio of shareholders' capital to medium- and long-term debt. Theoretically, the more standardised the firm's products, the higher the SUBB and SOLV ratios.

To these five ratios was added an economic profitability indicator (REOB) equal to the ratio of operating cash flow to invested capital. The latter is defined as the total amount of gross production assets and net circulating assets, which in turn are equal to: credit to customers + inventory − credit from suppliers. A breakdown into the main components was made by sub-period for average values of these six ratios by firm. The foreground of the analysis is reproduced in Figure 4.1. Generally speaking, the analysis reveals a liquidity management axis (the vertical axis) that refers to the firm's management of its market position (generic product vs. specific product) and a production management axis (the horizontal axis) reflecting the degree of product standardisation.

The statistical analysis of textual data from the annual reports to the boards of directors (BD)

For nine of the firms, the annual reports to the BD were 'scanned' on to a computer, representing about 220 texts of unequal length.[45] These texts underwent a technique of lexical analysis in which the sentences were compared, not on the basis of word count, but combinations of words held in common. The body of the text is divided into parts of approximately equal length (14–16 words). At the end of the statistical analysis, classes were compiled, grouping sentences that may be considered close to each other in meaning. For example, the programme grouped into one class (related to company product development) these two sentences: 'We have already called your attention to the fact that customers are demanding a small car benefiting from the tested experience of our brand' and 'Our technical service has obtained results that drew the most flattering praise from high military officials.'

These classes constitute 'core meanings' or 'lexical worlds' that express a semantic area. By expressing themselves in one of these lexical worlds, the speaking subjects (here the firm's management) give the meaning they consider relevant to their situation. They reveal the perspective behind their actions. We have called these worlds 'analytic registers'. For example, when the war ended, the firms which gave significant weight to the 'financing growth' world showed action oriented in that direction. To be satisfactory, the reconstruction of the results would require more room than we have here. We limit ourselves to describing the eight most important classes. The software cut the body of the text into 9,310 'basic context units' or BCU (the sentences), 66.3 per cent of which were grouped together into classes (representing a non-negligible loss of the semantic richness of the texts); 1,284 words were selected, of which 962 were used to define the classes, with the programme calculating by a χ^2 test the degree of correlation of the words to the classes. Nearly 67,000 occurrences were processed by the software. The latter reduced all derived words as well as the various word forms to their root; hence the + signs added to the words cited hereafter (such as *economi+* for the word 'economy' and all its derivatives).

First class: The overall situation (19.1 per cent of the BCU)

The most significant words in terms of χ^2 are especially affaire+ (sale), *chiffr+* (figure) the two components of the French word for *turnover, vente+* (sale), *situation+, economi+, crise+* (crisis), *exportat+* (export), *niveau+* (level), *pays+* (country), *ralent+* (slow), *enregistr+* (record), *constat+* (observ). This register is one of helplessness (*not being able*) developed as a general observation affecting *us* from the outside. The arguments use adverbs such as *despite, yet, however.*

Second class: Dividend distribution (24.7 per cent of the BCU)

The most significant words are, for example, *amorti+* (depreciat), *bénéfic+* (profit), *compt+* (account), *elev+* (rise), *exerc+* (year), francs, *impôt+* (tax), *pert+* (loss), *propos+* (propos), *réserv+* (reserv), *provision+* (provision), *reparti+* (allocat), *report+* (carry). The argument is expressed in terms of accounting (*nearly, about, instead of, compared to*) and deductive reasoning (*given, after, following*). The management speaks directly to the shareholders (*you*).

Third class: Product development (13.7 per cent of the BCU)

Among the most significant words may be noted *grand+* (major), *modèle+* (model), *clientèle+* (customer), *voiture+* (car), *appareil+* (device), *arme+* (weapon), *cylindre+* (cylinder), *étud+* (research), *haut+* (high), *marque+* (brand), *mitraille+* (machine gun), *moteur+* (motor), *nombreu+* (number), *perfection+*, *petit+* (small), *prototypy+*, *série+* (mass), *succes+*, *type+*, *réputation*, *progres+*, *technique+*. The argument takes place in the established order (*always*), moving towards quantitative progress (*more, as much, very*) as well as qualitative.

Fourth class: Financing capital growth (13.5 per cent of the BCU)

This class is characterised by words such as *capital+*, *action+* (share), *assemblée* (meeting), *réévalu+* (valu), *titre+* (share), *article+*, *autoris+* (authoris), *conform+* (comply), *décret+* (decree), *émission+* (issue), *emprunt+* (borrow), *loi* (law), *nominal+* (par), *obligation* (security), *rembours+* (repay), *millions*, *procéd+*, *ordonn+* (prescribe). The management explains the financial decisions made *by you*, the shareholders, *during an annual meeting* and therefore postulated as taken for granted by them.

Fifth class: Factory upgrading (10.4 per cent of the BCU)

This class is characterised by words such as *acquerir* (acquire), *atelier+* (workshop), *exécut+*, *fabrication+* (manufactur), *install+*, *outil+* (tool), *usin+* (factory), *programme+*, *achève+* (complete), *agrandi+* (enlarge), *aménage+* (improve), *bâtiment+* (building), *modernis+* (modernise), *terrain+* (land), as well as by various place names where factories are located. Here we are in the area of deliberate, localised productive action that we have undertaken here (*in*) and now (*at the moment, now*).

Sixth class: Operating cycle problems (8.5 per cent of the BCU)

The most characteristic words are *matière+* (material) and *premier+* (raw) (the two components of raw materials), *prix* (price), *revenir* (for 'cost' in 'cost price'), *cout+* (cost), *hausse+* (rise), *insuffis+*, *monnaie+* (currency), *produit* (product), *salaire+* (wage), *approvision+* (supply), *main+* (labour). The reasoning, which is negative as in class 1, implies more directly (*for, due to, by, so that*) and accusatory (*they* are the ones and that's *too much*).

Seventh class (6.3 per cent of the BCU)

This class is concerned more directly with, but without being limited to, the electrical industry and the railway. It seems to be a specific compromise between classes 3 and 5, joining product development to a deliberate, localised action, showing mastery over developments (syntax linking *in so far* to *what we have*).

Eighth class: Firm personnel (3.1 per cent of the BCU)

The most characteristic words are *personnel, entreprise*+ (firm), *concour*+ (contribut), *adress*+, *attribu*+, *remercie*+ (thank), *chef*+ (manager), *collabor*+, *comité* (committee, for works committee), *dévoue* (devote), *directe*+, *emploi*+ (employ), *ingénie*+ (engineer), *ouvrier*+ (worker). The firm's management speaks to its (*our*) personnel, thanking them on behalf of the shareholders for their devotion and collaboration (*a lot*).

The programme performs the factorial analysis of correspondence between tables by comparing the BCU and words (the presence of which has been quantified in the binary mode); the foreground of this analysis is reproduced in Figures 4.3 and 4.4. It also performs a descending hierarchical classification, making it possible to measure the degree of proximity between classes. This indicates a marked proximity between classes 1 and 2, which suggests that in their reports the firms tend to tie dividend distribution difficulties to the overall situation of economic crisis. Class 3 appears next in the classification, which may indicate that long-term product development could be considered a 'solution' to the crisis.

Classes 4 and 5 go together, because they have little connection to the previous ones, which underscores the correlation made by firms between factory modernisation and expansion and financing capital requirements. Class 6 comes next, linked to the two previous classes. Class 8 (personnel) comes at the end of the classification tree, a sign that the argument is separate from the other concerns of firms.

NOTES

1 1936 figures. Population census taken in March 1936.
2 R. Salais, 'Action publique, gouvernance et conventions de l'Etat: éléments d'un problème', in F. Godard, (ed.), *Le gouvernement des villes*, Descartes, Paris, 1997, pp. 255–86.
3 Based on unpublished work, F. Maurel and R. Salais, 'La conjoncture économique des années 1930 en France: une exploration par l'économétrie des modèles multivariés', Internal Memorandum GdR Institutions, Emploie et Politique Economique (IEPE), no. 67/87, June, 1987.
4 P. Villa, 'Une explication des enchaînements macroéconomiques sur

l'entre-deux-guerres', *Le mouvement social*, 154, March 1991, pp. 213–43, and P. Villa, *Une analyse macroéconomique de la France au XXème siècle*, CNRS Editions, Paris, 1993.

5   The limits of the Alceste software data handling capacity restricted the numbers involved (M. Reinert, 'Les mondes lexicaux et leur logique', *Langage et société*, December 1993, pp. 5–39). To gain an additional firm meant eliminating the 1939–44 period – which initial analysis showed to be quite specific. The nine firms selected maximised diversity.

6   The balance sheet analysis was undertaken by Yann Lhomme while studying at INSEE in 1996. The results are from his training report.

7   M. Storper and R. Salais, *Worlds of Production: The Action Frameworks of the Economy*, Harvard University Press, Cambridge, MA, 1997 (first published as R. Salais and M. Storper, *Les mondes de production. Enquête sur l'identité économique de la France*, Editions de l'EHESS, Paris, 1993).

8   See pp. 78–87 below.

9   P.-C. Haucoeur, 'Environnement macro-économique, transformations du système financier et financement des entreprises durant l'entre-deux-guerres en France', unpublished paper, Symposium on Historical Economy, Paris, December 1994.

10 D. Rousselier-Fraboulet, *Entreprises et occupation. La métallurgie dyonisienne 1937–1947*, PhD thesis, Ecole des Hautes Etudes en Sciences Sociales, 1995, 2 vols.

11 See Appendix 2 for the explanation and detailed results of the textual analysis.

12 'Material' expectations focus on the long-term evolution of technical and organisational systems.

13 At the request of the CGPF (Commission Générale de la Production Française), representing employers, Léon Blum on 5 June 1936 brought together at Matignon the CGPF and the CGT to reach an agreement that stopped the strikes and factory occupations. This accord, signed on 7 June, included: immediate collective bargaining agreements (modelled on the industrial agreement for metal industries in the Paris area, signed on 12 June); real salary rises of 15 to 17 per cent; worker delegates in firms with ten or more workers. Léon Blum promised to introduce the three social laws: the forty-hour work week; paid holidays (two weeks per year); collective bargaining agreements (see J. Danos and M. Gibelin, *Juin 36*, La Découverte, Paris, 1986, pp. 71ff.)

14 The entire group of material expectations define the sub-period 1925–9.

15 M. Margairaz, *L'Etat, les finances et l'économie. Histoire d'une conversion 1932–1952*, 2 vols, Imprimerie nationale, Paris, 1991, p. 421.

16 Ibid.

17 See Appendix 1 for details of the analysis.

18 Rousselier-Fraboulet, *Enterprises et occupation*, p. 21.

19 P. Gancarz, 'La métallurgie française face à la crise des années 1930 (1928–1938)', *Le mouvement social*, no. 154, January–March 1991, pp. 197–212.

20 Villa, 'Une explication'.

21 R. Frankenstein, *Le prix du réarmement français (1915–1939)*, Publications de la Sorbonne, Paris, 1982.

22 C. Didry and R. Salais, 'Troubles sur les produits d'Etat et écriture des conventions collectives de travail de 1936', in A. Jacob and H. Vérin (ed.),

L'inscription sociale du marché, L'Harmattan, Paris, 1995, pp. 112–35. P. Vennesson, 'La fabrication de l'armée de l'air en France: innovation institutionnelle et compromis socio-technique', *Genèses*, 15 March 1994, pp. 69–83.

23 E. Chadeau, *L'industrie aéronautique en France 1900–1950. De Blériot à Dassault*, Fayard, Paris, 1987.

24 The CGTU (Confédération Générale des Travailleurs Unifiés) split from the CGT in 1919, remained loyal to the Communist International and was controlled by Communist Party activists. The two branches were reunited in 1936. The CGT strongholds were the civil servants' trade unions; those of the CGTU were the metalwork industries.

25 C. Didry and R. Salais, 'L'écriture des conventions collectives. Entre le métier et l'industrie, un moment critique; les conventions collectives de 1936–1937', in A. Jobert, J.-D. Reynaud, A. Saglio, and M. Tallard (eds), *Les conventions collectives de branche: déclin ou renouveau?*, CEREQ, Etudes 65, Paris, 1993, pp. 77–94.

26 P. Fridenson, *Histoire des usines Renault. Naissance de la grande entreprise 1898–1939*, vol. 1, Seuil, Paris, 1972.

27 S. Schweitzer, *Des engrenages à la chaîne. Les usines Citroën 1915–1935*, PUL, Lyon, 1982.

28 Fridenson, *Histoire des usines Renault*, pp. 137–8.

29 R. Langlois, *Transactions-Cost Economics in Real Time*, Working Paper, University of Connecticut, May 1991.

30 A. Young, 'Rendements croissants et progrès économique', *Revue française d'économie*, vol. 5, no. 2, Spring 1990, pp. 85–109 (first published 1928).

31 Margairaz, *L'Etat, les finances et l'économie*, p. 414.

32 Fridenson, *Histoire des usines Renault*, p. 220.

33 In 1927, Lieutenant-Colonel Rimailho explained to the Commission Generale d'Organisation du Travail of the CGPF (CGOST became CEGOS in 1937) the system for rational allocation of overheads by 'work units' and 'homogeneous sections'. At Citroën, Mattern tried to link the measure of production costs to the rationalisation of task work with allocated time units (Schweitzer, *Des engrenages à la chaîne*, pp. 70ff).

34 The mission was organised by the Ordre National des Experts-Comptables et Comptables Agrées, the Association Française pour l'Amélioration de la Productivité and the Administration de Coopération Economique, in charge of economic relations between France and the USA. (Comité d'histoire de la comptabilité, 'La diffusion des coûts standards et du *direct costing* en France. L'exemple de Saint-Gobain, 1930–1960', n.d.)

35 Internal memorandum from the Financial Director of Saint-Gobain, dated 1951 (quoted in ibid.).

36 Salais and Storper, *Les mondes de production*, pp. 74–88.

37 Schweitzer, *Des engrenages à la chaîne*, pp. 95–7.

38 Cited in Margairaz, *L'Etat, les finances et l'économie*, p. 1203, note 7.

39 Charbonnages de France, Electricité de France, Gaz de France, Société Nationale des Chemins de Fer.

40 Interview with Jean Denizet, in F. Fourquet, *Les comptes de la puissance. Histoire de la comptabilité nationale et du Plan*, Editions Recherches ('Encres'), Paris, 1980.

41 The Centre d'Organisation Scientifique du Travail (COST) was created by Jean Coutrot (from the Ecole Polytechnique). It aimed to secure a positive link between economic modernisation and social humanism (M. Margairaz, 'Jean Coutrot 1936–1937: l'Etat et l'organisation scientifique du travail', *Genèses*, 4 May 1991, pp. 95–114.

42 Efficiency wages, introduced to economic theory by Alfred Marshall, designate a 'virtuous' dynamic balance between wage rises and increased labour efficiency, each one feeding the other due to a rising standard of living which has positive effects on labour skills.

43 Citroën had begun working on the 2CV as early as 1936; a pre-series was manufactured before the war (Fridenson, *Histoire des usines Renault*, p. 285).

44 Post-war patent applications reveal efforts to innovate in wartime, when patent applications were suspended Renault was preparing its popular 4CV, a combination of the Volkswagen and its own Primaquatre, during the war. In 1940, Renault considered that 'the postwar economy will . . . require very low-priced, mass-produced cars' (quoted by Fridenson, ibid.)

45 I would like to thank Martine Sennegon for her help in entering texts on to the computer.

5

AMERICANISATION AND ITS LIMITS

The reconstruction of Britain's engineering industries, 1945–1955[1]

Jonathan Zeitlin

INTRODUCTION

A central problem confronting all west European economies after the second world war was that of Americanisation. How far should European industry be reconstructed in the image of the United States, the dominant economic and military power of the postwar world? To contemporaries on both sides of the Atlantic, Americanisation of industry meant above all mass production – the high-volume manufacture of standardised goods using special-purpose machinery and predominately unskilled labour – together with its host of associated 'systematic' management techniques. Beyond the intrinsic appeal of such methods to Europeans aspiring to emulate American productivity, US policy makers actively sought to promote their diffusion through the technical assistance programmes and investment funds associated with the Marshall Plan. Recent literature on postwar Americanisation has tended to assume without much supporting evidence that this process proceeded relatively smoothly and rapidly, at least in its narrowly economic and technological dimensions. The real barriers to Americanisation, on this view, lay rather in the social, cultural and political spheres, where European elites and popular classes proved reluctant, to varying degrees and for different reasons, to embrace transatlantic models of labour management, welfare provision and mass consumption. Western Europe, as one influential formulation puts it, was only 'half-Americanised' during the postwar period; but the design and manufacture of industrial products in such accounts is squarely allocated to the 'Americanised' half. Even where the limits of industrial Americanisation are recognised, as for example in Maguire's otherwise valuable study of postwar British design and marketing policies, the persistence of 'pre-Fordist' production methods is taken to be a self-evident

101

indication of backwardness and complacency, an avatar of and contributory factor in the subsequent decline of domestic manufacturing.[2]

This chapter sketches out the contours of British debate about Americanisation and reconstruction in a key sector of manufacturing – the engineering or metalworking industries. Its central concerns are threefold. First, contrary to the claims of some recent historians,[3] it highlights the determined efforts – above all by government – to push British industry towards the adoption of American-style mass-production methods. Second, it re-examines contemporary objections to these proposals – some more prescient than others – and reassesses the practical impact of both on the reconstruction of British engineering. In so doing, finally, it questions the causal link between the limits of Americanisation and the subsequent decline of British manufacturing. For at a moment when American manufacturers themselves are struggling to respond to the challenges of new competitive strategies based on greater product diversity and productive flexibility, there can be little justification for considering mass production and systematic management as they were practised in the United States during the 1940s and 1950s as a universal model of industrial efficiency which other nations rejected at their peril.

In Britain as in other European countries, domestic debates about Americanisation of industry had a long history prior to 1945. From the 1890s, British observers monitored the evolution of mass-production techniques in American industry and considered their applicability to domestic economic conditions. While recognising the cost reductions and economies of scale theoretically obtainable from the American model, these discussions drew attention to the practical advantages of more flexible methods based on the use of skilled workers and general-purpose machinery in catering for the varied and fluctuating markets characteristic of British engineering. Concern was expressed about the inflexibility of special-purpose equipment, the overhead costs of bureaucratic management and the restrictive impact of standardisation on product innovation. However, British metalworking firms still selected certain features of American practice which could enhance product performance or productive efficiency without excessive loss of flexibility – such as new machine tools, payment systems and interchangeability of key parts – and used these piecemeal innovations to maintain or expand their position in domestic and international markets.

Promoting productivity, emulating America

The vast output and productivity of American industry during the 1940s reopened this debate and gave renewed impetus to British advocates of mass production. In the later years of the war, government planners, trade unionists and progressive industrialists put forward various proposals for the reconstruction of important sections of British engineering on mass-production lines. During the postwar productivity drive, official efforts to promote the adoption of American manufacturing methods reached their apogee through government standardisation campaigns, the transatlantic missions organised by the Anglo-American Council on Productivity (AACP) and the procurement policies of the nationalised industries.

Initially, the Labour government aimed to maintain full employment and boost output by 'manning up' key industries. By 1947, however, labour reserves were drying up, while capital investment was both constrained by material shortages and export priorities and could not be expected to yield rapid results. In the short term, increased output could only come from more efficient use of existing resources; raising productivity moved to the centre of Labour's economic objectives. The productivity drive encompassed policies aimed at improving the efficiency of British industry, from propaganda and exhortation, through the diffusion of work-study, operations research and human relations techniques, to public support for research and development.[4] Among the most important initiatives specifically directed at engineering was the promotion of product standardisation. In November 1947, Herbert Morrison, chairman of the Cabinet Committee on Production, proposed that the Board of Trade should consider measures to promote standardisation in British industry, including compulsory enforcement of dimensional standards for certain products. The Board of Trade commissioned an inquiry into efficiency gains achievable through standardisation. Despite its authors' enthusiasm for rationalisation, this concluded that reduction of product variety by itself yielded cost savings and output gains of only 5–10 per cent; larger savings of 25–50 per cent required much longer runs and heavy investment in new plant. 'Standardisation by the reduction of variety', concluded the Board, 'is not a panacea for the lessening of costs'; its report also underlined the attendant dangers of 'sterilization of design', reduced consumer choice and loss of ability to cater for diverse export markets. True to its voluntarist traditions, therefore, the Board rejected compulsory enforcement of standards except in cases of government procurement or public health and safety.

The Ministry of Supply (MoS), the department directly responsible for most engineering, was altogether more positive. While aware of the dangers cited by the Board of Trade, the ministry was convinced that greater standardisation in engineering would raise productivity. In November 1948, the ministry set up a Committee for Standardisation of Engineering Products under Sir Earnest Lemon, a pioneer of railway standardisation, to investigate the scope for the reduction of variety in the industry and the role of government in effecting it. After surveying domestic practice, revealing broad sectional variation, the Lemon Committee came down in favour of greater standardisation. Correctly applied, the committee contended, specialisation, simplification and standardisation should neither inhibit technical progress in design, impose uniformity on consumers nor result in a loss of markets at home or abroad. Designs could be altered periodically to accommodate technical advance; a reasonable variety of final products could be built up from standardised materials, parts and components; customers could be induced to accept standard articles through the vigorous use of price incentives. Despite these conclusions, however, the Lemon Report rejected compulsory enforcement of industrial standards as both impracticable and likely to produce 'serious rigidities and inefficiencies'. The British Standards Institution (BSI) should play a more active role in initiating new standards, receiving in return an increased public grant, but industrial standardisation must ultimately depend on the voluntary consent of private manufacturers. Government, the committee concluded, should encourage standardisation through a combination of public exhortation, tax allowances for capital investment and above all the purchasing policies of the nationalised industries, which consumed some 30 per cent of non-exported engineering.[5]

The Anglo-American Council on Productivity (AACP) was closely associated with the standardisation campaign and the Attlee government saw it as a means of devolving greater responsibility for the success of the productivity drive to business and labour. The AACP organised joint missions by British businessmen and workers to visit US plants, to investigate the sources of superior American productivity and to disseminate their findings. Most missions focused on individual industries, including engineering sectors, but specialist teams also studied key aspects of American practice such as product simplification, design for production, materials handling, production control and management accounting.[6]

The AACP missions concerned with engineering confirmed a substantial gap between American and British productivity and practice. However, the size of the gap was far from uniform across engineering as a whole. The contrast was sharpest in diesel locomotives and internal combustion engines, but scarcely evident in metalworking machine tools and woodworking machinery, with valves, pressed metal and electrical control gear somewhere in between. Contrary to the claims of some recent economic historians, the AACP engineering reports placed little emphasis on restrictive labour practices as a source of variations in productivity. Far more crucial, in their view, was the greater size and homogeneity of the American market, which made possible the longer runs that justified the fuller use of mass-production techniques. The reports also emphasised the active commitment of American engineering companies to the 'three charmed "S"s of high productivity': simplification, standardisation and specialisation. Even smaller firms tended to specialise on a narrow range of products, and high-production tooling was common on much smaller batches than in Britain. US manufacturers constantly sought to expand demand for their standard lines by 'making the market' through a combination of research, advertising and price discrimination against special orders. The effectiveness of mass production in US industry also depended on the application of systematic management methods such as standard costing, work study and production planning, as too did the success of labour policies like wage incentives and job evaluation.

But the practical message conveyed by the AACP productivity missions for the reorganisation of British industry was contradictory. Like the productivity drive itself, the AACP reports held out the prospect of efficiency gains through the adoption of American production methods; but the more radical the changes proposed in domestic practice, the more distant the potential benefits. On the one hand, the productivity teams highlighted the importance of inherently long-term measures such as reduction of product variety, greater mechanisation and automation, and the development of systematic management capabilities. On the other hand, many recommendations tended to focus on short-term measures which could be introduced within the existing organisation of production, such as better tooling, work study or incentive payment schemes. Paradoxically, therefore, at the same time as the AACP missions apotheosised American practice as a model for British industry, they also helped to circumscribe the scope of domestic reform.

BRINGING IT ALL BACK HOME

How did the various sections of the British engineering community respond to the Labour government's promotion of standardisation and Americanisation? On the business side, the reactions of peak associations like the Federation of British Industries (FBI) and the employer representatives on the Engineering Advisory Council (EAC) reflected their anxiety to limit the scope of state intervention in the private sector. Both organisations were extremely hostile towards compulsory standardisation, which they saw as the thin end of the wedge of state control; they opposed the Lemon Committee's proposal to give the BSI greater initiatory powers in establishing industrial standards. EAC employers also warned that 'it was particularly important to retain flexibility of production in order to combat American competition' and 'the standardisation of end products would be fatal from the selling point of view'. The employers' side agreed to recommend that engineering trade associations set up co-operative schemes for increasing production efficiency – including standardisation – while insisting that individual firms remain free to participate or not as they chose.[7]

Trade unions, by contrast, were more supportive. Like the FBI, the Trades Union Congress (TUC) sought to dispel what it saw as ill-informed foreign criticisms of domestic industry and emphasised the role of higher capital investment in raising productivity. But the General Council also pressed member unions to participate in AACP work; following a US team visit of its own, the TUC established a Production Department to train British trade unionists in productivity-enhancing techniques such as work study.

The reactions of individual unions were more complex but still positive. Jack Tanner, President of the Amalgamated Engineering Union (AEU), chief union spokesman on the EAC and a member of the TUC General Council, was an ardent supporter of the productivity drive, pressing government and employers for more vigorous measures. Tanner criticised the employers' disappointing response to the Lemon Report, while underlining the need to show the Americans on the AACP that the British were taking effective measures to increase standardisation, an objective central to the AEU's earlier proposals for postwar reconstruction.[8]

In 1945, the National Engineering Joint Trades Movement (NEJTM), an organisation uniting the AEU and the Confederation of Shipbuilding and Engineering Unions (CSEU), had campaigned for the continuation of wartime planning to promote productive efficiency and secure full employment after the war. The unions believed in the superiority of mass production and the urgent need for technical modernisation. Given the high levels of interwar unemployment, the NEJTM argued, British engineering had understandably become 'cautious and restrictive in its outlook. In technique, equipment and output per head many sections were far behind, for example, American standards.' Higher wartime productivity had occurred because the government became the main purchaser of engineering products, and because 'the organized workers played an important part in the drive for output and efficiency'. Without guaranteed bulk orders for machine tools, housing components and standardised consumer durables, the unions concluded, the advantages of mass production would be elusive. The NEJTM demanded that the new Labour government create a tripartite engineering board with executive powers to oversee the production and investment plans of private enterprise; this national body would form the apex of an articulated system of participatory planning stretching down to similar boards in the regions and joint production committees (JPCs) in individual factories. Such planning was not confined to capital: the unions requested that wartime manpower budgets be adapted to postwar economic management. The engineering unions' response to the productivity drive was to relaunch their campaign for participatory planning. *Engineering and the Crisis*, published by the CSEU in December 1947, attributed the government's economic difficulties to a 'lack of plan'; scarce raw materials and skilled labour were spread over too many non-standardised products, resulting in 'idle time coupled with low productivity' and 'ignorance of, or indifference to, the purpose of the production drive on the part of sections of the workers'. The CSEU demanded the transformation of the EAC into an effective planning body, buttressed by supporting sectoral, regional and district committees. The renewed planning campaign included a demand for statutory JPCs; as Tanner told the EAC in April 1948, 'there would not be a real response from the workers [to the productivity drive] unless they felt that they were not merely being consulted but were participating in the organisation of production'.[9]

The Labour government's reaction to the unions' proposals was unsympathetic. Unlike iron and steel, contended the MoS, engineering was not a basic industry; sectors such as locomotives and tin cans were too diverse to be governed by a single planning agency. Whereas the government embraced 'strategical' or 'democratic' planning for engineering, guiding the industry towards broad objectives using export quotas and raw material allocations, it rejected 'tactical' or 'totalitarian' planning which specified types of product, quantities and delivery dates in particular factories. Britain, officials emphasised, depended on being able to provide goods overseas. Customers were willing to buy in a competitive market in exchange for vital imports: 'Consequently, there had to be a good deal of flexibility, both in the broad outlines of planning and even more in the detailed picture.' Nor could ministers contemplate devolving executive powers to a tripartite body outside their control: this would represent both 'an abrogation of government' under British doctrines of parliamentary sovereignty and an unacceptable infringement of managerial prerogatives in privately owned firms. While ministers were unwilling to give unions more than an advisory role in industry-level planning, proposals to extend joint consultation in the factories enjoyed wider support; Cripps himself threatened employers with legislative sanctions if they did not voluntarily co-operate in the re-establishment of JPCs. However, the government rejected statutory compulsion as a result of opposition from the Ministry of Labour and, after some inter-union wrangling, from the TUC as well to such a permanent breach of voluntarist principles in peacetime. To avert more vigorous state intervention, the Engineering Employers Federation (EEF) encouraged its members to re-establish JPCs, whose numbers rapidly returned to peak wartime levels. But in the absence of any connection to wider economic planning or rights to information about the export targets fixed for individual firms, this second wave of JPCs inspired little enthusiasm among most engineering workers and shop stewards.[10] Rejected by the Labour government, the CSEU drew up its own *Plan for Engineering*, which it sought to promote through the TUC, with sector-by-sector proposals for the extension of public control, including bulk purchasing of utility products, the creation of statutory boards or development councils and selective nationalisations.[11]

The widest-ranging debate about standardisation, Americanisation and productivity was conducted by trade associations, engineering societies and the trade press. There were pronounced sectoral variations in attitudes towards the 'three Ss': a small survey of top industrial managers found, unsurprisingly, that manufacturers of intermediate goods or components for other businesses saw greater scope for standardisation than did those making complex capital equipment and finished consumer products. Beneath these sectoral variations, however, ran some common threads. British businessmen and engineers were well aware of the potential cost and productivity advantages of mass production, and the overall tenor of the debate was far more favourable to standardisation, simplification and specialisation than it had been in previous periods. However, prewar reservations about their commercial and technological limitations under domestic conditions had not been dispelled. Many respondents to the AACP and Lemon Reports emphasised the difficulties of imposing standard designs on varied export markets and the risks of excessive reliance on a narrow range of products under rapidly changing competitive conditions. Other commentators argued that 'the conditions which created a demand before the . . . war for a variety of products would return once the seller's market gave place to a buyer's market'; the ability to produce equipment like transformers or diesel locomotives to almost any specification was 'a priceless asset for overseas trade where individuality in requirements is even more marked than at home'. Further, excessive standardisation imposed constraints on technological innovation and design changes. These reservations were reinforced by acquaintance with American practice: one AACP team found that US woodworking machinery manufacturers froze their designs for up to ten years in order to amortize the costs of special tooling, while another reported that: 'A consequence of the large scale of production and widespread use of special purpose machinery is undoubtedly a tendency for design to become stereotyped and the combustion systems used by certain engine builders would certainly be considered out of date by British standards.'[12] These criticisms of postwar Americanisation were extensively documented in the influential trade journal the *Engineer*, which drew attention to the difficulties posed by trying to adapt American production methods to British practice and the possible benefits that might be derived from the study of Western European firms, who were Britain's real competitors in world markets.

Faced with these objections, standardisation advocates tended to turn from end products to components. Although this apparently promised to reconcile production economy with product diversity, standardisation of components raised nearly as many problems as it resolved. It increased production and inventory costs in the short run; it could also inhibit the development of new models because of the interdependence among their constituent parts. 'Even the standardisation of components for use in loco-motives of different overall design presents great difficulty', contended British manufacturers, 'since the modern diesel locomotive is so compactly built that even minor variations to meet a special requirement can cause repercussions throughout the structure.' Similar reservations were voiced by some of the most ardent domestic proponents of large-scale production. Sir Patrick Hennessy of Ford UK argued that 'if . . . all manufacturers had the same wheels, someone with a bright idea for an improved model might come along and be prevented from succeeding because he needed different wheels.' A preferable solution, a Board of Trade study concluded, was 'to decide on a good design and to make it in very large numbers which would give economies of scale both in components and in assembly, rather than attempt to make it with standard parts in a number of different designs'. Such arguments highlighted the tension between individual and collective standardisation, which meant, as contemporaries knew, that any attempt to pursue one was likely to undercut the other, at least in the medium term.[13]

Despite their admiration for American productive organisation, British commentators also criticised the high levels of stocks and work-in-progress on which it depended, anticipating more recent critiques of US manufacturing practice in comparison to that of the Japanese – as noted by B.E. Stokes, a British production engineer recently returned from a tour of US factories in 1952. Stokes identified 'the problem of the so-called "economic" batch': an 'erroneous idea of machine utilisation in which the machine requirements dominate the company requirements', leading production managers to insist on manufacturing components in long runs without reference to changing patterns of customer demand, the relative value of special and standard products, or the costs of immobilised capital. Stokes's proposed solution, like the 'just-in-time' system being developed by Toyota's Taiichi Ohno at that very moment, was to tailor production more closely to demand and reduce the costs of small-lot manufacture by increasing the speed and efficiency of machine changeovers. Such a strategy, however, required a system of production control capable of dealing with greater complexity and variety. As the AACP reports confirmed, however, few American firms had developed planning systems suitable for handling a greater variety of products manufactured in smaller quantities, while 'their immediate reaction, "increase the progress staff" [was] not unknown in Britain!'[14]

Among the central paradoxes of the productivity debate was its comparative neglect of Germany, Britain's major prewar competitor in most of the engineering industries. Postwar intelligence missions which inspected German factories were impressed by the skills and training of the labour force at all levels, from engineers and technicians to foremen and manual workers, but not by production methods and organisation, which they regarded as inferior not only to that of American firms but also of well-run British companies. 'Thus as regards the internal organisation of German industrial concerns we have very little to learn', concluded one specialist investigation of production control, a finding echoed in the reports of other intelligence teams dealing with aircraft instruments, machine tools and power presses. Yet German engineering exports grew rapidly during the 1950s, particularly to western Europe; by the middle of the decade, German machinery manufacturers had recaptured their prewar share of world markets, largely at British expense.[15]

FROM THEORY TO PRACTICE

Reconstruction planning and the postwar productivity drive touched off a far-reaching debate about the efficiency and organisation of British engineering; participants gauged the distance separating their indigenous manufacturing methods from American mass production on the one hand and German craft production on the other. What was the impact of this debate on product and production strategies in the British engineering industries during the postwar years? How did metalworking manufacturers decide in practice which American experiences were worthwhile and in what manner they could be adapted? To what extent did British engineering firms succeed in reconciling the countervailing demands of product diversity and higher productivity, complexity of manufacture and cost consciousness, flexibility and mass production? The most ambitious experiments with standardisation and mass production, predictably enough, were undertaken by the public sector. Both the MoS and the Central Electricity Board saw design standardisation as a key to overcoming backlogs in deliveries of power-station equipment; in November 1947 the MoS issued a statutory order limiting turbo-alternators for the domestic market to two standard sizes, 30 and 60 megawatts (MW). Similarly, the newly nationalised British Railways in 1948 developed a standard family of steam locomotives and coaching stock for use on all lines, followed by flow-line production of standard electric carriages for its southern commuter services during the early 1950s.[16]

The results of these initiatives proved disappointing even to their architects, vindicating many of the economic and technological objections raised by contemporary critics. The sizes and steam conditions selected for standard turbo-alternators turned out to be too small and too conservative to give maximum operating benefits, handicapping the thermal efficiency of British electricity generation during the 1950s and 1960s, in contrast to the French, who based more of their postwar re-equipment programme on sets of 100 MW and above, before standardising on 125 MW during the early 1950s. Real capital costs per unit of generating capacity declined substantially between 1948 and 1953, mainly because the nationalised electricity authority favoured the more advanced 60 MW and (after the withdrawal of the standardisation order in 1950) 100 MW sets. Little of this gain, conversely, was due to cost reductions associated with the replication of standard designs, since production economies of scale were undercut by the division of orders among many separate manufacturers, who remained reluctant to offer quantity discounts on collectively agreed prices. In 1950, the electricity authority persuaded one major manufacturer of power-generating equipment, C.A. Parsons Ltd, to withdraw from the group price-fixing agreement in exchange for guaranteed orders for standard designs. But the savings obtained satisfied neither party, and turbo-alternator manufacture at Parsons during the mid-1950s continued to be organised on jobbing lines, with a predominance of flexible, general-purpose machinery whose output was 'determined, to a large extent, by the skill, dexterity and, indeed, willingness of the operator to use [it] to the best advantage'.[17]

On the railways, too, investments in a new generation of standard steam locomotives helped to slow down the introduction of more efficient diesel models, raising rather than reducing operating costs in the longer term. The key problem here was uncertainty about the future advantages of competing traction technologies. During the 1940s, diesel locomotives had replaced steam on American railways; savings on maintenance and fuel charges more than offset their higher first cost. But dieselisation seemed less suitable for British conditions, with their shorter distances, denser and more diverse traffic and scarcer oil supplies; only in the shunting yards, whose near-continuous operations ensured cost-effectiveness, had diesel-electric engines been widely adopted. R.A. Riddles, the Railway Executive's Chief Mechanical Engineer, believed that steam would remain the power plant of choice for British locomotives until the relaxation of capital constraints made possible its gradual displacement by electricity as in continental Europe. He refused to compromise the proven benefits of standardisation, which he had personally experienced as a designer of wartime austerity locomotives for the MoS, by authorising trials of diesel engines on main-line services. Within a few years, however, changing patterns of fuel availability, growing power requirements and other unforeseen developments drove British Railways to convert to diesel, retrospectively confirming the earlier judgement of critics like the *Engineer* that a less ambitious standardisation scheme focused on fittings and components rather than complete steam locomotives might have been more prudent.[18]

The impact of Americanisation and the productivity drive on the private sector can be examined at both a collective and an individual level. Trade associations in various sectors, from motor vehicles, internal combustion engines and radio equipment to machine tools, textile machinery and railway rolling stock, established special committees to promote standardisation and productive efficiency through exchange of technical information and agreement on joint component specifications. In motor cars, a committee of chief engineers and purchasing managers from the 'big six' manufacturers began to publish common standards books for components such as brake shoes, whose designs were reduced from 136 to 10 basic sizes. Trade associations in aircraft, locomotives and cable manufacturing carried inter-firm collaboration further through the provision of common services such as testing, procurement of raw materials, sharing of equipment and tooling, and collection of information on foreign markets., The most widespread service was co-operative R&D, with the formation of new research associations for motor vehicles, machine tools, radio equipment, internal combustion engines and marine engineering. In the 1940s, many of these initiatives aimed at forestalling possible state compulsion and they proved most effective where the association's authority was reinforced by government, as in the case of aircraft where the MoS required the use of standard components on all military contracts. In motor vehicles, by contrast, designers remained free to deviate from common component specifications by invoking a 'failure to agree' provision; Nuffield and Austin broke off arrangements for the exchange of confidential information in 1949, following the revival of long-standing hostilities between their chief executives and the Labour Party's decision not to include the industry in plans for future nationalisation.[19]

At the level of the individual firm, the practical impact of Americanisation varied widely, depending, among other things, on sectoral patterns of demand and the strategic choices of top management. Thus, for instance, AACP follow-up reports found much greater willingness to standardise and invest in special-purpose machinery and tooling among manufacturers of valves, an intermediate good for which demand was large and rapidly expanding, than of diesel locomotives, a complex finished product for which the domestic market, unlike that in the USA, remained extremely narrow.[20] Within each sector, some firms were vastly more enthusiastic than others about the commercial prospects of mass-produced goods. One noteworthy case in point was Standard Motors, which reconverted its wartime shadow aircraft factory to high-volume production of standardised cars and tractors, using a single interchangeable engine for both types of vehicle and large numbers of automatic machine tools imported from the United States. To ensure adequate labour supplies and workforce commitment for the anticipated quantum leap in productive scale, the firm broke with the local engineering employers' association by agreeing a new wage structure with the unions based on a drastic reduction in job grades, shorter hours, a guaranteed weekly rate and higher output bonuses for large, self-organising gangs.[21]

At the level of the individual company, the reconstruction period saw a widespread rationalisation and narrowing of product ranges, involving mergers, amalgamations and reorganisation of existing firms. These tendencies were visible in motor vehicles, internal combustion engines and related components. The National Advisory Council for the Motor Manufacturing Industry (NACMMI) claimed that the number of basic models in 1948 would be reduced to 42 from 136 in 1939, with a drop in the number of body variations from 299 to 40. During this period, Austin replaced eight basic models and seven engines with three of each; the Nuffield Organisation pruned its range from eighteen to nine basic models, though the number of engines fell only from ten to eight. Despite Nuffield's hostility to the MoS's 'one factory, one model' campaign, its Board privately conceded that rationalisation was the right course to pursue. In 1949, the group appointed a corporate standards engineer and reorganised its production facilities, transferring the manufacture of Wolseley cars to Cowley and concentrating output of rear axles and front suspensions for Nuffield vehicles at the newly vacated Washwood Heath plant near Birmingham. After the two rivals merged in

1952 to form the British Motor Corporation, its new chief executive Leonard Lord reorganised production of mechanical parts, reducing the number of engines to three basic sizes, while retaining a larger number of body shells for the separate Austin and Morris marques.[22] American subsidiary firms like Vauxhall and Ford pursued even more radical policies along similar lines.

A major impetus towards standardisation came from component manufacturers themselves. Before the war, managers at Lucas, the dominant supplier of electrical and fuel injection equipment for British motor vehicles, were impressed by the efficiency of American component firms like Delco-Remy, whose manufacturing methods they sought to emulate. The company, whose staff made eighty-five visits to the USA between 1945 and 1949, formulated ambitious plans to double direct-operator productivity through further standardisation of design. Working through the NACMMI and the 'Big Six' standardisation committee, Lucas pressed car manufacturers to adopt common specifications for dynamos, starters, batteries, coils and headlamps. Managers envisaged that 168 current models could be replaced by 41 standard designs, yielding longer runs and lower costs, a point driven home by substantial price penalties on non-standard products. Lesser component firms such as Glacier Metal, suppliers of plain engine bearings for a variety of applications, likewise aimed to reduce costs, improve deliveries and justify investment in high-performance tooling by replacing some 20,000 customers' drawings with a standard list of designs and sizes manufactured for stock.[23]

Such applications of the 'three Ss' often paved the way for a far-reaching transformation of manufacturing methods. In some sectors, longer production runs and rising demand encouraged firms to install high-throughput special machinery and tooling, especially after constraints on capital investment eased from the late 1940s. The most spectacular example was the automatic transfer equipment introduced by car manufacturers like Ford, Vauxhall, Austin and Nuffield; mechanical-handling devices moved major components such as engine blocks, cylinder heads and gearboxes through a series of multifunction machining stations without any direct intervention by the operator. Austin was especially active in extending the use of both in-line and rotary transfer machinery; by 1953, the company had applied such equipment to a wider range of parts than in any other British automobile factory, stealing a march on the USA itself in the case of crankshafts. Where production volumes were insufficient to justify this level of mechanical integration, automatic multifunction machinery could none the less be employed on a stand-alone basis, as in the manufacture of fuel-injection equipment at Leyland and CAV, Lucas's commercial vehicle subsidiary. In body work, similarly, these motor vehicle firms invested heavily in special welding machinery, elaborate press tools and mechanical handling devices, as well as in new automatic rust-proofing plants and conveyorised paint shops. So did US-owned manufacturers of electrical appliances, like Frigidaire (a GM subsidiary), which retooled its Kingsbury factory with template dies, tangent benders and automatic spot-welding machinery for high-volume production of refrigerator cabinets. Hoover's new washing-machine factory at Merthyr Tydfil incorporated automatic anodising plant along with special-purpose equipment for pressing, shaping and welding the main shells.[24]

Less dramatic but equally significant was the reorganisation of production layouts along flow-line principles. Between 1946 and 1951, Austin replanned and mechanised its stores and assembly shops at Longbridge, integrating a maximum number of operations on to the lines themselves, and controlling the flow of materials by means of punched-card readers in each department. Many large manufacturers of cars, commercial vehicles, internal combustion engines and electrical appliances (Rover, Leyland, Perkins, Hoover and Frigidaire) also introduced power conveyors and mechanical handling systems to ensure progressive movement of work through assembly, machining and foundry processes. Other firms, however, often sought to obtain the benefits of flow-line layout through the use of less costly devices like roller conveyors and gravity slides, as in the cases of diesel-engine erection at Brush's McLaren subsidiary, twist-drill machining at the English Steel Co., electric cooker manufacture at GEC's Swinton plant, or even cylinder-head machining for Vauxhall's Bedford trucks.[25]

Above all, work study diffused rapidly through British manufacturing industry during the 1940s and 1950s. Work-study methods were used as a basis for production planning as well as for incentive payment systems, as in the case of valve manufacturers such as Glenfield & Kennedy and Walker, Crossweller & Co. or the motor vehicle firms discussed above. Occasionally, as at Perkins, rationalisation of production, job analysis and predetermined output targets could enable management to eliminate incentive bonuses altogether in favour of a flat hourly rate. More often, however, as with interwar task measurement and incentive systems like Bedaux, British engineering firms used work study to raise output and effort levels; this was easily 'added on' to existing production arrangements without the need for far-reaching reorganisation.[26]

OBSTACLES TO AMERICANISATION: SUPPLY AND DEMAND

Thus a significant stratum of British engineering manufacturers responded positively to official initiatives and the allure of Americanisation in hopes of raising productivity and tapping into potential markets for mass-produced goods. Some of these were local subsidiaries of American-owned multi-nationals, presaging a growing trend towards US direct investment during the 1950s and 1960s; but others, such as Austin, Lucas, Perkins or GEC, ranked among the leading indigenous companies in their sectors. However,

Britain's dire postwar economic position and the Labour government's broader policy choices combined to limit the scope for Americanisation in the short and medium term. Widespread, unpredictable shortages of fuel, power, labour and raw materials – above all steel – inhibited expansion plans and disrupted manufacturing programmes. Official restrictions on capital investment, based on 'make-do-and-mend', favoured expenditure 'directed to getting more output from existing plant rather than the creation of fresh capacity'. These problems were reinforced by the scarcity of foreign exchange for imported equipment and an export quota of 50 per cent for British machine tool output. Understandable though they were in the light of Britain's precarious balance of payments, export quotas of 50–75 per cent for many engineering goods, backed up by controls over steel allocations and adjusted at short notice, prevented manufacturers from building up stable home demand for standardised products, forcing them to disperse their output across a wide range of foreign markets, often based on short-run currency considerations rather than long-run commercial strategy. Although supply-side bottlenecks eased after 1948, permitting a relaxation of physical controls, they returned in 1950 as a result of the rearmament programme triggered by the war in Korea. Defence expenditure on metal and engineering goods more than doubled, to absorb nearly 16 per cent of British output and 18 per cent of employment by 1952–3, leading to acute shortages of labour and steel, as well as still higher export quotas and a further squeeze on the home market for consumer products like motor cars and electrical appliances.

Macro-economic uncertainty magnified the risks and exacerbated the difficulties inherent in the pursuit of mass-production strategies, as some British protagonists discovered. Among the most disappointing experiences was that of Standard Motors. After initial successes in export markets during the late 1940s, the firm's medium-sized Vanguard car encountered growing consumer resistance abroad during the early 1950s as competing models became more widely available, not least because its design had been shaped, as *The Economist* caustically noted, 'less by market research than by the desirability of using the same engine in it as in the Ferguson tractor'. By 1952, Standard had the worst export record of any of the 'Big Six' manufacturers, only managing to avert a cut in its steel allocations by introducing a new sports car model, which – unlike the firm's saloons – rapidly carved out a lucrative niche in the American market. The Ferguson tractor's development costs proved higher than anticipated, while production also increased more slowly and had to be sharply curtailed in 1949 due to a collapse in sales. Since more diversified firms like David Brown and others managed to increase tractor output during the same year, whereas that of Ford and Standard fell by a similar proportion, this reverse led some contemporaries to question 'whether the production programmes of the two largest manufacturers are too rigid', while highlighting for others the dependence of successful product specialisation on 'an accurate assessment of market requirements'. Even when sales did take off during the early 1950s, moreover, the tough licensing terms negotiated by Harry Ferguson ensured that Standard's profit margins remained thin. Although the company's innovative labour agreement delivered benefits in terms of industrial peace, workforce stability, reduced overheads and increased productivity, Standard never made the expected jump in volume or market share, and its wage levels gradually fell back towards those of other Coventry motor firms.[27]

Other would-be mass producers encountered analogous setbacks. At Glacier Metal, 28 per cent of production time in 1948 was spent on runs of ten days or less, for which elaborate press tools were uneconomic, as customers insisted on immediate delivery and were not prepared to wait for special machines to be built and set up, or demanded deliveries of small quantities over a period of time to avoid carrying large stocks. The firm's efforts to promote its standard bearings through price differentials carried little incentive, given the small share of this component in the total cost of a motor. Even firms with greater market clout, such as Lucas, found their standardisation programmes impeded by the necessity of manufacturing components and spares for a wide range of countries, often with different technical specifications, to which their customers' products were exported in hopes of meeting official targets. At Nuffield's Cowley plant, similarly, a combination of steel shortages, restrictions on domestic sales and difficulties in export markets reduced capacity utilisation on special-purpose equipment installed for the production of its Morris Minor and Oxford models to just 42 per cent in 1951 and 52 per cent the following year. Manufacturers of electrical cookers, refrigerators, washing machines, heaters and vacuum cleaners likewise found their ability to achieve long runs and production continuity impeded by materials shortages, erratic power supplies, export quotas and fluctuations in purchase tax on domestic sales during this period.[28]

THE PERSISTENCE OF SELECTIVE ADAPTATION

In this environment, many British metalworking industrialists preferred an incremental adoption of American-style manufacturing methods. Even those British metalworking firms which embraced mass production most enthusiastically often selectively modified US manufacturing methods to handle a wider range of products in smaller quantities through innovations similar to those later made famous by the Japanese. Austin built up its transfer machinery from various combinations of special unit heads manufactured in-house with interchangeable Archdale bases and mechanical handling devices; these standard elements could be reconfigured for work on new models with a minimum of scrapping, and design changes could be accommodated on existing equipment by adding new sections. Even firms with relatively short runs of repetition work had begun to utilise flow production techniques, observed Frank Woollard, a leading automotive engineer, by grouping similar components such as shafts, pulleys, gears and cams 'to permit a layout of the machines in operation sequence', and then adapting fixtures, jigs, tools and gauges 'to reduce the changeover time to a minimum'.[29]

In assembly as in machining processes, British engineering manufacturers adapted standard mass-production methods to accommodate greater product variety and shorter runs through practices similar to those developed by the Japanese. At Austin's new mechanically controlled assembly plant, opened in 1951, three different body and chassis types, as well as right- and left-hand drives, were put together on a single track; normal variations in assembly sequence could be introduced in 90–120 minutes, while colour changes involving operations remote from the line took no more than eight hours. At Nuffield Metal Products, too, four different body types could be assembled on multipurpose jigs without any resetting, allowing transfers of urgent work from one line to another in case of breakdowns. Rover carried this approach a step further by assembling several distinct models simultaneously on the same tracks, as did Leyland, which built all types of four-wheel chassis on a single three-section line, with extra stations for more-complex models. Even in the case of specialised machine tools, BSA Tools managed to assemble many different sizes and types of equipment on a single manual track, with machine bases pushed on trolleys from station to station.[30]

More significantly, some British engineering firms introduced production control systems aimed at minimising internal buffer stocks and work-in-progress, in line with contemporary critiques of American practice discussed earlier. Austin, for example, reduced floating stocks on the assembly lines, cut contingency stores to two days' requirements and achieved stock turnover ratios in some departments of more than fifty times a year by issuing parts for each vehicle in individual sets from a common 'marshalling yard', which served as 'an automatic progress chaser, a balancing mechanism and a reservoir with a small but effective "head"'. Similar systems were introduced at both Rover and Leyland, where sub-assemblies were produced only as required for immediate use on the chassis assembly lines. Both Austin and Rover sought to extend these systems of low-inventory manufacture beyond their own plants through 'frequent deliveries of relatively small quantities from outside suppliers'. While Austin did not always find it easy 'in the circumstances existing to-day . . . to obtain the necessary degree of co-operation', the *Automobile Engineer* reported, 'several companies have already realized that the system is good for both the supplier and user of the materials', and the car firm had designed special standardised trailers for transporting parts from outside factories.[31]

Although these British manufacturers were still attempting to push rather than pull components through the production process, their rationale for cutting inventories and stripping out buffer stocks closely resembled that of the 'just-in-time' system pioneered by Toyota and later adopted by other Japanese automobile companies. First, such British firms, like their Japanese counterparts, sought to hold down capital investments in stocks and work-in-progress, particularly since materials costs had risen much faster than those of other inputs in relation to prewar prices. Like Toyota, a number of British engineering companies saw the reduction of inventory as a mechanism for inducing continuous improvements in product quality and productive efficiency. At Austin, managers expected that the new assembly lines would exert an indirect pressure on upstream production processes 'since there is no means of switching a faulty component or sub-assembly and replacing it by another one', so that 'the quality of the product . . . will be obtained with much less rectification than hitherto'. At BSA Tools, 'the major advantage' of flow production was held to be that 'it throws into high relief any shortages which might jeopardise the time schedule for the production of the machine'. Among the benefits of manufacturing components on the 'group system', Woollard likewise noted, was that 'faulty work will be found almost immediately and the necessary adjustments made . . . since inspection will naturally be in line with the machines'.[32]

Such production systems typically required functional flexibility on the part of even semi-skilled operatives to cope with the variations in tasks and times involved in turning out different products on the same lines. '[I]n manning a continuously operated plant', advised Woollard, it was 'of very considerable help' to train 'operators to do several jobs . . . Operators who have had the opportunity of working on many and various machines and assembly lines make ideal flying-squad men', who could be frequently redeployed to overcome bottlenecks and imbalances in production. Often, demands for versatility extended beyond small squads of multiskilled operatives to embrace whole sections of the workforce; British manufacturers of motor vehicles, internal combustion engines, electrical appliances and other engineering products found the solution to this problem in group bonus systems which tied the earnings of each worker to the output of an entire production line. At Leyland, for example, not only assembly-line workers but also machine operators were remunerated according to 'a pooled bonus scheme based on the group output of completed parts. When necessary the operators move freely from one machine to another in the group. This is an important factor in maintaining an even flow of parts and in preventing an accumulation at any stage along the machining line.'[33]

CONCLUSIONS

Despite the Labour government's commitment to planning and stability as the basis for full employment and industrial modernisation, few periods have seen greater turbulence in product markets, factor supplies and technologies than that of postwar reconstruction. Under these conditions, some single-minded experiments with Americanisation and mass production came wholly or partially unstuck in both the public and private sectors, as foreseen by contemporary critics. Often, too, collective schemes for co-ordinated special-isation or industry-wide standardisation broke down in the absence of effective governance mechanisms capable of ensuring the compliance of indi-vidual enterprises, as for example in shipbuilding or motor vehicles. Hence most British metalworking firms tended to adopt cautious, incremental strategies of productivity improvement in which transatlantic techniques were selectively grafted on to indigenous manufacturing practices, as in the case of work study. A significant minority of domestic engineering manufacturers, including the local subsidiaries of US-owned multinationals, innovatively modified American-style mass-production methods to accom-modate greater variety and shorter runs, thereby adjusting to differences in the structure and stability of British markets. In some instances, these modifications built on practices known to American production engineers but rarely applied in US industry; in many respects, too, they closely resembled and may even have helped to inspire the techniques of reconciling product variety with productive efficiency, later deployed so successfully by Japanese manufacturers like Toyota and Nissan, such as quick tooling changes, mixed-model assembly and just-in-time component supply.

Despite its enormous ideological influence, the practical impact of the Americanisation drive on British engineering remained limited during the first postwar decade. It was only between the mid-1950s and the mid-1970s, as a massive wave of government-promoted mergers and takeovers transformed the structure of the industry, that British engineering companies decisively abandoned their indigenous model of productive organisation in favour of imported management techniques such as multi-divisionalisation and measured day work. Far from reviving its competitive fortunes, however, this putative Americanisation of British engineering was associated instead with a rapid loss of market share both abroad and at home, resulting in a steep decline of domestic production and employment. By the 1980s, ironically, the competitive difficulties of British engineering firms, like those of the Americans themselves, were frequently attributed to their inability to match the standards of product innovation and productive flexibility set by the Germans and the Japanese in meeting the demands of increasingly diverse and volatile international markets.[34]

NOTES

1 This chapter draws on J. Zeitlin, *Between Flexibility and Mass Production: Strategic Debate and Industrial Reorganization in British Engineering,*

1830–1990, Oxford University Press, Oxford, forthcoming, which contains fuller discussion and references.

2 M. Hogan, *The Marshall Plan*, Cambridge University Press, Cambridge, 1987, p. 436; P. Maguire, 'Designs on reconstruction: British business, market structures and the role of design in post-war recovery', *Journal of Design History*, vol. 4 (1991).

3 For example, C. Barnett, *The Audit of War*, London, 1986, and *The Lost Victory*, London, 1995.

4 See also N. Tiratsoo, Chapter 3 in this volume.

5 Public Record Office [hereafter PRO] CAB 134/639: 'Standardising and simplifying engineering products', memo by Ministry of Supply, 8 September 1948; Ministry of Supply, *Report of the Committee for the Standardization of Engineering Products*, Routledge, London, 1949.

6 A. Carew, *Labour under the Marshall Plan*, Manchester University Press, Manchester, 1987, ch. 9; N. Tiratsoo and J.Tomlinson, *Industrial Efficiency and State Intervention: Labour 1939–51*, Routledge, London, 1993, ch. 7.

7 PRO BT 195/1, Engineering Advisory Council [hereafter EAC] Minutes, 3 March 1949; BT 195/19: 'Production efficiency', EAC(49)67, June 1949; SUPP 14/141: 'Report of the Lemon Committee for Standardisation of Engineering Products: Comments from EAC', 2 January 1950; SUPP 14/333: 'Production Efficiency: Memo.', 28 July 1950

8 Tiratsoo and Tomlinson, *Industrial Efficiency*, pp. 133–42, 164–5; Carew, *Labour under the Marshall Plan*, pp. 147–56; PRO BT 195/1: EAC Minutes, 3 March 1949; SUPP 14/141: EAC Minutes 1 February 1950; BT 195/19: Leslie to Trend, 7 January 1949.

9 PRO SUPP 14/137: National Engineering Joint Trades Movement [hereafter NEJTM], memo. 'Post-war Reconstruction in the Engineering Industry', n.d., April and December (?) 1945; SUPP 14/138, NEJTM to J. Wilmot (Minister of Supply), 28 February 1946; TUC Archives, Modern Records Centre (MRC), University of Warwick, MSS 292/615.2/5: Confederation of Shipbuilding and Engineering Unions (CSEU), 'Engineering and the Crisis', 8 December 1947; PRO BT 195/6: EAC Minutes, 7 April 1948; J. Hinton, *Shop-floor Citizens: Engineering Democracy in 1940s Britain*, Edward Elgar, Aldershot, Hants, 1994, chs 8–9.

10 Hinton, *Shop-floor Citizens*, pp. 170–6, 184–94.

11 SUPP 14/141: memos etc., 1946–8; TUC Archives, MRC MSS 292/615.2/5: 'The Engineering Worker and Economic Recovery', 5 December 1949; TUC, Engineering and Shipbuilding NAC, minutes, 1 March 1950; CSEU, *Plan for Engineering*, 1951, 1953.

12 P.W.S. Andrews and E. Brunner, 'Productivity and the businessman', *Oxford Economic Papers*, 2, 1950; PRO SUPP 14/141: industry comments; British Productivity Council (BPC), *The Wheels of Progress: A Review of Productivity in the Diesel Locomotive Industry*, 1954, paras 35–6; PRO SUPP 14/330: meeting of PEP Engineering Group, 31 May 1948; Anglo-American Council On Productivity (AACP), *Woodworking Machinery*, London, 1952, p. 10; ACCP, *Internal Combustion Engines* (London, 1950), p. 40.

13 BPC, *Wheels of Progress*, p. 9; PRO BT 64/2379: 'Standardisation, Specification and Production of Variety' (1948); SUPP 14/330: Hennessy to PEP Engineering Group.

14 B.E. Stokes, 'The organisation of production administration for higher productivity', *Journal of the Institution of Production Engineers*, vol. 31, 1952, pp. 201–4, 211–14; BPC, *Production Control*, 1953. On Toyota, see M.A. Cusomano, *The Japanese Automobile Industry*, Harvard University Press, Cambridge, MA, 1985.

15 British Intelligence Objectives Sub-committee, *Investigation of Production Control and Organisation in German Factories*, Final Report 537, London, 1947, p. 8; A. Kramer, *The West German Economy, 1945–1955*, Berg, New York, 1991, ch. 6; A.S. Milward, *The European Rescue of the Nation-State*, Routledge, London, 1992, pp. 396–424.

16 L. Hannah, *Electricity before Nationalization*, Macmillan, London, 1979, p. 322, and *Engineers, Managers and Politicians: The First Fifteen Years of Nationalised Electricity Supply in Britain*, Macmillan, London, 1982, pp. 24–5; I.V. Robinson, 'Standardization of steam turbo-generating plant', *Proceedings of the Institution of Mechanical Engineers*, vol. 164, 1951; T.R. Gourvish, *British Railways, 1948–1973*, Cambridge, 1986, pp. 87–90; *Engineering*, 1 December 1950; F. Woollard, *Principles of Mass and Flow Production*, Iliffe, London, 1954, pp. 35–42.

17 Hannah, *Engineers*, pp. 104–10; *Engineer*, 21 November 1947, 17 March 1950; Robinson, 'Standardisation of Steam Turbo-generating Plant'; J. Henderson (Parsons), 'Some problems associated with the selection of machine tools for heavy engineering production', *Transactions of the Manchester Association of Engineers*, 1954–5, p. 323; Monopolies and Restrictive Practices Commission, *Report on the Supply and Exports of Electrical and Allied Machinery and Plant*, London, 1957, pp. 49–53, 82–6. For France, see F.P.R. Brechling and A.J. Surrey, 'An international comparison of production techniques: the coal-fired electricity generating industry', *National Institute Economic Review*, vol. 36 (1966).

18 Gourvish, *British Railways*, pp. 88–9; Johnson and Long, *British Railways Engineering*; PEP, *Locomotives*, London, 1951, pp. 10–11; *Engineer*, 21 January 1949, 21 September 1951.

19 PRO SUPP 14/141: industry comments; SUPP 14/333: 'Production Efficiency', EAC memos and associated papers; AACP, *Simplification in British Industry*, London, 1950, pp. 9–10; PEP, *Motor Vehicles*, London, 1950, p. 136; PEP, *Locomotives*, p. 20; *Engineer*, 28 January 1949, 31 March 1950; *Automobile Engineer* [hereafter AE] January 1952; BPC, *Wheels of Progress*, p. 11; T.R. Whisler, *At the End of the Road: The Rise and Fall of Austin-Healy, MG and Triumph Sports Cars*, JAI Press, Greenwich, CT, 1995, pp. 79–80.

20 BPC, *Wheels of Progress*.

21 N. Tiratsoo, 'The motor car industry', in H. Mercer, N. Rollings and J. Tomlinson (eds) *Labour Governments and Private Industry*, Edinburgh, 1992, pp. 170–3; S. Tolliday, 'High Tide and After: Coventry's Engineering Workers and Shopfloor Bargaining', in B. Lancaster and T. Mason (eds), *Life and Labour in a Twentieth-century City: The Experience of Coventry*, Cryfield Press, Coventry, 1985.

22 Ministry of Supply, *National Advisory Council for the Motor Manufacturing Industry: Report on Proceedings* (London, 1947), pp. 3, 10; PEP, *Motor Vehicles*; R.J. Wyatt, *The Austin, 1905–1952*, David & Charles, Newton Abbott, Devon,

1981, pp. 247, 287; Whisler, *At the End of the Road*, pp. 22, 79–80; *Engineering*, 10 November 1961.

23 H. Nockolds, *Lucas: The First Hundred Years*, vol. II: *The Successors*, David & Charles, Newton Abbott, Devon, 1978; AACP, *Simplification in British Industry*, p. 10; PRO BT 64/2314: 'Standardisation as an Aid to Productivity' (1949); *Engineer*, 5 August 1949.

24 Woollard, *Principles*, pp. 30–3, 147–50; *AE*, November 1947, July–October 1948, May 1950, July 1951, October 1951, June–July 1952, March–April 1953, August 1953; BPC, *Applying the Pressure: A Review of Productivity in the Pressed Metal Industry*, London, 1953; H.J. Graves, 'An outline of BMC developments in the field of automation', *Institution of Production Engineers Journal*, vol. 36, 1957; *Engineering*, 10 March 1950.

25 Woollard, *Principles*, p. 23; *AE*, September 1946, March 1947, February 1952, September 1951, August 1953; *Engineering*, 18 November 1949, 12 January 1951, 13 April 1951, 21 March 1952; AACP, *Final Report*, p. 33.

26 BPC, *Top of the Shop: A Productivity Review in the Valves Industry*, London, 1954, pp. 20–1, 27; 'Re-organization of a diesel engine works', *Engineering*, 3 July 1953. Also S.J. Dalziel, 'Work study in industry', *Political Quarterly*, vol. 27, 1956; Tiratsoo and Tomlinson, *Industry Efficiency*, pp. 148–50; H.F. Gospel, *Markets, Firms and the Management of Labour in Modern Britain*, Cambridge University Press, Cambridge, 1992, pp. 118–20.

27 Tiratsoo, 'The motor car industry', *Engineering*, 27 January 1950.

28 PRO BT 64/2379, 'Standardisation', app. A; Nockolds, *Lucas*, p. 92; Whisler, *At the End of the Road*, pp. 110–11; T.A.B. Corley, *Domestic Electrical Appliances*, Jonathan Cape, London, 1966, pp. 41–8.

29 *AE*, March–April 1953, August 1953; Graves, 'Outline of BMC developments'; BPC, *Applying the Pressure*, pp. 19–20; Woollard, *Principles*, pp. 42–3, 83, 150. See also Cusumano, *Japanese Automobile Industry*, pp. 88–97, 285.

30 Woollard, *Principles*, pp. 45–7, 84, 173–5; BPC, *Applying the Pressure*, p. 20; *AE*, September 1946, February 1951.

31 *AE*, September 1946, March 1947, February 1951, September 1951, August 1953; Woollard, *Principles*, pp. 21, 172.

32 *AE*, September 1946, March 1947, September 1951; Woollard, *Principles*, pp. 42–3, 47, 172.

33 Woollard, *Principles*, p. 82; *AE*, January 1951, February 1951; *Engineering*, 12 January 1951; AACP, *Final Report*, 1952 p. 34; BPC, *Applying the Pressure*.

34 P. Hirst and J. Zeitlin, 'Flexible specialization and the competitive failure of UK manufacturing', *Political Quarterly*, vol. 60, 1989.

6

TRAINING ENGINEERS IN
LORRAINE, 1890–1956

Françoise Birck[1]

Between the end of the nineteenth century and the beginning of the 1950s, the question of technical training was twice at the centre of national debate. Both these occasions followed a major historical calamity – the defeats of 1870 and the second world war – after which engineering was perceived as central to the future development of the country. In the first period (1880–1918), the development of applied sciences allowed the science faculty at Nancy to initiate the creation of schools awarding diplomas in engineering. Most institutes in Lorraine owe their existence to this historical legacy; half the current engineering diplomas awarded in the Lorraine region are from institutes created at the end of the nineteenth century.

By 1945, engineering schools in Nancy were training fewer students than they had at their inception. At the colloquium on research and scientific education held in Caen in 1956,[2] in the preparatory work towards the national Plan (Commission du Plan, 1952–3) and the work undertaken by the Conseil supérieur de la recherche scientifique, the findings of surveys undertaken by professional organisations were confirmed: France was suffering from a shortage of engineers. In reaction, Pierre Mendès-France evoked 'the inadmissable wastage of our national heritage of intelligence', rooted in the restrictive practices of an earlier period. The remark provides an insight into the adjustment of resources in engineering to the needs of the economy over more than fifty years.[3]

In this chapter, the example of Nancy will be used to examine the issue. Three engineering schools (the Chemical Institute created in 1889, the Electrotechnical and Mechanical Institute created in 1900–5 and the Ecole des mines in 1919) from their inception established different forms of commitment from their main partners: the state, the regions and industry. We shall describe how the complex system of practices implanted over the years influenced the reconstruction of the training of engineers in the immediate postwar period.

FRANÇOISE BIRCK

THE LEADING ROLE OF THE SCIENCE
FACULTY OF NANCY, 1880–1914

For a long time in France, universities played a marginal role in the training of managerial staff (*cadres*). From the French Revolution, training had been provided by *Ecoles speciales* created to respond to immediate requirements, such as the Conservatoire National des Arts et Métiers (1794) and various urban schools of arts and crafts (1806–1912). The Ecole des Arts et Manufactures for business leaders was formed in 1829, the prestigious Ecole Polytechnique in 1794, using the existing Ecole des Mines, Ecoles des Ponts-et-Chaussées and Ecole du Génie Maritime as subsidiary '*écoles d'application*'.[4] All trained civil and military engineers for public service. All recruited by selective examination but were not attached to the Ministère de l'Instruction Publique.

The Ministère de l'Instruction Publique, during the second empire, envisaged opening science faculties to non-matriculating students to study new disciplines, destined to prepare them for careers in industry and commerce. With the establishment of five new faculties underway – including that of Nancy – ministerial decrees established teaching in applied sciences parallel to the traditional syllabus. Whilst they did not carry university status, these courses, leading to a certificate of competence (*brevet de capacité*), were intended to provide serious scientific credentials for use in industry. In general this formula was not successful, even in Lille, where the young dean of the science faculty, Louis Pasteur, attempted to develop teaching in applied sciences in direct relation to the main industries of the area. The situation was no better in Nancy; only one candidate was registered in the first year (1856), followed by two candidates in 1857, who quickly dropped out. Teaching in applied science none the less continued, recruiting students from workers and artisans in the town to follow courses designed specifically for their needs.

The German victory of 1870 put applied science teaching in a different light. Celebrated scientists such as Pasteur and Berthelot drew attention to the shortcomings of the educational system and the decline of French science; these were blamed for the national disaster. Numerous studies extolled education and its achievements across the German border. Defeated militarily, France sought to reinforce its position among industrialised nations. The training of engineers became a national issue.[5] Republicans in government sought to reform the whole higher education system between 1880 and 1897.[6] The initiative mobilised support from local authorities and industrialists, resulting in the emergence of scientific centres on a regional basis.[7]

The science faculty in Nancy quickly became prominent in this movement. The Treaty of Frankfurt annexed Alsace and part of Lorraine to Germany; Nancy became the town nearest the new border, a reception point for immigrants from the new German territories, particularly from

Strasbourg and Metz. This helped stimulate new, prosperous enterprises, providing both capital and know-how to train staff. This dynamism was transferred to higher education; the migration to Nancy of institutions and teachers from the University of Strasbourg reinforced local research. These developments owed much to patriotic fervour, responding to the threat posed by a powerful neighbour. They resulted in the establishment of an institute specialising in chemistry, to train students in theoretical and practical aspects of the subject and to supply French industry with specialist expertise hitherto largely recruited from Germany. This project was initiated by senior members of the science faculty at Nancy and received active support from successive directors of training within central government.

State involvement, promoted by republicans, argued that government had a duty to promote such private or collective initiatives, rather than impose policies externally. In a speech delivered in 1881, Gambetta expressed this political vision:

> The great and elevated personality, the nation or the state, has a duty to intervene, not in order to impose upon any movement, nor in order to substitute itself for the free will of individuals but to encourage, support, help, and protect the free activity of the citizens.[8]

These principles underpinned the compromise between centralisation and autonomy which characterised the 1885 law on universities. They exemplify the relationship established by initiators of national policy on training at the two Nancy universities, A. Haller and F. Bichet, combining patriotic and republican values.

The Chemistry Institute and the Electrotechnical Institute

The threat of German industrial superiority was the reason invoked by the ministry when giving financial help to the new institute, based on Haller's scientific project, on condition that the local authorities matched the funding thus provided. Through membership of the Conseil Général of Meurthe-et-Moselle and the municipal council of Nancy, the university's spokesman, Bichet, used these assemblies as a platform to promote public action in support of this patriotic national project. In the final analysis, it was the financial aid provided by the state and the local authorities which together led to the founding of the Nancy Chemical Institute in 1889. Although the project called for closer links between industry and the university, industry was notable by its absence; the Institute was solely the product of republican politics operating at local and national level. It formed the model for various technical institutes in different academic centres at the turn of the century.[9] Initially, success was by no means certain.

It took over six years (1883–9) to raise the necessary funding. Only after several years was the Institute in a position to deliver more than a handful of diplomas (only three in 1896) and these were for chemists, not engineers. The new opportunities for training had difficulty finding its public.

From 1896, the teaching of applied sciences in Nancy accelerated. In four years (1896–1900) two new courses were developed, followed by two institutes to teach and research in applied electricity. As in the case of the Chemical Institute, the university promoted the initiative, this time with support from the Société industrielle de l'Est (Eastern Industrial Society) and the Société Solvay. In Nancy, in contrast to Montpellier or Toulouse, local assemblies were not the only important spheres of influence. The Société Industrielle de l'Est, created in 1833 by the Nancy Chamber of Commerce, recruited its members among industrial and business circles in the region. Membership included many of the business leaders who had moved to Nancy after 1870. The Society was not, however, very active prior to the establishment of the Chemical Institute, confining debates in the 1880s to the economic crisis and its social consequences. The idea of collaboration with the university only came on to the agenda when membership was extended to solicitors, journalists, consultant engineers and local councillors. Thereafter, academic scientific activity found an echo in local economic and political circles. The establishment of new networks created a multiplicity of initiatives in the applied sciences by the end of the century.

The Belgian industrialist Solvay was the most generous financier of the period. In 1872, Solvay created a successful sodium carbonate production process in his factory in Dombasle, near Nancy. The company possessed both a research policy and the means to carry it out. Much the same can be said of training policy. However, the enterprise found itself tied by the effects of industrial nationalism, which limited its development projects. The scale of its donations to the University of Nancy (FF870,000 over fifteen years) formed part of an image-building strategy, supported by academics willing to celebrate their benefactor's largesse. Nancy was not the only recipient of this patronage; aside from its support for an international congress in physics (1911–33), the company created the Institut International de Physique Solvay in Brussels in 1912. In a climate where the words 'science', 'nation' and 'industry' were closely associated with the local development of training in the applied sciences, the Electrotechnical Institute emerged, virtually unaided by the state.

In Nancy as elsewhere, the new form of training was linked to the application of electricity to a range of industries. The Institute aimed to develop technical expertise, academic research and the theoretical and practical instruction of future electrical engineers. In the latter case, questions of premises, programmes and the choice of teachers were quickly settled. The Institute opened in the autumn of 1900. Student recruitment was, however, problematic. It did not seem that there was room in Nancy for a new training college. The Chemical Institute, for example, took over ten years to fill all its places, and it succeeded only by recruiting non-matriculated students. The number of candidates presenting for the scientific baccalauréat in the region remained unchanged at 150. The problem was further complicated by the town's geographical location; it was difficult to attract students from the German territories, while the best local students tended to go to Paris.

The Institute was thus forced to liberalise student intake, selecting students both from the higher elementary and technical schools (*écoles primaires supérieures* and *écoles professionnelles*). Efforts were made to promote the Institute outside the region, particularly abroad. Fortunately, the German polytechnics were limiting recruitment of foreign students during this period and the French government was encouraging a new wave of students to consider provincial faculties.[10] Hence the student body at the Electro-technical Institute was, three years after its opening, larger than that of the Chemical Institute. When a mechanical section was added in 1905, the former was almost double the size of the latter. The proportion of foreign students rose, outstripping French students by 1910–11. The Chemical Institute recruited a large number of Russian students after 1906.

Inevitably, recruitment affected the organisation of studies. Open entry meant that selection (and elimination) took place during the first two foundation years, with specialisation in the third year. The discrepancy between the total number of students in all years and the number of diplomas awarded after the final year reveals the limits of the system. Of the 365 students registered in 1908–9, only 44 graduated. (In the same year the Chemical Institute delivered 42 diplomas out of a total of 143 students registered in the three years.) The system did have the advantage of opening access to higher education to students without the baccalauréat. The number of students continuing their studies after leaving higher elementary school in Nancy expanded in the years preceding the first world war.[11] But these were less numerous than foreign students, whose participation was essential to the very survival of the Institute. Republican reformers wished to diversify financial resources but this posed difficulties in ensuring long-term funding. It is hardly surprising that the institutes tended to recruit fee-paying foreign students. This situation was not peculiar to Nancy; this period witnessed the development of an international market in foreign students, Italy being accused of 'dumping' the costs of training elsewhere.[12] The science faculty in Nancy, however, maintained a lead over other provincial faculties, on the basis of its recruitment through the institutes. Numbering 357 foreign students over the year 1910–11, it surpassed Toulouse (163), Grenoble (44) and Lyons (35).[13]

The predominance of foreign students reflects the reputation and success of the Nancy institutes. However, it overstates the real interaction between scientific circles and their environment. The supply of university education from 1900 onwards fed an expanding local market, as regional economic development accelerated with the growth of metallurgical and mining industries. In research and the training of engineers, business enterprise followed this upward trend. In the pre-war period, the policy for the development of applied science teaching in Nancy was based on the lead given by the university, adapted by local influential industrial and political élites. This early success was more fragile than it appeared. The state progressively abandoned the initiating role it adopted in the early years of reform, supporters of 'pure science' – critics of the institutes – began to reconquer the universities.

The goal of the republican reformers in the 1880s had been to encourage the universities to abandon their traditional role in order to train future technicians; the science faculty at Nancy attained this objective. Courses in applied sciences, some awarding an engineering diploma, developed in a number of provincial universities before the first world war. In 1909 the *Revue internationale de l'enseignement* examined new trends in the science faculties. Its final report made a number of recommendations for the development of advanced technical training in universities.[14] The report was optimistic about the numbers involved: 'French factories can easily absorb twice the number of engineers they do now. Hopefully the new trends will open up even more opportunities. The development of our technical education is not only possible but indispensible for the industrial revival of the country.' The report compared the Nancy model favourably to the German:

> the new establishments of technical education can be organised in the same way as the German *technische Hochschulen*. Without needing to find foreign examples, the industrial institutes in Nancy, the municipal schools of physics and chemistry, and the Ecole supérieur d'électricité de Paris have achieved the good-will of all; these are more specialised and possess well-equipped laboratories.[15]

The Nancy science faculty was virtually the only one which responded positively to an inquiry undertaken by the *Revue internationale de l'enseignement supérieur* in 1916, following a debate initiated by Senator Goy on the creation of applied science faculties. In Nancy, this offered the chance to consolidate progress: 'the creation of an applied science faculty would have the advantage of providing a charter for these courses, providing them with more stability and would ensure accelerated growth.'[16] Although industrial finance had sponsored a number of new courses, such funding was sporadic and did not imply any future commitment. The university, for its part, had supported the science faculty in many of its undertakings, making available surplus funding. The other faculties all contributed to the finance of higher technical education; the emergence of alternative demands would throw this into question – especially as the institutes and their laboratories were expensive. In the absence of permanent finance, these relied almost entirely on student fees. Although foreign students compensated for low local recruitment, there was no way of predicting future numbers. The proposals of the Nancy science faculty during the inquiry published in 1916 therefore depicted the kind of policy required to ensure the permanence of the institutes created before the war. Two points stand out: first, the recruitment of non-matriculated students from the higher elementary schools had to continue – even at the risk of reduced provision of technical assistance provided by the faculties for recruits below degree level. Second, large state subsidies for staff and equipment were still required for both teaching and research.

The Ecole des Mines

In this case, the industrialists, or more precisely the ironmasters (*maîtres de forges*) of Lorraine, took the initiative to create a novel form of teaching in applied sciences. Previously annexed territories were returned to France following the Armistice. In June 1919, the Sarre territory was put under French control for fifteen years; the exploitation of the Sarre coalfield raised the question of replacing the 400 German engineers employed in its metallurgical and mining industries. The Ecole des Mines of Saint-Etienne, which trained engineers for these industries, had already publicised its inability to produce sufficient numbers, due to war casualties and the absence of students during hostilities.[17] With the shortfall estimated at six and half years' worth of students (thirty-seven engineers per year), it would have taken fifteen years to make good the shortage. During the war, a reconstruction report based on an inquiry into the pre-war mining industry had been used by the Ministre du Commerce, Clementel, to develop a debate on the industry's future.[18] The review of the Nancy Chamber of Commerce, *L'Union économique de l'Est*, brought this national debate to the local level by publicising the preoccupations of the local interests concerning postwar regional reconstruction. In this way, the project for an engineering school for mines and metallurgy was launched in Nancy.

Industrialists thought that they could build a local training school by calling upon those who had contributed to the financing of the prewar institutes. But they were not in the same position as the university, which articulated national values and interests; the *maîtres de forges* of Lorraine could only put forward arguments about their own immediate needs. Hence the new institute was funded by trade organisations in the autumn of 1919. Its advocates could count upon the support of the university as the latter still aimed to create an autonomous faculty of applied sciences. This would provide an additional asset to compete with the University of Strasbourg, now in French territory. In May 1919, the university council accepted the project submitted by the science faculty; the new Metallurgical and Mining

Institute would award the engineering diploma of the University of Nancy. Training would be subsidised by the main trade organisations linked to mining and metallurgy (the Comité de Forges de France, the Comité Central des Houilleres de France, the Comités des Forges et de Mines de Fer de Lorraine, the Société Industrielle de l'Est). In July 1919, the Ministre de l'Instruction Publique gave his official approval.

The combined resources of the local scientific establishment were made available to the new institute. Specialised courses took place in the different premises of the science faculty or in the institutes, taking advantage of existing facilities such as laboratories and collections. Given the high cost of laboratories, this operation would have been unthinkable in Metz, despite its closer proximity to industry. Industrialists were thus able to benefit indirectly from the investments made in the pre-war period. None the less, the university now had to deal with a powerful partner in the shape of the Corps des Mines whose co-operation was indispensible for the most specialised part of the teaching: mining. (The Corps des Mines was traditionally composed of the top graduates from the Ecole Polytechnique.) Management of the project was therefore shared between the university, represented by the dean of the faculty of sciences, and the Corps des Mines, represented by the chief mining engineer in the Nancy area. Both were responsible to an administrative committee made up of the Lorraine industrial elite. The influence of the Corps des Mines dominated the recruitment of students and the content of courses. The institutional framework underpinning the new Metallurgical and Mining Institute was closely patterned on the Ecole des Mines of Saint-Etienne, not on the other institutes in Nancy. The latter had adopted an 'open' system of recruitment accessible to non-matriculating students and to students from both higher elementary and technical schools. The supporters of the Ecole des Mines rejected this approach. Future engineers were recruited by competition at the same level as that required for the other *grandes écoles*. The only foreign students admitted were from Luxembourg, and they were not allowed to take the final examination.

Doubtless, such a system appealed to the industrialists because of its efficiency. Selective recruitment eliminated failure or withdrawal, facilitating rapid training at low cost. This did not mean, however, that graduates gained the same status as that endowed by the other major state institutions. Thus, for example, the administrative committee – dominated by appointees from the local chamber of commerce – was unable to replace the title 'institute' with that of '*école nationale supérieure*' as used by the Ecole des Mines de Saint-Etienne, whose recognition as an '*école nationale*' in 1908 had entitled it to award the same diploma of civil mining engineering as the Ecole des Mines de Paris.[19] The Nancy industrialists adopted the title '*école supérieure*', the amputation of the adjective '*nationale*' symbolising an important difference. For many years, ex-students demanded the addition of '*nationale*' in the hope of aligning their status with that of ingenueurs des mines de Saint-Etienne or de Paris.

In the short term, the status of this new establishment was uncontroversial, even for those schools in the area which might have been affected. None the less, this choice weighed heavily upon the development of other institutes (electrotechnical and chemical) and, upon the development of the whole of the local scientific system, when the question of the social status of engineers became more important than that of the quantity produced.

THE PROBLEMS OF THE INTERWAR PERIOD

In the short term, the two main institutes, preoccupied with demobilised soldiers, were unaware of the possible effects of the establishment of the local Ecole des Mines. The influx of students was so great that the Chemical Institute, whose places were limited by the number and size of its laboratories, had to establish an entrance exam based on the mathematics baccalauréat which selected 50 per cent of candidates for admission. Not subject to the same constraints, the Electrotechnical Institute admitted 400 students, or almost half the numbers in the science faculty.

Provided with state help for the renovation of buildings damaged during the war and for the modernisation of their facilities, the institutes were set to expand. The climate, however, was no longer the same; in the earlier period, the two major assets of the institutes had been the continuing commitment of the science faculty (and of Nancy University) and financial aid provided by industrialists. At the beginning of the 1920s, the Société Industrielle de l'Est continued to act as an intermediairy between the institutes and industry, establishing the Société des Amis des Instituts to promote continuity of funding via regular contributions. For the first time, this financial help was acknowledged in an explicit commitment by the university to ensure that 'all the teaching given would comform to the desires and wishes of industrialists'.[20] This could have resulted in the pooling of resources or, at least, in the negotiation of a common policy. However, the establishment of foundations specific to each institute – which collected and managed funds emanating from the tax on apprenticeship in various industries – meant that a unified policy could not emerge. (Industrialists who supported the development of technical training or who funded laboratories in pure or applied science were exempted from paying this tax, fixed at 0.2 per cent of wages in 1925.) Each institute established a separate policy at precisely the moment when the university was modifying its priorities. With the reconstruction of the University of Strasbourg underway, Nancy could no longer claim to be the 'frontier university'. There was no longer any advantage in underlining a regional specificity[21] and certainly little to gain from any association with the German model, given hostile opinion.

French criticisms of the position of German engineers were articulated before the war. During the conflict, they had become more virulent within the debates encouraged by Senator Goy's proposals. Whilst the usefulness of the industrial training provided in Nancy and Grenoble was recognised, the universities were warned against 'a Germany whom we are enjoined by everyone to imitate, a Germany where engineers go hungry'. One should avoid too great a number of graduates . . . throwing on to the streets a number of young people who would cry out in the same way as those in Germany'. Moreover, 'a graduate in the French system of higher education, whoever he may be, is persuaded . . . that he belongs to the intellectual elite and that consequently he should occupy an elevated rung on the social ladder of his country . . . Senator Goy's project, if pushed too far (would lead) to an overabundance of engineers which would be more disastrous to us than to our neigbours.'[22]

Controlling numbers and quality

How did the Nancy institutes approach the question of the status and quantity of the engineers they produced ? Although, the major mobilising themes of the earlier period pushed these issues into the background, they now became central since the very survival of the institutes was at stake.

The state underwrote both theoretical teaching and the operation of pure science laboratories, according to the principle of autonomy contained in the law of 1896. Responsibility for financing teaching in the applied sciences was left to the faculties themselves. This responsibility varied in accordance with the subjects taught and with student numbers. Two-thirds of the Electrotechnical Institute's budget, for example, came from fees (FF318,750 out of a budget of FF514,878). The state's contribution (FF124,250) made up much of the remainder and was three times bigger than that of the 'amis des instituts'. Although largely financed by industrialists, the situation was hardly different in the Ecole des Mines. In 1923 the employers' contribution was only slightly bigger than the amount raised by student fees (FF91,000 as against FF81,000).[23] These cases underline the importance of recruitment policy for finance, explaining why the Nancy institutes, together with those of Toulouse and Grenoble, opted for an 'open' system of recruitment. This principle consisted, in the words of the director of the Electrotechnical Institute of the 1920s, of permitting 'the entry of all students capable of following the courses together with serious foreign students likely to undertake propaganda in their own country in our favour'.[24] The financial advantages of recruiting foreign students was hidden behind political issues. These last considerations were not, however, unreal: in the early 1920s the government gave credits to help students from allied countries, notably Romania.

In general, this policy to maximise student numbers allowed the institutes to function well. The climate of the 1920s, however, threw doubt upon their value, despite the absence of problems of graduate placement. Associations of former students in the more reputable schools began to denounce the overabundance of engineers on the market and to throw doubt upon the value of the diplomas awarded. At local level, the mode of recruitment adopted by the Ecole des Mines provoked resentment. In this case, ex-student associations and certain members of the teaching staff advocated higher entrance requirements. In order to reconcile the quality of students with their quantity, the institutes tried to recruit more French students, whose initial level of training was thought superior to that of foreigners. The qualifications of foreign students had acquired a poor reputation. Before the war, Russian students were obliged to legalise their diplomas with the local French consulate, following the discovery of a counterfeiting operation in Paris. With the object of raising French recruitment, a preparatory course to first-year entry was proposed by the Lycée at Nancy. Nothing came of this, because of the attitude of *lycée* teachers – particularly those teaching the preparatory classes – who would not have been prepared to play along with the Nancy institutes. None the less, some years later, the same problem recurred. The Electrotechnical Institute suffered most, foreign students outnumbering the indigenous. Competitive entry was established in 1927, at the level of specialist mathematics classes – preparatory classes for candidates entering the *grandes écoles*, organised by the *lycées*, following the baccalauréat. This risked excluding a good proportion of the candidates from the higher elementary and technical schools in a period when the school-leaving age was being raised.[25] To avoid this problem, a preparatory year was established which, unfortunately, attracted mainly foreign students. Whilst the establishment of competitive entry failed to bring an influx of French students from secondary education, it meant that candidates from higher elementary schools who lacked the required level of mathematics were turned away. Competitive entry led to a sharp fall in student numbers. In the first year of its application the number of students fell from ninety-nine to forty-seven, French students remaining in the minority.

On the eve of the slump

The demographic decline of 1914–18 began to affect higher education from 1932 onwards.[26] At the same time, the emerging economic crisis was having repercussions on the institutes' funding. Les Amis des Instituts and the foundations were finding it more and more difficult to collect money from industrialists. It was difficult to find work for graduates; many ex-students were unemployed. Moreover, from the 1930s onwards, students from the Ecoles des Mines were experiencing great difficulty due to the crisis in the metallurgical and mining industries in the region. Students in the other two institutes were affected somewhat later. From 1931 onwards they were increasingly at risk of unemployment. Jobless graduate engineers were being produced at a rate of seven or eight a year and many ex-students were forced to accept employment which bore little relationship to their level of qualification. In addition, the Fédération des Associations, Sociétiés et Syndicats Français d'Ingénieurs (FASSFI) was campaigning for restrictions on the title of 'engineer' and raising doubts about the value of the diplomas awarded by the institutes.

For the Nancy schools and for the majority of engineers, this was a turning-point.[27] The engineers were realising that their status in companies scarcely differed from that of other salaried staff. This took some time to sink in. Writing in their newsletter in 1931, graduates from the Electrotechnical Institute hoped that 'industry in crisis did not disappear or jeopardize its existence, and abstained from laying-off good collaborators and loyal servants except as a final resort'. Similarly, in order to avoid its members having to submit 'to exasperating demands and formalities' in registering at municipal unemployment insurance offices, the French engineering unions succeeded in creating a state-subsidised system of unemployment insurance for 'intellectual workers'. This aimed to deliver benefits 'under the conditions of discretion and consideration compatible with the legitimate susceptibilities of the interested parties'.[28] This job situation influenced the recruitment policy of the three Nancy institutes.

The problem was to ensure the survival of the schools without placing too many engineers on the labour market. The Ecole des Mines was first to react. In 1931, the Conseil de Perfectionnement, consisting of a majority of representatives of industry, decided to cut the number of places available by competitive entry. Reduced from thirty to twenty-five, the number of places fell further, to twenty, in 1936. The Electrotechnical Institute attempted to maintain its financial equilibrium by privileging the recruitment of students to a fourth year of specialisation. The management of the Chemical Institute undertook a complete overhaul of its programme, establishing an entry examination as difficult as that of the Ecole des Mines. Entry requirements were tightened at the risk of rupturing traditional recruitment channels. Similar reforms in the Ecole des Mines led to a crisis in recruitment; the number of candidates fell from 315 in 1921 to 90 in 1936. The performance of the Chemical Institute proved little better: only fifty-one candidates attempted to gain entry to a first year consisting of a mere sixteen students, of which only fourteen graduated three years later. Competitive examination in 1937 and 1938 permitted the entry of twelve students, then nine, although there was a capacity to teach thirty students in each year.

Why did the Chemical Institute adopt a policy which, during the depression, jeopardised its very existence? One of the reasons cited was the necessity to adapt would-be chemical engineers to scientific and industrial advances by reinforcing their knowledge of mathematics and physics – but this could have been achieved through modifications to the university degree programme or through the extension of preparatory courses. Similarly, the attempt by the heads of the Electrotechnical Institute to permit all the Nancy schools to create a common 'centre polytechnique' could have been pursued, returning to the 'faculté des sciences techniques' promoted in 1916. The science faculty council was not opposed, but the Chemical Institute and the Ecole des Mines rejected the idea. Clearly, this was not a time for experiments. The Electrotechnical Institute refused to change its position. None the less, all these discussions had the same result: on the eve of the second world war, the three Nancy institutes trained fewer engineers than at their inception.

With the benefit of hindsight, it can be argued that the opportunity to consolidate the work of the founders had been missed in 1919 when the Ecole des Mines opened. The urgency of the situation and the weight of tradition pleaded in favour of a model based on the grandes écoles. Against this, the creation of a well-endowed centre polytechnique, financed by industrialists and by the pooling of existing resources, was possible. This could have trained students coming from specialised streams in higher primary or secondary education. This idea, which was circulating in the 1920s, was unsucessfully raised a number of times. The differences in status (in the Ecole des Mines) and the fear of producing too many engineers rendered the idea unworkable. It would none the less re-emerge after the second world war.

THE POST-WAR PERIOD

The Langevin–Wallon Commission and after

In the Langevin Commission, ideas developed within the Resistance movement were the focus for discussion. In January 1944, a commission for the reform of education was set up in Alger, to prepare the deliberations of a future constituant assembly. Its job was to re-establish the link with the reforms of the Front Populaire, while drawing lessons from more recent experience. The critique of élite attitudes during the war led to a close examination of their institutional formation. The system of grandes écoles and the preparatory classes were particularly singled out for analysis. In this, debates following the first world war, when doubts were raised about the system of grandes écoles, were repeated.[29] Now the ideological indictment was more serious: what was at stake was neither the acquisition of knowledge nor the multiplication of competences but the formation of the character and mindset of the leadership needed by the nation following the war. The commission therefore envisaged the transformation of 'the three or four years of university degree studies into a crucible within which the new elites could be created for the nation'.[30]

The commission chaired by Langevin condemned the duality of a system divided between grandes écoles and preparatory classes on the one side and university degree courses on the other. Against this background, the future of the university institutes was discussed. Technical schools and trade institutes could be linked to universities. Students would undertake theoretical education for two years, followed by technical training in specialized institutes. Preparatory classes would be integrated into the first two years of university education. Although simple, this idea came up against the heterogeneity of the existing system and was subject to virulent attack.

The reform proposed by the new director of the Electrotechnical Institute envisaged the creation in Lorraine of a 'powerful and modern *centre polytechnique* which would be more efficient than all the Parisian *grandes écoles*'. Here again the local situation was set against the Parisian monopoly, but the idea came from a series of inquiries undertaken in the United States. Following the American model, this would-be *centre polytechnique* would offer a range of options to students throughout their studies. In practical terms, this would have meant the creation at Nancy (where each school tended to function 'as a closed and isolated tower'[31]) of a federation of schools based on common recruitment procedures, the recasting of programmes and timetables and the constitution of a uniform central administration. On the first point, some progress had been made since 1936. In 1944, the Electrotechnical Institute, following the Chemical Institute, finally adopted a recruitment system based on an examination at the same level as that of the Ecole Polytechnique. In theory, this should have facilitated the two other points of the programme and led to the constitution of a regional centre of advanced technical education. In practice, the project collapsed due to the reservations of the Ecole des Mines, which was seeking to align itself with its prestigious fellows in Paris and Saint-Etienne.

At the national level, the Langevin Commission came up against the same difficulties. In 1947, it envisaged transforming the university institutes and the various technical training establishments attached to the universities into *écoles nationales supérieures*. The idea of abolishing the *grandes écoles* had been abandoned. Although this reform was a first step towards the general reorganisation of entry requirements into the *grandes écoles*, it did not resolve the quantitative problem: adjusting the training of engineers to the postwar industrial environment.

In the immediate postwar period, the Nancy schools continued to act as they had during the 1930s. Even the innovative director of the Electrotechnical Institute, Jean Capelle, limited the number of candidates for the entrance examination. A text in 1946, presenting the old institute as a *grande école* in the Lorraine region, betrayed this attitude:

> If French industry is adequately supplied with administrative, production and works engineers, it lacks skilled engineers for the direction of laboratories, and research and development establishments. This is precisely the class of engineers that the higher

electrotechnical and mechanical school trains in a limited quantity (30 per year). In this way, students can be individually supervised and take full advantage of the training offered by the school. Similarly, with the number of places offered being greater than the number of graduates, the question of placement presents itself in the form of too much choice.[32]

This situation was by no means unique. In 1950, a reunion of the standing committee of the ENSI favoured limiting the number of candidates admitted in order 'to maintain standards'. Some schools saw the number of students admitted fall below their target numbers. The old Electrotechnical Institute obtained authorisation for the admission of thirty-five students.[33] Even the Ecole des Mines, despite its close collaboration with industrial circles, was unable to expand, given the existing mode of recruitment. The uniform entrance exam to the three Ecoles des Mines, established during the war, was extremely restrictive. Out of 275 suitable candidates,[34] the Ecole des Mines obtained only thirty students. The situation was all the more risky in that the pool in the preparatory classes had shrunk, due to demographic factors.

Other schools, such as the prestigious Ecole Polytechnique, faced similar problems. Needing to fill out its classes in the postwar period, the Polytechnique sought authorisation from other schools to offer deferred entry to better candidates, allowing it to cream them off in the preparatory courses; this was not allowed. It none the less demonstrates the extent to which the future of the Nancy schools was linked to that of other establishments recruiting via a common entry exam. Indeed, the rivalry between schools was such that, in 1958, the Ministère de l'Education National set up a commission to look into the entry examinations in the *grandes écoles* in order to rationalise the examinations of 1959.

The Caen colloquium and state intervention

These examples illustrate the overlapping causes blocking an augmentation in the number of engineers trained in the Nancy area. The phenomenon, however, was more general and was brought to public attention during the Caen colloquium set up in 1956 by Pierre Mendès-France. This national colloquium into research and scientific education had been prepared by the Commission du Plan of 1952–3, by the Conseil Supérieur de la Recherche Scientifique and by experts involved in the reform of secondary education. In his inaugural speech, ex-Prime Minister Mendès-France deplored a situation of neglect which produced sharp contrasts in the quality of research and the training of engineers: 'In all fields of national activity, islands of exemplary productivity exist alongside stagnation, and miracles of innovation and daring with routine and impotence.'

Echoing the dramatic debates following the defeat of 1870, Mendès-France denounced France's handicap compared with foreign competitors: 'The men required are missing. We have not trained them.' The comparison of French statistics with those of countries such as the USSR or the United States was damning: whilst France possessed 62,000 researchers and engineers, the other two could boast 550,000 and 743,000 respectively. This said, Mendès-France did not rehearse the themes of over-restrictive entry practices but highlighted the rigidity of a system which reformers were at a loss to change. He introduced his particular notion of the role of the state as 'the only agent capable of giving a sufficiently vigorous impetus and, because of its ability to adopt long-term projects, of promoting necessary reforms'.[35] This statement implies a politics undermining the compromise between centralisation and local autonomy established by the republican reforms of the 1880s. Although such an interpretation can hardly be based upon a single statement, Mendès-France also argued that he 'did not conceive the role of the state differently in the scientific domain than he did in the economic domain'. He was aiming 'in the direction of greater freedom' by attacking 'redundant institutions, compartmentalisation, in order to facilitate the smoother functioning of the mechanism . . . All competent people would thereby be used in the service of the country, notwithstanding their training, diplomas or convictions. Local authorities, public establishments, nationalised industries, and universities would share the responsibility between them.'

In some senses, this political project seems to be compatible with the republican ideas of the turn of the century. But the economic situation was completely different. Whilst turn-of-the-century reformers were acting in the context of the great depression of the 1880s, the 1950s was a period of unprecedented, state-sponsored economic expansion. Between 1953 and 1955 industrial growth averaged 8.5–9 per cent. From 1945 to 1951, the Lorraine region utilised Marshall Plan aid to re-equip mines and staple industries. The state therefore possessed the wherewithal to pursue its policies. The demand for engineers was rising in all sectors. A study in 1956 estimated a shortfall in future supply of 8,000 in 1955, growing to 22,000 in 1960 if the situation remained unchanged.[36] These estimates helped shape the Third National Equipment Plan for the years 1957–61 and, by implication, determined the demands raised by the higher education sector.

Given that P. Donzelot, the ex-director of the Chemical Institute, was appointed to the key post in the ministry, the Nancy schools were not disadvantaged. From this moment, new perspectives opened up for the existing institutes, who found themselves caught up in a growth spiral. The Fourth Plan predicted an unprecedented expansion in the number of students in higher education, because the overall increase in the length of education in the postwar period coincided, in the years 1964–5, with a demographic explosion.[37] The commission projected an expansion of *écoles nationales supérieures* from 4,650 engineering students in 1961 to 12,490 in 1969–71.[38] Proportionate increases were envisaged for the Nancy schools. These changes coincided with global plans to reorganise higher scientific education. The latter was inspired by the principles advocated by the Langevin–Wallon Commission, partly realised by the decrees promulgated in 1947. The idea was to establish a common foundation year for science faculties and for preparatory courses leading to the *grandes écoles*; a common course would facilitate access to both. The state relied upon schools similar to those which, as in Nancy, were linked to the universities in order to increase the number of engineers. This procedure was thus the opposite of that undertaken by the Ecole des Mines and the Chemical Institute in Nancy, since both had established an entrance exam similar to that of the state-run schools. In the 1930s, the institutes, which had been based on open recruitment, chose to merge into the 'closed' system of preparatory classes for strictly scientific reasons. In this way, they proved that the university could also train engineers, but by somewhat different methods.

Too many engineers?

The growth in the number of engineers trained by the *écoles nationales supérieures* and the existing schools did not meet the demand estimated at a variety of different levels. New institutions were created which recruited, 1930s-style, on the basis of the possession of the *baccalauréat* or the *brevet de technicien*. In 1957 the first Institut National des Sciences Appliquées, created in Lyons, recruited from outside the usual channels based on the preparatory schools. The democratic pretensions of the Langevin–Wallon Commission were thus put into practice through a mobilisation of all forms of national intelligence.

This new policy was received with considerable trepidation by organisations representing engineers, who feared for the status of the profession. The line of defence had not changed: 'one must at all costs avoid a massive increase in the number of engineers in order to avoid forcing them to accept inferior work outside their domain.'[39] Although this might seem to be a case of history repeating itself, the example of Nancy serves to illustrate alternative outcomes. The absence of strong direction in the interwar period facilitated the explosion of diverging interests and this led to a preoccupation with élitist issues and the status of managerial qualifications. Arguably, our current debates have moved on. As in the 1930s, the engineers have discovered that, given unemployment, their status in an enterprise is scarcely more enviable than that of other salaried staff; the real question at issue is whether they can take their place in society. Is there no other choice than that between 'wasted people' and that which leads towards a 'wastage of intelligence'?

NOTES

1 This chapter uses material from interdisciplinary research 'Villes et institutions scientifiques', Programme interdisciplinaire de recherche sur les villes du CNRS, presented at a colloquium: 'Enseignements industriels et formations technico-scientifiques supérieures en Lorraine XIXe–XX siècles', organised by the Mission histoire industrielles of the Archives départementales de la Moselle in Metz, December 1995.

2 Papers published in *Les cahiers de la République*, December 1957.

3 A. Grelon, 'La question des besoins en ingénieurs de l'économie française. Essai de repérage historique', *Technologies, idéologies, pratiques*, Université de Provence, vol. VI, 1987.

4 A. Grelon, *The Training and Career Structures of Engineers in France, 1880–1939*, Cambridge University Press, Cambridge, Maison des sciences de l'homme, 1993.

5 A. Grelon, 'Les universités et la formation des ingénieurs en France (1870–1914)', *Formation et emploi*, nos 27–8, 1989.

6 G. Weisz, *The Emergence of Modern Universities in France, 1863–1914*, Princeton University Press, Princeton, NJ, 1983.

7 M. Grossetti, 'Villes et institutions scientifiques. Genèse des pôles scientifiques français', *Annales de la recherche urbaine*, nos 62–3, June 1994.

8 C. Nicolet, *L'idée républicaine en France. Essai critique*, Gallimard, Paris, 1982, p. 454.

9 'Villes et institutions scientifiques', final report, p. 82.

10 M.J. Nye, *Science in the Provinces: Scientific Communities and Provincial Leadership in France, 1860–1930*, University of California Press, Berkeley, CA, 1986, p. 27.

11 J.P. Briand and J.M. Chapoulie, *Les collèges du peuple*, INRP, Paris, 1992, p. 191.

12 See the note of the director of the school in 1914 in Archives de l'institut électrochimique'.

13 Nye, *Science in the Provinces*, p. 29.

14 H. Le Chatelier, A. Croiset and F. Larnaude, 'Rapport fait au nom de la Société de l'enseignement supérieur', *Revue internationale de l'enseignement* [*RIE*], Paris, 26 June 1909.

15 Ibid.. pp. 47 and 50.

16 *RIE*, 1916, pp. 301–7.

17 Correspondence of the director of the school, Friedel, in *L'union économique de l'Est*, no. 3, 16 February 1918.

18 The final report (1919) in three volumes is based on work undertaken by the consultative committee of the Arts et Manufactures and various commissions set up by the Ministry from 1917. The Comité des Forges published a report on the Lorraine industries by R. Pinot, in Bulletin de l'industrie minérale, vol. 1, 1917.

19 Archives of the school, minutes of the Conseil d'administration, 1920.

20 Archives of the Institut électrotechnique: letter by the dean of the science faculty (Petit), 10 November 1920.

21 Archives départementales de Meurthe-et-Moselle, W1018 (218), report of the recteur, 1921.

22 *RIE*, documents and enquiries, 'Pour notre enseignement technique supérieur', vol. 72, 1918, pp. 124–34; p. 291.

23 Archives de l'École des Mines, Budget de l'école, 1926.

24 'Discours du directeur Vogt', *Bulletin de l'association des anciens élèves de l'Institut électrotechnique de Nancy*, no. 32, 1923, p. 16.

25 A. Prost, *Histoire générale de l'engeignement et de l'éducation en France*, vol. 4, Nouvelle librairie de France, Paris, pp. 222, 225.

26 Ibid., pp. 219–22.

27 A. Grelon (ed), *Les ingénieurs de la crise: titre et profession entre les deux-guerres*, Ecole des Hautes Études en Sciences Sociales, Paris 1986; Grelon, 'La question des besoins', p. 8.

28 *Bulletin de l'association des anciens élèves de l'Institut électrotechnique de Nancy*, no. 71, March 1933.

29 L. Guillet, *L'Enseignement technique supérieur à l'après-guerre*, Preface to H. Le Chatelier, Payot, Paris, 1918.

30 Archives Nationales (AN), 74 AJ63; 'Commission pour l'étude des problèmes d'après-guerre, section des questions intellectuelles', minutes of meetings 1942–1944.

31 Conference paper given by Jean Capelle, in the *Revue de l'association des anciens élèves de l'IEN*, Nancy, no. 101, February 1947.

32 Ibid., no. 98, 1946.

33 Archives de l'Ecole, Conseil de la Fondation, minutes of 20 June 1950.

34 Archives départementales de Meurthe-et-Moselle, dossier W 1018, bundle 128, Letter of Marcel Demonque, 26 November 1946.

35 Op. cit., p. 35.

36 'Perspectives et besoins en ingénieurs en France', *Notes et études documentaires*, La documentation française, no. 2581, Paris, 1959.

37 Prost, *Histoire générale*, pp. 251–5.

38 'La planification de l'enseignement en France', *Notes et études documentaires*, La Documentation française, no. 2935, Paris, 1960, p. 30.

39 Grelon, 'La question des besoins', p. 15.

7

TECHNICAL TRAINING OF YOUTH IN BRITAIN

Keith Burgess

INTRODUCTION: THE 'YOUTH PROBLEM'

The extent of young worker employment in 'blind alley' occupations was seen by contemporaries as one of the most disturbing aspects of the problem of 'under-employment' in Britain during the interwar period. Especially during the 1930s, these jobs were to be found not only in the growing distribution sector of the economy, but also in traditional industries like printing where apprenticeship was in decline, and in the expanding mass production industries.[1] This concern was not new in the interwar period, however; the assumptions of policy makers continued to be influenced by the pre-1914 context. The question of juvenile labour had been subsumed beneath a wider concern about the so-called 'youth problem' which had surfaced in Britain at the beginning of the twentieth century.[2] This was related to a perceived erosion of British economic competitiveness, the consequent need to improve national efficiency, and fears arising from the threat of urban degeneration in the years preceding the first world war. The demand for juvenile labour actually rose during the late Victorian and Edwardian periods because of the increased subdivision of work in industry and the growth of sectors like transport and distribution that relied heavily on juveniles. Although juvenile labour was still cheap relative to adult labour, its price was rising and job opportunities were abundant. There was a high level of labour mobility among juveniles. Anxiety was expressed about what would happen to them in later life, couched in the moralising language of 'fecklessness' and 'an easy labour market', relating, in turn, to the labour unrest of the period.[3] An alarming picture was drawn of the degeneration of Britain's large cities that relied on 'living on human capital' in an economically wasteful and socially threatening way, whilst depending increasingly on rural immigration for their 'best workers.'[4]

The policy response to this situation before 1914 was idealistic, muddled, occasionally repressive. That youth needed to be better educated was frequently asserted, yet even a radical social critic like R.H. Tawney was silent on what should be taught.[5] It became almost a truism among contemporaries that juveniles needed education (training?) to become 'adaptable' workers; but what was meant by 'adaptable' and how was it to be achieved? The contemporary meaning of adaptability involved a conflation of economic and social (moral?) issues:

> In the minds of reformers, being 'adaptable' suggested both individual fulfilment and a sense of community loyalty and, therefore, social and occupational cohesion. In effect, the concept implied a commitment on the part of the employee to *work* as a moral good in its own right, irrespective of wages, conditions, or personal (selfish) satisfaction.[6]

The dilemma for policy makers in Britain before 1914 was the fundamental one of resolving the economic and social evils of juvenile labour, whilst at the same time adhering to a key principle of political economy: the free market in labour. This problem was to persist into the interwar period.

Despite these strands of continuity, the first world war transformed the context if not the assumptions of public policy in regard to the adolescent in Britain. The immediate effect of the war was to increase further the demand for juveniles by creating labour shortages; the termination of hostilities brought this to an abrupt end. At the same time, the demands of war disrupted established apprenticeship systems, with more enduring consequences. More than half the total number of juveniles thrown out of work at the end of the war were unable to find alternative employment in the short term, although the dearth of reliable statistical evidence makes it impossible to quantify the magnitude of this problem during the 1920s and 1930s.[7] Problems specific to adolescents were overshadowed in the short term, however, by the determination of successive British governments to stabilise the postwar social order. Yet whom was stabilisation to serve, and for what end? According to one historian:

> Stabilization meant not so much preserving liberal procedures as re-establishing the overlapping hierarchies of power, wealth and status that can be loosely termed 'capitalist'. In an age of mass suffrage, these challenged hierarchies had to be defended less in terms of custom than results – that is, their performance for society as a whole. Increasingly, performance included the maintenance of economic welfare.[8]

Postwar stabilisation involved a twin-pronged strategy of production and political legitimation, but successive governments did not find it easy to meet both these conditions at the same time.

In the economic sphere, the search for stability required 'a strategy of production' as well as one of political legitimation, and this impinged directly on British youth. Much of the optimistic appraisal of the working experience of juveniles during the interwar years has been based on relatively low *measured* rates of juvenile unemployment. Apparently both adult women and juveniles were able to find 'well-paid' work during this period, compensating for comparatively high levels of unemployment among adult men.[9] No doubt the redistribution of labour from declining export sectors to expanding home-based industries was accomplished primarily through the recruitment of adolescents.[10] Yet a case study of interwar Slough shows that adult women and juveniles were only preferred to adult men because they were cheaper; other things being equal, the employer's preference was for young labour since it was even cheaper than that of adult women.[11] In the London labour market, despite high juvenile participation rates and relatively low levels of youth unemployment, employers' determination to select the cheapest labour simply shifted the unemployment 'bulge' to the adjacent higher age range, peaks being registered by the age groups 55–9 *and* 25–9.[12] The classic effect of 'blind alley' jobs on the later working lives of juveniles appears as valid for the interwar years as for the pre-1914 period.

Concern about the extent of juvenile unemployment intensified following the world depression of the early 1930s, leading to major investigations into the problem. A detailed study of conditions in Lancashire and Cumberland, based on an inquiry of directors of education and head teachers during the autumn of 1932, showed that many so-called 'unemployed' youth simply did not register as seeking work following a period of peak unemployment.[13] Ministry of Labour statistics underestimated the number of unemployed juveniles between the ages of fourteen and sixteen who did not appear on the registers – equivalent to about one-third of the total number who did register. Further, the academically best qualified school-leavers were in fact the *least* successful in finding employment, confirming contemporary fears about how far 'blind alley' employment fostered low levels of educational attainment. Whilst these problems might be expected to be serious at the depth of the depression, investigations undertaken later in the decade highlighted their persistence in the face of economic recovery. A study of youth unemployment in five Lancashire towns between Easter 1934 and the middle of 1936 discovered that no more than 56 per cent of juveniles had found jobs which their schools regarded as acceptable, and that a large proportion of juveniles entering the retail trade faced unprogressive and badly paid employment.[14] Again, the negative correlation between educational attainment and employment was revealed; those juveniles who had been the least successful at school entered the highest-paid jobs, yet mainly in staple industries like coal mining where unemployment or short-time working were frequent and the prospects of permanent work at adult rates were remote.[15]

By the late 1930s, despite evidence of economic recovery, anxiety about the unprogressive character of juvenile employment and the extent of youth unemployment was no longer confined to the depressed regions of the British economy. In 1935, for example, out of a total of 4,865 jobs created in the Birmingham engineering trades, only 899 required a period of systematic training; this situation was replicated in other expanding towns in the West Midlands such as Wolverhampton. Yet it was the increasing army of juveniles employed in the distributive trades which was the cause of the greatest concern. The total labour force in this sector rose from 1,143,350 to 1,766,730 between 1923 and 1936; 21 per cent of its insured workers were below the age of eighteen in 1934. The distributive trades were the single largest occupational grouping for juveniles 'placed' by the Ministry of Labour's Juvenile Advisory Committees, accounting for more than one-third of all vacancies in large cities. The retail sector also suffered high rates of unemployment among youths over eighteen years old as they were replaced by younger and even cheaper labour. Youth unemployment was linked to the rising incidence of crime and homelessness and the deleterious effects of over-work and industrial accidents on the physical well-being of youth. In London, the 'Mecca of youth labour', similar developments were also to be observed.[16]

THE RESPONSE: POLICY INITIATIVES

How effectively was the 'youth problem' tackled in policy-making terms? On the industrial aspects of this question, attention has centred on the quality of apprenticeship in interwar Britain and the extent to which it responded to changing economic conditions. Was the traditional style of apprenticeship, in light of its demise since the end of the nineteenth century, still the most suitable means of preparing young people for employment? Recent research shows that apprenticeship was a market-oriented form of training; it did not command most employers' attention since, with the exception of a few large firms, they relied heavily on well-developed external labour markets.[17] Yet technological change during the interwar period created new needs for trained manpower that traditional-style apprenticeships could not meet. Employers had limited capacity to meet these needs themselves thanks to market fluctuations, their continued commitment to labour-intensive technologies which did not require investment in human capital and their weak organisational capacity to plan and integrate new forms of training.[18] A Ministry of Labour survey of apprenticeship in the 1920s revealed that apprenticeship systems were uneven in quality, that during economic slumps employers neglected training and used apprentices as a source of cheap labour.[19]

Yet doubts remain about the validity of such a sweeping indictment for the whole of the interwar period. There has been little research into the ways in which technological change affected employers' perceptions of their man-power requirements, although there were sectors of the British economy in this period which were both technologically innovative and had a substantial input of skilled labour, such as gas and electrical engineering, and which recruited highly skilled manpower, such as the heavy chemical industry.[20] In this respect, it has been noted that there have been few studies of the ways individual firms constructed specific relations with the network of local technical institutions during the interwar years. The importance of why and how such relations were constructed casts doubt on generalisations about employers' perceptions of their manpower requirements based exclusively on the macro-economic conditions faced by entire industries.

If the industrial dimension of the 'youth problem' has not been satisfactorily resolved, its treatment from an educational perspective has also been unconvincing. Sanderson has argued that the basic problem was not so much the lack of formal alternatives to apprenticeship as the unwillingness of employers to recruit from such institutions.[21] There was an alleged lack of compatibility between employers and educators. This assertion is made without detailed reference to developments during the interwar years, including the 1930s, except that it is argued – somewhat inconsistently – that the output of the junior technical schools did not meet the demand. The latter also stand accused of failing to develop curricula sufficiently distinct from those 'other sorts of secondary schools', although there are no references to curriculum development in this period and Sanderson seems unaware of the fact that one of the advantages cited for the junior technical schools was that they were *not* tied to the regulations and system of examinations governing secondary schools.[22] The crux of the problem seems to have been that the flexibility they enjoyed also implied a lack of parity of esteem in the eyes of the public, in comparison with the traditional forms of post-primary education.

Educational historians agree that the interwar period was one of 'missed opportunities' in the sphere of innovative policy making.[23] Yet this view fails to do justice to the efforts made to develop new initiatives in order to improve the employment prospects of young people in the 1930s. The task of adapting existing institutional structures was daunting. Problems arose from the haphazardly developed and loosely co-ordinated educational system, ill-suited to the promotion of systematic manpower policies. Although the defects of public provision can be traced back to the nineteenth century, the 1902 Education Act had separated secondary education controlled by the county councils from locally provided elementary education, and this proved damaging.[24] The lack of parity of esteem between technological subjects and the traditional curriculum was reinforced when the introduction of the School Certificate and Higher School Certificate in 1917 excluded technical subjects from 'secondary' education.[25] Financial constraints undermined the ability of the local authorities to develop alternative forms of post-primary education during the interwar period. Under the terms of the 1918 Education Act, the provision of grants to the local authorities increased central control over their expenditure, which in effect meant control by the Treasury.[26] As a result, the numbers enrolled in the secondary schools increased steadily during the 1920s and 1930s in response to middle- and lower-middle-class aspirations to 'black-coated' occupations. The educational system lacked both flexibility and resources to develop new forms of post-primary education, despite the ambitious proposals of the Hadow Report.[27] In the 1930s, seven out of ten children still entered employment directly from elementary schools at the age of fourteen. This was seen by contemporaries as the root of the 'youth problem'.

Policy making in this sphere was not helped by conflicting priorities between the Board of Education and the Ministry of Labour.[28] The latter's responsibility for the 'industrial side' of the question implied an adherence to the orthodoxy of the free labour market. The ministry viewed training as the responsibility of the employer; its thinking was also constrained by uncertainty over Treasury funding, the apathetic response of potential consumers, and fears of 'flooding' labour markets during a period of high unemployment.[29] Yet these constraints were not the sole factors impeding policy development. There was a fundamental theoretical question of proving the connection between investment in education and training and improved economic efficiency. According to the assumptions of *laissez-faire* orthodoxy, investment in training normally means that the costs borne and the benefits received involve different individuals: parents or firms who pay to train workers have no guarantee that the cost will be recovered.[30] This implies that a market for human capital consisting of individual consumers cannot theoretically be proved to exist, and the price mechanism cannot allocate resources optimally without a market. This difficulty of demonstrating that more investment in education and training would lead to improved economic efficiency was a crucial obstacle faced by policy makers grappling with the 'youth problem' in the 1930s.

Technical training: the West Midlands experiment

The Board of Education (unlike the ministry) was not hampered by the grip of such orthodoxies. The forward-looking perspective of the Board's officials was demonstrated in their positive response to the recommendations of a wide-ranging report on education for the West Midlands Metal Working area, published in 1930.[31] This report revealed that little full-time vocational education was provided in the region. Of the 23,327 students enrolled at junior technical schools, 20,143 attended part-time evening classes, 1,973 attended part-time day classes and only 1,211 attended full time. The fragmentation of different institutions also created staffing problems; the principals of some colleges also acted as heads of department at another institution in an adjacent district. 'Comparatively few' students completed the full series of junior, senior and advanced courses; high wastage rates characterised evening and part-time instruction. Only about 100 full-time teachers were employed on this work in the area, in comparison with almost 2,000 part-time staff. The report commented favourably on the small number of firms in the area who released their apprentices during working hours to attend day classes without loss of wages: fifty-seven in Birmingham, twenty-eight in Coventry, six in Dudley, four in Smethwick, fourteen in Walsall and twenty-seven in Wolverhampton. It also noted the presence of employers and workers on the advisory committees or college committees of management, which advised on the curriculum, provided equipment and used their influence to persuade young people to attend classes. Although the institutions reflected the range of industries in the region, they were concentrated in Birmingham and, to a lesser extent, Coventry. This contributed to the high wastage rates on courses remote from the homes of those students' who attended mainly in the evenings.

Yet the report emphasised the small proportion of the occupied population enrolled in courses. In Birmingham, over 153,000 were employed in the metal industries, according to the 1921 census, but only 401 boys were enrolled in the city's two junior technical schools in 1927–8. The most successful junior technical school was in Coventry. Since its establishment in 1919, about 90 per cent of the boys passing through it had entered the engineering industry, and 60 per cent had continued their studies either in part-time or evening classes at the town's technical college. Small numbers attended classes, although the number of traditional apprenticeships was low and increasing responsibility was expected of semi-skilled workers. The majority of students taking courses were destined for posts of 'responsibility', i.e. foremen, supervisors and higher administrative posts. In commercial occupations, little advanced work was being done other than by students taking the professional qualifications connected with commerce, such as accountancy; the lack of day-time instruction in foreign languages was regarded as especially serious. Finally, the report noted that too many of the courses were over-specialised and recommended that they should be broadened to include subjects like factory administration, costing, statistics and applied economics.[32]

To promote action on the report, it was agreed that copies should be sent to all the relevant local authorities, rather than directly to the employers' and workers' associations, to secure local co-operation in implementing its recommendations. Representatives of the local authorities were invited to attend a conference in Birmingham in November 1929, to be addressed by the President of the Board, Sir Charles Trevelyan. Trevelyan argued for closer relations between the schools and industrial and commercial organisations, urging greater co-operation between local authorities to realise this objective. He also indicated a new departure in the Board's policy in proposing that the 'rank and file' of industry should also be served by any new initiatives. Yet progress in implementing the report was slow. The most important obstacles seem to have been financial; authorities required compensation if their institutions enrolled students from other areas. The independence of county boroughs like Birmingham and their suspicion and jealousy of neighbouring towns were major problems in which the Board had little power to intervene.

The Board's lack of legislative powers to enforce rationalisation and its reliance on voluntary co-operation meant that it was not until October 1933 that officials believed they had collected sufficient information about local conditions to bring the issue to a conference of chairmen of education committees. There were obvious cases of duplication of facilities by adjacent authorities; for instance, the number of students enrolled at Aston Technical School fell because classes in the same subject had started in West Bromwich without any consultation with Birmingham. The Board's Technical Branch repeated the need for more co-operation between the local authorities in concentrating specialist courses in the most suitable centres, and called for more extensive facilities for the interchange of students but the outcome was inconclusive, owing largely to Birmingham's opposition to any encroachment on its freedom of action. Detailed administrative machinery as proposed by the Board was not agreed until May 1935. Two committees composed respectively of heads of institutions and Her Majesty's Inspectors (HMIs), on the one hand, and directors of education on the other were to be advised by the new West Midland Advisory Council for Further Education, consisting of representatives of educational institutions, HMIs and co-opted representatives of industry and commerce.

The perseverance of the Board of Education's officers in implementing the 1930 report on the West Midlands, in the face of early apathy and hostility from the local authorities, testifies to the Board's awareness that changing circumstances required new initiatives in the sphere of education for employment. Despite its own limited powers, it eventually succeeded in devising an administrative structure that could promote the expansion of vocational education in one of the most important industrial regions in Britain. Official commitment to provide sufficient funding and more co-operation from employers was still required. As the Chairman of the new Advisory Council made clear, government could not be expected to fund the additional facilities and teaching staff if expensive equipment was to be used for only two or two and a half hours during one evening a week: firms had to be persuaded of the benefits of full-time instruction during the day.[33]

The success of the Board's intervention in the case of the West Midlands has not been examined in a study of the government's commitment to expand technical education following the general election of November 1935.[34] Based on Inspectorate reports, the Board estimated that this commitment would cost almost £12 million for England and Wales alone, to be borne in part, of course, by the local authorities themselves. Again, as was the case in the West Midlands, many local authorities were reluctant to take on this burden in the late 1930s despite the Board's energetic promptings. In particular, the rearmament boom was inflating the price of land, labour and materials; local authorities had to compete for scarce resources with the more pressing demands of other government departments. By 1939, progress had been made on only twenty-one of the 300 or more projects identified in the initial HMI survey.[35] Thus the Board was unable to use its earlier success in the West Midlands as a 'model' for the rest of the country. Given limited powers, it had to depend on persuasion; above all, it failed to secure the required degree of co-operation from employers in encouraging young workers to undertake day-time study, which was essential if ambitions to expand technical education were to succeed. The West Midlands episode suggests that the Board's difficulties were not rooted in any lack of determination on its part nor in its subordination to an anti-industrial or anti-technological ideology. Rather, they sprang, first, from the reluctance of industrial and commercial interests to support its claims to scarce resources and, second, from its relative impotence in relation both to the local authorities and other central government departments.

BRITISH RESPONSES IN INTERNATIONAL PERSPECTIVE: THE ILO SURVEY

Concern regarding the 'youth problem' was not confined to Britain during the 1930s. Policy makers were increasingly aware of similar conditions in other countries as a result of Britain's membership of the International Labour Office (ILO) – set up in response to a British initiative during the Versailles peace negotiations after the first world war to secure worker collaboration in the transition to peacetime conditions in the face of the bolshevist threat.[36] A product of tripartite corporatism, the ILO saw the international extension of collective bargaining rights as a major objective; here, it was concerned at what it regarded as the continued exploitation of young people who were not usually included in 'collective bargaining'.[37] At its first session in 1919, the ILO adopted a convention forbidding the industrial employment of children under fourteen years of age; during the interwar years a number of further conventions were adopted, including Convention 33, introduced in 1932, that prohibited the employment of children under the age of fourteen in non-industrial occupations.[38] As the leading instigator of the ILO, Britain was embarrassed when in a number of ILO publications the conditions of its young workers were revealed as especially deficient. In 1935, Britain had, after Italy, the highest rate of juvenile unemployment among females of all developed countries in the age group 14–24 (44.2 per cent), despite this being under-recorded in the official statistics. Britain also lagged behind some other countries in preparing young people for employment. Whilst in Germany, for example, 33 per cent of all boys and girls finishing the compulsory eight years in full-time education continued their education for a ninth and tenth year, in Britain only 23 per cent of boys and 17 per cent of girls attended full-time schooling when registered as unemployed. The ILO's report was particularly concerned about the effect of prolonged unemployment on the psychology and future capabilities of young people. To attack the problem of 'blind alley' jobs, the report urged that employers be required to recruit their young workers through public exchanges. Finally, while recognising that the falling birth rate would eventually reduce the number of juveniles entering the labour force, this was no reason for complacency since the highest rates of unemployment were found among the age group 25–39, indicating the classic effect of 'blind alley' work on young people in later life.[39]

The ILO's continuing concern about the employment of young people led in June 1938 to a decision to place the question of technical and vocational education and apprenticeship on the agenda for the twenty-fifth session of the International Labour Conference due to meet the following year. In order to facilitate discussion, a committee was established consisting of sixty members, thirty of whom were government representatives, and fifteen from each of employers' and workers' organisations. This was asked to prepare a questionnaire to be sent to the appropriate government department of each member country, to gather more information on existing forms of education and training and how these might be improved. In the discussion of the form that the questionnaire should take, several significant differences of opinion emerged among the government, employers' and workers' representatives; this helps to explain why the Board of Education's drive to expand this area of its activities had produced such limited results. While several representatives emphasised the necessity for more co-operation between the interested parties, it was also stressed that education should avoid premature specialisation and cultivate qualities of adaptability in young workers. In commenting on the latter point, it is noteworthy that the British government member asked for due consideration be given to 'the special conditions in each branch of industrial activity', and argued that governments could usefully reply to a number of questions 'only if the particular needs of the various branches of industry and of the various trades were taken into account'.[40] This important difference in emphasis indicates the extent to which the British still assumed that the provision of education for employment was market-led. In fact, the British delegation submitted a memorandum to the conference amplifying its views on this question. Moreover, the British employers' delegation objected strongly to the inclusion in the questionnaire of a section on apprenticeship and pre-apprenticeship training, which they maintained were strictly industrial matters that should not be subject to public scrutiny.

This discussion over the questionnaire highlighted the 'exceptionalism' of the views expressed by the British delegation. The employers' representatives again objected to the inclusion of a sub-section in one of the questions asking whether teachers responsible for 'practical training' should be required to take regular 'refresher' periods in industrial or commercial employment. This was resisted on the grounds that it might be required of employers who could not afford to employ them. The British employers also opposed the inclusion of a question proposed by Scandinavian government members that educational schemes should not charge fees and that they should be protected against cutbacks in periods of economic depression. Such inclusions, it was claimed, implied 'intervention' in government budgetary policy. A compromise was finally reached that made the charging of fees optional. Both the British government and employers' representatives also opposed the ILO's original text that time spent in attending courses should be included in normal working hours: because of 'certain practical difficulties', 'should' was substituted by 'desirable'.[41] This objection reflected the small number of firms in Britain who allowed their young workers day-release on full wages. Yet it was the section on apprenticeship that caused the most acrimony because the British employers' representatives insisted that these were 'industrial' rather than 'educational' questions. Most of the ILO's original text was eventually accepted by majority vote, with the exception of the right of apprentices to belong to trade unions. This was excised.

These differences of opinion in the preparation of the ILO's questionnaire cast doubt on the likelihood of a generally agreed tripartite approach to the issue of education for employment. British employers, in particular, appeared reluctant to accept this as part of the 'public sphere' of policy making at all. Furthermore, there was some inconsistency in the views expressed by the British government members. Whilst their separate memorandum showed a preference for industry- and trade-specific education, one of the British government's representatives subsequently argued that because of the increasing rate of technical progress, a worker's training 'should be as wide and fundamental as possible', to encourage adaptation to new jobs in later life.[42] These inconsistencies became even more striking in the response to the questionnaire made by government departments and industrial interests in Britain.[43] The National Confederation of Employers' Organisations (NCEO) was 'highly sceptical' about many of the proposals and thought that all questions on apprenticeship should deliberately not be addressed. The NCEO also viewed proposed measures 'for ensuring central control and uniformity' in regard to standards and curricula as 'both unsound and impractical', and was especially opposed to any attempt to make compulsory the attendance of young workers at day or evening classes. Both the Board of Education and the TUC were also opposed to specialisation of a 'pre-vocational nature' during the period of compulsory school attendance, although, interestingly, the Scottish Education Department favoured this recommendation. On the other hand, the Board responded to a question on whether part-time vocational education for young workers should be voluntary or compulsory by stating that 'the alternative in this question is not a real one as many young workers who have received full-time vocational education before they enter employment continue afterwards to receive part-time vocational education'. In light of the Board's actual experience during the 1930s, this statement was a rather optimistic reading of the situation. Finally, both the Board and the Juvenile Department of the Ministry of Labour regarded the ILO's proposal to set up a network of vocational schools related directly to the economic needs of localities as an industrial rather than an educational question, although the TUC's response was more positive.

The ILO's questionnaire also dealt with gender relations; here, some noteworthy differences of opinion appear. Whilst the Board, the TUC and the Scottish Education Department responded affirmatively to proposals that young women as well as men should have the same entitlement to vocational education, the Industrial Relations Department of the Ministry of Labour

> doubt whether a case can be made for the grant of equal facilities to girls since in industry generally the skilled operatives are recruited in the large majority from the male sex and women are employed on semi-skilled or process work for which a technical training is not required.[44]

This stereotyped view of Britain's skill requirements expressed by a major government department helps explain why so little was done to resolve the 'youth problem' during this period. Differences between the Board and the Ministry of Labour also arose over proposals for collaboration between public agencies and industrial and commercial interests in promoting vocational education. The Board thought that this was of the 'highest importance', as did the TUC and the Scottish Education Department, but the ministry, on the other hand, believed that initiatives in this area should be left to employers. However, the questions on apprenticeship provoked the most serious disagreement; all the government departments and the TUC were in favour of some kind of public supervision of standards and curricula whilst the NCEO's attitude was adamantly negative, holding the view that:

> many of the matters dealt with go far outside the ordinary sphere of educational training, and fall deeply into the field of industrial organisation. All the matters dealt with . . . are completely inappropriate to be dealt with in relation to vocational education and the Confederation is strongly opposed to their inclusion in any resulting recommendation.[45]

Finally, differences of opinion on the extent of the 'public sphere' are also evident in the replies to a question on systematic provision for regional, national and international exchanges of students and apprentices. Both the TUC and the Scottish Education Department responded positively but the ministry's Juvenile Department thought that this was an industrial question which should be left to the discretion of workers and employers.[46]

These contrasting responses to the ILO's questionnaire reveal not only the divergent views of the NCEO and the TUC, which is perhaps hardly surprising, but also the divisions between the Board of Education and the Ministry of Labour. Whilst these two government departments clearly overlapped on the question of education for employment, their responses demonstrate a conflict of priorities, with the ministry generally favouring 'Home Rule for Industry' whereas both the Board and the Scottish Education Department wanted greater public regulation. The tensions between the educational and industrial departments of policy making, dating back to the 1910 Choice of Employment Act, persisted on the eve of the second world war. The important exception was in the sphere of apprenticeship, where the NCEO was isolated in its opposition to the prevailing view that public regulation was required. The ILO's report did indeed highlight the 'exceptionalism' of the British model of education and training for employment.[47] In contrast to market-led and trade-specific education and training that was still the norm in Britain, the report supported the view that, despite the growth of mass-production industries, modern technologies required greater knowledge of the principles of production – not narrow manual skills; these could only be acquired from an extensive *general* education in the 'technical humanities'. Specialisation in vocational schools should be limited and the deleterious effects of an extensive division of labour in the workplace were emphasised. The priority of avoiding undue stratification in educational provision contradicted the hierarchically organised schema indicated in the memorandum submitted to the ILO by the British government. Above all, the report urged that day-time study for young workers should be generalised, although, as the Board's experience with the West Midlands had shown, this was exceptional in Britain. Finally, its findings on comparative apprenticeship systems stressed that Britain was almost unique among developed countries in its lack of restrictions on the right of employers to take on apprentices, regardless of the quality of the training and the absence of generally agreed standards of curricula and examinations.[48]

CONCLUSIONS: THE SECOND WORLD WAR AND AFTER

These deficiencies of provision in the sphere of education for employment, together with the lack of a consensus among interested parties, resurfaced during the second world war. As had been the case during the first world

war, the short-term focus of policy makers shifted from youth unemployment to the regulation of the conditions of employment of young people,
how best their capacities could be improved in light of their declining
numbers and their possibly enhanced value. Government's various restrictive
orders regulating the employment of juveniles during the war, through
employment exchanges or juvenile employment bureaux, meant that the
choice of work for more than 80 per cent of elementary school-leavers was
now subject to direct public control. This, it was argued, would give the
child 'an opportunity for choosing his occupation more really than was often
the case before the war'.[49] At the same time, however, the competition for
juveniles was so intense that 'it may not always be the best or the most suitable jobs which will carry the highest wages'.[50] This reflected a widespread
concern that the longer-term interests of young people were in danger of
being sacrificed to the short-term needs of the war effort. A highly critical
report on the provision of youth education and training was published by
the Institution of Electrical Engineers in January 1942, accusing industry
of not taking sufficient responsibility for the education and training of its
employees, whilst the local authorities were also criticised for providing
courses of instruction that were too narrow or 'abstract' for the majority
of school leavers.[51] Official statistics showed that only 20 per cent of those
leaving the junior technical schools were retained in craft employment, the
majority proceeding to non-manual occupations; the reliance on evening
classes was described as limited and inadequate.

At the same time, wartime priorities confirmed the weakness of the Board
of Education, both in relation to the autonomy of the local authorities and
to the claims of more powerful government departments.[52] This led to the
Board's officials taking a position of extreme caution. A long memorandum
prepared for R.A. Butler in April 1941, for example, argued that an extension
of education along the lines of the junior technical school would be
mistaken, on the grounds that there was little demand for it: provision should
be strictly 'vocational', limited to 'well-defined trades' organised on a regional
basis.[53] The ILO's plea in 1938 for an extension of studies in 'technical
humanities' had made little impact on the Board's thinking. Legislation
obliging employers to train young workers was dismissed on the grounds
that it would provoke 'bitter opposition' from the majority of firms, would
not be supported by the Ministry of Labour, and 'would have awkward
repercussions on industrial politics in many directions'.[54] The outlook of the
Ministry of Labour was similarly circumspect, despite its establishment of
a wartime Committee on the Recruitment and Training of Juveniles for
Industry. The views presented to the latter by both employers and trade
unions showed neither much understanding of what 'vocational education'
meant nor any clear idea of how it might be developed, but there was
unanimity on the question that education was no substitute for 'apprenticeship in the works'.[55] Moreover, whilst employers accepted that some form of

state supervision of adolescents up to eighteen years of age should be retained in the postwar period, the majority favoured a widening of existing systems of apprenticeship, as attendance at an educational institution could not replace work experience.[56] Much seems to have been expected of the aborted scheme for part-time continuing education in Young People's Colleges, which it was hoped would be created by the 1944 Education Act. Yet the ministry's committee had no definite proposals about what might be taught in these institutions, except that their curriculum should be 'general' and aim to improve the 'adaptability' of the young worker.[57]

This research suggests that the relative failure of policy makers to develop new initiatives in the sphere of education for employment was the consequence of interacting ideological, institutional and intellectual factors. Despite the enthusiasm for technical education shown by the Board of Education's Technical Branch officials and HMIs, there is some truth in the often-repeated claim that Britain's educational establishment remained unconvinced that the study of subjects with 'a more realistic bias' was compatible with the standards of academic rigour associated with the traditional curriculum of the secondary school.[58] It is difficult to ascertain precisely whether this was a result of ignorance or of prejudice; it was probably a mixture of the two. An idealistic framework of social theory permeated the educational system with an 'anti-vocational' bias,[59] which was divorced from economic thought and lacked detailed knowledge of technology and industry. This ideological obstacle was a powerful disincentive to policy innovation, given the disorganisation and fragmentation of the structure of industry. As the Permanent Secretary to the Board of Education remarked: 'neither Industry nor Commerce are [sic] found to exist as some corporate entities with which the education service can establish relations, or for which it can provide some common-form services'.[60] Indeed, the example of the West Midlands illustrates the magnitude of the outlay in both time and effort that was required for the Board to establish a working relationship between education and industry in just one area of the country.

How far was government responsible for the limited progress that was made during this period to resolve the 'youth problem'? The relative weakness of the Board of Education clearly did not encourage policy innovation, but the hostility of employers to state initiatives was also important. The Board can be faulted for the passive reliance of its senior officials on proving a prior need before they were prepared to implement new initiatives. Only some technical educationalists and the Board's Technical Branch recognised that young people needed a greater understanding of the principles or fundamentals of production processes. This had to be more widely disseminated *before* economic progress could begin to eradicate the blight of 'blind alley' employment. Finally, even after the 1944 Education Act had strengthened the powers of the new Ministry of Education in relation to the local authorities, the determination of the latter to assert their independence did not resolve earlier difficulties in ensuring local co-operation.[61] Vocational education remained marginalised in the tripartite structure of grammar, modern and technical schools established under the terms of the 1944 Act. Efforts to assimilate existing junior technical schools into the new system of secondary education were impeded by the continuing lack of parity of esteem associated with so-called 'technical' subjects. It was this together with the relatively high costs of technical schools that dissuaded most local authorities from establishing them according to the provisions of the 1944 Act.

Above all, the economic orthodoxy of the Treasury made it difficult to prove that more expenditure on the education and training of young people would necessarily lead to improved economic efficiency. Human capital theory was not readily adaptable to conventional analyses of how labour markets functioned, and even recent statistical research can be criticised for its assumption that educational attainment, as measured by the number of years of schooling, for example, is an adequate proxy for investment in human capital,[62] whilst alternative measures like the 'white-collar' share of employment are equally suspect.[63] Policy making suffered from a lack of knowledge of how changes in industrial structure and production processes affected the balance of cognitive, interactive and motor skills required of young workers, which the repeated emphasis on 'adaptability' served only to disguise. Thus it has been argued more generally that the reliance of young people for education and training on the vagaries of the 'free market' is more their problem than their salvation.[64] The findings of this research do little to contradict this contention. Forced into a premature dependence on impersonal labour markets, all but the most affluent and capable lacked the resources, qualifications, social connections and, above all, the institutional support without which genuine freedom of choice in employment is not possible.

NOTES

1 See W.R. Garside, 'Juvenile unemployment and public policy between the wars', *Economic History Review*, vol. XXXI, 1977, pp. 322–3. For examples drawn from contemporary literature: J. and S. Jewkes, *The Juvenile Labour Market*, Gollancz, London, 1937; J. Gollan, *Youth in British Industry*, Gollancz, London; J. Jewkes and A. Winterbottom, *Juvenile Unemployment*, Allen & Unwin, London, 1933; A.E. Morgan, *The Needs of Youth*, Oxford University Press, Oxford, 1939.

2 Harry Hendrick, *Images of Youth: Age, Class, and the Male Youth Problem, 1880–1920*, Clarendon Press, Oxford, 1990.

3 Michael J. Childs, 'Boy labour in late Victorian and Edwardian England and the remaking of the working class', *Journal of Social History*, vol. 23, no. 4, 1990, pp. 784, 792–3, 797–8.

4 R.H. Tawney, 'The economics of boy labour', *Economic Journal*, vol. XIX, December 1909, pp. 536–7. See also Hendrick, *Images of Youth*, pp. 143–7.

5 R. Szreter, 'A note on R.H. Tawney's early interest in juvenile employment and misemployment', *History of Education*, vol. 19, no. 4, 1990, p. 382.

6 Hendrick, *Images of Youth*, pp. 234–5.

7 Garside, 'Juvenile unemployment'.

8 C.S. Maier, *In Search of Stability: Explorations in Historical Political Economy*, Cambridge University Press, Cambridge, 1987, p. 181.

9 Nick Bosanquet, 'From Bermondsey to Canary Wharf: the social context of change in industrial relations, 1880–2000', *British Journal of Industrial Relations*, vol. 30, 1992, pp. 240–1.

10 Carol E. Heim, 'Structural transformation and the demand for new labour in advanced economies: interwar Britain', *Journal of Economic History*, vol. XLIV, no. 2, 1984, pp. 590–1.

11 Mike Savage, 'Trade unionism, sex segregation, and the state: women's employment in "new industries" in interwar Britain', *Social History*, vol. 13, no. 2, 1988, pp. 227–8.

12 Barry Eichengreen, 'Unemployment in interwar Britain: new evidence from London', *Journal of Interdisciplinary History*, vol. XVII, 1988, no. 2, pp. 348–51.

13 Jewkes and Winterbottom, *Juvenile Unemployment*, esp. p. 18 and Table 1, p. 21.

14 Jewkes and Jewkes, *The Juvenile Labour Market*, pp. 36–44.

15 Ibid., pp. 89–91.

16 Gollan, *Youth in British Industry*, esp. pp. 62–3, 125–9, 187–8, 234, 240 and ch. XII.

17 Howard Gospel and Reiko Okayama, 'Industrial training in Britain and Japan: an overview', in Howard F. Gospel (ed.), *Industrial Training and Technological Innovation: A Comparative and Historical Study*, Routledge, London, 1991.

18 Ibid., p. 21.

19 Ibid., p. 24. See also Bernard Elbaum, 'The persistence of apprenticeship in Britain and its decline in the United States', in ibid., p. 203.

20 J.F. Donnelly 'Science, technology and industrial work in Britain', *Social History*, vol. 16, 1991, p. 197.

21 M. Sanderson, 'Education and economic decline', *Oxford Review of Economic Policy*, vol. 4, 1988, pp. 38, 44.

22 Ibid.

23 Peter Gordon, Richard Aldrich and Dennis Dean, *Education and Policy in England in the Twentieth Century*, Woburn Press, London, 1991, pp. 59–60.

24 G. Timmons, *Education, Industrialization and Selection*, Routledge, London, 1988, p. 74.

25 S. Curtis, *Education in Britain since 1900*, Andrew Dakers, London, 1952, pp. 90–1. See also Gordon *et al.*, *Education and Policy*, pp. 300–2.

26 D. Thoms, 'The Education Act of 1918 and the development of central government control of education', *Journal of Educational Administration and History*, vol. VI, no. 2, 1974.

27 See, in particular, Marian Bartlett, 'The state and the problem of technical education in Britain, 1914–1926', DPhil thesis, University of Oxford, forthcoming.

28 Garside, 'Juvenile unemployment', p. 329.

29 R. Lowe, *Adjusting to Democracy*, Clarendon Press, Oxford, 1988, pp. 223–4.

30 E.C. Evans and N.C. Wiseman, 'Education, training and economic performance: British economists' views 1868–1939', *Journal of European Economic History*, vol. 13, 1984, p. 145.

31 Board of Education, *Education for Industry and Commerce: The West Midlands Metal Working Area*, Educational Pamphlet no. 74, HMSO, London, 1930, whence information in the following paragraphs is taken.

32 Ibid., p. 11.

33 Public Record Office [PRO] ED 46/11, 1929–1935, 'Report on Education for Industry and Commerce in West Midlands'. This follow-up file documents events described here.

34 Bill Bailey, 'The development of technical education, 1934–1939', *History of Education*, vol. 16, no. 1, 1987.

35 Ibid., p. 61.

36 Robert W. Cox, 'ILO: limited monarchy', in Robert W. Cox and Harold K. Jacobson (eds), *The Anatomy of Influence: Decision-making in International Organization*, Yale University Press, New Haven, CT, 1974.

37 Kathleen Gibbard, *ILO: The Unregarded Revolution*, Dent, London, 1937, pp. 89–90.

38 Ibid., appendix 11.

39 International Labour Office, International Labour Conference, Nineteenth Session, Geneva, 1935, *Unemployment Among Young Persons*, ILO, Geneva, 1935, whence the following statistics are taken.

40 International Labour Conference, Twenty-Fifth Session, Geneva, 1939, *Technical and Vocational Education and Apprenticeship*, ILO, Geneva, 1938, p. 4.

41 Ibid., p. 11.

42 Ibid., pp. 18–22.

43 The following is based on the replies to the questionnaire invited by the Ministry of Labour: see PRO LAB 19/49, 1938–42.

44 Ibid., pp. 5–6.

45 Ibid., p. 7.

46 Ibid., p.8.

47 International Labour Conference, Twenty-Fourth Session, *Technical and Vocational Education and Apprenticeship*, ILO, Geneva, 1938.

48 Ibid., pp. 12–17.

49 Ministry of Labour and National Service, *The Young Worker*, Juvenile Employment Service Pamphlet No. 1, HMSO, London, 1944, pp. 9, 11.

50 Ibid., p. 11.

51 PRO, ED 136/669, Board of Education, 1940–1944. Technical Education – Miscellaneous, 'A Critical Review of Education and Training for Engineers', pp. 1–2.

52 Peter Gosden, 'From Board to Ministry: the impact of the war on the education department', *History of Education*, vol. 18, no. 3, 1989.

53 PRO, ED 136/669, 'Some Problems in Technical Education', Wallis to Butler, 17 April 1941.

54 Ibid., p. 10.

55 PRO, LAB 19/106, 1942–1945. Sub-committee on Post-war Apprenticeship and Technical Education. See esp. meeting 29 March 1943, pp. 2, 4.

56 Ibid., Discussion of Second Interim Report, 19 December 1944. Summary of replies.
57 Ibid., Draft Recommendations, 22 January 1944.
58 See, for example, Board of Education, *Curriculum and Examinations in Secondary Schools: Report of the Committee of the Secondary School Examinations Council Appointed by the President of the Board of Education in 1941* (Norwood Report), HMSO, London, 1943, p. 3.
59 Jose Harris, 'Political thought and the welfare state, 1870–1940: an intellectual framework for British social policy', *Past and Present*, vol. 135, 1992, esp. pp. 138–41.
60 PRO, ED 136/669, Wood to Butler, 24 February 1942, p. 1.
61 Gordon *et al.*, *Education and Policy*, pp. 62–3.
62 N. Crafts, *British Economic Growth during the Industrial Revolution*, Clarendon Press, Oxford, 1985, p. 176.
63 S. Broadberry and N.F.R. Crafts, 'European productivity in the twentieth century: introduction', *Oxford Bulletin of Economics and Statistics*, vol. 52, 1990, p. 384. For a critique of conventional measures of human capital, see David R. Howell and Edward N. Wolff, 'Technical change and the demand for skills by US industries', *Cambridge Journal of Economics*, vol. 16, 1992.
64 William Lazonick, *Business Organization and the Myth of the Market Economy*, Cambridge University Press, Cambridge, 1991, p. 72.

Part II

REGULATING LABOUR MARKETS

8

ARBITRATION IN CONTEXT

Socio-economic conditions and the
implementation of the law on conciliation
and compulsory arbitration in the Parisian
metal industries and light engineering in
the Arve Valley

Claude Didry

The establishment of conciliation and compulsory arbitration in France between 1937 and 1939 is frequently seen as a policy primarily designed to adjust the purchasing power of wage earners. From this perspective, policy appears as a response to the inflation that followed the French franc's instability on international currency markets.[1] The system helped to establish collective agreements following the strike movement of May–June 1936, which it helped to prolong. Legally reinforced collective agreements became the chief instrument and basis for a wages policy. The main objective was to adjust wages in line with the economic potential of each sector, particular account being taken of possible productivity gains capable of maintaining profit levels in a non-inflationary environment. In the workplace, the arbitration procedure thus challenged traditional systems of managing productivity issues (*les conventions de productivité*) embodied in established production systems.[2] It outlined a means to 'share productivity gains' which, for economic theorists, was to be the source of growth for the three decades of postwar expansion.

To qualify what in many ways can be considered as a teleological interpretation of the establishment of conciliation and compulsory arbitration, the diversity of existing forms of production must be taken into account. Social unrest at the end of the 1930s stemmed from a plurality of economic situations; there was little sign of the anticipated Keynesian economic agenda aimed at maintaining workers' purchasing power. Misunderstandings resulted when agreements, established in the metal industries of the Paris region, were superimposed on radically different productive environments.

Arguably these misunderstandings were one of many sources of social unrest. The question of wage readjustment and the re-examination of traditional conventions governing productivity frequently led to the introduction of conciliation and compulsory arbitration procedures. However, our hypothesis here is that the parties in dispute, and the arbitrators, moved towards the clarification of working practices (*conventions du travail*) and the associated unemployment conventions (*conventions du chomage*)[3] by focusing on the particular features of the local economy within which 'collective disputes' developed.

We will discuss this hypothesis with reference to the metal industries of the Paris region and light engineering in the Arve Valley in the alpine *département* of Haute Savoie. This paper will demonstrate how the law of 31 December 1936 led to 'situational arbitration'[4] – namely, the adaptation of these new procedures to specific locations. We will refer to 'superarbitration' awards selected from the first 200 such cases published in the *Journal Officiel* of 1937. These 200 awards provide important evidence through which the procedure can be evaluated. They are an important source for historians and sociologists; they were also the basis for discussion at the Confédération Générale du Travail (CGT) congress of 1937. Awards varied in scope, ranging from disputes concerning a single company to disputes that involved the whole of a trade in a particular area. This diversity reflects the haphazard development of agreements aimed at ending the wave of factory occupations in May–June 1936.

CONCILIATION AND ARBITRATION IN 1936: FROM PRACTICAL APPLICATION TO LEGAL RECOGNITION

The strikes of May–June 1936 marked a revival in the workers' movement following a period of decline which started in the 1920s. They were prompted by major economic changes brought about by rearmament. Characteristic French forms of production, notably luxury goods for export, (such as silk and 'Parisian' articles, organised in production systems along the lines of a *fabrique collective* or Alfred Marshall's 'district'), retained their post-first world war levels. Rearmament led to the extension of more industrial, factory-based forms of production, notably in the metal industries.[5] Noiriel emphasises how, in the Paris region, this development led to a clearer separation between home and the workplace.[6] The transformation in workers' living conditions meant that Communist Party efforts to infiltrate and organise were directed both at the expanding factories and at tenants in poor-quality and insecure housing in the Parisian suburbs.

This strong polarisation between the workplace and the home was manifest in the factory occupations of May–June 1936. The importance of worker processions in the strikes of the 1880s contrasts significantly with factory occupations as the location of working-class activism in the mid-1930s, although both forms of protest re-emerged later in the decade. Such movements gained support from an idea expounded in two articles (one by Benoît Frachon on collective agreements, the other by Ambroise Croizat on factory committees) published in July 1935 in *Métallurgiste*, the organ of the Consolidated Metal Workers Federation (Fédération Unitaire des Métaux). In pursuit of the 1920s' Bolshevik strategy to inflitrate factories, the workplace became the prime site of working-class struggle. Factories became the focal point of demands concerning trade union freedom and worker representation. Worker solidarity was thus primarily linked to the workplace. The importance of workplace occupation can be seen again during the strikes of 1936, as these conflicts were finally resolved when employers acknowledged that branch collective agreements were binding, whether agreement was pending or had already been ratified. The contrast with strikes carried out at the turn of the century, which were political events marked by processions, appears in Léon Blum's defence strategy in the trial of Riom:

> From the point of view of public order, this form of strike [the sit-in] has undeniable advantages. The workers occupy the factory but it is also true that the factory occupies the workers – the workers being there, not elsewhere. They were not on the street. From the moment they were grouped together in the factory, they were not forming processions with songs and red flags which clashed with police barricades, provoking the violent and sometimes bloody incidents of all known strikes.[7]

From the first strikes in 1935 and in May–June 1936, factories in the metal industries predominated in the application of this strategy, even though the marked diversity of that sector had to be taken into account. In the Paris region, two forms of production co-existed: Citroën's adoption of 'American methods' – and factory-based mass production – on the one hand, and a multitude of small workshops on the other. The aircraft industry, which spearheaded the union movement, was characterised by the coexistence of variously sized companies, the majority of whose workers were highly skilled and were referred to as 'specialists'. Such companies often consisted solely of research departments producing prototypes. At the other extreme, a strategy of diversified production systems meant that aeronautical construction might become a division in a large enterprise, as in the Renault factories.[8] In this way the impact of the trade cycles found in the automobile sector could be mediated. Within this productive universe, the factory regime was counterbalanced by the significant movement of specialist workers from one establishment to another, in an environment where people frequently knew each other.

THE SPIRIT OF THE LAW OF
31 DECEMBER 1936

Beyond monetary considerations

Coinciding with the devaluation of the franc and continuing monetary instability, article 15 of the law of 1 October 1936 established a procedure for compulsory arbitration. Arbitration and conciliation, however, were further discussed during the economic recovery and during the spontaneous resumption of industrial disputes in the autumn of 1936.[9] These issues were the focus of a meeting, organised by Léon Blum on 14 September 1936, between employers' representatives and CGT leaders. The conciliation and compulsory arbitration procedures which emerged during these negotiations involved two issues. First, the definition of a mechanism for maintaining the purchasing power of the wage-earner formed part of a quasi-Keynesian demand management agenda, which was crucial in an inflationary context. Second, procedures to defuse strikes – which were tending to break loose from union control – were urgently needed.

Following this meeting, negotiations between representatives of the CGT and the Confédération Générale de la Production Française (CGPF), organised by Blum, led to the drafting of the law of 31 December 1936. This detailed precise conciliation and arbitration procedures, establishing the system's autonomy from the macro-economic outlook which dominated the Blum cabinet. The widespread victimisation of workers' representatives by employers caused Léon Blum to resolve the crisis by resorting to a vote in the National Assembly, rather than by reopening industrial negotiations. The passing of the law permitted the application of a text which, although agreed by negotiation, had been rejected by the employers' confederation. Whilst the law was being debated, the Chambres Syndicales Patronales du Nord had repudiated an arbitration award, proposed by Blum, to settle a dispute stimulated by an earlier sacking of workers' delegates.

For trade union leaders at least, the new law therefore had a significance which went beyond the adjustment of purchasing power in the context of monetary and economic policy. Being aimed at the resolution of 'collective disputes', the procedure codified a traditional practice of official intervention in organising negotiations between the two sides. The procedure conferred a crucial role on joint conciliation commissions, which performed this function. It fell to these commissions and, in the second stage of the procedure, to the arbitrators and 'super' arbitrators,[10] to establish for themselves the scope of their jurisdiction in cases which they judged to be 'collective'. Resort to arbitration only occurred when conciliation broke down. The structure of conciliation commissions was complicated, ranging from the *département* and trade level (where the commissions could be organised in accordance with the particular provisions of the collective agreement), to the Commission

Professionnelle National and finally the level of the Commission Paritaire Interprofessionnelle. At each of these levels it was possible to initiate official arbitration once the opposing parties considered that conciliation procedures had been exhausted.

Applying the procedure: the ambiguity over 'collective disputes'

The limits of the conciliation commission's jurisdiction were defined by the category of 'collective dispute' with which it dealt. However, such terms were not closely defined by law. A perusal of parliamentary debates indicates that the term *différend collectif* generally designated disputes that could lead to a strike or to a collective dispute. The term's lack of precision implied the existence of a large margin for manoeuvre, marked variations depending on the trade or locality involved. The importance of this margin to allow different interpretations was reinforced by the fact that the final arbitration could not be challenged. In effect, this meant that the enforcement of the judgement was almost entirely dependent on the good will of the parties involved. In this sense, an agreement by both sides to resume work was proof that an award had been accepted and a final settlement reached.

Conciliation and arbitration across diverse systems of production

The superarbitration award of 7 February 1937 concerned the Parisian metal industries; it was based on the maintenance of purchasing power in the context of a reduction in working hours which sprang from work-sharing. One of the first to be published, and the tenth recorded, this award applied to a sector which, as we have noted, acted as a catalyst to the disruptions of May–June 1936. Brought in to adjudicate upon a demand raised by the workers' union and contested by the employers, Professor W. Oualid made an award which resolved a dispute linked to conciliation and arbitration proceedings begun in December 1936, that is, before the law was passed, under a procedure inaugurated by Article 15 of the monetary law of 1 October 1936. Faced with the workers' demand for an adjustment of wages following price rises, the employers proposed an extension of overtime in order to compensate for their greater financial outlay.

The workers' demands were accepted by the superarbitrator, with the proviso that relative price stability was a precondition to the implementation of an award:

> the increase in wages is justified owing to a marked rise in the cost of living, but it would be impossible to establish an immediate and complete parallel between changes in retail prices and wages levels without condemning the economy to an instability incompatible with trade agreements and to a never-ending wage–price spiral.[11]

Oualid adopted an argument which relied in part on the quantity theory of money. He was thus antagonistic to adjustment mechanisms which he judged to be over-reactive, and which would lead to instability in income distribution:

> Any unforeseen retroactive element involved in the application of these new rates represents a threefold inconvenience: it would force those liable to pay to pay out immediately, upset their cost price calculations and throw into circulation a number of monetary signals which would accelerate price increases.[12]

In this way, the purchasing power of wages had to be adjusted within the framework of specific institutions aimed at the maintenance of workers' living standards: family allowances thus became a wage-adjustment variable integrated into a policy for maintaining both purchasing power and the national birthrate. (The superarbitrator's interest in family allowances as the means to adjust purchasing power waned somewhat following a memorandum from the Ministre du Travail which underlined the diversity of family allowance funds and the resulting difficulty of establishing uniform procedures for wage adjustment.) These two elements were linked, since the definition of purchasing power implies that the conditions of the family are taken into account. Thus for the superarbitrator:

> As the increase in the cost of living hits working families more than single people or households without children, it is advisable to encourage, in the Paris region, the birth of first, second and third children in order to raise the French birthrate. Existing family allowances are abnormally low . . . [13]

The employers' overtime proposal also became a focus of discussion and this was reflected in the award. The employers' proposition was rejected by the superarbitrator after an enquiry based on the records of the indemnified unemployed, held by the Office Publique de Placement de la Seine, in the metal trades around Paris.

The application of the law of 21 June 1936, which established the forty-hour working week, was implemented in December 1936. For the arbitrator ('in order to favour the current economic recovery'), the law had to be applied in conformity with its objective, namely, 'the express aim . . . to put pressure on employers to make them use less capable or older workers, who make up the majority of the unemployed, it being granted that rising unemployment gave employers the opportunity to select their work force, the older and less able workers being targeted for dismissal first'.[14] Oualid's analysis thus leads to the hypothesis that unemployment affects those whose productivity is the lowest (the least able) and whose remuneration was most clearly above their productive potential (the elderly). This implies that the 'concrete' work supplied by each worker was not considered as a uniform commodity. Economic recovery would bring about the reverse effect, provided that recourse to overtime did not upset this balance.

Oualid's superarbitration award utilised the notion of establishment (*établissement*), familiar in the world of the Paris metal industries. This trend appeared in the organisation of the labour movement itself, the communist component applying the Bolshevik strategy of factory infiltration, which led the communists, through the CGTU militants, to stress the importance of workplace 'implantation' in the conflicts which foreshadowed the movement of May–June 1936. The importance of the factory and the 'establishment' also appears in the registration procedures for the unemployed in the Paris region. The question of a wage readjustment led to a debate on the classification of workers within the different establishments, capable of taking account of the fringe group of unemployed working outside any given establishment.

The employers' promotion of an adjustment in purchasing power which relied on greater recourse to overtime thus led to the superarbitrator's defence of work-sharing, established in the law introducing the forty-hour week. The award, and the arguments of the two parties, reveal the commitment of the worker representatives and the superarbitator to a redefinition of the contract of employment based on the notion of belonging to an establishment. This concept also appears in the definition of unemployment as an absence of 'places' in an establishment – and hence was implicitly rehearsed across different arguments.

The Paris metal industries' agreement as a model for light engineering in the Arve Valley

Out of the first hundred arbitration awards, the one concerning light engineering in the Arve Valley[15] stands out because of its length (three pages in the *Journal Officiel*). The size of this award is explained by the fact that, prior to the appearance of the collective dispute bound by the procedure, there was no pre-existing collective agreement beyond one dated July 1936, which defined three geographical areas for wage-rates and established a schematic preliminary classification. The concern here was to determine the scale of an increase in wages, taking into account price-levels and the specific features of production in the valley: 'The differences in wages between the three areas established by the agreement of July 1936 are justified by the cost of living, above all in housing, which is less expensive for Cluses and Sallanches workers, and even less expensive for the mountain and rural areas.'[16] Hence it was necessary to determine the conditions under which a wage rise could take place, and thus to establish a 'convention' (the expression used by the superarbitrator) – or at least its guiding principles – by making reference, in conciliation and in the first stage of arbitration, to the text under discussion. Clauses from this text were sometimes cited by the award.

The Arve Valley is located between Annemasse and the Mont Blanc range. It was marked by the development of light engineering in small-scale enterprises (around ten people in the 1930s, and approximately twenty nowadays). Following the incorporation of Savoy into French territory, contacts with Geneva diminished, leading to a decline in the clock- and watch-making industry in the region. From the last century onwards the industry began, therefore, to reconvert to light engineering. The first world war played an important role in the development of this regional industrial activity, as much by sustaining clock- and watch-making specialisation through research and development in delayed-action clock mechanisms, as by encouraging light engineering activity itself, coupled with mechanical construction. The 1930s were marked by the growth of light engineering which was linked to the development of other metal industries in France, particularly the car industry, and to the continued decline in clock- and watch-making.[17]

An economist and assistant lecturer at the Grenoble Law Faculty, the superarbitrator, Robert Mossé,[18] moved with ease from general economic models to the particular forms of production in the valley. His macroeconomic view echoed the principal aim of workers' demands for wage readjustment to compensate for rising prices. The superarbitrator justified the merits of these demands by referring to an economic analysis that refuted the validity of the price–wage spiral: 'Wages being only a fraction of production costs (around 40 to 50 per cent in the industries under consideration) a wage increase of around 12.5 per cent, for example, leads to an increase of only 5 to 6.5 per cent in production costs.'[19] He also recognised the principle of an index of wages capable of simultaneously taking into account price and production levels defined as follows:

> Employer and worker delegations, in talks with the superarbitrator, together with the unanimous decision of three arbitrators, have approved the principle of a wages forecast index. This index is to be based on an combined index that allocates a coefficient of 2 to the cost of living and a coefficient of 1 to the volume of production in the mechanical engineering industries.[20]

The choice of this index was based on an economic analysis justifying postwar policies for sharing productivity gains:

> The raising of wages augments the purchasing power of consumers in that it represents the transfer of incomes from social categories which would have hoarded it, to social categories liable to reinject

it rapidly into economic circulation. Following a rise in incomes, and a consequent rise in demand, there is some reason to believe that an increase in production would facilitate a reduction in cost prices, especially in the industries under consideration, which are, for the most part, highly rationalised.[21]

The argument was thus almost explicitly based on a conception of work approximating to that of the 'industrial world'. The increase in the number of units produced due to greater demand takes place in the context of important economies to scale.

Though the superarbitrator adopted a 'macro-economic' approach to economic phenomena, he none the less acknowledged in his award the specific nature of the economic universe he was addressing, but at the price of numerous disparities between his economic analysis and specific proposals. The question of unemployment in the valley was the decisive element leading the superarbitrator to take the industry's unique character into consideration. Whereas for Oualid the problem in the Paris region was to encourage establishments to take on unemployed workers in response to an increase in production during economic recovery, the problem for the light engineering industry was to cope with relatively regular slack seasons during which work relations could become strained. To deal with this, Robert Mossé's award introduced a measure based on the assumption that employment contracts could be extended for a period of six months even if no work was given by the employer to the worker. This measure 'targets not so much the major economic fluctuations, which produce unemployment lasting longer than this period, but the seasonal work fluctuations which can to a great extent be attenuated by rational work arrangements'.[22] This was presented as a translation of the clause relating to re-employment priorities contained in the collective agreements on the metal industries in the valley:

> Article 29 of the present agreement places no obstacles in the way of a suspension of the obligation to pay wages and ancillary benefits and . . . the non-breaching of employment contracts is primarily aimed at giving a legal basis to priority in re-employment as established by Article 29.

The support for employment contracts thus rehearsed the collective agreement of the Parisian metal industries, whilst exploring a somewhat different interpretation – through which the employment contract could extend beyond the period during which the worker was physically engaged in work. It aimed at taking into account the fact that:

> In the particular case of the industries in Faucigny, there are small and medium-sized firms which have every interest in remaining in

contact with a labour force that could prove indispensible the moment production had to be increased.[23]

This clause was implicitly linked to the fact that, within an industry where domestic production and piecework played an important role, employers and workers belonged to the same 'community of uncertainty' (that is, one based on shared conventions concerning unemployment) where participation in the trade is rooted in the locality. Here, specialist workers emerge with skills which are irreplaceable for specific enterprises. The framing of such an arrangement in terms of seasonal fluctuations formally embodied existing practice: from the turn of the century, domestic workers did not declare themselves 'unemployed' so long as the machines set up in their homes by the merchants remained there. Such perspectives evoke the concept of unemployment developed by Auguste Keufer (general secretary of the Syndicat du Livre) during the debates on unemployment insurance at the Conseil Supérieur du Travail in 1894. He distinguished between seasonal, predictable fluctuations in activity and more radical economic uncertainty (which leads to genuine unemployment calling for state intervention).[24]

The particular nature of the work contract and its heterogeneity, given the diversity of the forms of employment in the valley, gave the superarbitrator the arguments needed to institute area zoning of wage rates. Whereas the establishment of wage zones in the collective agreement of the Parisian metal industries was justified by differences in the cost of living from one area to another, wage zones in the valley reflected levels of urbanisation. Clearly the cost of living was higher in urbanised areas, since wage earners were reliant on retail outlets, whereas rural inhabitants could produce for themselves. The degree of urbanisation was thus an indicator of the level of 'subordination' of workers. The difference in remuneration between urban and rural areas corresponded, in fact, to the degree of autonomy experienced by workers with respect to their work: 'Considering . . . that a reduction in workers' wages in the countryside is compensated for by the relative liberty which they enjoy to undertake agricultural work'.[25]

In other respects, the difference in remuneration evolved from the survival in rural areas of small and medium-sized enterprises, faced with competition from the larger companies in the urban areas of Annemasse and Cluses. The superarbitrator presupposed the preservation of a diverse but unified industrial infrastructure, since such diversity facilitated complementarity between producers. This diversity was thus not limited to quantitive differences, but was linked to the relative nature of subordination[26] contained in the employment contract. The factory work of some complemented the relative freedom of others.

From analyses of this kind, the superarbitrator pragmatically accepted the workers' demands for uniform wage levels, the degree of urbanisation leading, as we have seen, to differences in remuneration. He was thus led to consider the question of wage equality between men and women, on a parallel to the question of the territorial harmonisation of wage levels. If, according to the superarbitrator, such an alignment of wages were, in itself, desirable: 'an increase in the wages of female personnel in line with the principle of 'the same wages for the same work' would, given the size of this particular workforce, run the risk of undermining their interests by increasing their liability to be made redundant'.[27] An increase in wages for female workers would thus be detrimental to the employment of women. The inequality in wages between men and women was all the more acceptable given that: 'one must not neglect the fact that, for many female workers between eighteen and twenty-five years of age, wages merely represent supplementary income for the working family'.[28] Female work was less well paid than male work; the family and, by extension, the woman herself, was less dependent on the wage alone. The award also reflected the importance of female domestic employment, which facilitated the combination of productive activities and household tasks ('reproductive activities' in Marxist terminology). The superarbitrator accordingly pointed out that 'work at home presents many advantages, both for the employer [who was thereby relieved of overheads] and for those [generally females] who work at home who, by staying at home, can significantly increase household earnings'.[29]

The maintenance of differentials in remuneration for work in rural and urban areas and for female labour and male labour could have been called into question by the workers' demands for an increase in piecework wages relative to hourly wages. Piecework was, in fact, more common among domestic outworkers, being a form of work that was more generally rural and undertaken by women. In this case, the superarbitrator echoed employers' demands for an 'average piecework wage' above the hourly rate fixed by collective agreement. The average wage was then defined by the undertaking of a normal task under the following conditions:

> A 'normal task' used for the calculation of piecework wages is one which can be carried out by one worker in three, under the supervision of an overseer or shop foreman. The workers are designated by drawing lots for the control test, and are unaware of being involved in a test.[30]

The conversion of piecework into hourly paid work was thus only possible in urban factory work. In this way the wage differential between rural and urban areas could be maintained and the economy of light engineering in Savoy preserved.

In his search for a way to transpose the model of the agreement of the Parisian metal industries, the superarbitrator entrusted members of the trade with the task of establishing the precise mechanisms for enforcing the more general measures. In this, he was led to involve worker delegates in consultations over working conditions similar to that undertaken by factory inspectors. Worker delegates thus became responsible agents in the detailed application of more general measures.

The application of a system classifying each worker, based on the general categories contained in the Parisian collective agreement which distinguished specialised workers and skilled workers, was handed over to a joint commission made up of two employers, two workers and a technician. This procedure gave some satisfaction to workers in that it offered protection against the risk of deskilling by employers in an attempt to lower wages. It also aimed at resolving a major dilemma in the classification of worker skills. The 'skilled' category was defined in the Parisian agreement by the completion of an apprenticeship or by the possession of a technical diploma (*certificat d'aptitude professionnelle*) obtained through study. Many workers in the region were thus left out of the specialist worker category on the grounds that they had not obtained the necessary diploma. This point was settled by reference to precedents established in Lyon and Grenoble 'by the requirement of a month's trial period dealt with under Article 31 giving full guarantees to the employers'.[31]

In the same way, the enforcement of the forty-hour week did not at first give rise to the prior fixing of an across-the-board working week; the implementation was delegated to worker representatives. In the relatively diverse environment of the Valley, 'the superarbitrator considered . . . it was only possible to organise consultation with representatives'.[32]

CONCLUSIONS

The setting up of compulsory arbitration procedures in France from the autumn of 1936, channelled workers' demands towards the defence of wage-earners' purchasing power against the risks of inflation. Established to resolve collective disputes, the first law on conciliation and compulsory arbitration was confronted not only with a multitude of claims, but also with the transposition into other worlds of production of agreements forged in the pilot sector of the Parisian metal industries. This proved to be difficult. Through the scope which it gave to arbitrators, particularly to the super-arbitrator at the end of the procedure, the law provided a framework within which the economy of work conventions in each productive situation could be clarified.

Within this framework, the Parisian collective agreement and the union activity in this sector acted as benchmarks. Here, the application of arbitration and conciliation procedures had developed in an exemplary fashion: Oualid's superarbitration award ended a negotiation procedure which accompanied the framing of the law itself. This award confirmed that the metal industries in the Paris region were developing towards mass production. Here, the problem of unemployment and wage increases could be placed in the context of a 'labour market', in terms of its interactions with other markets, through the price–wage spiral and in the adjustment of labour supply to demand.

On the other hand, the award concerning the light engineering industry in the Arve Valley drew on the co-existence of diverse forms of employment in a productive environment subject to regular fluctuations. Working practices, notably those concerning unemployment, took a specific form here; both workers and employers shared the burden of fluctuations in production. However, this form of 'flexible' production did not lead to the oppression of the waged workforce in these small enterprises (said to be characterised by a somewhat dated paternalism). The mere existence of superarbitration awards bore witness to a high level of worker activism drawing upon solid union organisation. In these circumstances, the collective agreement of the Parisian metal industries became the reference point for negotiators, though its relevance for employment in light engineering was not immediately apparent. The demand for an adjustment in wage purchasing power committed those involved, both workers and employers, to the task of transposing established agreements derived from the Paris collective agreement and the Matignon accord to the specific situation of the Arve Valley. Parisian metallurgy was not, however, simply the 'spearhead'[33] for a pre-existing national workers' movement. The agreements and the procedures which took shape there appeared rather as an organisational model, appropriated and adapted by agents in other spheres of production.

Consequently, the 'anchoring'[34] of those affected by collective disputes in the reality of specific production systems can be understood as the consequence of the independence conferred on the superarbitrator by the law of 31 December 1936. Not completely bound by the general rules of a higher tribunal, the superarbitrator could anchor his award to the particular production relations within which the dispute began. He could thus produce an effect within this situation. The law led to collective disputes which, over and above questions linked to the readjustment of wages, created problems of transposing established agreements (worker representation, the forty-hour week, paid holidays, etc.) into worlds of production where factory-based employment was not common. On the other hand, the hypothetical existence of a higher court[35] implied that the superarbitrator would have had to take into account not only the existing legislation but also the consequences of his award for future arbitration, together with the risk that it might be overturned. Consequently, in later months, the role of arbitrator underwent a certain 'normalisation', and was integrated into a structure which extended from the general rules laid down by the higher court's awards to the more specific norms of arbitration.

NOTES

1 J.P. Rioux, 'La conciliation et l'arbitrage obligatoire des conflits du travail', in R. Rémond and G. Bourdin (eds), *Edouard Daladier, chef du gouvernement*, PFNSP, Paris, 1977.

2 R. Salais, 'Incertitude et interactions de travail', in A. Orléan (ed.), *Analyse économique des conventions*, PUF, Paris, 1994, pp. 371–401.

3 Ibid.

4 This notion is inspired by the concept of 'theatre of situation' developed by J.P. Sartre.

5 P. Fridenson, *Histoire des usines Renault*, vol. 1: *Naissance de la grande industrie 1898–1939*, Seuil, Paris, 1972; D. Phan, 'Productivité, emploi et salaires ouvriers chez Renault autour des années 30' *Le mouvement sociale*, no. 154 March 1991; C. Didry and R. Salais, 'Troubles sur les produits d'Etat et écriture des conventions collectives du travail en 1936', in A. Jacob and H. Vérin (eds), *L'inscription sociale du marché*, L'Harmattan, Paris, 1995.

6 G. Noiriel, *Les ouvriers dans la société française, XIXème–XXème siècle*, Point Seuil, Paris, 1986.

7 A. Supiot, *Critique du droit du tranvail*, PUF, Paris, 1994, p. 154.

8 Phan, 'Productivite'.

9 D. Borne and H. Dubief, *La crise des années 30, 1929–1938*, Point Seuil, Paris, 1989; and G. Lefranc, *Juin 1936*, Julliard collection archives, Paris, 1966.

10 That is, arbitrators adjudicating settlements on a regional or trade basis.

11 *Journal Officiel de la République Française* [henceforth *JO*], documents administratifs, 1937, p. 625, col. 1.

12 Ibid., col. 2.

13 Ibid.

14 Ibid., col. 3.

15 Award no. 63, dated 16 March 1937, ibid., p. 665.

16 Ibid., col. 3.

17 C. Courlet, B. Pecqueur, and G. Sanson, *Diagnostic d'actions et de développement local : le cas de la Vallée de l'Arve*, report of IREPD for the CRIDEL, Grenoble, 1992.

18 The author of a work on collectivism (1939) which analysed the Soviet Union in term of Hayekian marginalism. He also published in 1929 a work on compulsory unemployment insurance.

19 *JO*, p. 625, col. 2.

20 Ibid., p. 667, col. 1.

21 Ibid., p. 665. col. 3.

22 Ibid., p. 668, col. 2.

23 Ibid.

24 F. Birk, 'Le positivisme ouvrier et la question du travail' in J. Luciani (ed.), *Histoire de l'Office du Travail*, Syros, Paris, 1992.

25 *JO*, p. 666, col. 1.

26 In the sense given to the term by labour law specialists, see G. Lyon-Caen, *Le droit du travail non-salarie*, Sirey, Paris, 1990.

27 *JO*, p. 666, col. 1.

28 Ibid., p. 667, col. 3.
29 Ibid., p. 666, col. 1.
30 Ibid., p. 665, col. 2.
31 Ibid., p. 666, col. 2.
32 Ibid., p. 668, col. 2.
33 A spearhead whose emergence prefigured a social movement which could be identified with an 'explosion' or a reaction taking place within a homogeneous milieu.
34 We have borrowed this term from E. Goffman, *Frame Analysis: An essay on the organisation of experience*, Harvard University Press, Cambridge, MA, 1974, Chapter 8 and p. 100: 'a third series of doubts (the first relating to the framing of an activity, to its grammar, the second to the moulding that an activity may be subjected to) is linked to the anchoring of the context, particularly with respect to the biographical identification of the different scenic elements including, above all, the human elements.'
35 Such as the Cour supérieure d'arbitrage which came into existence following the law of 4 March 1938.

9

COLLECTIVE AGREEMENTS IN FRANCE IN THE 1930s

Products, territories and scales: the Saint-Etienne example

Michelle Zancarini-Fournel

The institutionalisation of collective bargaining between employers and workers, initially introduced in the particular circumstances of the first world war in the French defence industries, became widespread in 1936–7 and standard practice after the second world war. By fashioning legal forms and forums for negotiation, state intervention in industrial and social affairs, visible from the turn of the century, led to the codification of work relations in private companies. This intervention, initiated by socialists in the government, was not isolated from the economic situation or from social pressures. Strike action in 1917–19, in 1935–6, during the post-Liberation period and in 1947–53 helped trigger procedures designed to resolve such conflicts. What principles and terms of reference served as a basis for negotiation? Did the process of negotiating and drafting collective agreements modify market forces and executive authority? Does it reveal the emergence of 'industrial democracy' in private firms? Were the practices of the various parties – businessmen, trade unionists, the workers themselves and state representatives – modified by the drafting and the implementation of the agreements which paved the way for arbitration and worker representation? How far did the political, economic and social situation affect the process of compromise? Did industrial agreements contribute to the social construction and institutionalisation of age and sex divisions within the workforce?

The study of work agreements in the industrial area of Saint-Etienne during the years 1936–9 provides at least partial answers to these questions. The area selected for observation combined different scales, both local and national. A large production and marketing company, the Manufacture d'Armes et Cycles de Saint-Etienne (MFAC – the Saint-Etienne Arms and Cycles Factory), which was headed by Etienne Mimard from 1885–1944,[1] combined several worlds of production in a single area of employment

178

around the town. The area contained diverse industrial and commercial branches – the textile, metallurgical and food industries – which are studied with reference to the Parisian metallurgical industry, whose 1936 agreement was considered the model for collective contracts.

The choice of social micro-history allows us to test the models suggested by Robert Salais and Claude Didry on the drafting of agreements.[2] Thanks to exceptional archives (minutes of the daily meetings of the joint committee in 1917; minutes of the tripartite meetings on the development of the metallurgical agreement in the Loire in 1936; accounts of the proceedings of the committee for conciliation and arbitration in 1937–9), the ways in which the various parties constructed and formalised a set of procedures and rules can be analysed. Local issues relating to production, which sometimes differ from national issues, can be traced: the cost of working out the agreement and how that agreement transformed – for a brief time – the relationships between the parties concerned can be estimated. To this local examination of a single geographical area is added an even more detailed perspective: the study of a company where different agreements were enforced. From December 1936 to December 1937, a long conflict took place in this company: a 'hundred-day' strike, including sit-ins and violence, both individual and collective, a conflict that was linked to the passage of the agreements.

ORIGINS: ARBITRATION, COLLECTIVE CONTRACTS AND JOINT COMMITTEES

Collective agreements, the election of delegates to control their enforcement and mandatory conciliation and arbitration procedures were the three components that comprised state organisation of work relations in the 1930s. These measures were not entirely new. The practice of worker delegation – apart from associations (*amicales*) and unions – already existed before 1914 in the Saint-Etienne metallurgical industry, even though this was not formally recognised by employers.[3] Legislation on conciliation and arbitration had been passed as early as 1892 but it remained relatively inefficient, in part because it was voluntary – as opposed to mandatory – and its enforcement was temporary or limited. Arbitration and conciliation procedures, as defined by that law, failed because they were not obligatory; discussions on the bill, however, made the creation of a mandatory category possible – for companies working on contracts for the state, the *département* or the commune.[4] The Millerand decree of 10 August 1899 required companies in receipt of state contracts to account for the working conditions of their waged workforce and to observe all existing legislation. In the Saint-Etienne area, this applied to the Manufacture d'Armes de Saint-Etienne (MAS), which was a state arsenal.

Albert Thomas, Ministre de l'Armement, was an advocate of *union sacrée* and of 'industrial unity for social peace'. For him, the war was, until December 1917, a laboratory for the foundation of new work relations based on arbitration, tripartite negotiation and the election of worker delegates. During 1917, however, this socialist minister faced massive strikes, both in Paris and in the provinces, especially in the Loire. In January 1917, a decree made arbitration compulsory for disputes involving companies contracting for the state, particularly munitions factories. At that time, the Saint-Etienne area was France's arsenal, employing more than 100,000 male and female workers. On 30 April 1917, a ministerial decision entrusted joint committees with the task of setting minimum wages for the duration of the war in organisations that were working for national defence. The Prefect of the Loire – in the government's name – assembled delegates from the employers and the workers in the presence of the controller of the military workforce and one ministerial representative (Colonel Dhé, Deputy Chief of Staff), whose presence indicated the significance of these negotiations. The procedure used shows that tripartite negotiation had not yet been fully accepted: the Prefect convened the employer and worker delegations separately. Etienne Mimard, the MFAC director, headed the employers' group; his proposals for wage categories and scales formed the basis for negotiation.[5] The workers' delegation was headed by Clovis Andrieu, the leader of Syndicat des Metallurgistes, ex-leader of Syndicat des Charpentiers en Fer (steelworkers) of the Seine before the war, a revolutionary who belonged to the anti-militarist minority and the charismatic leader of the Loire unions in 1917–18.[6] During final discussions which preceded the signing of the agreement, the employer and worker delegations were kept apart from the state's representatives. The principles of tripartite discussion were not yet accepted; the representative of the state in the Loire was only there to facilitate negotiations. Formally speaking, this was a contract between two parties: the legal formula governing collective contracts that had been adopted by the Chamber of Deputies in 1913 and was voted by the Senate in 1919.

The written agreement, which was signed by worker and employer delegations in June 1917, and which was made known to the waged workforce when official notices were posted in the war factories, constructed categories linked to the organisation of production. Those who were not paid by piecework were qualified as 'skilled workers' (*professionnels*); for the others, the minimum or basic wage was linked to the total value of collective production, to which a bonus was added; the bonus could never be less than 10 per cent of basic salary (or 20 per cent in the engineering industries). For workers with high output, wages could exceed those in the skilled category. As for the female workers – none of whom was classified as skilled – 'for the same work performed in the same conditions by men and by women, the piecework rate cannot be less than that paid to men'. In 1917, unlike in 1936, there was not yet a formal distinction between men and women for piecework – the women workers in 'male trades' being indispensable in wartime – although the work stations were kept separate in the workshops.

This apparently egalitarian classification may be interpreted in two ways: first, as the result of the strikes led in the armaments factories by the *munitionnettes* (the name given to these female war workers) and the attempts made by leaders of the metal workers union to organise them by creating female branches in each workshop, second, alternatively, as the result of the constant refusal by trade unionists to accept women's rates in their sector, the demand for equal pay at that time – if it was indeed achieved – did nothing to raise wages for women's 'normal' work, which was habitually underpaid.[7] Both views co-existed within the metalworkers' union on the Loire. In the drafting of the collective contract, the classificatory categories revolved around piecework, and thus job rationalisation, not sex: the conciliation and arbitration committee specified that basic piecework scales should be the same for all, irrespective of age or gender.[8]

According to the order of 24 June 1917 (signed by Albert Thomas), women in the workplace were given voting rights and became eligible to stand as workshop delegates (unlike foreign and 'colonial' workers who were also present in great numbers in the same factories). Hence one form of citizenship, the right to vote, was introduced into the workplace at a time when political citizenship was denied to French women – and was suspended for everyone during the war. The state representative on the conciliation and arbitration committee (i.e. the military controller) declared himself in favour of incorporating traditional bonuses (adjusted by seniority, work effort, family size) in the basic salary, overriding the views of Etienne Mimard, who wanted to abolish such payments. By late 1917, Minister Loucheur of the new Clemenceau government had abandoned the joint committees and unilaterally created cost-of-living bonuses, which were revalued during 1918 as prices continued to rise. In April 1918, faced with the government's decision to call up the oldest mobilised servicemen from the war factories, the Syndicat des Métaux de la Loire requested the enforcement of the principle 'equal pay for equal work' for the new young employees.[9] As was the case for women in 1917, the union's concern here was that wages would be cut by the introduction of underpaid minors (under age 18) to replace conscripts being called to the front. At the end of the war, with demobilisation, the laws governing the munitions factories were suspended.

The Senate passed the law of 25 March 1919, defining 'the collective working agreement' as: 'a contract on work conditions, concluded between representatives of a syndicate, or any other organisation of employers contracting for their members, or even of a single employer, commitment undertaken by each of the parties towards the other party'. The text of the agreement had to be filed at the record office of the Conseil des Prud'hommes (industrial tribunal) or at the registry of the local court of justice. Thus, it was the terms of 'the trade' that prevailed here, i.e. that of the contract made between two parties before the trade's representatives, a commitment restricted to those who accepted it.[10] It was also the logic of a liberal economy: once the law was passed by the legislature, the state stepped back. The flourishing of collective agreements in 1919, a result of the social movements of 1917–20, was short-lived: their number progressively decreased and became negligible after 1930.[11] In the Loire, except during 1920 when seventeen agreements were signed, these were very few. There was none in the Saint-Etienne metallurgical industry before 1936: the CGTU majority in the Syndicat des Métaux de la Loire established a tradition of conflict that lasted until 1935 with the victorious strike of the Forges et Aciéries de la Marine (Iron and Steel Works of the Navy) in St Chamond.[12] This militant culture was exemplified by the strikes of 1919, 1920 and especially that of the metallurgical industry of 1924.[13] There were no collective agreements in the Saint-Etienne mines, in contrast to practices observed in the collieries of northern France: in 1933, 51 per cent of the northern colliery companies had signed agreements, a phenomenon that was linked in part to the practice of electing safety delegates for the mines following the law of 28 June 1894,[14] and also to the campaigns of Abbé Lemire, député du Nord and a promoter of workers' gardens, who favoured collective contracts as a means to promote harmony and social peace. This concern was echoed *a contrario* in the debate that took place in the CGT after the first world war: contractual agreement or revolution? This debate was especially heated in the Saint-Etienne area, the 'small homeland' of revolutionary trade unionism.[15]

The economic depression hit the Loire early, where the exporting industries – such as ribbon manufacturing,[16] arms and cycles – experienced a drop in exports and in production, and also a market transformation as early as 1927. In addition to national union policies and strikes to secure national or even international goals, the depression explains why the CGTU's activities were no longer concentrated solely within firms but also outside them, in the organisation of unemployment committees, anti-expulsion committees and hunger marches, under the direction of the Secrétaire de Metaux, Marcel Thibaud. In 1929, in the Prud'hommes elections for the metallurgical industry, the CGTU won 47 per cent of the vote, the CFTC 28 per cent and the CGT 25 per cent.[17] With the advent of economic recovery, especially from early 1935 in the air force and naval armaments industries, and with the prospect of reunification with the CGT, the CGTU again experienced active militancy within companies in these sectors, as illustrated by the symbolic strike of the *Aciéries de la Marine* in St Chamond at the end of 1935.[18] An indirect result of this strike was the election of a proto-Popular Front municipal council in Saint-Etienne – close to St Chamond – in 1935, thanks to closer ties between the CGT and the CGTU: between communists and socialists, on the one hand, and the Catholic labour movement, on the other.

1936: THE GENDER OF AGREEMENTS.
THE EXAMPLE OF THE SAINT-ETIENNE
METALLURGICAL INDUSTRY

The movement of strikes and sit-ins came belatedly to Saint-Etienne – Antoine Prost has noted the same thing in other regions – starting after the Matignon accord of 7 June 1936: strikes broke out on 8 June in the mining and construction industries, and on 9 June in the metallurgical industry of the Gier and Ondaine valleys, close to Saint-Etienne. On 12 June the Saint-Etienne metallurgical industry was hit. The first meeting between the unions and the employers' federation took place on 17 June at the prefecture, and about thirty meetings were necessary before an agreement could be reached.[19] The agreement of the Parisian metallurgical industry of 24 June 1936 may have served, if not as a model, at least as a reference point for regional agreements; in July 1936, l'Union des Métaux published an 'agreement standard' of twenty-five articles. First, the point was to define the minimum wage in the six main categories, which were themselves divided into two branches, the iron industry, on the one hand, and the cycle and light engineering industries, on the other: 'specialist (skilled) workers, manufacturing trades, tool and precision trades, then unskilled or specialist female workers, young boys and young girls'. At the end of July 1936, the situation had reached an impasse; there was a wide gap between the workers' delegation and the employers' delegation, which was under strict orders from its constituent members.

After separate interviews with both sides, the Prefect broke the deadlock by making counterproposals, which the workers' unions accepted for the women, the young men and the young girls, but which they turned down for the male specialist and trade workers, the only categories for which the union was fighting. As the employers' federation kept refusing to yield to pressure, the unions appealed to the Ministre du Travail to secure an agreement, signed on 12 September, to be enforced immediately in all factories.[20] It was followed by numerous other meetings, which led to a classification of trades and an official scale of qualifications. While in 1936 the state of the market was very different from one product to another (cycle sales were rising, while arms sales dropped by a third), arms and cycles were classified in the same category, establishing the significance of 'the trade' whose ideal type was the skilled worker working independently. No female workers were classified as skilled. For two categories of female workers, however, the arms engravers and the cycle spinners, whose salaries before the agreement were actually 'superior to the highest category in the collective contract, it is not possible to settle within the said contract the position of female workers exercising this function'. This means that in 1936 there was no statutory recognition of qualification for women, even when such qualification was recognised *de facto* in terms of salary before the signing of the collective agreement.[21] An immediate consequence of this was, in accordance with the collective agreements, a decrease in salary for the cycle spinners, for instance, who were classified as 'standard decorators'. For other categories, such as white-collar workers, technicians and supervisors in the metallurgical industry, there was no gender distinction in the classificatory categories, but there was a wage difference between men and women performing this work. Here, then, equal work meant unequal pay and gender distinctions in appointments. In addition, when an employee position was assigned to a woman, output was always specified (a hundred words a minute for an invoice shorthand typist, forty words a minute for a regular typist).

There was thus consensus between the state representative and both sides of industry to formalise a gendered division of labour and the institutionalisation of a masculine working class, parallel to rationalisation. The drafting of collective agreements in the metallurgical industry in 1936 contributed to the definition of categories which institutionalised age and gender divisions within waged work, while arbitrarily assigning qualifications. Paradoxically, the definition of those categories may have, as in the Aciéries de Saint-Etienne, contributed to the restructuring of factory production by clarifying the actual positions held by workers so as to be able to classify them, stimulating the renovation and rationalisation of production,[22] a process in which the worker delegates were involved, willingly or not.

A LARGE COMPANY: MULTIPLE WORLDS OF PRODUCTION. FROM AGREEMENT TO CONFLICT

The Manufacture des Armes et Cycles de Saint-Etienne (MFAC) was affected by the metallurgy agreement, but the situation was complex because this company of 1,800 salaried workers combined several worlds of production. It manufactured arms and cycles and was thus linked to strong trade practices with a union dominated by the CGTU, as well as to a job market peculiar to the Saint-Etienne area, characterised by a workforce which moved between the various companies and between small crafts and big industry. The MFAC was also a mail-order company which marketed throughout the world, especially in the colonies, not only the products it manufactured but also numerous other items – such as sewing machines or typewriters – which were bought elsewhere but labelled and packaged in Saint-Etienne. Hence the company employed many male and female office and store workers; the female workforce was superior in number and had few union members (except a small minority at the CFTC). The unity of the company was assured by a highly centralised chain of command and a bureaucratised hierarchy.

In the negotiation of agreements, the management distinguished not only workers, clerical staff, technicians and the metallurgical supervising staff, but also within the category of clerical workers itself, between shop workers, who were sales people, and office employees, who reported to the central administration. This division between the productive, commercial and administrative sectors was not unprecedented. During the discussion of the enforcement of laws on social insurance and family benefits, Etienne Mimard had succeeded, thanks partly to his political connections, in having his various workshops and services considered distinct establishments, each of which was only gradually subjected to these laws, while the MFAC was classified as a single commercial establishment for fiscal purposes, a status that was more advantageous in terms of taxation. Whereas the more militant metalworkers obtained social insurance and family allowances in October 1933, the office personnel did not obtain the same rights until 1936. An identical managerial tactic, which aimed at division, stalling and buying time, was applied to the implementation of the Popular Front government laws and the drafting of collective agreements. The drop in business that followed the economic depression of the 1930s, the determination to lower costs by cutting wages and the refusal to allow state legislative interference explain Etienne Mimard's uncompromising attitude during negotiations on the various agreements. As a matter of fact, the company combined several trades: the metallurgical trades, which manufactured the arms and cycles that made the company's and the city's reputation, the printing trades (through the printing of the famous *Tarif Album*, the catalogue that was circulated worldwide, and the *Chasseur Français* magazine, as well as the countless leaflets and order forms typical of a centralised, hierarchical company), and, in fewer numbers, the woodworking and furniture trades, which manufactured both engravings for the catalogue illustrations and boxes for packaging. Each sector of the factory then came under the jurisdiction of a specific trade agreement which, whether it was negotiated at the local or national level, was always adapted to the company.

Aside from the metalworkers, the first agreement was a trade-wide collective contract, signed on 13 November 1936, between the Confédération Générale de l'Ameublement en France (the French furniture confederation) and the CGT's Confédération Générale des Travailleurs du Bois (wood-workers confederation). The MFAC was represented in the negotiations by the management of its Paris commercial subsidiary, a distributor of products manufactured or marketed by the MFAC. Stormy discussions lasted four months, and the final draft reflected a compromise, although it was heavily loaded with trade practices linked to direct action: Articles 8 and 9 can be interpreted as permitting each member of the workforce to submit his or her *réclamation* (claim or request) – and not his or her *revendication* (demand), a term rejected by businessman Etienne Mimard – without referring to the delegates, who could be dismissed at any time. Hiring was associated at the same time with public placement offices, union placement offices and direct hiring; apprenticeship was regulated and progressive; arbitration was effected within the trade, without state interference, by the unions' and employers' federations; and the worker provided his own tools. The compromise was reflected in the mode of payment: hourly rates remained unaffected; for payment by piecework, a secret vote was to take place at a later date in order to determine whether it was acceptable or not, and the employers' delegation pledged to examine the possibility of eliminating it. Unlike the metallurgical sector, work rationalisation was not accepted; traditional trade practices prevailed. This agreement, negotiated with the CGT, was also signed by the CFTC on 20 November 1936, but Article 3 specified that, while union rights were granted, workers pledged not to engage in harassment of non-unionised personnel, which reveals the state of mind prevailing in the trade.

The collective work agreement that was signed on 17 September 1936 between the master-printers' federation and the CGT's Fédération des Travailleurs du Livre (print unions) was extended in May 1937 to the whole of France. More than any other, it strictly regulated weekly work schedules (Saturdays being potentially free, as well as Mondays, a vestige of the traditional 'Saint Monday'). Any hours between 7 p.m. and 7 a.m. were considered night work and paid at overtime rates; salaries were indexed according to the cost of living; apprenticeship was regulated, to define the ratio of apprentices to workers, in order to contain competition. Here we are dealing with something that closely resembles a statute. The procedures for elections of delegates, unlike other agreements, were listed as appendices, a sign of the union's mistrust of this new institution, which also indicates how far back in time collective contracts go in the printing industry (the end of the nineteenth century).

Conflict broke out in the company in December 1936, after the employers decided to implement the forty-hour work week law in the metallurgical sector. Etienne Mimard did not want to extend it to the office and store employees. After a brief one-day factory sit-in, when the personnel revived the united action in workshops and stores that had not occurred since 1920, Etienne Mimard gave in, but then in retaliation refused to add to the new minimum wages the bonuses and commissions formerly paid to the employees; and while implementing the two-week paid vacation, he eliminated the special days off he had granted previously. Furthermore, he was to fight every inch of the way for a year, from December 1936 to December 1937, to establish a separate agreement for the sales personnel of the MFAC. To the latter, he wanted to apply the collective agreement for Saint-Etienne's retail trade, which was signed on 25 June 1937, and which was considerably less advantageous than the metalworkers' agreement passed on 10 March 1937. According to the latter agreement, pay was to be adjusted according to the formal qualifications and age of each worker (between ages of fourteen and twenty-two, which was a recognition of a kind of apprentice-ship), to gender, as well as – a novel feature of the Loire agreement as compared to the Parisian one – to seniority in the company and in the job, which rewarded faithful employees. This reveals the intertwining of several training patterns: those traditional to the trade, through apprenticeship and seniority, and that of training by the state, as indicated by diplomas – from the CAP (vocational training certificate) to secondary studies in technical schools; pay could be doubled accordingly.

Distinctions were also drawn among supervising staff: team heads, foremen and workshop heads, the hierarchy being defined according to the number of workers involved and the nature of the responsibility; the workshop head might supervise a hundred workers and could initiate improvements in production. The collective agreement for Saint-Etienne's trade, which Mimard wanted to apply to his sales personnel and which was the source of the long conflict, was negotiated with the CGT and the CFTC but actually left the unions little room. Hiring was conducted directly by the employer; pay was monthly or hourly; and minimum salaries included all commissions. In order to implement it in his company, Mimard wanted to eliminate the sliding scale for salaries, the seniority premium and, for young people, the protection of their jobs until the return from military service; he also wanted to insert an additional article over and above those guaranteeing union rights and freedom of opinion, 'that is the laws protecting property and the freedom to work', including a reference to 'fair play'.

Company archives include the various drafts of the agreements, annotated in Etienne Mimard's writing; through what is crossed out and reworded, managerial thought in action can be discerned. Certain terms were banned, such as *'syndicat'* (union) and *'revendications'* (demands), which he replaced with *'délégués du personnel'* (personnel delegates) and *'réclamations'* (requests). Altering the model of the Paris agreement, he systematically substituted the term *'ancienneté'* (seniority), which implied bonus payments, with *'collabo-ration ininterrompue'* (uninterrupted service). Etienne Mimard refused to comply with the various arbitration rulings; an arbitration award of July 1937, which was unfavourable to the employees, stated that out of 717 office and store employees, 675 came under the jurisdiction of the retail trade agreement and 45 under that of the metallurgical trade contract [*sic*]. The company was then occupied by the workers on 1 August 1937, that is, at the beginning of the hunting season, which was catastrophic for arms and ammunition sales; the strike lasted until 11 November 1937, hence its nick-name, the 'hundred-day' strike. All personnel were laid off, the company was evacuated by force, and court action was taken. The waged workforce was cut by about a third, not only to get rid of strike activists, but also to re-establish a balance between the company's turnover (sales of weapons for hunting dropped by a third between 1930 and 1937) and the overhead costs, which had been raised by the more generous wages granted after the

Matignon accord and by the implementation of the subsequent agreements, in the context of a business slump.

In November 1937, Mimard declared:

> before the 1936 strike we had two general sets of regulations in practice in our establishment, one for our white-collar workers and one for our workshops. Today we have as many collective contracts as sales operations, as many collective contracts as we have worker categories, a contract each for white-collar workers, for technicians and for supervising staff in the metallurgical industry, and a retail contract. What a wonderful mess![23]

From regulations to collective contracts, the evolution of the terms underscores the retreat of absolute executive authority in the company, and also its resistance. This appraisal has not taken into account the strategy of dividing interests and the delayed implementation of the 1936 laws, and it obliterates the fact that the agreements contributed to the process of defining groups and categories, thereby institutionalising the gender and age divisions and endorsing, with few exceptions, the rationalisation process, which had begun in the company in 1921 with the introduction of piecework. It also underscores, however, the complexity and the heterogeneity of the jobs actually performed and formalised in just one company, and the constraints preventing all work and administrative processes being rendered uniform.

IMPLEMENTING THE AGREEMENTS (1937–1939): CONCILIATION AND ARBITRATION

The law of 31 December 1936 on mandatory conciliation and arbitration was passed after the interruption of talks with the Confédération Générale du Patronat Français (CGPF: General Federation of French Management). The unions had supported the establishment of agreements and the recourse to arbitration in view of managerial defiance, and also to achieve a peaceful solution to the conflicts, which had multiplied in the autumn of 1936, and to bring an end to continuing unrest. For the CGT in 1937 this was a 'temporary pause'. Beyond these national and general explanations, peace was promoted through the regular practice of conciliation and arbitration during the long bi-monthly meetings of manager and worker delegates at the Prefecture of the Loire, with repeated appeals to 'a spirit of goodwill' by the labour inspector who presided over these meetings in the name of the Prefect, and through the common language the participants eventually agreed upon – a reasonable rhetoric that prohibited abuse. All these factors help to explain why, on 28 February 1938, the head of the managers' delegation, who had also negotiated the metallurgical agreement in 1936 (and had then spoken of an unbridgeable gulf between the two sides), observed 'an atmosphere of collaboration and harmony'.[24]

Solutions were found through joint work: for instance, the CGT agreed to the dismissal of a female union delegate in a cycle company who constantly questioned the foreman's authority; in return, the head of the managers' delegation promised to hire her in another company belonging to the cycle employers' federation.[25] The practice of placing workers in another company in cases of conflict was used several times: it allowed the manager to save face and honour while preserving employment for the worker. This agreement between union and management leaders even led, in May 1938, to a tactical alliance between the managers' delegation and the CGT representatives to exclude the CFTC from representation in a hat factory of Chazelles/Lyon: 'unquestionably, the CGT is the only representative organisation', in the words of the head of the management delegation.[26] This decision was legitimised by the committee on the basis of legal judgment: 'since the matter is a modification of the existing agreement, those organisations that took part in the first discussion should be the ones to renegotiate', this allowed for the exclusion of the CFTC, which had not signed the initial agreement (the CGT counted 1,100 votes and the CFTC 500).

This climate of agreement was not always upheld by constituents: in December 1936, a bank director resigned from the managers' union because it supported the signing of a national agreement. The Chambre Syndicale des Tissus Elastiques (Federation of Elastic Fabrics) disowned its president, who had signed an agreement, and replaced him.[27]

The arbitration commission had been involved in the negotiations on collective agreements – for instance, on 4 June 1937, the classification of trades in the clothing industry, or, on 23 July, the definition of the price lists of velvet and elastic ribbons manufactured outside Saint-Etienne. It also became involved in conflicts: in the case of layoffs in salting factories, a novel solution was put forth by the secretary of the Syndicat des Métaux (to rotate teams on two-week shifts, to avoid unemployment for some). In a ruling dated 17 March 1937, which aimed to suspend a strike at the Saint-Etienne collieries, the committee eventually sided with the striking miners because of the director's authoritarianism, a decision unanimously approved by those present. This collaboration and compromise between union and management representatives lasted until the law was modified on 4 March 1938. In July 1938 the committee was divided into three sections: workers (with four CGT and one CFTC delegates), engineers, and collaborators (three CGT, three CFTC, and three independent delegates). The role of the plenary committee was then restricted to registering and signing a report of recourse to arbitration; sessions were shorter and seemed to have been more formal. A traditional logic resurfaced: instead of the conciliation and arbitration procedure, the Conseil des Prud'hommes was used.[28] After the general strike of November 1938, disagreement clearly set in and took the form of a legal battle; in the arguments exchanged, the union representatives appropriated a legal argument based on operational categories; the managers' representative stated that the metallurgical agreement was illegal because it was signed by the unions' central organisation and not by the individual unions themselves. The unions' representative retorted by rejecting the definition, for one day's strike did not mean that the work contract had been broken (legally, this required two consecutive days). In 1939 the national and international political agenda weighed more than local issues for both sides. Later, local debate was to take place in a different framework and the Vichy regime used other agents to achieve agreement.[29]

CONCLUSION

State intervention in industrial relations could only be achieved, in the first place, thanks to exceptional circumstances, such as war and *union sacrée*. It was not until 1936, with the Popular Front government and the accompanying social movements, that the agreement procedure gradually took root, although not without difficulties and backtracking. At the local level, some managers could barely tolerate state intrusion in the industrial relations of their companies, and they devised strategies for bypassing or resisting it. The representatives of employers' and unions' federations of each *département*, convened under the aegis of the Prefect and the labour inspectorate, found territory for agreement in 1936–8. Union action, however, was driven forward by another model – that of the skilled metal worker – whereas the unions, especially the CGT, which was the privileged negotiating partner for the authorities, portrayed themselves as representative of the whole working-class population. Within this process of negotiation and contractual agreement, the unions thus contributed, in the process of rationalisation, to formalising and institutionalising the sexual division of labour.

(Translated by L. Parrott and F. Brunet)

NOTES

1 Archives Manufrance [AM], MFAC, dossier conventions collectives [collective agreements' file] 1917–37.
2 C. Didry and R. Salais, 'Troubles sur les produits d'Etat et écriture des conventions collectives de travail', in A. Jacob and H. Verin (eds), *L'inscription sociale du marché*, L'Harmattan, Paris, 1995; R. Salais and M. Storper, *Les mondes de production. Enquête sur l'identité économique de la France*, EHESS, Paris, 1993.
3 D. Colson, 'Bourse du Travail et syndicalisme d'entreprise avant 1914: les Aciéries de Saint-Etienne', *Le mouvement social*, vol. 159, pp. 73–4.

4 A. Engel, *L'arbitrage et la conciliation en matière de conflits collectifs entre patrons et ouvriers: la réforme de la loi du 27 XII 1892*, Giard & Brière, Paris, 1908.

5 AM, MFAC, dossier Guerre [war file] 1914–18, commission mixte [joint committee] 1917–18.

6 Biography of Clovis Andrieu, *Dictionnaire Maitron*. A general strike broke out in December 1917 in the area when Clémenceau ordered the call-up of Andrieu to the front, because of his union activities. The strike was successful, and Andrieu remained the head of the Syndicat des Métaux of the Loire until 25 May 1918, the date of his arrest along with about fifty other militants.

7 L. Auslander, and M. Zancarini-Fournel (eds), *Différences des sexes et protection sociale*, PUV, Paris, 1995 esp. the essay by Ava Baron.

8 13 August 1917, MFAC, dossier commission mixte [joint committee file].

9 Letter of 26 April 1918: military inspector to Etienne Mimard, MFAC, dossier commission mixte [joint committee file].

10 Pierre Laroque, in *Les conventions de travail*, Imprimerie nationale, Paris, 1934, emphasises the difference from German jurisprudence that was in effect in Alsace, where a union signature meant a commitment to 'work peace'.

11 Pierre Laroque, 'Tableau de l'évolution du nombre des conventions de 1919 à 1933', ibid., p. 73.

12 See Didry and Salais, 'Troubles sur les produits d'Etat'. We should emphasise the important role played in the strike and the negotiation by the local CFTC, which was influential and very combative.

13 AM, MFAC, dossier grèves [strike file], 56-page report: 'Grève de la métallurgie à Saint-Etienne', March–April 1924.

14 P. Laroque, *Les rapports entre patrons et ouvriers*, Editions Montaigne, Paris, 1938.

15 Henri Barreau, *Histoire inachevée de la convention collective de la métallurgie*, Editions de la Fédération des travailleurs de la métallurgie CGT, Paris, 1976; for the 1919 theory debate in the CGT, see p. 41. For the Saint-Etienne area, see D. Colson, *Anarcho-syndicalisme et communisme*, Centre d'Etudes foréziennes, Saint-Etienne, 1986.

16 B. Reynaud, *L'industrie rubanière dans la région stéphanoise*, Centre d'Etudes foréziennes, Saint-Etienne, 1991, pp. 215–20.

17 Héritier, Bonnevialle, Ion, Saint-Sernin, *150 ans de luttes ouvrières dans le bassin stéphanois*, Ed. Le champ du possible, Saint-Etienne, 1979, p. 170.

18 Ibid., p. 186: the strike was monitored by national union officials, Croizat and Timbaud for the CGTU, Pérez for the CFTC. At the delegate elections on 12 June 1936, the reunited CGT received 2,010 votes and the CFTC 518.

19 Archives Départementales de la Loire, M Sup 922, office of the Prefect.

20 Pamphlet: *Contrat collectif de travail entre l'Association des syndicats métallurgistes patronaux de la Loire et les Ouvriers sur Métaux représentés par les Syndicats Ouvriers des Métaux de la région de Saint-Etienne, adhérants à la CGT*, 1936.

21 After a spinners' strike in 1935, the cycle industry employers hired women *en masse*, which resulted in a downward pressure on salaries; this explains why neither bosses nor unions fought for the classification of women as skilled J.P. Burdy, M. Dubesset, and M. Zancarini-Fournel, 'Rôles, travaux et métiers de femmes dans une ville industrielle Saint-Etienne 1900–1950', *Mouvement Social*, vol. 140, July–September 1987.

22 D. Colson, 'Grille de qualification et émergence du social dans l'entreprise: les Aciéries de Saint-Etienne et les accords de 1936', in Yves Cohen (ed.), *Les chantiers de la paix sociale*, Presses de l'ENS, Saint-Cloud-Fontenay, 1995.

23 AM, MFAC, dossier grève de 1937 [1937 strike file], assessment by Etienne Mimard.

24 Archives Départementales de la Loire, M Sup 899: n.b. This appraisal was made when the workers' delegation agreed to congratulate the head of the employers' delegation for the award of Legion of Honour that he had just received!

25 Archives Départementales de la Loire, 29 November 1937. Agreement was doubtless facilitated by the fact that it involved a female delegate and that the competition for employment in the cycle industry was fierce, due to the depressed state of the market.

26 Ibid., committee meeting, 24 May 1938.

27 Ibid., 30 December 1937.

28 Ibid., 25 July 1938.

29 Jean-Pierre Le Crom, *Syndicats nous voilà! Vichy et le corporatisme*, Editions de l'Atelier, Paris, 1995.

10

FRANCE AND UNEMPLOYMENT INSURANCE FROM 1920 TO 1958

The myth of social security

Philippe-Jean Hesse

When the notion of unemployment was invented at the turn of the century,[1] there was no legal definition of the term.[2] Supporters of compulsory insurance existed in France[3] but they could not make their voice heard, as Léon Bourgeois noted in 1910 at the conference in Paris on unemployment: 'We regret seeing so many ideas 'conceived in France' bear more fruit abroad than in France itself.'[4] If this initial hesitation is understandable, the persistent inertia is surprising. Certainly France was less affected by unemployment than its neighbours. Cahen-Bernard noted that France suffered infinitely less from unemployment than England or Germany; for the interwar period, E. Weber emphasises: 'The economic crisis hit Great Britain and Germany like a blizzard; in France it was experienced rather as an irritating shower.'[5] In 1935 unemployment was three times worse in England and four times worse in Germany, not only because of differences in statistical measurement.[6] Likewise, the period of reconstruction that followed the Liberation was marked by labour shortages, not unemployment – reflected in appeals to the public by the tripartite government and, in particular, the Communist Party and the Confédération Générale du Travail (CGT).[7]

Even so, it is astonishing that the question of unemployment relief remained unsettled at the turn of the century, when public assistance was reorganised.[8] Not until 1945 was a comprehensive plan for social security adopted, as advocated in the programme of the Conseil National de la Résistance: 'A complete plan of social security to ensure for all citizens the means of subsistence in all eventualities where they are incapable of procuring this for themselves by work.' The first article of the programme states: 'There is to be established a social security scheme aimed at protecting workers and their families against any reduction or loss of their capacity to earn.'[9]

There had certainly been a great demand for a comprehensive welfare state, but governments had responded without any marked enthusiasm. It is therefore necessary to enquire into this lack of action under the Third and Fourth Republics. Two answers are possible: the first is suggested by a remark of Garraty about England: '[they were] more interested in increasing the rate of unemployment benefits than in increasing employment'.[10] Would not France, on the contrary, seek to boost employment rather than simply to give help to the unemployed? But unable to ignore poverty entirely, the treatment of unemployment under public assistance programmes still implied that many of the victims were responsible for their misfortune: 'Unemployment was for long the worst misfortune for the worker; it meant poverty and humiliation: poverty because he [*sic*] had no money and humiliation, since it was his fault, due to his lack of initiative and his laziness.'[11]

ERADICATING UNEMPLOYMENT: A MAJOR PRIORITY?

According to the experts, unemployment could not arise in a country suffering a demographic deficiency: low birth rate and large numbers killed in two world wars. The fault lay in economic organisation, and it was there the government should apply a remedy. The measures should be quantitative, to lower the demand for or increase the supply of work, and qualitative – to adapt one to the other.[12]

Limiting the demand for work

Three approaches were tried: lowering the number of applicants for jobs; limiting the span of an active working life, and reducing working hours. The priorities chosen were as much for political and ideological reasons as for economic ones.

As foreigners were recruited when manual labour was required,[13] so they were excluded when unemployment rose. The law of 10 August 1932, finalised in 1935, gave a general preference to native manual labour; other laws protected the higher professions, doctors or lawyers.[14] Foreign workers were encouraged to return to their country of origin. In 1931–3, more than 500,000 people were repatriated through the offices of the Service de la Main d'Oeuvre Etrangère, which pursued the unemployed and also ousted foreign workers from positions which could be restored to French nationals. Temporarily restrained by the Popular Front, the movement recommenced later in an even more xenophobic and anti-Semitic atmosphere.[15]

Women formed the other target category. The Church, the bourgeoisie and also the revolutionary unions had always looked askance at a woman who left the home to work in a factory: she was a perfidious competitor who lowered wages, a destabilising influence due to her feminine charms, and better adapted to the domestic than the industrial scene. The exclusion of women, already proposed by the unions at the beginning of the crisis, was introduced in 1940 and helped reduce the figures from 1,100,000 unemployed in 1940 to 88,000 in 1942. The law of 11 October 1940 established measures in the public sector to make married women and those over fifty years of age redundant, to prevent the appointment of female assistants, and to limit their promotion. The law for the private sector was not passed but the Préfets asked businessmen to put equivalent discriminatory practices into effect. Unsatisfied demands from women for employment grew as a result.[16] Visible unemployment became female; it is necessary to add the hidden unemployment of women who did not seek work. Under the rules of l'Etat Français (travail, famille, patrie) they had a right to a family but not to work.

Efforts to reduce the working lifespan never progressed much beyond the proposal stage. The law on old-age benefits had fixed retirement age at seventy in 1905, that on workers' pensions (1910) had reduced it to sixty-five, with possibilities of retirement at sixty in legislation of 1912, 1928 and 1930.[17] Some plans, such as that of Pétrus Faure on the eve of the war, were proposed to open up work opportunities for young people, and advocated a retirement age of fifty-five for unemployed people, financed on a co-operative basis. Without going so far, the regime of Marshal Pétain tended to put retirement of salaried staff at sixty within the limits of the Allocation aux Vieux Travailleurs Salariés. This was in line with a proposal for social insurance presented by the Ministre du Travail, Réne Belin, from October 1940.[18] The other temptation was to raise the school-leaving age, thereby also raising educational standards. This option, advocated by the CGT in 1931 and by the Paris Chamber of Commerce in 1935, resulted in the raising of the school-leaving age to fourteen. There were also indirect measures taken by Vichy through youth work schemes, Chantiers de Jeunesse, the Centres de Jeunes Travailleurs et Travailleuses and the Centres d'Assistance par le Travail, for youths from fourteen to twenty years of age who had finished their studies but not found employment.[19]

The reduction of working hours has always been an objective of workers, to raise the quality of life. Successive laws imposed a six-day working week, then the eight-hour working day. The reformist CGT, after splitting from the CGT Unitaire, included the forty-hour week and paid holidays in its programme: the employers pleaded the impossibility of such measures. Strikes and factory occupations forced them to bend to shop-floor pressure, which was supported by the newly elected government (1936). The statutory forty-hour week and fifteen days paid holiday had an important psychological impact; the effects on the workplace were more limited. According to Paul Reynaud, the forty-hour week would ruin the positive effects of the devaluation of September 1936:

working hours fell from an average of 46 hours in October 1936 to 39.9 hours in May 1937 and 38.7 hours in March 1938 . . . the recruitment of the unemployed was due to make up the difference. A false hope. Total activity (in man hours) fell from 71.6 in October 1936, to 64.9 in June 1937 . . . In October 1938 the number of unemployed on assistance was only 26,000 less than in 1935 and 25,000 men had been taken on by the public, civil and military services.[20]

The government on the eve of the war did everything to increase working hours to what they became with the general adoption of overtime after the war, a system organised by law in February 1946.[21] The overall effect of the policy in reducing the demand for work was feeble; implementation of a later school-leaving age and earlier retirement was limited, as the exclusion of women and foreigners was late – and their effects were barely exceeded by the reductions in working hours. In reducing annual working hours from 2,496 to 2,000, 25 per cent more employees should have been taken on to maintain the same output. According to Reynaud's calculations, the impact was an increase of only 10 per cent.

Increasing the work supply

Whether spontaneous mechanisms or deflationary measures were preferred, the direct reduction in the cost of work – salaries and indirect social charges – had at the time strong supporters in the economic as much as in the political field. J. Rueff, a prominent liberal intellectual, argued in his article in the *Revue d'économie politique* (1931) that all workers were assured of finding salaried employment determined by the market; there could not be permanent unemployment unless the minimum wage was frozen above the point at which it would settle spontaneously. French governments – of Laval and Flandin – moved towards policies of this sort for ideological reasons and to support the currency, which remained a fundamental objective. Once contract prices – and among them officials' salaries – and expenses were restrained, a snowball effect was expected on private-sector prices and so a general recovery would begin.

The same shift in economic conceptions appeared in the choices made to increase the demand for goods, priority being given to external factors. Everyone demanded an increase in customs tariffs, then the fixing of import quotas for foreign products.[22] Unions and businesses also led a campaign against imported goods, appealing to growing nationalism. The Paris Chamber of Commerce favoured invisible earnings, in particular tourism, whilst the government tried to relaunch the export of luxury goods by abolishing the special tax of 12 per cent in 1934.

Consensus was less evident over promoting economic recovery by major public works, following Roosevelt's New Deal, advocated by the liberals and the English Labour party. To the ignorance of multiplier theory was added the poor reputation of the national workshops of 1848 and the desire to maintain budgetary equilibrium. Local initiatives remained timid. In Bordeaux in 1921 some jobs were created for roadsweepers; between 1926 and 1927 the mayor outlined more important projects and asked the state for help. In the 1930s demands became more pressing and *La Petite Gironde* approved the plan adopted by the government in 1934, but which was soon perceived to be a drop in the ocean.[23]

The CGT, within the general Popular Front campaign, now relaunched the claim that the latest events had pushed back into second place, despite the 20 milliards of civil works programmed by the law of 20 August 1936 and directed towards rearmament.[24] The few large workshops answered poorly to the needs of a workforce deprived of instruction and badly disciplined. This was why some advocated more re-educative programmes. Yvonne Becquet, foreshadowing the work camps adopted by Vichy, proposed that:

> Special work camps should be established where unemployed workers will be enrolled. In these camps great works of afforestation, drainage of marshy ground, and the construction of dykes to reclaim land will be carried out . . . the workers employed there will be fed, lodged and clothed and can even earn a small wage. Great emphasis must be placed on physical fitness, cultural and professional improvement, and common recreation.[25]

The idea that technical progress caused unemployment and could be combated by returning to a pre-industrial economy is a permanent feature of French ideology. It supported initiatives to return to the land, since unemployment seemed an urban phenomenon. In the 1930s, sending the unemployed back to the land[26] was popular; it was decided to give those who chose to return to rural areas transport coupons, an allowance for six months and help to find lodgings. The measure adopted in 1935 achieved, within four years, the removal of thirty-nine unemployed workers from the Paris area. Despite this, the French state made this one of the cornerstones of its social and economic policy.

The other aspect of this fear of technology consisted of proposals to block modernisation: the creation of a tax upon inventions, the adoption of a fiscal policy which penalised the rapid processing of material, the institution of a fund which bought inventions but did not divulge their secret except for the purposes of production and the possibility of consumption.[27] Such a policy of systematic procrastination might seem suicidal and in industrial matters the government did not follow these lines, but there was no hesitation in attacking other innovations. High-yielding cornfields and vineyards were forbidden in 1931; the development of new modes of distribution was impeded between 1935 and 1936, measures supported by the workers' movements.[28]

Organising the job market

All the above remedies deal with the question in a quantitative fashion – increasing the supply of work or reducing the demand – but it is possible to see things differently. Unemployment is a mirage arising through lack of information and/or unsuitability of qualifications. In his course of lectures, Oualid addressed 'the job market and its organization' and identified three headings: training, job placement, unemployment.[29]

The crisis witnessed the opportunity for relaunching the idea of raising the capacities of manual labour; such moves marked the 1930s, in particular the law of 30 October 1935, providing for rehabilitation centres organised by industrialists, municipalities, educational institutions, employers' and workers' organisations and specialist associations.[30] Bordeaux opened a training centre for unemployed metalworkers between eighteen and thirty years of age; its success was limited because most were over the age limit.[31] In Nantes, where these institutions functioned even before the adoption of this regulation, difficulties were numerous. Of forty admitted to the National Technical College, only six were still enrolled some months later.[32] Apart from its cost, this approach seems limited; there were few job vacancies and the period of instruction gave no guarantees that the number of jobs envisaged would be available when the course finished.

The idea of resolving the problem of unemployment by organising information on job vacancies and worker placement came not only from economic circles, but also from the unions. They advocated systems of travel assistance which permitted the unemployed to go where more jobs were available. In England the Labour Exchanges Act of 1909 had tried to install a national placement system. France, in the same period, was content to struggle with a surplus of private agencies and to encourage initiatives taken by the unions and the municipalities, through the bourses du travail. These organisations confronted a dual problem: first, local initiatives took only a local approach to the job market; second, exchange of information between them was almost neglegible for ideological and financial reasons. Employers', workers' and municipal systems were reluctant to collaborate and lacked personnel as well as equipment – as noted by the controller of unemployment institutions for the northern regions in August 1939.[33] Some progress was made following the ruling of 25 May 1945, article 6, which required all workers seeking employment to register with the departmental service for manual labour. But job placement had to wait for the Agence National de l'Emploi before it assumed a national dimension, through a decree – once more a reform bypassing Parliament – in the summer of 1967. France – a so-called centralised state – took sixty years to organise a national job market. Common measures to eradicate unemployment were thereby considerably delayed, as was the adoption of unemployment insurance.

FINANCIAL AID FOR THE UNEMPLOYED

Didier Renard rightly insists on the central importance of public assistance – in contrast to compulsory social insurance – in the French system of social security. But his focus on retirement and health neglects family allowances and unemployment. The specificity of these areas does not undermine the relevance of his analysis.[34] We will examine three policy areas: charitable and public assistance, voluntary insurance and compulsory insurance – although only the first two were ever adopted for the unemployed.

Private charity and public assistance

Charity may appear outdated for the years 1920–50, but the term has the advantage of covering both private and public provision while drawing attention to the conventional moralising attitudes evoked by the subject of unemployment. The idea that unemployed people are responsible for their difficulties is deep-rooted. Those who wanted to help the unemployed had to eliminate the idle from their proposals.[35] Bertrand Poiret-Delpech remembers: 'at the time unemployed persons and tramps were sometimes described in the same terms'.[36] The Nantais writer Marc Elder, in an unpublished manuscript in 1933, summarised the dominant opinion of the bourgeoisie, emphasising that 'from the moment that society permitted the lame to live, the lame have gobbled up society'. This distrust explains why private charity and public intervention remained limited: assistance had to be selective and of low value.

It is not necessary to dwell on the diversity of religious charities; the tradition led the faithful and the clergy to minister to all in misfortune. The convents distinguished themselves, as did the organisations of St Vincent de Paul, and also the Christian unions connected to youth movements and the mutuelles.[37] The work of the charitable bureaux (bureaux de bienfaisance) should also be mentioned, although it is difficult to discover what assistance they gave to the unemployed.[38] More specifically, voluntary unemployment funds, created by municipalities, were widespread. On 2 August 1914, Puteaux, at the gates of Paris, created the first fund and some days later a circular from the President of the Council set out plans for a national fund for unemployment to give state subsidies to the localities.[39] This temporary fund, which lasted until after the war, divided the money between various organisations, proportionate to their activities. Participation was very variable and took the form of partial reimbursements for sums advanced largely by the municipalities, taking account of administrative delays.[40]

Decrees of 1918 and 1926 tried to standardise the management of departmental and municipal funds, as much in the conditions governing access to this assistance as in the total amounts involved. The 1930s witnessed a new beginning: from 1930 to 1932 funds increased from twenty-six, of which two were departmental, to 1,100. This movement then slowed down; in 1936 there were 1,569 funds, of which seventy were departmental, covering 60 per cent of Frenchmen. Understandably some pressed for standardisation of treatment. In February 1936 Albert Sarraut proposed the creation of regional unemployment funds. Léon Blum considered obliging each locality to create a fund, but abandoned the idea.[41] So the interwar period ended with a mere updating of laws issued since the turn of the century (6 May 1939). However, the state's financial role had grown; from one-fifth to one-quarter, it rose to one-third to one-half, sometimes reaching 90 per cent of funding.[42] Overall, credits multiplied by a factor of 1,600 between 1926 and 1934, the sharp rise before 1932 showing the severity of the problem and the impossibility of resolving it in any other way.[43]

Where they functioned, the funds were accused of drifting aimlessly; humanitarian certainly, but still unacceptable. A report drawn up in August 1939 for the North, the Pas-de-Calais and the Somme clearly explains the reasons for this. Since it was necessary to refer the elderly unemployed to the law on assistance of 1905, and as the latter was of little help to the beneficiaries and costly for the local councils – because assistance for the elderly was not centrally subsidised – an agreement was reached to allow workers over seventy to be classified as unemployed. In some areas they constituted a third of the claimants and were sometimes more than eighty years old. Certainly, the circular from the Minister for Labour of 15 June 1933 made the payment of unemployment benefit to those over seventy conditional on a test of physical and professional aptitude, but doctors were very willing to provide such certificates.[44]

Unemployment certainly did not give any automatic right to assistance; it was necessary to be poor, moral and also lucky. Not only did unemployment have to be involuntary, which eliminated strikers, those dismissed for professional incompetence, and those who refused work offered, but – with rare exceptions – the claimant had to be destitute. The person had to have belonged both to the local area and to his trade for a number of years, and still only had a right to assistance for a limited period.

These rules necessitated multiple controls: in Bordeaux the combined intervention of the Office de Placement, the Division de l'Assistance Publique and the Commissariat Central eliminated half the requests for assistance.[45] Again, having obtained assistance did not mean that all was well, since if subsequent enquiries showed assistance had been wrongly granted the money could be recovered. Although less scientific, criteria employed by charities were also restrictive. Sadoul, disguised as an unemployed worker for his enquiry, came up against public hospices which had 'suspended assistance'. The distribution of soup rations often stopped before all had been satisfied, and night shelters were full more quickly than the home set up by *L'Intransigeant* for dogs abandoned by the unemployed.[46] The recipients of help were hardly advantaged; aid was of short duration while the lack of work tended to become prolonged. Shelters accepted people for three or four nights; financial assistance for the unemployed was only given for between thirty and 120 days per year. Once suspected of not genuinely seeking work, the unemployed worker was considered incapable of managing what was given to him. This often translated into payments in kind rather than cash, and – if possible – as consumable goods under the control of benefactors.[47] All agreed on the distribution of soup to the poorest of the unemployed. As early as 1921, the mayor of Bordeaux decided to 'act quickly to help the genuine poor and to prevent disturbances'. He began food distribution using the municipal provisioning service which allowed bread, beans, potatoes, sardines, herrings and meat to be bought at a reduced cost. Later, free meals were given to school-age children of unemployed workers; non-municipal organisations – restaurateurs and CGT unions – extended this to adults.[48] M. Verret, alluding to the uniformity of contemporary political solutions, summarises it thus: 'Red soup or white soup, nothing but soup in any case.'[49] It was still necessary to offer an act of allegiance by saying a prayer, reciting canticles or presenting a union card.

So assistance, although useful, was insufficient because budgets were so limited. Sardoul remarked bitterly that Paris, in 1932, doubled the soup kitchen budget – from FF46,000 to FF92,000, while the subsidies for the theatres were FF2,000,000 and to the police FF500,000,000. In the same year Saint-Nazaire, a town savaged by unemployment, provided 9,000 free meals and put FF4,000,000 into the unemployment fund[50] and Besançon, not content with giving financial assistance through unemployment funds, used the army to distribute hot meals and construct shelters.[51] In these circumstances, the idea of using insurance to prevent the unemployed from going with 'head bowed and hand held out' – in the expression of deputy Mouret – reappeared in the form of voluntary insurance, subsidised by the state, or as compulsory insurance.

Subsidised voluntary insurance

Subsidies to voluntary unemployment insurance first appeared at the end of the nineteenth century. Central government first decided to support these funds with the finance law of 24 April 1905, later modified by the decree of 6 May 1939. It was hoped that voluntary insurance would expand, but the results did not live up to expectations. Even before central government took any interest, the municipalities supported union initiatives. From 1896 Dijon took responsibility for deficits, while Moulins gave an annual subsidy shared between existing funds, later called the Ghent system when the Belgian town adopted it in 1901. The Conseil Supérieur du Travail, when consulted in 1903, was divided on the question of unemployment between free choice, subsidised voluntary insurance and obligatory insurance; finally it decided on free-choice state aid by twenty-six votes to three with ten employers' abstentions. The idea of state subsidies was taken up again the following year and Parliament introduced a line of credit in the 1905 Budget, leaving the administrators to decide the conditions governing the allocation of resources. What had been envisaged originally as benefit to salaried workers alone was later extended to other vulnerable groups; under the decree of 28 July 1932, subsidies were provided to funds to protect self-employed workers and small businesses.[52]

The system assumed that trade union initiatives would develop in this area. But revolutionary syndicalists did not want to prop up capitalism: employers should be responsible for society's malfunctioning. Protection against accidents at work should now be extended to unemployment; paternalist employers were already moving in this direction.[53] As for the reformist CGT, it hesitated. It was only concerned with a small section of waged workers, mostly skilled men who were not at risk of unemployment. It had difficulty in collecting subscriptions and feared a drop in membership if these were raised. In addition it was ill-prepared to play an administrative role. With the exception of the printers' union (Fédération du Livre), union unemployment funds were unsuccessful. There were attempts on the fringes by Catholic and corporatist organisations of employers' unions; for example, a plan covering unemployment, illness and old age was tried at the Saint-Nazaire workshops in 1923 by the technicians' unions and the Confederation de l'Intelligence et de la Production Française.[54] The lack of enthusiasm explains why state subsidies for unemployment funds did not increase much. In some years they were only partially spent: in 1925 out of FF567,000 credited only FF201,000 was spent. The availibility of assistance apparently killed off the initiative of 1905.

Undoubtedly the slump provoked a revival of interest – there were up to 200 funds – and required the mobilisation of large sums to save existing funds.[55] The prohibition of unions by Vichy tolled the knell of union-based insurance and the almost complete disappearance of unemployment during the postwar years did nothing to stimulate its renaissance.

Compulsory unemployment insurance

The myth of social protection was always present in spirit but never in fact. It is necessary to follow its periodic resurgence since Millerand, in 1904, abandoned his initiative not in principle but for financial reasons.[56] Following the first world war, the need to reconstruct France on more egalitarian foundations, while at the same time developing a policy of social insurance comparable to that of newly recovered Alsace-Lorraine, led to proposals for social insurance laws and a new will to implement them on the government's part.[57] It was necessary to reform the poorly enforced law on pensions and to establish cover for the sick – like the protection against occupational disease (the law of 1919) – and for the unemployed. From the start different influences were traceable in this area; Fernand Philippart, mayor of Bordeaux and social progressive, declared in 1921: 'The worker must be insured against illness and also against unemployment, for he must not suffer from those events against which nothing can guard'; he thus allied himself to the Socialist Party's programme. The idea was taken up by Mouret who laid out his proposals on 8 May 1923.[58]

Under the terms agreed by the deputies in 1924, an allowance for the unemployed was granted, at a rate of 40 per cent of salary, with appropriate contributions. Benefit would be paid from the eighth day following the declaration of unemployment and was available for up to sixty days per year. In seasonal industries penalties for insufficient contributions were increased, this difference in treatment being excused by the higher salaries paid in these sectors to compensate for the intermittent character of the work.[59] However, as usual the Senate chose a different interpretation of the law from the lower chamber. The sleight-of-hand was admirable and can be left to the words of Doctor Chauveau, chairman of the High Assembly:

> Along with illness, invalidity and old age, there is a fourth social risk, in the sense in which we understand the word, unemployment: that is to say the state of the salaried worker without employment through involuntary lack of work. Like the other risks envisaged in the proposal, does not unemployment here entail the cessation of that work necessary to the existence of the individual and his household? In addition, it is necessary to reflect that the guarantee with which this proposed law covers the expected risks is subject to the fulfilment of conditions regarding duration of payment and rate of contributions, and that, if these conditions are not fulfilled, the insured party will be punished for default. To benefit from sickness insurance, for example, the worker must have contributed for fifty days at least in the three months that precede the illness . . . How can he do this if he has been unemployed? The normal application of social insurance policy would find itself, therefore, to a certain extent contradicted by this failure to observe the conditions of payment. For all these reasons the extension of social insurance to involuntary unemployment is an indispensable development. So the Senatorial commission, at the suggestion of M. Peyronnet, has incorporated this condition in the proposal. On the other hand, what we propose is less an insurance against unemployment than a regulation of payments in the event of unemployment.[60]

This option was taken up by the law of 5 April 1928 in article 1: 'Social insurance covers the risk of illness, premature invalidity, old age, death, and involves contribution to domestic costs, maternity expenses and those due to involuntary unemployment . . . '. Article 21 defines the nature of this contribution. Social insurance only covered French workers with a contract of employment: those finding themselves involuntarily unemployed would have their contributions maintained, up to 10 per cent of their wages, under regulations established by the sickness insurance code. In this way, a real compulsory unemployment insurance policy ran aground. Assistance for the unemployed continued into the Vichy period, with family allowance in the case of full or partial unemployment.[61]

The parliamentary exchange could not satisfy the supporters of obligatory insurance, who repeated their demands; from 1930, when President Doumergue travelled to Loire-Inférieure, the deputy-mayor of Saint-Nazaire complained that social insurance should be complemented by proper protection against unemployment,[62] as the CGT demanded. The establishment of a comprehensive system was in the programme of the Socialist Workers International, while elements close to the Communist Party, like the CGTU, demanded that this insurance should not mean contributions paid from wages.[63] In Parliament, proposals introduced in 1933 did not adopt compulsory insurance, which seemed impossible to implement when the situation was so grave and when England itself was returning to public assistance with the Unemployment Act of 1934.

The war witnessed a progressive reabsorption of unemployment. There was no real problem until the first years of the decade[64] and the solution that prevailed, influenced by the increasingly detailed diktats of the occupying power, involved departure for the workshops of the Organisation Todt, then into the Reich factories for a growing number of French workers, first as volunteers, then forced volunteers, and finally under the auspices of Compulsory Labour Service. The problem of unemployment did not, therefore, win attention from organisations established under the *Charte du Travail,* like the social committees.[65] Compulsory insurance seemed a remote possibility to Vichy. Leaving on one side some patches of unemployment following the Liberation,[66] the difficulty lay later in finding manpower for the economic recovery, the occupation of Germany and the colonial wars. Meanwhile France could not run its economy on a theory and the different proposals from clandestine parties and unions, ending up in the programme of the Conseil National de la Résistance, naturally had to focus attention on the consequences of the right to work.[67]

The man of the moment was Pierre Laroque to whom Alexandre Parodi, Ministre du Travail et de la Securité Sociale, officially passed the Direction Generale des Assurances on 5 October 1944.[68] Public opinion, after the years of trial, looked for security, and the decree of 4 October 1945 aimed to satisfy this expectation by covering workers against risk, including unemployment.[69] It seemed proper to introduce a system of unemployment insurance into social security at that time; but there was nothing in the initial proposals, or in the law of 22 May 1946, or when its reorganisation was discussed the following year. Laroque was critical of the Beveridgian model, which he described as a 'vast nationalised system of unemployment insurance',[70] but it was the state's involvement that he disliked; he reaffirmed the necessity of 'extending social security to those areas which it has not reached . . . , in particular to unemployment'.[71]

The obstinate exclusion of a comparatively cheap extension (in the short or medium term) to the French system requires explanation. Several factors come to mind: scant public interest in a minor issue? Trade union rejection of workers' contributions? Refusal of business to accept another scheme when they had been powerless to prevent the extension of previous ones?[72] Inability to clarify the definition of unemployment?[73] Popular feeling that this, like the right to work, remained essentially the responsibility of state-subsidised public assistance?[74] A little of each and perhaps, above all, the dominant realism which led to setting ambitious long-term objectives probably encouraged a certain number of reforms to be delayed.[75] In any case, when '1945 seemed like a unique chance which should not be missed',[76] it was well and truly muffed, and the 1950s opened with France still unable to handle the unemployment insurance question clearly. Contrary to the advice given by Beveridge in his famous 1942 report, France moved more towards minor adjustment than revolution.[77]

Separated from social security, the issue continued to be discussed as France signed the International Agreement on Unemployment in 1951. Voluntary insurance could no longer be relied on; the unemployment funds, which had numbered over 200 in 1936, had shrunk to one. The decree of 12 November 1951 undertook to modernise the traditional system of assistance by taking into consideration seasonal unemployment, at that time the only prevalent type.[78] This law gave national responsibility to central government for public assistance; it took up no position on compulsory insurance.[79] There was a shift of opinion away from an organised statutory scheme and it was through a national collective agreement on 31 December 1958 that, outside the social security system and against the wishes of the Ministère du Travail,[80] that employers' and workers' representatives introduced a trade-based scheme organised through unions and associations, ASSEDIC, grouped under a national unit, UNEDIC. Privately financed and privately administered by elected representatives from employers' associations and trade unions, this unemployment insurance cut itself off from the social security scheme – with its elected directors and state involvement at various levels. Unemployment insurance also remained distinct from the state's labour services which inspected job placement, working conditions and lay-offs. Hence, a conventional system prevailed, a French-style 'collective agreement', signalling waning enthusiasm for the idea of a welfare state of which General de Gaulle and his chief ministers, recently come to power, had never been great supporters.

Employers were reasserting their authority. This reaction had begun with new retirement rules and it progressed; however, this was not a matter of building a second pillar of the social security system. Unemployment insurance was the essential element that eluded the state. Compulsory insurance carried the day in the end, but by a detour away from public intervention.[81] Further, it remained confined to salaried workers, excluding both new labour market entrants and those hit by the diminution of independent activity.

CONCLUSIONS

For decades France pursued the most diverse policies to address the problem of unemployment, hovering between the exclusion of the 'parasite' (as the unemployed were perceived by the bourgeoisie and peasants), the provision of compulsory workshop placements (a solution dear to the moralists), the guarantee of 'the right to work' recognised by socialists, unions and – theoretically – the Constitution, the reservation of jobs for the most worthy (male workers of French nationality), private and public assistance, and compulsory insurance. All possibilities were discussed and tried. In the current crisis, all have resurfaced in the same confusion, accentuated by the fact that today there are at least four official definitions of unemployment.[82]

From this historical viewpoint and the multifaceted French response to the problem of unemployment, several questions arise. First, why – and unemployment is only an extreme example of a more general phenomenon here – the preference for assistance?[83] Was it the Republicans desire to fight Christian charity on its own ground, with the aim of winning the allegiance of large sections of the population to the regime? Or a continuation of French economic backwardness, Sauvy's explanation for France's incapacity to face the 1930s crisis? Lack of faith in social insurance as a German invention? This did not prevent the adoption of 1928 and 1930 laws and, in the sphere of unemployment, the invention was English. Second, the struggle against unemployment and its consequences remained outside the province of the state throughout this period, calling into question the idea of permanent centralised official action in this field. Government and Parliament looked to the localities to organise public works, job placement, training and public assistance both through traditional form and through the creation of special unemployment funds. They also turned to voluntary agencies; the unions were called on to manage job placement bureaux and unemployment funds, before they joined businessmen in creating and regulating unemployment insurance. The image of '*l'Etat dirigiste*' is completely reversed, the more striking if the comparison is made with the centralised system developed in Britain, which stimulated critical remarks from Laroque in 1946.

Finally, and perhaps above all, how was it that, within a system of social protection designed to address the problems of waged workers,[84] the ultimate risk to which waged workers were exposed – that is unemployment – was not really taken into account? It could be reasoned, in simplistic fashion, that on losing work the unemployed lost the status of salaried workers and – with this – their rights to social protection specific to salaried workers. Perhaps admitting that the unemployed have rights implies the acceptance of urbanisation, when the rural electorate and ideal were so politically important, and not just on the conservative side.[85] It also meant recognising the victory of industry and capital over craft and commerce, the latter so dear to the Radical Party and the left. It meant reinforcing the rights of workers against a *patronat* which was hostile to the development of social protection determined by the state.[86] This would have involved radical change in the position of waged workers, for long considered socially inferior. When this stage was superseded, at the end of the 1950s and beginning of the 1960s, the moment came to adopt a system of compulsory social insurance, and social groups accomplished it. So France entered the era of the waged worker just when the status of waged workers began to be undermined by heavy unemployment and new types of work – a historical irony.

NOTES

1 C. Topalov, 'L'invention du chômage: terminologie, classification et réforme sociale, 1880–1910', *Rencontres d'Oxford*, Mission Recherche (MIRE), Paris, 1995; R. Salais, N. Baverez, and B. Reynaud, *L'invention du chômage. Histoire et transformations d'une catégorie en France des années 1890 aux années 1980*, PUF, Paris, 1986; M. Mansfield, R. Salais, and N. Whiteside, *Aux sources du chômage, 1880–1914*, Belin, Paris, 1994.

2 C. Willmann, *Essai d'identification juridique du chômeur*, Thèse droit Paris X, 1994.

3 A. Cambriel, *Les subventions de l'Etat, des départements et des communes aux caisses de chômage*, Thèse droit Paris, 1908.

4 Quoted in J. Cahen-Bernard, *Assurance contre le chômage involontaire en France et à l'étranger*, Thèse droit Nancy, 1913.

5 E. Weber, *La France des années 30. Tourments et perplexités*, Fayard, Paris, 1995, p. 50.

6 W. Oualid, *Législation industrielle*, Cours de doctorat, Paris, 1927, pp. 342–51.

7 A. Besson, *Le droit social dans la période du gouvernement tripartite, 1945–1947*, Mémoire de DEA de droit social, Nantes, 1991.

8 D. Renard, 'Les rapports entre assistance et assurance dans la constitution du système de protection sociale français', *Rencontres d'Oxford*, MIRE, Paris, 1995.

9 P. Laroque, 'Le plan français de sécurité sociale', *Revue française du travail*, 1946, no. 1.

10 J.A. Garraty, *Unemployment in History: Economic Thought and Public Policy*, Harper Colophon Books, New York, 1979, p. 193.

11 M. Verret, *L'ouvrier français. Le travail ouvrier*, A. Colin, Paris, 1982, p. 67.

12 In 1931 the government estimated the number of unemployed at 100,000; the Paris Chamber of Commerce at 420,000; Léon Blum at 650,000; others declared the figure to be 4 or 5 or even 7 million. Garraty, *Unemployment in History*; F. Fouquet-Lapar, *La crise du chômage en France*, Rapport à la Chambre de Commerce de Paris, 1935; G. Hereil, *Le chômage en France. Etude de législation sociale*, Thèse droit Paris, 1932; G. Sadoul, *Les religions et le chômage. La croisade de charité*, Bureau d'Editions modernes, Paris, 1932; A. Sauvy, *Histoire économique de la France de l'entre-deux-guerres*, Fayard, Paris, 1965.

13 R. Trempé, 'Vichy et le problème de la main d'oeuvre étrangère dans les mines', in *Convergences. Mélanges offert à Marcel David*, Calligrammes, Quimper, 1991.

14 J. Malivoire de Camas, *La France et le chômage*, Thèse droit Paris, 1933.

15 P. Durand, 'L'emploi des travailleurs étrangers (loi du 27 août 1940)' *Droit Social*, 1941, Garraty, *Unemployment in History*; P.-J. Hesse and J.-P. Le Crom, 'L'indemnisation des chômeurs dans les années 1930', in *Les sans-emploi et la loi*, Calligrammes, Quimper, 1988.

16 See M. Bordeaux, 'Vichy en plein travail, 1940–42', in *Les sans-emploi et la loi*, Calligrammes, Quimper, 1988. Taking all the regions together the following results were reached: in September 1940, 338,000 (33.5 per cent); in September 1941; 150,000 (60 per cent); in September 1942, 59,000 (67 per cent).

17 Renard, 'Les rapports'.

18 Archives Nationales [AN] 2 AG 499. R. Belin, *Du secrétariat de la C.G.T. au gouvernement de Vichy. Mémoires, 1932–1942*, Albatros, Paris, 1978; E. Biron, *Les péripéties de la retraite de vieux: la politique française de la vieillesse du Front Populaire à l'avènement de la IV République*, Mémoire de DEA de droit social, Nantes, 1993.

19 Bordeaux, 'Vichy en plein travail'.

20 Paul Reynaud, *France Saved Europe*, New York, 1947, vol. 1, p. 376

21 Besson, *Le droit social*.

22 A. Gueslin, *L'Etat, l'économie et la société française, XIX–XXe siècles*, Hachette, Paris, 1992.

23 J.-M. Benaben, 'L'aide aux chômeurs de Bordeaux (1920–1940)', *Colloque d'histoire de la Sécurité Sociale*, AEHSS, Bordeaux, 1979.

24 J.-P. Rioux, 'Le Front populaire et son échec', *L'Histoire*, no. 88, 1988, pp. 88–93.

25 Y. Becquet, *The Organization of Workers' Leisure*, Pedone, Paris, 1939, p. 77.

26 J. Perret, *Le cancer du chômage. Toxiques, narcotiques, remèdes*, PUF, Paris, 1936.

27 A. Sauvy, *La machine et le chômage. Le progrès technique et l'emploi*, Dunod, Paris, 1980.

28 R. Dufraisse, 'Le mouvement ouvrier "rouge" devant la grande dépression de 1929 à 1939', in D. Fauvel-Rouif, *Mouvements ouvriers et dépression économique de 1929 à 1939*, Aassen, 1966.

29 Oualid, *Législation industrielle*, pp. 296–373.

30 G. Latellier, J. Perret, H. Zuber, and A. Dauphin-Meunier, *Enquête sur le chômage en France*, vol. 1: *Le chômage en France de 1930 à 1936*, Sirey, Paris, 1938; Hesse and Le Crom, 'L'indemnisation des chômeurs'.

31 Benaben, 'L'aide aux chômeurs de Bordeaux'.

32 Perret, *Le cancer du chômage*.

33 AN 72 AJ 576.

34 Renard, 'Les rapports'.

35 J. Alber, 'Government responses to the challenge of unemployment', in P. Flora and A.J. Heidenheimer (eds), *The Development of Welfare States in Europe and America*, Transaction Books, London, 1984.

36 B. Poirot-Delpech, 'Interview', *Lire*, no. 108 1984, p. 87.

37 P.-J. Hesse, 'Maître, patron ou employeur: des oeuvres sociales à la protection sociale complémentaire', *Revue de l'économie sociale*, no. 24 1991, pp. 19–38; P.-J. Hesse, 'Des rendez-vous manqués: les travailleurs chrétiens de Nantes', in J. Deniot and C. Dutheil (ed.), *Métamorphoses ouvrières*, L'Harmattan, Paris, 1996.

38 Hesse and Le Crom, 'L'indemnisation des chômeurs'.

39 Hereil, *Le chômage en France*; M. Lautier, *Assurance- chômage et assistance (Législation comparée et droit français)*, Thèse droit, Rennes, 1936.

40 Benaben, 'L'aide aux chômeurs de Bourdeaux'.

41 Association de Recherches et d'Etudes sur le Mouvement Ouvriers dans la Région de Saint-Nazaire (AREMORS), *Etude et documents sur Saint-Nazaire et le mouvement ouvrier de 1920 à 1939*, Aremors, 1983; Lautier, *Assurance*.

42 M. Barbance, *Saint Nazaire. Le port, la ville, le travail*, Crépin Leblond, Moulins, 1948; Benaben, 'L'aide aux chômeurs de Bourdeaux, M. Daclin, *La crise des années 30 à Besançon*, Les Belles-Lettres, Paris, 1968; B. Gallinato, *Le budget social d'une ville moyenne. Libourne, 1811–1940*, AEHSS, Paris, 1984; Lautier, *Assurance*; F. Valette, 'Etre pauvre à Nancy entre les deux guerres', *Annales de l'Est*, 1988, n.1.

43 Fouquet-Lapar, *La crise du chômage en France*.

44 AN 72 AJ 576.

45 Benaben, 'L'aide aux chômeurs de Bourdeaux'.

46 Sadoul, *Les religions et le chômage*.

47 But at Nantes in 1935 material assistance only represented 4.4 per cent.

48 Benaben, 'L'aide aux chômeurs de Bourdeaux'; cf. also Gallinato, *Le budget social*; Y. Marec, *Le 'clou' rouennais des origines à nos jours (1778–1982): du Mont de Piété au Crédit Municipal. Contribution à l'histoire de la pauvreté en province*, Editions du P'tit Normand, Rouen, 1983.

49 Verret, *L'Ouvrier Français*.

50 Barbance, *Saint Nazaire*, p. 611.

51 Daclin, *La crise . . . à Besançon*.

52 Cambriel, *Les subventions de l'Etat*; Cahen-Bernard, *Assurance contre le chômage involuntaire*; Hereil, *Le chômage en France*.

53 Hesse, 'Maître, patron ou employeur'.

54 Barbance, *Saint Nazaire*.

55 AN 72 AJ 576, Report of August 1939.

56 Cahen-Bernard, *Assurance contre le chômage involuntaire*.

57 H. Hatzfeld, *Du paupérisme à la sécurité sociale. Essai sur les origines de la Sécurité sociale en France, 1850–1940*, A. Colin, Paris, 1971.

58 G. Antonietti, *Histoire contemporaine politique et sociale*, PUF, Paris, 1986; Benaben, 'L'aide aux chômeurs de Bourdeaux'; J. Cavignac, 'Le syndicalisme girondin face aux assurances sociales (1925–1930)', *Colloque d'histoire de la*

Sécurité Sociale, Nancy, AEHSS, Paris, 1978; L. Gueneau, *Les dernières crises de chômage et la question de l'assurance obligatoire*, Thèse de droit, Lyon, 1924.

59 Gueneau, *Les dernières crises*, p. 113.

60 C. Chauveau, *Les assurances sociales*, Payot, Paris, 1926, pp. 91–2. The option-ally insured worker was excluded from unemployment insurance since he was not salaried; this echoes the theory developed by Castel on the setting up of social security systems: R. Castel, 'Le modèle de la société salariale comme principe d'une comparaison entre les systèmes de protection sociale du Nord et en Europe du Sud', in *Rencontres de Florence*, MIRE, Paris, 1997.

61 Cf. AN 72 AJ 476.

62 C. Kahan and J. Landais, *Les années folles à Nantes, 1920–1930*, Ouest-Editions, Nantes, 1995.

63 Antonietti, *Histoire contemporaine*; Garraty, *Unemployment in History*; P. Laubier, *La politique sociale dans les sociétés industrielles, 1800 à nos jours. Acteurs – idéologies – réalisations*, Economica, Paris, 1984.

64 Bordeaux, 'Vichy en plein travail'; Y. Durand, 'S.T.O. – Vichy au service de l'Allemagne', *L'Histoire*, no. 167, 1993, pp. 14–23.

65 J.-P. Le Crom, *Syndicats, nous voilà! Vichy et le corporatisme*, L'Atelier, Paris, 1995.

66 J. and Y. Pilven Le Sevellec, *Les délaissés de la Libération. La vie de tous les jours dans la poche de Saint-Nazaire: août 1944–11 mai 1945*, Ouest-Editions, Nantes, 1995.

67 H.C. Galant, *Histoire politique de la Sécurité sociale française (1945–1952)*, A. Colin, Paris, 1955; J. Le Goff, *Du silence à la parole. Droit du travail, société, Etat, 1830–1989*, Calligrammes, Quimper, 1989.

68 P. Laroque, *Au service de l'homme et du droit. Souvenirs et réflexions*, AEHSS, Paris, 1993.

69 A. Barjot, (ed.), *La Sécurité sociale. Son histoire à travers les textes*, vol. 3: *1945–1981*, AEHSS, Paris, 1988; N. Kerschen, 'L'influence du rapport Beveridge sur le plan français de sécurité sociale de 1945', *Rencontres d'Oxford*, MIRE, 1995; F.-X. Merrien, *Etude comparée de l'édification et de l'évolution de l'Etat protecteur en France et en Grande-Bretagne*, CRSST, Université Paris-Sud, Paris; B. Pequignot, '1945: la Sécurité sociale. Naissance et contradictions', *Prévenir*, no. 5, 1982, pp. 21–39; Y. Saint-Jours, 'La France', in H. Zacher, P. Kohler, and P.-J. Hesse (eds), *Un siècle de sécurité sociale – 1881–1981*, CRHES, Nantes, 1983.

70 Merrien, *Etude comparée*, p. 250.

71 P. Laroque, 'Sécurité sociale et assurances sociales', *Informations sociales*, 1945, n. 7, pp. 111–14.

72 Hatzfeld, *Du pauperisme*.

73 Salais *et al.*, *L'invention du chômage*; R. Salais, 'La fléxibilité économique et la catégorie "chômeur": quelques enseignements de l'histoire', in *Les sans-emploi et la loi*, Calligrammes, Quimper 1988; C. Topalov, *Construction de la catégorie de chômeur. France, Grande-Bretagne, Etats-Unis, 1900–1940*, Rapport MIRE and MIRE-Info, 1990; Topalov, 'L'Invention du chômage'; M.-T. Joint-Lambert, *Politiques sociales*, FNSP and Dalloz, Paris, 1994.

74 F.-X. Schaller, *Le droit au travail*, Aux portes de France, Porrentruy, 1946.

75 Besson, *Le droit social*; Galant, *Histoire politique*.

76 Kerschen, 'L'influence du rapport Beveridge'.
77 P. Durand, *La politique contemporaine de sécurité sociale*, Dalloz, Paris, 1953.
78 J. Doublet and G. Lavau, *Sécurité sociale*, PUF, Paris, 1957; A. Philbert, *La Politique sociale de la France*, La Documentation Française, Paris, 1960.
79 J.-J. Ribas, 'Sécurité sociale et classes sociales en France', *Droit social*, vol. 15, 1952, pp. 477ff.
80 Gueslin, *L'Etat, l'économie et la société française*.
81 Merrien, *Etude comparée*; Willmann, *Essai d'identification juridique*.
82 Y. Rousseau, 'Le statut des chômeurs', in *Les sans-emploi et la loi*, Calligrammes, Quimper, 1988; Willmann, *Essai d'identification juridique*.
83 Renard, 'Les rapports'.
84 F. Calcoen, D. Greiner, and J. Verly, 'Nouvelles formes d'emploi et protection sociale. Une approche européenne comparative', *MIRE-Info*, n. 31, 1994; R. Castel, *Les métamorphoses de la question sociale. Une chronique du salariat*, Fayard, Paris, 1995; Castel, 'Le modèle de la "société salariale"'.
85 Merrien, *Etude comparée*.
86 H.W. Ehrmann, *La politique du patronat français, 1936–1955*, A. Colin, Paris, 1959; Hatzfeld, *Du pauperisme*.

11

THE EVOLUTION OF THE CONTRACT OF EMPLOYMENT, 1900–1950

The influence of the welfare state

Simon Deakin

INTRODUCTION

The concept of the contract of employment expresses an ambiguity which is characteristic of modern labour law in general. Notions of 'service' or 'employment' which imply the 'subordination of the individual worker to the capitalist enterprise'[1] are set within a framework of contractual rights and obligations which are, supposedly, the product of mutual agreement between the parties. If the purpose of subordination is somehow to legitimise or underpin managerial prerogative, it is unclear what the role of contract might be. Does contract, by stressing the need for agreement and reciprocity of obligation, place limits on the notion of subordination, or is it a 'figment of the legal mind' which, no matter how 'indispensable', simply serves to conceal the exercise by the employer of unilateral power?[2] The ambiguity is deepened by the use of the same concept of the contract of employment to define and limit the scope of legislative intervention designed for the protection of the individual worker. Those employment relationships which are based on dependent or subordinated labour are deemed to be appropriate subjects for regulation and taxation under legislation of the welfare state which aims, in various ways, to collectivise and redistribute certain social and economic risks. Statutes governing occupational health and safety, employment protection and unemployment insurance tend to exclude 'independent' or 'autonomous' labour from the scope of regulation, or at least from the core of protective rules.[3] From a legal point of view, then, 'subordination' is both the expression of the worker's subjection to managerial prerogative,[4] and also the gateway to social protection.

This chapter traces the evolution of the concept of the contract of employment in British labour and social security law in the first half of the twentieth century, the period in which an extensive system of statutory and collective regulation of the employment relationship was slowly built up. At the start of this period, it is difficult to find anything resembling the concept of the contract of employment as it is now understood. That is to say, the nineteenth-century law on employment did not recognise the modern distinction between dependent employment and self-employment; nor did it consistently see the obligations of the parties to the employment relationship as 'contractual'. Most industrial workers were still subject to a model based on master and servant relations, which was not only explicitly hierarchical, but was shaped extensively by external statutory and judicial intervention. This 'service model' faded only gradually, as collective bargaining and arbitration over wages and conditions of employment became more widespread and as early social insurance and workmen's compensation legislation imposed certain social obligations on employers. These influences were together responsible for the emergence of the modern contract of employment, as a concept which embraced all forms of wage-dependent labour and also expressed the reciprocal rights and obligations of the parties. The 'contractualisation' of the employment relationship was a result, very largely, of the socialising influence of the legislation of the welfare state.

THE NINETEENTH-CENTURY LEGACY

Kahn-Freund dated the emergence of the contract of employment to the nineteenth century and ascribed its development to the twin forces of industrialisation and the demise of the pre-modern forms of statutory wage regulation.[5] Most modern accounts of the contract of employment follow Kahn-Freund in assuming that a coherent common law of employment existed prior to the passage of protective legislation. The generally prevailing view is that with the advent of the welfare state the influence of contract waned,[6] although some maintain that this process has still not gone far enough to prevent contractual concepts continuing to exercise a malign influence on modern labour law: 'the dead weight of tradition in the common law accounts in part for the survival of the simple contractual account of the employment relation'.[7]

This received wisdom exaggerates the unity and doctrinal clarity of the nineteenth-century common law of employment and presents a misleading picture of the evolution of contract within it. A better view is that

> well into the twentieth century, even as late as the Second World War, work relations were not legally expressed in the form of contract at all . . . the end product of the nineteenth-century development was not the myth of the employment contract but a fundamentally different and specific legal concept of service.[8]

This is not to deny that some significant nineteenth-century doctrines took a contractual form, such as the principles governing deductions from wages,[9] or the assumption by the worker of the risk of injury at work caused by a fellow servant (the doctrine of common employment).[10] However, these were isolated and somewhat opportunistic uses of contract law. For workers subject to the jurisdiction of the magistrates under the master and servant legislation, the relevance of contract as a source of reciprocally binding rights and obligations was negligible.

The Master and Servant Acts of 1747, 1766 and 1823 grew out of the system of wage regulation and discipline contained in the pre-modern Statute of Artificers, and outlived the repeal of those parts of the Statute which had guaranteed protection for the skilled trades and provided for the setting of minimum wages. The Master and Servant Acts gave the local magistrates jurisdiction to resolve employment disputes and powers to fine and imprison workers for various offences, including refusing to enter into an agreed hiring, absconding from work and quitting before the end of the agreed term. Tens of thousands of convictions were handed down each year prior to the repeal of the criminal jurisdiction in 1875.

However, the magistrates' disciplinary powers did not extend to independent contractors, on the one hand, or to higher status workers, on the other. An Act of 1867 clarified the case-law of the time by specifying that the jurisdiction covered only the classes of 'servant' and 'labourer'. These groups were identified by the test known as 'exclusive service': 'the statute . . . applies only to cases of contracts to serve. There may indeed be a service, not for any specific time or wages, but to be within the contract there must be a contract for service by the party exclusively.'[11] In practice, the courts were able to extend this notion to cover most skilled and semi-autonomous craftsmen, in particular where they found evidence of long notice periods in the terms of hiring, or of formal commitments to serve, such as the 'pit bond' which operated in parts of the mining industry. By these means, most industrial and agricultural workers were brought under the disciplinary range of the Acts; however, professional, managerial and clerical workers remained outside. In their case, a more clearly contractual model began to develop: the 'employee' (a term reserved to this group) had the right to sue for damages for wrongful dismissal and for the failure of the employer to provide work as agreed.[12] But similar actions by servants or labourers for damages for breach of contract or for wages due as earned under the contract tended to fail; among various restrictive rulings, the courts decided that the magistrates' statutory powers to abate the wages of servants for breach of discipline overrode any contractual rights which the worker might have had under the terms of his or her hiring.[13]

According to Meyers, the repeal of the Master and Servant Acts meant that 'after 1875, at least at formal law, employer and employee had identical and only civil resources for breach of employment contracts'.[14] However, the law was not so even-handed as this might suggest. Magistrates continued to have powers over the contracts of agricultural and industrial workers which exceeded those of the regular civil courts and which continued to shape the service relationship. The relevant legislation was contained in the Employers and Workmen Act 1875, which, in common with the master and servant model, excluded higher-status workers – employees – from its scope.[15] The Act granted the county courts and magistrates' courts powers in addition to those of the common law to supervise the terms of the contract and the worker's manner of performance, including the power to grant specific performance.[16]

At this point, then, the principal division in the law of employment was not between dependent and autonomous workers, but between different groups of wage- or salary-earners according to their social rank and status; and in the case of the service relationship, disciplinary legislation backed up by special judicial powers, and not the common law of contract, was the basis for the exercise by employers of managerial prerogative. A 'contract of employment' embodying bilateral, reciprocal rights and obligations can only be said to have developed for a relatively small group of higher-status workers, employed in clerical, managerial or professional positions.

REDEFINING THE EMPLOYMENT RELATIONSHIP: THE ROLE OF SOCIAL LEGISLATION

The first decades of the twentieth century saw the rapid development of social legislation which attached obligations of compulsory insurance, contribution and compensation to the employment relationship and began to regulate terms and conditions of employment. The first Workmen's Compensation Act was passed in 1897 and the first National Insurance Act in 1911. The Trade Boards Act 1909 set up the first minimum wage controls in the 'sweated trades', and the Factory and Workshop Acts were extended at about the same time to provide a more effective framework for the protection of occupational health and safety. These Acts at first relied on the status-based distinctions within the employment relationship which were to be found in the common law as well as in the restrictive, nineteenth-century legislation which was still in force. Salaried, non-manual workers were differentiated from manual workers paid by the hour or by piece rates, and the latter were distinguished from outworkers, casual workers and others with irregular working arrangements. These distinctions were only slowly effaced as social legislation became more comprehensive and more egalitarian in its outlook and as the impact of restrictive legislation declined under the influence of the same values.

The term 'workman' as used in early social legislation had a specific meaning which was related to manual employment. The Employer's Liability

Act 1880, which introduced some limited exceptions to the doctrine of common employment, adopted the definition used in the Employers and Workmen Act 1875, and the two Acts, one protective and the other restrictive, were subsequently interpreted in tandem. The same definition was later extended to the Truck Acts. The courts gave the term a restricted meaning. In *Morgan* v. *London General Omnibus Co.*,[17] a claim for damages for personal injury under the Act of 1880, the Court of Appeal held that a bus conductor, who 'earns the wages becoming due to him through the confidence reposed in his honesty', was outside the Act : '"labourer" cannot in its ordinary acceptation include an omnibus conductor . . . The mere fact that a man works with his hands is not enough to constitute him a workman within [the Act].' In *Cook* v. *North Metropolitan Tramways Ltd*[18] a claim by a tramcar driver failed for the same reason; similarly, a locomotive guard was held to be outside the Truck Acts,[19] while a sales assistant[20] and a hairdresser[21] were outside the Employers and Workmen Act.

The effect of these decisions was to exclude a large class of workers from the scope of the protective legislation of the time. With this in mind, the Workmen's Compensation Act 1897 was provided with an extended statutory formula, according to which a workman was to be defined for the purposes of that Act as including 'any person who is engaged in an employment to which this Act applies, whether by way of manual labour or otherwise'.[22] The relevant employments were the railways, mining and quarrying, factory work and laundry work. However, the widened formula failed to achieve its aim, receiving instead a hostile reception from the courts. *Simpson* v. *Ebbw Vale Steel, Iron & Coal Co.*[23] concerned a claim for compensation by the widow of a colliery manager who had been killed in an underground accident. The Court accepted that a non-manual worker could come within the scope of the Act, but the victim 'must still be a workman'; and the legislation, being paternalist and regulatory in nature, could not have been intended to cover the case of a senior employee:

> [the Act] presupposes a position of dependence; it treats the class of workmen as being in a sense 'inopes consilii', and the Legislature does for them what they cannot do for themselves: it gives them a sort of State insurance, it being assumed that they are either not sufficiently intelligent or not sufficiently in funds to insure themselves. In no sense can such a principle extend to those who are earning good salaries.[24]

Counsel for the employer felt able to put the issue even more clearly in terms of social class: 'the Legislature were contemplating a class of workers who may be described as belonging to the working class in the popular sense of that term – a wage-earning class'.[25]

The next Workmen's Compensation Act, in 1906, had to establish a new scheme of definition; the one it adopted came to form the model for the bulk of social legislation in the pre-war and interwar periods. A 'workman' was now defined as 'any person who has entered into or works under a contract of service or apprenticeship with an employer, whether by way of manual labour, clerical work or otherwise, and whether the contract is expressed or implied, is oral or in writing'.[26] This was then followed, however, by several important exclusions, including those for non-manual workers with an annual remuneration in excess of £250; casual workers employed 'otherwise than for the purposes of their employer's trade or business'; outworkers; and family workers. By these means, the traditional exclusions for high-status workers, on the one hand, and casual workers, on the other, returned by the back door.

The health insurance part of the National Insurance Act 1911 also applied, initially, to persons employed under contracts of service or apprenticeship, but excluded non-manual workers earning in excess of £160 per year; casual workers not dependent on their employer's business; commission agents; and a large class of public sector workers, including teachers, military personnel and civil servants, who were already covered by separate state-run schemes.[27] Male and unmarried female outworkers were brought under this part of the Act[28] and at a later stage the Insurance Commissioners exercised delegated powers to bring married female outworkers within the Act too,[29] but both male and female outworkers were to remain largely outside the unemployment insurance legislation. The first unemployment insurance scheme only covered the more stable industrial trades,[30] and its subsequent history up to the 1940s is one of only gradual extension: legislation of the 1920s set lower contribution rates (and lower benefits) for women workers, and agricultural employment was not brought into the system until the Unemployment Insurance Act 1935.

The control test

The clarification of the statutory formulae following the Acts of 1906 and 1911 focused the courts' attention on the concept of the 'contract of service'. In filling out the concept, the principal criterion adopted by the courts was that of the employer's 'control' over the way in which the work was performed. Kahn-Freund's well-known critique argued that this test was

> based on the social conditions of an earlier age . . . It reflects a state of society in which the ownership of the means of production coincided with the possession of technical knowledge and skill and in which that knowledge and skill were largely acquired by being handed down from one generation to the next by oral tradition and not by being systematically imparted in institutions of learning from

universities down to technical schools. The control test postulates a combination of managerial and technical functions in the person of the employer.[31]

The implication of this passage is that the control test was derived from a pre-capitalist model of personal employment relations, and that its survival and use into the twentieth century can largely be put down to the common law's resistance to change. A closer analysis reveals that the control test had little to do with a pre-capitalist, personal model of employment, and that its adoption by the courts coincided with, and did not significantly pre-date, the welfare state legislation of the early twentieth century. Rather than being an anachronistic survivor of a previous age, the control test was taken up precisely because of its value to the courts in classifying employment relationships for the purpose of determining which should fall within the compulsory contribution and compensation provisions of social legislation.

The leading twentieth-century cases in which the control test was put forward were *Simmons* v. *Heath Laundry Co.*[32] and *Underwood* v. *Perry*[33] in the field of workmen's compensation, and *Scottish Insurance Commissioners* v. *Edinburgh Royal Infirmary*[34] and *Hill* v. *Beckett*[35] in national insurance. The nineteenth-century cases cited as authority for the test were rather obscure, and involved subjects outside the normal range of employment disputes. *R.* v. *Negus*,[36] in which the court had referred to 'control' as the principal test, concerned the definition of the term 'servant' under the Larceny Acts. *Yewens* v. *Noakes*,[37] a case which was later much relied on, was a tax case which concerned a statutory exemption from inhabited house duty where premises were occupied by a 'servant or other person . . . for the protection thereof'. The Court of Appeal held that a clerk earning £150 per year did not fall within this definition. In both cases, the judges saw control as associated with a unilateral power of direction on the part of the employer and with a corresponding duty of obedience on the part of the worker. In *Negus* Mr Justice Blackburn held that

> the test is very much this, whether the person is charged and bound to obey the orders of his master. He may be so without being bound to devote the whole of his time to this service; but if bound to devote his whole time to it, that may be very strong evidence of his being under control.

Lord Justice Bramwell seems to have had the same idea in mind when he said in *Yewens* v. *Noakes* that 'a servant is a person who is subject to the command of his master as to the manner in which he shall do his work'. Lord Justice Thesiger thought it obvious that a salaried clerk was not a 'servant' in this sense, any more than were 'the manager of a bank, a foreman with high wages, persons in the position almost of gentlemen'. The status or 'position' of such workers was seen as limiting the scope of the orders which the employer could legitimately give.

Why did courts several decades later light upon these cases as authoritative guidance to the classification of employment relationships? It seems unlikely that they simply adopted a test which was already well established in the common law. 'Control' was far from being the principal test even in the nineteenth century; 'exclusive service' had been the criterion used to set the limits of the Master and Servant Acts. Nor was 'control' particularly important in determining the scope of the vicarious liability of employers in the common law of tort. Although it is mentioned as a possible criterion for identifying the service relationship in some tort cases,[38] it was not definitively established as the main criterion. Distinguishing between servants and independent contractors was not, in fact, a major issue for the common law of tort in the nineteenth century, because actions against employers tended to be restricted on other grounds, namely the 'unholy trinity' of defences of common employment, contributory negligence and assumption of risk.

A more convincing explanation is that the use of the control test was a doctrinal innovation which enabled the courts to give a restrictive interpretation to social legislation whose element of compulsion, as *Simpson* v. *Ebbw Vale*[39] made clear, they found repugnant. The control test narrowed the scope of the new legislation in two ways: on the one hand it reinforced the status-based distinction between the 'labouring' and 'professional' classes, while on the other is excluded casual and seasonal workers to whom the employer made a limited commitment of continuing employment.

This process can be seen at work in *Simmons* v. *Heath Laundry*.[40] The plaintiff was a laundry worker who, having injured her hand at work, made a workmen's compensation claim for loss of earning capacity in respect of piano lessons which she had been giving in her spare time. The Court of Appeal concluded that she was not a 'workman' for the purpose of giving the piano lessons, so this portion of her claim failed. Rather than simply saying that she was an independent contractor for the purposes of what was clearly a subsidiary occupation, the Court used the control test to place her in the category of autonomous workers:

> the question to be asked is what was the man [*sic*] employed to do; was he employed upon the terms that he should within the scope of his employment obey his master's orders, or was he employed to exercise his skill and achieve an indicated result in such manner as in his judgment was most likely to achieve success?[41]

In other cases in this line, a lecturer, chemist, nurse, doctor and poor-law officers were held to be excluded.[42] These middle-class employees were outside the service relationship because they were perceived as enjoying a high degree of autonomy and discretion in the way they carried out their work, autonomy which was not compatible with the status of servant or workman. The exclusion of medical professionals had the added advantage, from the courts' point of view, of minimising the liability of poor-law guardians and hospitals at a time when health services were only partially funded by the state and many organisations were perceived as having an insecure financial base.[43]

The position of casual workers was complicated by the prevalence of sub-contracting in many industries. The contract system of hiring labour through an intermediary was still the predominant form of industrial organisation in road-building, construction, shipbuilding, mining and quarrying, and iron and steel. This meant that there might be no contractual nexus between workmen hired by the butty worker or foreman and the ultimate owners of the site, plant or materials on which they worked. The control test, as applied by twentieth-century courts, often had the effect of classifying foremen as independent contractors, given their responsibility for hiring their own gangs;[44] while the gang workers or labourers themselves had no claim against the ultimate users of their labour since the latter did not 'control' the performance of their work.[45] Piecework payments were also treated by the courts as strong evidence of independent-contractor status, notwithstanding clear statutory signals that this was not to be the case.[46] Share fishermen – inshore trawlermen who were paid on a proportion of the profits from individual voyages – were found to be outside the social insurance legislation.[47]

Seasonal and casual workers who were directly employed by the ultimate employer were the subject of particular statutory provisions, specifying that they were to be included in the legislation where they were economically dependent on their employer's business. This did not prevent considerable litigation arising. The courts held that a single, one-off hiring was not necessarily outside the scope of the Acts,[48] and were also prepared to include seasonal workers who returned to their employer on a regular basis[49] and part-time workers with long service.[50] However, in other cases they excluded workers under task contracts,[51] temporary workers[52] and casual workers with short-term service.[53] Trainees and unemployed workers receiving instruction and work experience at government training centres were also beyond the scope of the legislation.[54]

The adoption of the control test enabled employers to avoid responsibility for the social risks of illness, injury and unemployment which it had been the aim of social legislation to impose, at least in part, upon them. The drawing of fine distinctions to defeat the legislation in this way was not universally accepted. The Scottish courts, influenced, perhaps, by the civilian tradition of giving a purposive interpretation to social legislation, were on occasion reluctant to allow employers to contract out of the Acts by these means (just as, in the nineteenth century, they had been reluctant to accept the doctrine of common employment which held that the worker impliedly accepted the risk of a fellow servant's negligence[55]). In *Paterson* v. *Lockhart*,[56] a case concerning the status of a foreman, Lord McLaren considered that

> it would be a serious restriction of the scope of the Act if it were possible by introducing some condition into an agreement to take it out of the category of a pure contract of service, and so to avoid liability under the Act . . . It is quite in accordance with custom for a superior workman to choose his own assistants. An engineer may choose his own fireman or a mason his hodman. But that does not prevent their being servants paid by a common employer.

In *Dunlop* v. *M'Cready*,[57] Lord Adam said of a group of gang workers that 'to call them independent contractors is . . . a mere playing with words'. These were, however, isolated examples of a more tolerant judicial attitude. More typical of the case-law as a whole was the finding of the Court of Session in *Littlejohn* v. *Brown*[58] to the effect that a rivet boy, hired by the head riveters in a shipyard, had no contract of service with the main employer:

> if the test is the direct and immediate selection, payment and control and power of dismissal, the evidence is all one way, namely, that [the plaintiff] was in the service of Gammell and Lacey, John Brown & Company being only indirectly connected with the boy's employment.

The 'unitary' model of the contract of employment which, in modern labour law, extends to all categories of wage-earners, only came into being when further reforms were enacted to social legislation, in particular the extension of social insurance which took place in the National Insurance Act 1946. A major aspect of the Beveridge Report was the abolition of distinctions between different categories of employees: henceforth, all wage- or salary-earners, regardless of their annual income or of their professional status, would come under the same contributory classification.[59] Accordingly, the 1946 Act established two principal classes of contributors: Class I covered 'employed earners', defined as 'any persons gainfully occupied in employment . . . being employment under a contract of service', and Class II covered those employed on their own account. The latter paid a lower rate of contribution and were excluded from the unemployment insurance part of the scheme. In this way the fundamental division between *employees* and the *self-employed* was established. The same distinction was adopted for the purposes of income taxation[60] and, in due course, in the employment protection legislation which was introduced first in the early 1960s.[61] The ending of the old divide between manual and non-manual workers was epitomised by the merging of the concepts of the contract of *service* and of *employment*: for statutory purposes, these were now synonymous.[62]

Faced with this new situation, the courts abandoned the old distinction between low-status and high-status employees when seeking to identify the contract of service.[63] The control test itself came to be regarded as excessively artificial, and gave way to the tests of 'integration' and 'business reality'. These stressed economic as opposed to personal subordination as the basis of the contract of employment. The test of the worker's 'integration' into an organisation was used to explain how professionals such as doctors and journalists could be classified as employees, notwithstanding the high degree of autonomy they enjoyed in their work.[64] 'Business reality' had the effect of extending protection to casual workers and outworkers who were dependent on the business of another, as opposed to being entrepreneurs with a business and employees of their own.[65] By these means, a more inclusive notion of the employment relationship came to be established for the purposes of determining the scope of employers' liabilities in respect of personal injuries, employment protection and social insurance.

THE IMPACT OF COLLECTIVE BARGAINING

At the same time as changes to social legislation were cementing the 'unitary' contract of employment in place, the growth of collective bargaining, supported indirectly by the state, was contributing to the same process. Its impact was felt first of all in the marginalisation of the practice of labour-only subcontracting. In addition to the role played by technological change and by economies of scale and scope, the spread of collective representation to the lower occupational grades and ranks played a role in the emergence of the modern, integrated form of corporate organisation. In iron and steel, for example, the organisation of the sub-contracted underhands, beginning at the turn of the century, and their gradual integration into the wage-setting and arbitration procedures first established by the skilled unions were important steps in this process.[66] In coal mining, the butty system was only finally brought to an end in some regions with the nationalisation of the industry in 1946.

The spread of collective bargaining helped to undermine the old status distinctions in a second sense. Collective arbitration of labour disputes gradually displaced resort by employers to the quasi-disciplinary powers of the magistrates under the Employers and Workmen Act 1875. That Act was only formally repealed in the 1970s; however, its use by employers appears to have declined rapidly after 1918 and just a few reported cases, in the coal industry prior to its nationalisation, can be found for the 1940s. Already in 1928, F.W. Tillyard wrote that the relevant provisions of the 1875 Act were 'practically a dead letter'; the reason was that 'contracts of service are determinable more and more by short notice, so that powers to rescind and powers to enforce performance for unexpired periods of service are in practice rarely if ever wanted'.[67] Unions had pressed for a shortening of minimum notice periods in trades where collective bargaining had become established, precisely in order to avoid the disciplinary impact of the 1875 Act and to lessen the risk of liability in tort for inducing breach of contract when organising industrial action. Tillyard argued that as a result of collective bargaining and of legislation setting pay and conditions of work:

> the inferior status of the worker has disappeared. This is absolutely true as regards the administration of the law, but it is also largely true of other means of settling disputes. On Boards of Conciliation, on Trade Boards, on Courts of Referees, and on other bodies dealing with trade interests, working men and employers meet on an equality.[68]

The third effect of collective bargaining, supported by employment legislation, was to stabilise the employment of industrial workers, by discouraging lay-offs and other suspensions of work initiated by the employer and by attacking the practice of workers being hired by the day. Although the common law made some progress towards recognising the individual worker's right to wages during lay-off caused by lack of work,[69] short-time working and lay-off without pay remained widespread during the interwar years. In part this was because workers could claim unemployment benefit for short periods without work, so that the risk of short-time working could effectively be displaced on to the unemployment insurance system.[70] However, the wartime Essential Work Order[71] helped limit this abuse in the case of 'scheduled' or essential work, by requiring the employer to find work for the employee and restricting the power of both sides to terminate the contract of employment at will. At the same time the Ministry of Labour actively encouraged the growth of collective bargaining over Guaranteed Week Agreements, and these spread to a number of industries after 1945.[72] Collective bargaining at sector level received significant statutory support through Order 1305, which provided for compulsory arbitration over the application of sector-level terms and conditions to non-union firms, and which remained in place for several years after the end of the war.[73] Casual labour practices in the docks were dealt with through legislation which, somewhat unusually, placed the hiring process on a statutory footing.[74]

These legal controls over hiring and the more general move away from short-term notice periods were central to the postwar conception of full employment. The memorandum of evidence submitted by Political and Economic Planning during the preparation of *Social Insurance and Allied Services* argued for 'greater job security and better organisation of man-power ... by a compulsory notice period (at least two weeks) in every contract of employment, and compulsory notification of every vacancy and registration of every worker during the period of notice'.[75] In similar vein, Beveridge argued in *Full Employment in a Free Society* in 1944 that:

> in one special field, return to the old ways of engaging labour should be definitely made impossible. Industries like docks and harbour services which by practising casual employment have been the main generators of chronic under-employment in the past, have been transformed in the war. It may be assumed that the main principle of the transformation will remain in peace, that the men following such occupations will have guaranteed weekly wages, and that this will lead in due course to the organisation of regular work as well as of regular wages, with men working for a single employing agency or for groups of employers, in place of taking their chance with single employers at a number of separate taking-on places. It may be hoped that in many other industries, the former position in regard to the employment of men will be transformed by the substitution of weekly for daily or hourly engagements.[76]

As it was, the proposal for compulsory notice periods had to wait until the Contracts of Employment Act 1963, and notification by employers of vacancies has never been made mandatory. Indeed, in many ways, the process of applying labour standards to the employment relationship remained incomplete after 1945. The regulatory role of labour legislation was confined, with collective bargaining at sector level remaining the principal source of regulation of terms and conditions. Sector-level collective agreements, while providing an effective floor of rights for hourly-paid workers in a majority of industries from the 1940s onwards, did not significantly widen the subject-matter of bargaining, so that there remained a significant gap between manual and non-manual groups in the quality of occupational benefits, notwithstanding their single status as employees for legal purposes. The employment protection legislation of the 1960s and 1970s marked a further step towards standardisation, in that it introduced important protections in the areas of income security and termination of employment for both manual and non-manual employees. Its impact was nevertheless limited by qualifying conditions which allowed for the exclusion of certain part-time, temporary and casual workers from protection. Even prior to the deregulatory policies of the 1980s and 1990s, large areas of the workforce were employed in unorganised firms or sectors, or in casual forms of employment which fell outside the scope of effective institutional regulation; here, the concept of the contract of employment could only with difficulty be applied.

CONCLUSION

This chapter has traced the impact of social legislation upon the concept of the contract of employment during the formative years of the welfare state in Britain in the first half of the twentieth century. We have seen how the redistributive and protective goals of the welfare state gave rise to forms of regulation and taxation which were focused to a large extent on the institution of wage-dependent labour. The legislation sought to establish on a general basis the responsibilities of employers for sharing and spreading social and economic risks arising out of employment (injury, ill-health, unemployment, lack of income in retirement). At first, the courts were reluctant to apply this form of regulation to relationships which, in their eyes, were more akin to the relationship of employer and independent contractor. This category included, on the one hand, intermediary suppliers of labour services, such as butty men and gang leaders, and, on the other, high-status workers such as managers, professionals and skilled clerical staff. The juridical form given to these status-based distinctions was the 'control' test. Gradually, however, these distinctions faded as the legislation took hold, and the previously separate models of 'service' and 'employment' began to merge into one another. The control test was eclipsed by the 'organisation' and 'economic reality' tests. The modern, 'unitary' contract of employment was the result: legally, at least, all employees now had a single status, which was differentiated from that of independent contractors who genuinely worked 'on their own account'.[77]

The impact of the welfare state, then, was to add a layer of protective 'status obligations' to the employment relationship,[78] in addition to those supplied by the older, hierarchical tradition of master and servant.[79] Far from being inimical to a contractual conception of employment, collective bargaining and social legislation, by stabilising the employment relationship, made it possible for a contractual model to develop which was based on the recognition of reciprocal rights and obligations and the sharing of economic risk. Even the core of common law rules, the judge-made implied terms, were affected by this process, as the courts gradually came round to the view that the employer, as well as the employee, was bound by the implied duty of co-operation and by the requirement to act in good faith.[80] Common law doctrines, such as the concept of incorporation of terms, were used to give effect to the normative terms of collective agreements (albeit with variable success).[81] In so far as this process of 'contractualisation' was a partial one, it failed to go further, not so much because of any doctrinal rigidity within the common law, but by virtue of the selective and partial nature of the legislation itself and the preference for voluntarism in industrial relations. There was no equivalent in British labour law to the concepts of social citizenship which helped to ensure the general application of labour standards in France during the same period, no commitment to a universal statutory minimum wage, nor any attempt to place the regulation of working time on a general statutory footing. Variations in the bargaining power of different groups continued to be reflected in the inter-occupational structure of wages and conditions as it developed in the postwar period, and the division between white-collar and blue-collar status remained intact within pay and benefit structures at company level, notwithstanding that it had ceased to have any legal significance. Nevertheless, the process of stabilising the employment relationship was slowly carried forward by employment protection legislation, and as late as the mid-1980s sector-level collective agreements were still being used in some sectors to bring about reductions in the basic working week and to extend the duration of annual paid leave entitlements.

The contract of employment is often seen as having survived into the modern period *in spite of* the growth of collective bargaining and regulatory legislation; this chapter has suggested that the opposite is the case, that the contract of employment as we know it today is largely the *product* of the welfare state. As such, it also reflects the welfare state's shortcomings. The regulation and standardisation of the employment relationship may have achieved greater security only at the cost of reproducing certain rigidities and inequalities which are now seen as unsustainable. These perceptions add fuel to the debate over the 'fragmentation' of the contract of employment in the face of growing labour flexibility. Yet, as we have seen, the debate over flexibility is nothing new. The construction of the modern labour market began in the 1890s and 1900s under conditions of extreme economic insecurity which mirror those of our own time. It seems unlikely that the contract of employment will have no role to play in future attempts at reconstructing labour law.

NOTES

1 B. Hepple, 'Introduction', in B. Hepple (ed.), *The Making of Labour Law in Europe*, Mansell, London, p. 11.
2 O. Kahn-Freund, *Labour and the Law*, 3rd edn, ed. P. Davies and M. Freedland, Stevens, London, p. 8.
3 See S. Deakin and G. Morris, *Labour Law*, Butterworths, London, 1995, p. 162, for further discussion of this point.
4 Lord Wedderburn, 'Companies and employees: common law or social dimension?', in his *Labour Law and Freedom: Further Essays in Labour Law*, Lawrence & Wishart, London.
5 O. Kahn-Freund, 'Blackstone's neglected child: the contract of employment', *Law Quarterly Review*, vol. 93, 1977, pp. 508–28.
6 P. Atiyah, *The Rise and Fall of Freedom of Contract*, Clarendon Press, Oxford, 1979.
7 H. Collins, 'Market power, bureaucratic power and the contract of employment', *Industrial Law Journal*, vol. 15, 1986, pp. 1–15, esp. p. 14.

8 K. Foster, 'The legal form of work in the nineteenth century: the myth of contract?', paper presented to the conference on *The History of Law, Labour and Crime*, University of Warwick, 1982; see also A. Merritt, '"Control" v. "economic reality": defining the contract of employment', *Australian Business Law Review*, 1982, pp. 105–24; 'The historical role of the law in the regulation of employment: abstentionist or interventionist?', *Australian Journal of Law and Society*, vol. 1, 1982, pp. 56–86.

9 S. Deakin, 'Logical deductions? Wages law before and after *Delaney* v. *Staples*', *Modern Law Review*, vol. 55, 1992, pp. 848–57.

10 *Bartonshill Coal Co.* v. *Reid* (1856) 3 Macq. 266; see Wedderburn, 'Companies and employees', pp. 99–101.

11 *Lancaster* v. *Greaves* (1829) 9 B. & C. 627, 631–32 (Parke J.).

12 *Emmens* v. *Elderton* (1853) 13 CB 495; *Turner* v. *Goldsmith* [1891] 1 QB 544.

13 *Lilley* v. *Elwin* (1848) 11 QB 472; *R.* v. *Biggins* (1862) 5 LT 605; see Deakin, 'Logical deductions?', for analysis of these cases.

14 F. Meyers, *Ownership of Jobs: A Comparative Study*, University of California Press, Los Angeles, 1964, p. 19.

15 Under the Employers and Workmen Act 1875, s. 10, a 'workman' was defined as including a 'labourer, servant in husbandry, journeyman, artificer, handicraftsman, miner, or [person] otherwise engaged in manual labour'.

16 See Deakin, 'Logical deductions?', for an account of the distinctive features of the Act.

17 *Morgan* v. *London General Omnibus Co.* (1884) 13 QBD 832.

18 *Cook* v. *North Metropolitan Tramways Ltd* (1887) 18 QBD 683.

19 *Hunt* v. *Great Northern Railway Ltd* [1891] 1 QB 601.

20 *Bound* v. *Lawrence* [1892] 1 QB 226.

21 *R.* v. *Louth Justices* [1900] 2 Ir.R. 714.

22 Workmen's Compensation Act 1897, s. 7.

23 *Simpson* v. *Ebbw Vale Steel, Iron & Coal Co.* [1905] 1 KB 453.

24 *Simpson* v. *Ebbw Vale Steel, Iron & Coal Co.* [1905] 1 KB 453, 458 (Collins MR).

25 *Simpson* v. *Ebbw Vale Steel, Iron & Coal Co.* [1905] 1 KB 453, 456.

26 Workmen's Compensation Act 1906, s. 13.

27 National Insurance Act 1911, s. 1 and Sched. 1.

28 National Insurance Act 1911, Sched. 1, Part I, para. (c).

29 National Insurance Act 1911, s. 1(2); SR & O 1912/921; SR & O 1914/880.

30 They were named as building; construction; shipbuilding; mechanical engineering; ironfounding; vehicle construction; and sawmilling. National Insurance Act 1911, Sched. 6.

31 O. Kahn-Freund, 'Servants and independent contractors', *Modern Law Review*, vol. 14, 1951, pp. 504–9, esp. p. 505.

32 *Simmons* v. *Heath Laundry Co.* [1910] 1 KB 543.

33 *Underwood* v. *Perry* [1923] W.C. & I. Rep. 63.

34 *Scottish Insurance Commissioners* v. *Edinburgh Royal Infirmary* 1913 SC 751.

35 *Hill* v. *Beckett* [1915] 1 KB 578.

36 *R.* v. *Negus* (1873) LR 2 CP 34.

37 *Yewens* v. *Noakes* (1880) 6 QBD 530.

38 e.g. *Sadler* v. *Henlock* (1859) 4 E. & B. 570.

39 *Simpson* v. *Ebbw Vale Steel, Iron & Coal Co.* [1905] 1 KB 453; see above (p. 216).

40 *Simmons* v. *Heath Laundry Co.* [1910] 1 KB 543.

41 *Simmons* v. *Heath Laundry Co.* [1910] 1 KB 543, 553 (Lord Justice Buckley).

42 See, respectively, *Waites* v. *Franco-British Exhibition* (1909) 25 TLR 441; *Bagnall* v. *Levinstein* [1907] 1 KB 531; *Dow* v. *McNeil* [1925] W.C. & I. Rep. 32; *Murphy* v. *Enniscorthy Guardians* [1908] 2 Ir. R. 609; *re South Dublin Union Officers* [1913] W.C. & I. Rep. 245.

43 The courts were also prepared to use the control test to divide the functions of medical employees into those for which the employer was responsible and those for which it was not: see *Hillyer* v. *St Bartholemew's Hospital* [1902] 2 KB 820, in which the hospital was held not to be liable for negligence of a nurse in the performance of her professional, as opposed to her administrative, duties.

44 The courts reached opposing outcomes in different cases. Butty workers and foremen were found to be within the protection of the Workmen's Compensation Acts in *Evans* v. *Penwelt Dinas Silica Brick Co.* (1901) 18 TLR 58 and *Paterson* v. *Lockhart* (1905) 42 SLR 755, but outside them in *Simmons* v. *Faulds* (1901) 17 TLR 352, *Hayden* v. *Dick* (1902) 40 SLR 95 and *Vanplew* v. *Parkgate Iron & Steel Co.* [1903] 1 KB 851.

45 *Crowley* v. *Limerick County Council* [1923] 2 Ir. R. 178; *Littlejohn* v. *Brown & Co. Ltd.* 1909 SC 169; although cf. *Dunlop* v. *M'Cready* (1900) 37 SLR 779; *Doharty* v. *Boyd* 1909 SC 87.

46 Workmen's Compensation Act 1906, s. 13; National Insurance Act 1911, Sched. 1, Part II, para. (h).

47 *Scottish Insurance Comrs.* v. *M'Naughton* 1914 SC 826.

48 *Boothby* v. *Patrick & Son* [1918] W.C. & I. Rep. 340.

49 *Smith* v. *Buxton* [1915] W.C. & I. Rep. 126.

50 *Dewhurst* v. *Mather* [1908] 2 KB 754.

51 *Alderman* v. *Warren* [1916] W.C. & I. Rep. 266.

52 *Stoker* v. *Wartham* [1919] 1 KB 499.

53 *Knight* v. *Bucknill* [1913] W.C. & I. Rep. 175; *Withams* v. *Larsen Ltd* [1928] W.C. & I. Rep. 323.

54 *Broome* v. *Ministry of Labour* [1927] W.C. & I. Rep. 232; *Watson* v. *Government Instructional Centre* [1929] W.C. & I. Rep. 265; *re Leeds Corp. and Chadwick* (1928) 44 TLR 797 (cf. Unemployment Insurance Act 1920, s. 47(1)(6); Unemployment Insurance Act 1927, s. 15 and Sched. IV); *McGeachy* v. *Dept. of Health for Scotland* 1938 SC 282.

55 It was not until the House of Lords decided *Bartonshill Coal Co.* v. *Reid* (1856) 4 Macq. 266 that the Scottish courts accepted the doctrine, which had its origins in decisions of the English courts.

56 *Paterson* v. *Lockhart* (1905) 42 SLR 755, 757.

57 *Dunlop* v. *M'Cready* (1900) 37 SLR 779, 782.

58 *Littlejohn* v. *Brown* 1909 SC 169, 174.

59 *Social Insurance and Allied Services*, Cmd. 6404, London, HMSO, 1942, para. 314.

60 The modern division between self-employment and dependent employment in the law of taxation emerged only gradually. The Income Tax Act 1918 drew a distinction between earnings from public-sector employment (Schedule E) and

earnings and profits from all other employment (Schedule D). Then the Finance Act 1922 (s. 18) in effect transferred earnings from dependent employment in the private sector from Schedule D to Schedule E. This left just the self-employed in Schedule D. Later, employees, but not the self-employed, were subjected to automatic deductions of tax under the 'Pay-As-You-Earn' system (Income Tax (Employments) Act 1943). The cumulative effect of these changes was to institute radically different tax regimes for the two groups.

61 The first such statute was the Contracts of Employment Act 1963; the relevant provision is now contained in the Employment Rights Act 1996, s. 230(1).

62 See, in the context of social insurance, *Vandyk* v. *Minister of Pensions and National Insurance* [1955] 1 QB 29.

63 See, in particular, *Stevenson, Jordan & Harrison* v. *McDonald & Evans* [1952] 1 TLR 101.

64 *Cassidy* v. *Minister of Health* [1951] 2 KB 343; *Roe* v. *Minister of Health* [1954] 2 QB 66; *Beloff* v. *Pressdram Ltd* [1973]] 2 All ER 241.

65 *Market Investigations Ltd* v. *Minister for Social Security* [1969] 2 QB 173; *Lee Ting Sang* v. *Chung Chi-Keung* [1990] ICR 409.

66 F. Wilkinson, 'Collective bargaining in the steel industry in the 1920s', in A. Briggs and J. Saville (eds), *Essays in Labour History*, vol. 3: *1918–1939*, Croom Helm, London, 1977.

67 F. Tillyard, *Industrial Law*, 2nd edn, A. & C. Black, London, 1928, pp. 328–9.

68 Ibid., pp. 17–18.

69 Most notably in *Devonald* v. *Rosser & Son Ltd* [1906] 2 KB 728.

70 On the 'OXO' system of working, see E. Szyszczak, *Partial Unemployment: The Regulation of Short-time Working in Britain*, Mansell, London, 1990, p. 76.

71 The Essential Work (General Provisions) (No. 2) Order, SR & O 1942/1594.

72 Szyszczak, *Partial Unemployment*, pp. 82–3. At the same time, the scope for using the unemployment insurance system to subsidise short-time working was gradually restricted, but it was only with the introduction of statutory guaranteed pay in the Employment Protection Act 1975 that the practice was effectively ended: ibid.

73 On Order 1305 and its successors, see Lord Wedderburn, 'Class, struggle and ideology in British labour law', in *Labour Law and Freedom*, pp. 8–15.

74 Dock Workers (Regulation of Employment) Act 1946. The Wages Councils Act 1945 also aimed to combat casualisation by a series of extensions to the powers of the Wages Councils, most notably the power to set minimum conditions relating to annual paid leave. (The principle of annual paid leave had been intro-duced by the Holidays with Pay Act 1938, but its implementation had lapsed with the outbreak of war.)

75 *Social Insurance and Allied Services*, Cmd 6405, HMSO, London, 1942, p. 36.

76 William Henry Beveridge, *Full Employment in a Free Society*, Allen & Unwin, London, 1944, 2nd edn, 1960, para. 231.

77 See M. Freedland, 'The role of the contract of employment in modern labour law', in L. Betten (ed.), *The Employment Contract in Transforming Labour Relations*, Kluwer, Deventer, 1995, p. 21.

78 W. Streeck, *Social Institutions and Economic Performance*, Sage, London, 1993, ch. 2.

79 A. Fox, *Beyond Contract: Work, Power and Trust Relations*, Faber & Faber, London, 1974.

80 See Deakin and Morris, *Labour Law*, pp. 296–301.

81 Ibid., pp. 232–9.

12

INDUSTRIAL RELATIONS IN IRON AND STEEL, SHIPBUILDING AND THE DOCKS, 1930–1960

Roy Mankelow and Frank Wilkinson

INTRODUCTION

It is impossible to talk about a British labour market *model* or to summarise neatly some general tendency in the labour market. Like Topsy, labour markets and industrial relation systems just grew under the shaping influence of product and labour structures and organisation; techniques of production and methods of working; the enactment, interpretation and enforcement of labour law and how these and other factors interacted and changed. The three industries chosen here – iron and steel, shipbuilding and the docks – show how factors specific to particular sectors resulted in wide differences in institutional and organisational developments.

The iron and steel industry developed an *internal* labour market, shipbuilding a *craft* market and the docks a largely *secondary* labour market within which privileged segments evolved. The form of industrial relations adopted by the iron and steel industry can be described as *voluntary joint regulation*. This originated with the introduction of joint conciliation and arbitration boards which concluded agreements on the terms and conditions of employment and accepted binding arbitration as the final stage of procedure. Shipbuilding industrial relations typified developments in engineering and related metalworking trades in which the institutions and outcomes were importantly shaped by the unresolved clash between the traditional rights to regulate their trade claimed by craft workers and the right to manage their shops demanded by the employers. These struggles resulted in a system of collective bargaining in which employers made unilateral decisions on claims submitted by unions, leaving the latter the option of taking it, leaving it or resorting to industrial action. This collective bargaining system was typified by the procedure embodied in the 1922 National

Engineering Agreement by which disputes and grievances could be processed through a series of stages to a national conference where 'the employers sat in judgement'.[1] This system can be described from the workers side as involuntary employers' conciliation. The form of industrial relations in the docks resulted from initiatives taken by the unions under the 1919 Industrial Courts Act and later by government, which established a semblance of joint regulation that was never fully accepted, particularly by the employers. This can be described as *involuntary joint regulation.*

WORK, LABOUR MARKET ORGANISATION AND INDUSTRIAL RELATIONS IN IRON AND STEEL, SHIPBUILDING AND THE DOCKS

Industrial structure and organisation, 1930–60

By the interwar years both iron and steel and shipbuilding were in decline, and in an attempt to reverse this the government introduced trade protection and measures to encourage industrial rationalisation. Protection enabled iron and steel to recover quickly from the 1929 slump and by 1938 steel output was 8 per cent above its 1929 level. Trade, however, recovered slowly, depressing the demand for ships and the flow of goods through the docks. By 1938 shipbuilding was still 30 per cent below its 1929 peak, imports had yet to recover their 1929 level and exports were 30 per cent down. By 1947, steel production was 22 per cent up on 1938, shipbuilding had risen by 14 per cent and imports and exports by 25 and 8 per cent respectively. By 1960 steel output had risen 100 per cent, imports by 75 per cent and exports by 100 per cent above 1947 levels. Shipbuilding performed less impressively: output peaked at 25 per cent higher than 1947 in 1955 but by 1960 had fallen to 90 per cent of the 1955 peak.

Government intervention to rationalise shipbuilding and iron and steel in the interwar years was only partly successful. Plants were closed, others were modernised and some concentration of ownership took place. Nevertheless, the industrial structure remained fragmented with a long tail of small and obsolete plant.[2] The docks also retained their fragmented industrial structures and outdated methods. From 1938 rearmament and wartime priorities took precedence so that by 1945 the wartime failure to maintain and renew plant had exacerbated the problems inherited from pre-war. The steel industry responded to postwar growth in demand and productive capacity was expanded and extensively modernised, without, however, fundamentally transforming the structure of production. Shipbuilding was even less effectively modernised and remained poorly placed to take advantage of growth in world demand. This was disguised whilst demand from

British ship-owners kept ahead of domestic shipbuilding capacity, but as they increasingly turned to the lower prices and more reliable delivery times of foreign producers the fundamental weakness of British shipbuilding was exposed.[3] There was no serious attempt to modernise the docks. During the war some American cargo-handling practices were introduced but to a surprising extent the docks in 1960 were operated in much the same way as they had been before the first world war.[4] An understanding of these matters is crucial to any analysis of post-1930 labour markets.

Importantly, then, during the period 1930–60 the industries studied here had largely retained their pre-1930 structure and organisation, an inertia complemented by lack of change in labour market structures, work organisation and industrial relations.

Work organisation and labour market structure

The three industries share a strong continuity of worker organisation inherited from older traditions and maintained as they developed from the mid-nineteenth century. In each industry, skilled workers were of central importance in the organisation of production. It was common practice for firms to cede managerial authority by contracting production to skilled workers who controlled and organised production and employed and paid their own underhands.[5] When contracting was replaced by direct employment this control was largely transferred to the directly employed skilled workers.

Iron and steel is a process industry consisting of a series of production stages and supporting ancillary services, each using different technologies that required specific skills and experience. Technical change reduced the importance of the skills and knowledge of the leading process workers and transformed labourers into machine operators, and this, with the growing organised power of the underhands, put an end to contracting. Next, pressure from the underhands for access to skilled jobs transformed the external craft markets of the contractors into markets internal to the firm. Promotion became by seniority in lines organised around production techniques and operated by trade union branches.[6] Promotion lines provided on-the-job training and guaranteed access to higher levels of skill and earnings for members, but restricted labour mobility to the lowest occupations.

Shipbuilding is essentially a construction industry that requires a succession of different skills, which proliferated as ships became more complex. Some skills were specific to shipbuilding but most of the ninety-five trades working in shipbuilding were general to engineering and other metalworking trades.[7] The fine division of labour, high degree of trade specialisation, the sequencing of each trade's input and the small number of ships produced in each yard resulted in a high level of labour mobility between yards along skill lines. The horizontal divisions in the labour market hardened as the shipbuilding trades became organised into craft unions which protected their members' skilled status and their 'right to trade' their craft in opposition to employers, lower-skilled workers or other craft grades. As a consequence, demarcation and dilution disputes were endemic, and were especially triggered by the introduction of new equipment, materials and processes.[8] Entry into shipbuilding trades came to be by apprenticeship training, maintained and administered by the unions. The attempted substitution of apprentices for journeymen led to union-imposed restrictions on the numbers of apprentices. Apprentice training was narrowly based, trainees receiving little or no technical instruction,[9] and training took place within the multi-craft teams. These organised and undertook production so that the skills needed to co-ordinate the production process were also acquired through practical apprenticeships.[10]

Dockwork involved moving cargo to and from the ships and their loading and unloading. The demand for labour was irregular because of the uneven flow of shipping into the ports, the proliferation of employers and the cut-throat competition between them. The response was a casualisation of the dock labour force organised around the *call-on* system, whereby workers presented themselves for work each day and were selected if needed. Only a small proportion of dockworkers had permanent employment with one employer, and generally dockworkers worked for a large number of employers.

As a casualised industry without entry qualifications, the docks became an employer of last resort, providing the possibility of occasional work to any with the strength to push a barrow. None the less, there was a hierarchy of dockers. The elite of the dockworking labour force were the stevedores, who had the skill, knowledge and experience for the loading and unloading of ships. The dockers worked on the quays and included both workers who regularly presented themselves at the calling-on stands and those who came to the docks on the off-chance of picking up occasional work. There were also divisions between the strong, physically fit, mainly younger workers, the 'blue-eyed boys' who worked hard and quickly and were rarely without work, and older and less-fit men who were less frequently employed.

The regular men lived in permanent communities, close to the docks. These served to reproduce the dock labour, structure entry into its ranks and form the basis for trade unionism. The dockers and stevedores received no training from their employers; the skills of the job were passed on from father to son. As dockwork became strongly unionised the regular men were able to exercise much greater control over job access, and in time only those who carried a 'ticket' were allowed to work in the docks, and only union card carriers could obtain a dockers' ticket. The unions gave first preference to their members' sons, and next to other relatives. Some men also gained entry as employers' nominees. The dock labour force was thus recruited and trained almost entirely through local communities of dockers.

The large numbers seeking casual work at the docks, and the poor quality of many casuals, led to registration schemes in Liverpool in 1912 and in Bristol soon after. But the impetus for registration only gained pace from the 1920s as unemployment increased. London introduced registration in 1921. There, although the average number of men required for work amounted to 34,000 per working day, the register was set at 61,000 registered dockworkers. Registration was a step towards controlling the chaos of the call-on but did little to end casualism,[11] which remained the normal employment system up to decasualisation in 1967.

Industrial relations and wage determination

As early as 1869 the iron masters and their contractors in the north-east iron district had set up a board of arbitration and conciliation to agree terms and conditions of employment. This form of joint regulation progressively extended throughout the industry. With the ending of contracting, as all process workers became employed directly by the firms, process worker unions increasingly repudiated joint boards and demanded face-to-face negotiations. But the change was more apparent than real. The contractor's tonnage rate was divided by agreed proportions between all members of the production team, so individual contracting was replaced by group contracting and joint regulation survived the transition to direct negotiations.[12]

The iron and steel industry adopted a two-tier system of wage determination. Base tonnage rates and manning levels were negotiated at plant level but these were subject to centrally agreed general adjustments. It became the established practice for the general wage level to vary with product prices, the formula for which was agreed by collective bargaining. Agreed industry-wide procedures were also established for processing and arbitrating local disputes. These maintained industrial peace but did not prevent earnings drift or secure for the employers control over manning and work practices. It became accepted that base rates could only be revised if changes in technology or working conditions were 'substantial'. Claims were taken piecemeal through the procedures but it proved difficult to establish that they were radical enough to merit adjustments in rates, manning or work practices. Consequently, base rates were sticky, earnings drifted upwards with output and varied widely with plant productivity, and working practices and manning were difficult to alter.[13] Breaking the link between productivity and earnings required united action by the employers, but this threatened the established procedures. Such common cause proved impracticable because of the threat it posed to the long industrial peace; moreover, changes in wage determination which mainly benefited the most progressive firms gave them a further edge over their less-efficient competitors.[14]

National negotiations over the length of the working day in steel plants took place in 1918–19. These negotiations were important both because they established a national eight-hour working day and because they breached the convention that base rates were fixed locally. This latter change resulted from the agreement that although the weekly pay of workers with base shift earnings of less than fifty shillings (£2.50) per shift were to be protected by leaving the shift rates unchanged, the shift rates of workers earning 120 shillings (£6) were reduced by 33 per cent, and between these limits the reduction in base rates was the greater the higher the base rate. In effect, the highest-paid workers paid for the reduction in their hours whilst the employers met the cost for the lowest paid.[15] The innovation of the highest paid contributing to the cost of national wage settlements was further developed in the 1920s.

Until the first world war, tonnage rate payment and product-price-related sliding scales were confined to process workers whilst maintenance workers and ancillary workers were paid time rates which did not vary automatically with product prices. During the first world war, iron and steel workers were awarded *war bonuses* to compensate for consumer price inflation. After 1920, as iron and steel prices collapsed, the war bonuses were converted into sliding-scale increments and the wages of all iron and steel workers were subjected to product-price fluctuations. Steel prices continued to fall sharply, driving the wages of the lower-paid – who were not on tonnage rages and who had not benefited from post-1914 tonnage increases – below their pre-war real value. Under pressure from the lower-paid and the general unions, which organised many of the ancillary workers, the Iron and Steel Trades Confederation (ISTC) negotiated an increase in base rates for the lowest-paid workers and an extension of tonnage bonuses to include non-process workers; in return they conceded a reduction in the tonnage rates of the highest-paid steel workers and a relaxation of weekend working rules.[16]

A national minimum basic shift rate was agreed in 1937. In 1939 product-price-related sliding scales were frozen and cost-of-living sliding scales introduced. Following the second world war, wage determination was further complicated by nationally agreed general wage increases. Thus by the 1950s, earnings of most workers in iron and steel varied automatically with plant output and the index of retail prices. They were also adjustable by national and local bargaining.

National bargaining in shipbuilding developed as, under pressure from trade unions, the shipbuilding employers came together to form the Shipbuilders Employers' Federation (SEF). The unions – which were already concerned at the effects of demarcation disputes on their membership and funds – responded by forming the Federation of Engineering and Shipbuilding Trades (FEST). Negotiations were carried on at a number of levels. For example, FEST was empowered to negotiate pay and conditions common to the whole industry, but had no powers in respect of particular crafts.[17] The national 1908 Edinburgh Agreement included the provision that, while local differences in wages and hours were to be preserved, '*general fluctuations'* in the activity of the industry as a whole were to be met by alterations in the wages of all trades and all districts simultaneously.[18] During the first world war the general wage level in shipbuilding was supplemented by war bonuses and in the first half of the 1920s the employers imposed a succession of national lock-outs to reduce wages.[19] From 1930, however, National Uniform Plain Time Rates (NUPTR) were negotiated for skilled and unskilled workers.[20] Nevertheless, wage determination in shipbuilding became increasingly complex. During the war nationally agreed time rates were enhanced by bonus additions, which were consolidated into the NUPTR in 1950. These were increased at regular intervals in the 1950s. Concurrently the continuing expansion of piece-rates, in lieu, overtime and other special payments, affecting over 80 per cent of skilled workers, guaranteed wide variations in take-home pay.[21]

At the shipyard level, work allocation and the use of machines remained contentious issues.[22] Job control was seen as crucial by both sides; whilst the employers tried to assert their authority, in general they failed. They attempted to operate machines with semi-skilled labour, reduce manning levels and cut wage rates. The unions made concessions but the employers' dependence on the technical expertise of their skilled workers enabled craft unions to capture the operations of new machines and classify them as skilled. Thus, despite changing technology, the strength and organisation of the trade unions left the craftsmen firmly in control of the workplace and of the organisation of work.

No formal negotiating procedures for resolving local wage, work organisation and demarcation disputes to cover the whole shipbuilding industry were ever instituted.[23] Long-standing procedures did exist but not all unions were party to them. The Boilermakers and Shipwrights also refused to sign the 1912 demarcation agreement, on the grounds that demarcations were exclusively union business. The result of negotiations, which took place separately at national, district and yard level and between the SEF and FEST as well as separately with the Boilermakers, Shipwrights and Engineers, made for interminable disputes over demarcation and wage differentials.

In the docks the 1889 strike established a minimum time rate of six pence per hour and a minimum of four hours' work for casuals taken on at the call. However, the dockers and their newly founded unions were soon locked in a bitter struggle against the employers, who unilaterally repudiated the terms of the 1889 settlement. In 1911 the dockers and several other unions amalgamated to form the National Transport Workers Federation (NTWF), and in 1919 this Federation put forward national wage demands for the dockworkers, using the procedures laid down in the Industrial Courts Act. The employers responded by forming a provisional national body (which subsequently became the National Council of Employers of Dock and Riverside Labour, and later still the National Association of Port Employers) to represent them at the Shaw Inquiry set up to investigate the NTWF's demands.[24] Lord Shaw's Award (1920) conceded the dockworkers' claim for a national time rate of sixteen shillings for an eight hour day and gave strong support to the expansion of pieceworking in the docks as a means of guaranteeing output.[25] These latter proposals were not initially supported by the unions; nevertheless, piecework spread rapidly through the dock industry. Shaw also recommended the establishment of a national joint negotiating body, and out of this emerged the National Joint Council for Dock Labour (NJC). The NJC was involved in all national negotiations and disputes, but any matters not national in scope were handled by local joint councils or direct by individual employers and the unions. The influence of national bargaining on earnings declined in the depressed 1920s as employers forced down national minimum wage rates to ten shillings per day and as piecework spread, increasing the importance of locally agreed wage supplements.

The Dock Labour (Compulsory Registration) Order 1940 required port employers and dockers to register and, in 1941, the Essential Work (Dock Labour) Order guaranteed a weekly minimum wage to men available for work at the full eleven turns in the week. As the second world war drew to its close, the need for a scheme to replace the 1941 Order was widely accepted by government, employers and unions alike; none of them wanted a return to the pre-war system. Following unsuccessful negotiations between employers and unions, the government introduced the Dock Workers (Regulation of Employment) Order 1947 (S.R. & O. 1189). This came into operation as the National Dock Labour Scheme (NDLS) under the direction of a new joint body, the National Dock Labour Board.[26] The Scheme retained in large part the provisions of the wartime Order, and although it did nothing to end casualism, it made it illegal for any Scheme port to employ non-registered men except as temporary workers under certain laid-down conditions.

The NDLS established a guaranteed minimum wage for registered dockworkers who presented themselves for work at the eleven call-ons per week. But local negotiations grew in importance, frequently handled by local unofficial leaders, so that the wide differentials between earnings of men both within the same port and in other docks were maintained. In the London docks, the London Ocean Trades Employers' Association is said to have maintained a list of more than 5,000 different cargo-handling piece-work rates.[27] Overtime was widely abused – usually with the tacit approval of management – 'cons', payments for special skills or unpleasant working conditions also flourished, widening pay differentials and creating dissatisfaction.[28]

INDUSTRIAL DISPUTES, 1930–60

By 1930 all three industries had well-established national bargaining institutions. But only iron and steel had developed effective procedures for resolving local disputes, the likelihood of which had increased with the proliferation of payment by results and special payment systems. During the 1930s the lid had been kept on industrial relations at the local level by high unemployment. But economic recovery from the mid-1930s and the full employment achieved during the war dramatically transformed the supply side of the labour market, giving local unions unprecedented bargaining power.[29] This is reflected in the strike record. In the period 1930–8 the average number of working days lost per 1,000 insured persons in the docks was 285, and in 1947–55 this reached 3,134. A similar pattern of change took place in shipbuilding, with working days lost per 1,000 insured persons rising from 328 to 890.[30] Table 12.1 shows the trend of strike activity in the immediate postwar period up to 1959. Comparing 1949–52 with 1953–9, workers involved in strikes as a percentage of workers in employment increased threefold in all industries and services, as did working days lost per 1,000 workers. Strikes in iron and steel and related industries broadly followed this pattern, whilst in shipbuilding the increase was closer to fivefold. In the ports and inland waterways, a sector which largely consists of the docks, strike activity declined somewhat but remained at a very high level.

The underlying continuity in the pattern of industrial disputes and their resolution or non-resolution can be illustrated by a brief consideration of key industrial relations problems from each of the three industries: maintenance

Table 12.1 Strike activity in British industry, 1949–59

	Workers involved as a percentage of employees in employment			Working days lost per 1,000 employees in employment		
	1949–52	1953–9	1949–59	1949–52	1953–9	1949–59
Shipbuilding and marine engineering	4.3	21.3	15.1	272.7	1,928.6	1,326.5
Ports and inland waterways	21.2	14.6	17.0	1,685.5	1,139.6	1,338.1
Iron and steel and other metals	1.6	5.6	4.1	71.4	240.7	179.1
All industries	0.1	2.6	2.0	56.0	162.7	123.9

Source: J.W. Duncan, W.E.J. McCarthy, and G.P. Redman, *Strikes in Post-war Britain*, London, George Allen & Unwin, 1983.

craftsmen in iron and steel; welding in shipbuilding; and the Dock Labour Scheme.

A long-running dispute between the craft unions and the Iron and Steel Employers' Association (ISTEA) accounted for a significant proportion of the strikes in iron and steel in the postwar period. The maintenance craftsmen were dissatisfied with the wide differentials between their earnings and those enjoyed by the highly paid process workers, but they were reluctant to accept compulsory arbitration or to continue to follow the pattern of wage settlements set by the negotiations between ISTEA and the ISTC, the process workers' union. The employers insisted on compulsory arbitration but chose for comparators similar workers in other industries who tended to be lower paid than skilled maintenance workers in steel. The ISTC had traditionally supported the employers and, moreover, could be expected to make a comparability claim if the craft unions received special treatment.

In 1949 the National Joint Craftsmen's Iron and Steel Committee (NJCISC) signed an agreement which improved the relative pay of craftsmen, and set up a National Joint Committee for negotiating craftsmen's pay and conditions. A procedure was agreed which included arbitration as a final compulsory stage and stipulated, in clause 8, that any breach in procedure anywhere in the industry would mean an industry-wide withdrawal from negotiations by the other side. This was designed to secure national control over negotiation by preventing craft unions operating on a local as well as national front. From 1949, the NJCISC met with little success in its objective of improving the relative pay of maintenance craftsmen at national level, where its claim twice failed at arbitration, or at the local level because of clause 8.[31] As a consequence, in 1956 the NJCISC withdrew from the 1949 procedural agreement, turned down a wage increase previously awarded to the process workers and supported its claim for a higher wage increase by an overtime ban. This escalated into a strike and the Ministry of Labour intervened with a Court of Inquiry. The findings of this inquiry, at which the process workers' unions gave evidence in support of the employers, recommended the acceptance of the employers' wage offer and the continuation of compulsory arbitration.

In 1959 the craft unions signed a new procedural agreement under which arbitration was voluntary and which confined retaliatory action for a breach of procedure to the works at which the breach took place. Nevertheless, it was not until 1964 that any substantial progress was made on the craftsmen's claim. This agreement created five grades of maintenance workers with promotion conditional on skill acquisition between the first four grades (the fifth grade was reserved for apprenticed craftsmen) and extra payments determined by length of service. The importance of the promotion and seniority elements in the 1964 pay settlements forestalled any counterclaims by the process workers but it also had the effect of creating an internal labour market for craft workers in the iron and steel industry. The sixteen years of bargaining leading up to 1964 demonstrated the ability of the iron and steel employers to maintain effective national control over bargaining at all levels, even when confronted by the craft unions. The continued inability of the shipbuilding employers to exercise such control is illustrated by negotiations over the introduction of welding.

Welding became a central issue in bargaining in the shipbuilding industry in the early 1930s. By then welding had begun to replace riveting in ship construction and it promised to transform shipbuilding technology. Given the high levels of unemployment and the radical changes to shipbuilding methods it would bring, welding provided a unique opportunity to transform work organisation. Lorenz's study demonstrates both the employers' realisation of the potential for reform provided by welding but also their failure to grasp the opportunity.[32] A committee of the SEF explored the possibility of establishing a new craft grade of ship welder, who would be paid the National Uniform Time Rate for skilled workers and require two years' training; the grade would be located outside the established union structure. The committee's deliberations went further and considered using the introduction of welding to break up the squad contracting system, creating a more detailed division of labour, confining skilled workers to skilled work, and substituting cheap non-apprenticed workers on the simpler jobs. However, the committee disagreed about the more radical changes, and they were not included in the report put to the unions. This report also back-tracked on the two years' training in favour of a five-year apprenticeship to include the more general shipyard skills required for the skilled workers' traditional role as organisers of production. The unions rejected this watered-down version and by 1942 the boilermakers had established jurisdiction over welding in hull construction and established a wide pay differential for welding over other skilled wage rates. But the boilermakers' claim for jurisdiction beyond hull construction was opposed by the shipwrights, plumbers and coppersmiths, and others. The consequence was a plethora of demarcation disputes which grew to epidemic proportions with the prefabrication of ship sections, which moved much ship construction from the berths to the shops. Lorenz attributes the failure of the employers to use welding in order to radically reform work organisation to the fact that only the large, vertically integrated armaments firms had the managerial capabilities for such changes. These firms had experience in general engineering when contracting for warships, and were subject to Admiralty control which required them to improve their planning, manufacturing and accounting expertise. Smaller producers had no similar outside constraints, and their lack of managerial capabilities and continued dependence on the craft workers meant they were incapable of introducing the changes required to take full advantage of the opportunities offered by welding.

The continued importance of old antipathies between labour and capital and the central importance of managerial expertise for improving industrial relations is also illustrated by the working of the Dock Labour Scheme.[33] The Scheme was imposed on the docks by the government after the unions and employers failed to agree an alternative. It was based on the continued employer preference for casual labour and incorporated Bevin's old 'work or maintenance' proposals. The Dock Labour Boards (DLB) consisted of an equal number of docker and employer representatives and were responsible, amongst other things, for overseeing the registration of dockers and employers, labour allocation within the docks and discipline. Under the Scheme, if dockers were not engaged at the first call they were allocated by the DLB to wherever labour was in short supply; if no jobs were to be found they were paid the guaranteed minimum wage rate. But operating time was lost as the workers moved from dock to dock under the direction of the DLB and through the unions' insistence on a full gang before work could begin. The DLB's disciplinary function also proved difficult to discharge because of the traditional hostility between dockers and employers. These were embedded in the appeals procedure because the equal representation of employers and workers frequently resulted in stalemate, the system was overloaded by the large number of appeals, and the operating employers failed to discipline their workers effectively. The Scheme shifted the expense of maintaining workers who were not employed and of running the Scheme on to the employers, who complained of the high cost. But real underlying problems remained: the very large numbers of often very small employers, their lack of skill in personnel and other management, the poor working conditions they provided, the intensity of competition between them which in periods of high employment led to the bidding up of wages, their ready agreement to special payments, and their tolerance of indiscipline. The Scheme also established the DLB as the legal employer, separate from the operating employer, and thereby exacerbated the problems of developing mutual interests between employers and workers that were built into the system of casual employment.

SUMMARY

Until the first world war product wages (wages adjusted for product prices) were highly flexible. This was institutionalised in iron and steel by product-price-related sliding scales and in shipbuilding by the national agreement that locally agreed rates should fluctuate according to the state of trade. In the docks employers retained, in large measure, unilateral control of wages. During the first world war a cost-of-living element was introduced into wages by the war bonuses. This fixed element in pay proved a contentious issue in the 1920s when the unions were unable to resist employer pressure for reductions, although they did succeed in establishing national minimum wage rates to protect the lowest paid. In the second world war and after, the cost of living again dominated national bargaining, the iron and steel industry switched from product-price to cost-of-living sliding scales. More widely, rising consumer prices were compensated for by regular national wage increases. The introduction of a cost-of-living element did not necessarily mean that product wages became inflexible. This depended on the ability of firms to pass on wage rises in price increases. These economic conditions prevailed during the early postwar period. Wages were also variable with output because of payment by result, originally confined to skilled workers but progressively extended. Widening the scope of payment by result in the 1920s was closely linked to the introduction of national minimum wage rates and was designed to increase incentives and help prevent the widening of differentials between the high and low paid.

The employers in the three industries enjoyed a high degree of short-term labour force flexibility. In iron and steel this was secured by promotion by seniority, which concentrated job insecurity on the short-service workers and tied the economic interests of long-service workers to their immediate employers. In shipbuilding and the docks, where the workforces were highly casualised, job insecurity was more equally shared but at the cost of stunting any build-up of mutual interests between the firms and the workers they employed.

The workforces in the three industries exercised and continued to exercise significant control over production. No doubt this ceding of managerial authority economised on fixed costs and saved the expenses of establishing organisational structures and employing qualified managerial staff. But the vesting of power in the hands of skilled workers made it difficult to introduce new methods, reduce manning and change working practices. The employers were also effectively excluded, or, perhaps more precisely, they excluded themselves, from the social reproduction of the labour force. In shipbuilding, the unions ran the apprentice system; in iron and steel, skills were acquired by learning by doing in promotion lines; and in the docks, skills were transmitted within families and dockland communities. In shipbuilding regionally based union branches increased the efficiency of local labour markets by serving as labour exchanges whilst inter-regional union links facilitated mobility of workers between shipbuilding areas. In iron and steel, union control of promotion ensured orderly labour allocation whilst the union ticket in the docks helped reduce the chaos of casualisation. Union provision of a wide range of welfare benefits also helped keep the workforce together in shipbuilding regions during recessions; community solidarity served the same function in the docklands; whilst temporary demotion down iron and steel promotion lines during recessions kept together the key members of production teams and preserved their skills and experience for the employers. These systems lifted responsibility for training and labour allocation from the employers and preserved the pool of skilled labour in industries where labour demand fluctuated widely, but it also reinforced worker solidarity and made the technical upgrading of training systems difficult.

British firms adopted short-term employment and pay strategies which shifted a considerable degree of risk to their workforces by making jobs and pay highly uncertain. They nevertheless developed a long-term dependency on the skills, knowledge, experience and organising ability of their skilled manual workers which in turn bestowed upon these workers considerable bargaining power. In iron and steel the resulting problems were ameliorated but by no means completely removed by joint regulation which built up a foundation of strong procedures and collective bargaining expertise. These facilitated the resolution of major conflicts, such as the low-pay disputes in the 1920s and the maintenance craftsmen's disputes in the 1950s and 1960s, without industrial disruptions. Nevertheless, the local fixing of rates, manning and work organisation and the difficulties in changing them through industry-wide procedures created wide earnings differentials which were closely linked to plant productivity. Inefficient plants were preserved by their ability to continue to pay low wages; at the efficient end of the industry strongly entrenched workers were well placed to maintain tonnage rates, despite productivity increases, and to protect manning levels and archaic forms of work organisation. The failure of bargaining in iron and steel to equalise earnings across the industry and to adjust manning and work organisation to changing technology effectively subsidised inefficiency and imposed a tax on technical progress. This reinforced the structural factors which made adjustment to changed circumstances difficult, reduced the overall efficiency of the industry, lowered its competitive performance and therefore its ability to grow and to generate new jobs.

These structural weaknesses also persisted in shipbuilding and the docks, preserved by the ability of firms to shed labour readily and to get wages down. But these problems were exacerbated by the intractability of both sides which ruled out the development of effective collective bargaining institutions. Employers in the docks and shipbuilding mounted militant campaigns at national level when unemployment was high and the unions were at their weakest only to lose the initiative when faced with equal intransigence at the local level as the product and labour markets tightened. Consequently in the docks and shipbuilding, militancy, on both sides, compounded fundamental organisational weaknesses and led to a failure to develop effective procedures. In these circumstances the employment, wage and work organisation effects of technical and other changes could not be seriously considered, let alone resolved.

The result was intense job insecurity and alienation which, when coupled with worker power in the labour process, led to the development of practices that protected labour but restricted management. A further effect was the building of vested interests into local organisation, which guaranteed a militant response to employer initiatives. On the employers' sides, weakness in management organisation and a lack of expertise, training and profession-alism amongst managers were major obstacles to the initiation of change and to seeing it through.[34] In the early years of the second world war, civil servants and government ministers were shocked at the 'technical ineptitude and autocratic attitudes displayed by managers'.[35] Managerial weakness and the paucity of their training were highlighted in the Devlin report on the docks[36] and the Geddes and Booz-Hamilton reports on shipbuilding.[37] The Donovan report also queried whether the quality of personnel management was sufficient to carry through its recommended reforms of company bar-gaining. The failure of British management either to break shop-floor power or to effectively incorporate it into organisational structures left management dependent on 'foremen' or 'supervisors' who were usually promoted from the shop floor as intermediaries between senior management and production workers. But whilst foremen were expected to act as managers, they were rarely treated as such and frequently lacked the administrative and other skills necessary to perform their work effectively.[38]

The general attitude of employers towards skills and skilled workers reflected a wider class antipathy towards both work and workers.[39] The lack of regard of employers for the skills of the workforce led to a continuous pressure for deskilling, but in general employers had neither the technical expertise nor the authority to impose the work organisation necessary to break the hold of the craft workers. On the other hand, training was disputed territory and controlled by the workers, so the employers had neither the incentive nor the capability to reform it. For the workers, training was protective and thus largely closed to the requirements of changing tech-nology. The 'them and us' attitudes of both employers and workers created by this history destroyed any basis for effective co-operation[40] and created endless possibilities for dispute. The balance between these opposing forces was maintained by periodic high levels of unemployment which operated to reduce the bargaining power of labour, but not by enough to enable the employers to secure control. This uneasy equilibrium was broken by the long upward swing in economic activity from the 1930s onward, and because so little had changed, or was to change, in the underlying forces structuring industrial relations, the consequences of prolonged prosperity were escalating industrial disruption.

CONCLUSIONS

With hindsight it is possible to detect that, during the period under review, two modern labour market forms were emerging in the industrialised economies. One originated in developments in the USA and has been described as the Fordist system. This was rooted in individualism and unregulated competition and was strongly influenced by Smithian notions of the division of labour and a progressive deskilling of the workforce. In the creation of the Fordist system American management destroyed the effectiveness of craft unions, asserted its unilateral right to manage and, by organising the labour process along Taylorist principles, secured control of the conception and execution of work. The industrial unions which reorganised the workforce in the 1930s came to accept managerial prerogative in the organisation of work, negotiated comprehensive company wage and benefits agreements, but left management free to implement changes at shop-floor level to enhance productivity.

In the northern European *corporate* states the modern labour market took an alternative form. These economies were strongly influenced by the notion that social justice bestows on individuals employment rights as citizens. Regulated, rather than unrestricted, competition is a second European tradition influencing institutional organisation of product and labour markets. This resulted in strong and active employers' associations which engaged with trade unions as they developed so that centralised bargaining became the norm. State intervention in this process set the stage for tripartite decision-making in labour market policy. Individuals came to enjoy extensive statutory rights: of free association, to representation and to strike; employment contracts and conditions were carefully regulated by law and active labour market policies were targeted at high levels of training and assisted labour mobility. In turn, the unions, whilst opposing deskilling and faster working, co-operated in the introduction of new technology.[41]

The underlying relationships and managerial philosophies in the docks and in shipbuilding more closely approximate to those in the US labour market model, but British employers had neither the collective strength to break union control nor the capabilities to reorganise the labour process, and so the development towards Fordism stalled. In iron and steel the incorporation of the trade unions within effective collective bargaining institutions promised the development of labour market conditions closer to the northern European model. But fragmentation on both the unions' and the employers' sides prevented the emergence of sufficiently strong central organisations to impose the industry-wide wage and labour regulation necessary to ensure the effective introduction and exploitation of technical change. As a consequence, the strong collective bargaining institutions developed in steel merely served to build in and reinforce those structural features responsible for economic decline.

NOTES

1 K. Coates and T. Topham, *Trades Unions in Britain*, Spokesman, Nottingham, 1980, p. 175.

2 E.H. Lorenz, *Economic Decline in Britain: The Shipbuilding Industry*,

1890–1970, Clarendon Press, Oxford, 1991, pp. 59–60; and D. Burn, 'Steel', in D. Burn (ed.), *The Structure of British Industry*, vol. 1, Cambridge University Press, Cambridge, 1958, pp. 260–305.

3 Lorenz, *Economic Decline*.

4 G. Phillips and N. Whiteside, *Casual Labour: The Unemployment Question in the Port Transport Industry, 1880–1970*, Clarendon Press, Oxford, 1985, p. 265.

5 Pollard has noted of the contract system: 'if it was not a method of management it was at least a method of evading management': S. Pollard, *The Geneses of Modern Management: A Study of the Industrial Revolution in Great Britain*, Edward Arnold, London, 1965, p. 11.

6 F. Wilkinson and B. Elbaum, 'Industrial relations and uneven development: a comparative study of the American and British steel industries', *Cambridge Journal of Economics*, vol. 3, no. 3, 1979, pp. 288–92.

7 S. Pollard and P. Robertson, *The British Shipbuilding Industry, 1870–1914*, Harvard University Press, Cambridge, MA, 1979, p. 153.

8 G. Roberts, *Demarcation Rules in Shipbuilding and Ship Repairing*, Cambridge University Press, Cambridge, 1967.

9 Pollard and Robertson, *British Shipbuilding Industry*, p. 156.

10 Lorenz, *Economic Decline*, pp. 59–60.

11 A. Bullock, *The Life and Times of Ernest Bevin*, 2 vols, Heinemann, London, 1960, vol. 1, p. 125.

12 F. Wilkinson, 'Collective bargaining in the steel industry in the 1920s', in A. Briggs and J. Saville (eds), *Essays in Labour History 1918–39*, Croom Helm, London, 1977, pp. 103–5.

13 Ibid.

14 Wilkinson and Elbaum, 'Industrial relations', p. 299; see also J. Hodge, *Workman's Cottage to Windsor Castle*, Sampson Low & Marston, London, 1931, p. 107, for a discussion of the question of competitive advantage in influencing the degree of inter-firm support for wage rate reduction and the union attitude to technical progress. His general view was that the steel workers supported technical change provided they got a fair share of the plunder.

15 A. Pugh, *Men of Steel*, Iron and Steel Trades' Confederation, London, 1951.

16 Wilkinson, 'Collective bargaining'.

17 *Shipbuilding Inquiry Committee 1956–66: Report* [Geddes Report] (Cmnd 2937), HMSO, London, 1966, p. 100.

18 Pollard and Robertson, *British Shipbuilding Industry*.

19 H.A. Clegg, *The History of British Trade Unions since 1889*, 3 vols, Oxford University Press, Oxford, 1985, vol. 2, p. 374.

20 D.J. Robertson, *Factory Wage Structures and National Agreements*, Cambridge University Press, Cambridge, 1960, pp. 71–4.

21 K.G.J.C. Knowles and D.J. Robertson, 'Earnings in shipbuilding', *Bulletin of the Oxford University Institute of Statistics*, vol. 13, 1951, p. 360; and Robertson, *Factory Wage Structures*.

22 F. Wilkinson, 'Demarcation strikes 1901–72', ch. 5 (unpublished working paper); and E.H. Lorenz, 'The labour process and industrial relations in the British and French shipbuilding industries from 1880–1970: two patterns of development', unpublished PhD thesis, University of Cambridge, undated, ch. 7.

23 Geddes Report, pp. 106–8.

24 G. Adams, *Organisation of the British Port Transport Industry*, National Ports Council, London, 1973, p. 54.

25 D.F. Wilson, *Dockers: The Impact of Industrial Change*, Fontana/Collins, London, 1972, p. 226.

26 Ibid., p. 122.

27 M. Mellish, *The Docks after Devlin: A Study of the Effects of the Recommendations of the Devlin Committee on Industrial Relations in the London Docks*, Heinemann, London, 1972, pp. 17–18.

28 *Final report of the Committee of Inquiry under the Rt Hon. Lord Devlin into certain matters concerning the Port Transport Industry* [*Devlin Report*], Cmnd. 2734, HMSO, London, 1965, p. 6.

29 Bullock, *Ernest Bevin*, pp. 211 and 208.

30 Devlin Report, p. 4.

31 This account is based on a study of wage bargaining in steel made in the 1960s which included a study of contemporary wage determination in Corby iron and steel works. This research confirmed the ISTEA's success in controlling the level of local wage settlements. See F. Wilkinson, 'Craftsmen in the iron and steel industry', 1969, unpublished.

32 Lorenz, 'The labour process', chapter 6.

33 This account of the Dock Labour Scheme is taken from R. Mankelow, 'The effects of modernisation and change in the London docks: with particular reference to the Devlin reforms and events since 1967', unpublished thesis, University of Cambridge, 1994.

34 D.R. Shiman, 'The role of managerial inefficiency in the decline of the British economy', paper presented at the November 1989 Social Science History Association's conference, Washington, DC, pp. 9–13.

35 N. Tiratsoo, 'British management, 1945–64: reformers and the struggle to improve standards', in A. Abe and T.R.G. Gourvish (eds), *Britain and Japan in the Age of the Corporate Economy*, Oxford University Press, Oxford, 1997.

36 Devlin Report, pp. 9–11.

37 Geddes Report, and *British Shipbuilding 1972: A Report to the Department of Trade and Industry by Booz-Allen and Hamilton International BV*, HMSO, London, 1973, p. 173.

38 R.B. McKersey and L.C. Hunter, *Pay, Productivity and Collective Bargaining*, Macmillan, London, 1973, p. 217.

39 For a view of the attitude of a 'gentleman' to the world of work and money, see P. Cain and A. Hopkins, *British Imperialism: Crisis and Deconstruction, 1914–1990*, Longman, London, 1993, p. 299.

40 Lorenz ascribes the decline of British shipbuilding to the failure of British management to institute proper management planning and control, and argues that it was not possible for employers to bring about major change because of the resistance of craftsmen and their unions, which had its roots in mistrust of the employers: E. H. Lorenz, 'An evolutionary explanation for competitive decline: the British shipbuilding industry, 1890–1970', *Journal of Economic History*, vol. 51, no. 4, 1991, pp. 911–35.

41 B. Strath, *The Organisation of Labour Markets: Modernity, Culture and Governance in Germany, Sweden, Britain and Japan*, Routledge, London, 1996.

13

STATE REGULATION AND INDUSTRIAL ORGANISATION

The London workshop trades, 1911–1960

James Gillespie

In 1926 R.H. Tawney made the triumphant claim that minimum wage regulation under the trade board system 'represents, with the sole exception of the extension of public education, the most successful piece of social legislation of the past quarter of a century'.[1] Others who had led the campaign against 'sweated' labour before the first world war concurred. James Mallon and Edward Lascelles argued that the boards had been second only to the registration of dockers in transforming the economic structure of the poverty-stricken and demoralised East End of London.[2] The problem of the 'sweated trades', predominantly the London clothing industry, had led to the largest experiment in minimum wage policy in British industrial history. Legally enforceable minimum wages in the sweated trades, they argued, had forced employers to mechanise and had driven production out of the small insanitary workshops and homeworkers' rooms, opening the way for factory production. At the same time, the representative structure of the boards had forced both sides of industry to organise for the first time. These two achievements, industrial restructuring and organisation, had been the principal aims of the National Anti-Sweating League and the public campaign for minimum wage legislation before the first world war. By the mid-1920s the campaigners were claiming victory on both counts.

While the basis of this analysis shifted considerably in the three decades before the first world war, the central principle remained constant. Low wages were not the result of the normal workings of the labour market, but were an aberration that called for short-term state intervention to correct unusual local circumstances. The first Act, in 1909, was directed narrowly at setting minimum rates in trades designated as 'sweated'. The anti-sweating campaigners confidently believed that if the state enforced higher minimum wage levels, bad employers would be forced out of business. Increased labour costs would force surviving firms to invest in machinery, raising productive efficiency and ending the parasitic status of the industry.

The anti-sweating movement had relied on a flawed analysis of poverty in urban areas dominated by workshop trades and sub-contracting. As with Beveridge's contemporary analysis of casual labour markets, the emphasis was placed on lack of organisation on the supply side. By enforcing a minimum wage rate for the lowest paid, a new norm of labour contract could be imposed on these highly fragmented labour markets, regularising employment. Minimum wages, it was argued, would either force these trades to reorganise and mechanise production or drive them out of existence. Either outcome would be a net gain to welfare. This attempt to force restructuring through setting a floor on the price of labour ignored two key features of the workshop trades. Except for 'slop clothing', the so-called 'kaffir trade' to the colonies, by 1909 low wage rates were not a problem to most employed in these industries. It was the seasonality of employment – a result of swift changes of fashion in product markets – which was the key problem.[3]

There is a now a considerable literature on the formation of the first trades boards, and the agitation around 'sweated labour' that provided its political background.[4] Few historians have gone beyond the study of the origins of minimum wage policy; the assumption has been that once the 1909 reforms were in place, little further needs to be explained. Hart has recently put this dominant position: 'from New Years Day 1910, when the Trades Board Act of 1909 came into force, until the passage of the Wages Act of 1986 little changed in British minimum wage policy'.[5] She judges this policy a dismal failure, as the gender-specific nature of 'sweating' was lost in the minimum rates set by the new boards. Other historians have been no less critical of the trade boards' record. In Lowe's account, the limits imposed on the boards were an index of the failure of the early Ministry of Labour to realise its promise. For Davidson, they were an effect of the limited social intelligence collected by the state, and a conscious avoidance of the political consequences of a wider intervention in the workings of the labour market which a coherent attack on low wages would require. Each of these critiques has relied on an institutional analysis – with the forms taken by state intervention in Britain bearing most of the explanatory burden, whether it be the peculiarities of the British constitution (Hart) or bureaucratic politics (Lowe).[6]

The approach taken here also stresses the importance of institutions, but set in a wider framework. Instead of assuming a set of essentially arbitrary objectives which can then be judged, such as 'the end of sweating', the boards are seen as sites of shifting conflict in which their aims were continually redefined. Placed in the context of the labour markets that they regulated, a far more important point becomes the extent to which they were appropriated by existing labour practices. Contemporary attempts to reform casual labour markets fell foul of deep-seated labour market practices which appropriated new forms of state intervention. The trade board system successfully entrenched itself in the workshop-based trades of London because its powers over wage rates did not challenge the main structures of these trades, seasonality of employment and the widespread use of sub-contracting. Instead, the boards gave organised labour and employers the power to limit competition. Employers practising unfair competition by paying low wages could be driven out of business without upsetting the practices that sustained the fragmented industrial structures: the features that the architects of anti-sweating legislation had seen as their primary target.[7]

TRADE BOARDS AND THE CLOTHING TRADES

These features of the boards can be seen in the case of the tailoring trades, by far the largest industry included in their scope. Interwar developments in tailoring did not effect the simple transformation of this complex set of trades. Changes in product markets were central to industrial change as innovations in retailing opened the way to factory production in limited areas of the industry.

Three major developments – none of them reducible to changes in the payment systems of labour – marked the interwar years. First, a shift in product markets appeared, pioneered by the new retail bespoke factories of Leeds and north-east London. Firms such as Burtons developed close linkages between retail chains and final consumers, offering the higher quality of personal measurement of men's suits with the low costs of subdivided factory methods. This innovation was dependent on stable fashion, and attempts to extend these methods into ladies' tailoring were less successful. While wholesale bespoke tailoring did not abolish sub-contracting – even the most developed factories of Leeds still relied on smaller workshops in peak periods – they represented a major innovation in industrial organisation. These years were also marked by a reshaping of the rigid sexual division of labour which had always characterised the clothing trades. Factory work opened up new possibilities for younger women. The higher-skilled and strategic areas, such as cutting, remained male preserves, but making-up in the factory became largely female, with far greater regularity and better pay than any alternative employment. A wage economy based on relatively steady earnings and a comparatively high level of trade union organisation followed. By the mid-1920s, the Leeds factory sector provided most of the leadership of the National Union of Tailors and Garment Workers, a union which was soon divided by a gulf between the attitudes of the factory-based sector and the workshops.[8]

For large areas of the industry, these factory methods proved to be of marginal advantage. The bulk of employment remained in the highly seasonal workshop trades. These were not mere survivals from an under-developed stage of industrial organisation – as the proponents of industrial efficiency argued. The original targets of anti-sweating agitation, the 'slop' clothing workshops and homeworkers of London's East End, had indeed vanished by the end of the first world war: the emergence of competitive clothing industries in the colonies, especially South Africa and India, destroyed their markets.

New sectors, however, emerged to take their place, based on new product markets and labour forces. Ladies' tailoring, a largely Jewish, London-based trade, began to develop just before the war. Dominated by seasonal fashion, it relied on labyrinthine networks of sub-contracting to maintain flexibility. Low capital barriers to entry as a 'master' and the use of family labour meant that the line between worker and employer was unusually blurred, even for a sub-contracting trade. When the East End United Ladies' Tailoring Trade Union (ULTTU) was contemplating its future in the late 1930s, although a modernising, largely communist-led faction argued for amalgamation with the national tailoring union, a substantial minority held out for a union with the masters' association: 'in order to run better strikes' against the real enemy, the wholesale buyers for retailers. Unlike earlier homeworkers, in no sense could ladies' tailors be called 'sweated'. Earning high wages, when working, the problems of their industry centred on the effects of seasonal closure. As a result, the ULTTU was highly suspicious of the trade boards. These sub-contracting trades remained largely male preserves, except for some marginal and poorly paid processes. Nothing like the feminisation of the wholesale bespoke trade occurred in ladies' tailoring.

INDUSTRIAL ORGANISATION AND COLLECTIVE BARGAINING

It is difficult to assess the effects of the trade boards on wage rates in the tailoring trades. The first rates in tailoring were set on the eve of the first world war. Their impact cannot be disaggregated from the general impact of the war economy on the industry. About the postwar years it remains difficult to reach any firm conclusion, especially as enforcement levels remained low. Even the most consistent defenders of the boards admitted that there were persistent weaknesses in inspection, and that in many areas employers could flout minimum rates with impunity. On the other hand, the boards' most bitter critics within the trade union movement did not call for their complete abolition.

From the outset the enforcement machinery had been criticised for its ponderous inefficiency. As the responsibilities of the boards increased, these administrative inadequacies were compounded. In July 1915 the six trade boards set minimum rates covering half a million workers, and, with 12,000 employers on their lists, had a total inspectorate of twelve. By December 1922 the number of workers covered had increased sixfold and the number of firms was up to 180,000. To cope with this increase the inspectorate had only been raised to thirty-six officers. This weakness was exacerbated by administrative difficulties of co-ordination. As independent bodies, trade boards set rates but played no direct role in enforcement. This function was taken over from the Board of Trade by the Office of Trade Boards at the Ministry of Labour. Hence the boards were unable to monitor the working of their own policies in any direct sense. The Home Office's factory inspectorate was loath to be involved in trade board work and passed on very few complaints.[9] From January 1922 to June 1923 the East London Division of the Factory Inspectorate filed a total of eleven complaints; eight other London divisions sent in none at all.[10] As trade board inspectors could only perform two thorough inspections a day, this meant thin coverage. Infringements by employers were almost invariably identified after a direct complaint by workers, usually made through their trade unions. The response of the ministry to infringements was to conciliate; very rarely did it take legal action, and usually suggested a quiet payment of arrears with no pubic admission of wrongdoing. In cases involving the Retail Bespoke Board the ministry did not even inform workers when such an order was made, pleading the cost of the additional clerical work involved. Privately, departmental memoranda argued that publication of the arrears would create 'friction between worker and employer', particularly if the ministry had settled by compromise, without full repayment.[11]

The weakness of inspection was compounded by the many strategies open to employers to evade paying the minimum rates. A thorough study of inspection in 1923 argued that a 2 per cent inspection rate was all that could be achieved during the first ten years of the boards' jurisdiction, and that evasion was flagrant, particularly in the homeworking trades. This was made worse by the reluctance of the ministry to prosecute, the lenience of the courts, and a fear of victimisation that deterred potential witnesses.[12] There was a gradual improvement of the inspection rate during the 1920s, but, given the small size of the inspectorate, much of this increase in quantity required a further sacrifice of quality. Consequently, the system relied on the vigilance of trade unions and rival employers to report undercutting. To follow the *New Survey of London* in ascribing improving conditions in the clothing trades to the trade boards is to ignore their ramshackle inefficiency. They merely presided over and helped to smooth an industrial transition already well under way, and provided a *de facto* collective bargaining structure for the industry.[13]

Both the 1909 and 1918 Acts maintained the fiction that, as trade boards regulated industries too weakly organised to establish voluntary collective bargaining without state assistance, they were merely advisory bodies composed of individuals familiar with the interests of either capital, labour or the community. Although nominated by the organised interests within the industry, members were ministerial appointees, and final responsibility for approving and implementing their decisions rested with the Ministry of Labour. Appointed members held the balance of power, representing the public interest. Initially, the board itself was seen as filling the functions of a surrogate trade union. Gertrude Tuckwell argued that instead of merely setting minimum wage rates for the worst exploited workers, the boards should set rates for all classes of workers in an unorganised industry, 'the state to do what the unions are doing in organised trades'.[14] Herbert Gladstone echoed these views in a Cabinet memorandum on the first draft of the Sweated Industries Bill:

> Speaking generally, the idea of the Wages Board is to organize and induce agreement between the employers and employed in what are known as 'sweated trades'. The State comes in to give these scattered, unorganized and miserably poor workers a certain measure of advantage which powerful labour combinations have obtained for themselves.[15]

The main beneficiaries of anti-sweating legislation were the most difficult to organise, and representation of their interests quickly passed into the hands of other groups. The trade board was to be a substitute for independent trade unionism rather than its midwife.

The major test of the boards was the extension of the system into tailoring. Of the trades chosen under the 1909 Act this was by far the most complex and national in scale. Given the lack of organisation on both sides of the industry, the Board of Trade appointed all forty-nine members of the original Tailoring Trade Board. It argued that none of the tailoring unions had wide enough coverage to represent all the workers in the industry, and was faced by an almost complete absence of organisation on the part of employers. Twenty-two representatives were selected from each side of the industry, the remaining five 'independent' members were government nominees. The prospect of state intervention had an immediate effect on employers. In London alone they formed three organisations inside a few months; the London and District Wholesale Clothing Manufacturers' Association, the predominantly Jewish Master Tailors' Organization, and a London based association of sub-contractors, the Association of Makers of Ready-made Clothing for the Shipping Trade, which covered many of the prime targets of anti-sweating legislation in the export slop trade.[16] Organisation was far slower on the union side, in part because the existing unions were based on workers whose wages were already so high that they would not be affected by the introduction of a minimum wage.[17]

The Board of Trade retained a veto over rates set by the new board, and any manufacturer or union could protest before the new rate was implemented. After six months of discussion the new rates became obligatory. Initially confined to the wholesale and wholesale bespoke trades, the

Tailoring Trade Board was extended in 1912 to include the bespoke trade. In 1919 the complexity of setting rates in such a diverse industry was recognised when the Board was split into separate Wholesale and Wholesale Bespoke, Retail Bespoke and Costume and Mantle Boards.[18]

The first minimum rates were set during a protracted process of bargaining that lasted from the Board's first meeting in late 1910 until its final approval by the Board of Trade in August 1911. From the outset, rate setting took the form of modified collective bargaining. Tawney noted that:

> The elements of economic strength, bluff and skill in bargaining are not ruled out but merely limited by the fact that the participation of both parties in the work of the Trades Board does something to moralize economic relationships, and that the ultimate decision rests with the appointed members whose duty it is to represent the public economic conscience.[19]

The war years saw a major extension of state regulation of the tailoring trades, mainly to the benefit of the workforce. Rather than dilution and attacks on skilled males' privileges within the industry, state regulation had the effect of undermining managerial prerogatives and authority within the workplace. Instead of being fired on the spot for breaches of discipline, workers were now protected by the Munitions of War Act. Just as importantly, the Garment Workers' Union, previously confined to the factories of Leeds, amalgamated with several small London unions and began to recruit those seen previously as unorganisable.[20]

This new balance of power was formally registered with the restructuring of the boards at the end of the war. Their new role was defined in the ambitious Whitley scheme for reorganising industrial relations. Joint industrial councils were to be established in industries where organisation was already well established. Trade boards were to form the lowest rung of this edifice, a transitional stage before an industry could regulate itself without direct state involvement. The Trade Board Act of 1918 embodied this expanded vision. It increased the numbers of industries covered by boards and extended their rate-fixing powers. Instead of merely confining themselves to minimum rates they could now set rates for different grades within a trade. Consequently membership of the appropriate trade boards became far more important for trade unions. In the joint proposals of the Ministries of Reconstruction and Labour, however, the ambulance role of the trade boards remained predominant. As their wage determinations were enforced by the state, they could not be treated as normal agents of collective bargaining; the Ministry of Labour retained its veto on all rates set by the boards:

> The question of whether an Industrial Council should be formed for a given industry depends on the degree of organization achieved

by the employers and workers in the industry, whereas the question of whether a Trade Board should be established depends primarily on the rates of wages prevailing in the industry or in any part of the industry.[21]

In the aftermath of the first world war, the trade boards were expanded, both in their powers and the number of trades they covered. More importantly, however, their objective shifted from setting a minimum floor to wages: from the anti-sweating goal of the 1909 Act, the analysis now focused on broader questions of industrial organisation. If industrial conditions set insuperable obstacles to this organisation emerging spontaneously, then the state would impose a period of tutelage. Under the 1918 Trade Boards Act, the boards were seen as a first step towards modern industrial relations, on the model of mature industries such as engineering. Once this period of tutelage had been served, it was expected that the board would be replaced by a joint industrial council, a voluntary body of employers and workers, to enable a peaceful and co-operative settlement of industrial relations. Despite the changed criteria of the 1918 Act, the shift from an anti-sweating model was not immediate. The Ministry of Labour still hoped that minimum wages could be used as a lever to enforce more fundamental labour market reform.

By the end of 1921 the numbers of boards had gone from the prewar thirteen to sixty-three, and the workers covered from 500,000 to a temporary peak of 3 million. But this momentum died as minimum wage regulation came under severe attack during the postwar depression. The National Council of Employers' Organisations orchestrated resistance to the expansion of the boards to new industries, especially in the distributive sectors. This assault pulled up short when it was clear that few on either side in the manufacturing trades covered by minimum wage regulation wanted its outright abolition. Most employer critics were satisfied with minor changes in procedure: speeding up the rate-setting process, restricting ministerial discretion in extending board coverage to new areas of industry, or allowing greater regional variation in minimum rates. Attempts at abolition were repulsed by an alliance of employer groups, anxious to regulate unfair competition out of existence, and unions, aware that without state enforcement of trade board rates their influence over wage rates and conditions would vanish. James Mallon, as secretary of the TUC Trade Boards Advisory Committee, played a key role in isolating opponents of the system and meeting trade union complaints. Industrial organisation, on both sides of industry, remained dependent on the coercive powers invested in the boards.

The unions quickly recognised some of the possibilities inherent in the new stronger trade boards. Even without ambitious schemes of industrial reorganisation, it seems likely that there would have been a move away from merely setting a general minimum wage. In the case of tailoring, a general rate would be too high or too low for some occupations. The prevalence of piecework created further problems for a system based on a minimum hourly wage. As trade unions and employers negotiated minimum rates for each occupation either the trade boards' minimum would soon become irrelevant or there would be pressures to extend the system to settle differentials, including those of the skilled workers. The board would set legally enforceable minimum rates for occupations that no one had ever suggested were 'sweated'.[22]

In effect, this was a clash of rival industrial strategies. The unions saw the boards as a means of establishing the conventions of collective bargaining over the industry, protecting the position of organised workplaces from wage competition. While there was some criticism, particularly from industry, of the shift from simple anti-sweating principles, the Ministry of Labour adhered to the Whitley strategy. The boards were no longer simple safety nets for the most disadvantaged. Instead, they were instruments of reorganisation. Wages policy was to foster wider changes in capital investment and the regularisation of employment.

The differences between the ministry and producer groups soon became apparent. The first major trial of strength came during the postwar depression, when the tailoring boards succumbed to pressure for wage reductions. In April 1921 the Wholesale Mantle and Costume Manufacturers' Federation (WMCMF) and the Tailors and Garment Workers Trade Union (TGWTU) made a joint application to the Wholesale Mantle and Costume Trades Board. After lengthy negotiations they agreed to a wage reduction of two pence per hour for all male workers, and one penny for all female workers. By side voting, combining the employers' and TGWTU votes they were able to outvote the combined independent representatives, the Master Ladies' Tailors Organization (which represented the sub-contractors) and rival unions. Ministry of Labour officials responded angrily. At a meeting with Andrew Conley of the TGWTU and C.J. Healy of the WMCMF, Sir David Shackleton, from the Ministry of Labour, 'referred again to the fact that Trade Boards are established in trades for the purpose of giving workers the protection afforded by a minimum wage and not for the purpose of enabling organisations to make their agreements binding throughout any trade'.[23]

Noting the prevalence of similar practices in wholesale and men's ready-made tailoring, Humbert Wolfe, the secretary of the Office of Trade Boards within the ministry, argued that registration of the agreement would mean official connivance at the use of trade board machinery to ensure compulsory adherence to voluntary agreements by those not party to the original negotiations. He pointed with particular vehemence to the marginalisation of the role of the independent state appointees in formulating wage levels. As no one was suggesting that organisation was now at such a level that trade boards could be withdrawn without the industry sinking into its former chaos, decisions about rates could not be entrusted to the largest organisations in the industry. This met with a hostile reaction from the representatives of the industry, as employers and union warned of a mass secession of their members if the agreement was not ratified. Faced with the prospect of the obstruction of attempts to set any wage levels other than those agreed to by the Federation and the TGWTU, the Ministry backed down. Reiterating the view that, however desirable they may be in principle, voluntary agreements should not depend on the trade board for enforcement, the ministry referred the agreement back to the board to allow full consideration by minority interests. The new rates were then officially confirmed.[24]

Despite the chiding of Wolfe, this set the pattern for industrial relations within the industry. Agreements reached in private negotiations between the TGWTU and the employers' associations were then ratified and made legally enforceable by side voting on the board. Instead of a consensual instrument reflecting opinion across the industry, the trade board had become the vehicle for particular sectional interests.[25] This pattern typified trade board industries: a 1930 TUC survey found that in workshop trades covered by the Act, unions saw the boards as the key to enforcing collective bargaining, even if some warned that this reliance on the state set a bureaucratic distance between unions and their members. The boards moved from concentrating on minimum rates. Most of their energies now went on negotiating differentials throughout the trade, setting legally enforceable terms and conditions for all workers, from the highly exploited, who were the original target of regulation, to highly paid skilled workers. By the mid-1930s a TUC survey found that very few male workers were on trade board minimum rates. The old union fear that the minimum would become the standard rate had also been realised more for female than for male workers. The boards had ceased to be isolated preventative bodies and were integrated into the wider system of collective bargaining.[26]

This had immediate consequences for the women workers, who made up the vast majority of the workforce in trade board industries. Although the problems of underpaid female labour had provided the basis for the anti-sweating campaign, the trade boards subverted this objective. By the end of the 1920s there was a marked change from the optimism with which many women trade union organisers had greeted the postwar extension of the boards as 'a short cut to full organisation'.[27] For the worst-paid women workers, the decisions of the boards remained, at best, remote and weakly enforced, at worst they provided a threat to the employment of older women. As boards set differential wage rates for skilled, largely male classifications within a trade, this set a legal sanction on sexual divisions of labour. A Hat, Cap and Millinery Trade Board Order (England and Wales) confined its rates for skilled cutters, blockers and stiffeners in this predominantly female trade to 'male persons', provoking an attack that the trade boards had become 'a huge machine for awarding little more than half the male wage rate to the great majority of women workers'.[28]

Throughout the interwar years trade union strategies in the workshop trades relied upon state intervention to enforce wage agreements. In the clothing trades, the TGWTU remained in the anomalous position of never organising more than a minority of workers in the industry, yet being enmeshed in detailed collective agreements with employers concerning every branch of the industry. The weaknesses of the Office of Trades Boards inspectorate meant that much of the enforcement of minimum rates was left to the unions. In well-organised and militant workshops the legal power of the minimum rate was frequently invoked. Union criticisms of the boards could be intense when particular demands were not met, but stopped well short of a demand for abolition, calling instead for a strengthening of the inspectorate and trade union access to the firms' books.[29] A TUC survey of industries covered by trade boards in the late 1930s found that 'the Boards [in this case in boot and shoemaking] had become the sheet anchor of the various agreements of the national union'.[30] Unions remained wary of the tendency of minimum rates to become standard, but saw the boards as braking wage changes, slowing falls in slack times, but setting procedural constraints on rises when conditions improved. For most of the interwar years the boards were seen as a 'very effective weapon for maintaining rates in time of depression, a useful instrument for supplementing ordinary Trade Union efforts' and a 'safeguard when times are slack'.[31]

As this suggests, these conditions were common across a variety of workshop-based, seasonal trades. Employers led the successful push for minimum wage regulation in the furniture trades in the late 1930s by warning that 'some of the Federation have reason to fear that, unless a change in the wage position at the bottom end of the trade comes about soon, there will be a definite and spreading movement of withdrawal from Federation membership'. The main object of regulation was to 'reduce, and ultimately eliminate, the competition that is endangering the present wage standards of good Employers and the continued existence of the Federation themselves'.[32]

WAR, INDUSTRIAL CONCENTRATION AND THE FAILURE OF PLANNING

The interwar trade boards had little impact on goals of industrial restructuring, and became state-backed agents of collective bargaining. A second and, in the short term, more successful attempt at industrial restructuring was made during the second world war. The focus was on product markets (through the utility clothing scheme), on the organisation of production (through licenses on the release of raw materials, the enforced integration of rival business units and the geographical dispersion of industry), and on the labour market (through manpower controls). Again, however, although the coercive powers available to the Board of Trade and the Ministry of Labour had a short-term impact, this proved transitory. With the return of peace, and especially as rationing and production controls were eased, older labour practices reasserted themselves.

Although the immediate motive for concentration was the manpower and munitions crises of the early war years, there were wider objectives in play. In the late 1930s political attention had again focused on the industrial conditions of crowded inner cities, especially London. The *Report of the Royal Commission on the Distribution of the Industrial Population* (the Barlow Report), which was published at the outbreak of war, had pointed to the geographical imbalance of employment in London as a major strategic and economic problem, foreshadowing plans to weaken the industrial concentrations of the inner city. The concentration scheme embodied Barlow's assumptions about the need to break down regional concentrations of industry. It also contained an implicit criticism of the ethnic homogeneity of London's East End and its base in the predominance of workshop trades.[33]

At the production end, there was a radical attack on the concentration of the clothing trades in the traditional centres of workshop production – especially in the East End of London – and on the sub-contracting system. To obtain raw materials, firms were issued with 'nucleus certificates', which compelled them to combine to concentrate production in units of more than fifty employees and with not less than 75 per cent of their production being on government contracts. Workplaces employing fewer than fifty had to 'band together' to form a nucleus over this threshold. By March 1944 in the East End, 502 concentration schemes incorporated 1,227 firms, 1,436 were excluded or outside.[34] Severe restrictions were placed on firms licensed to continue outworking. They could work for no more than three principals and the nucleus firms had to submit full lists of all outworkers to the Board of Trade.[35] As with minimum wage regulation, once the Board of Trade had indicated its intentions, opposition to the concentration scheme from within the industry dissipated. Medium-sized and larger firms – the easiest targets for regulation – pressed the Board to use its full statutory powers to prevent evasion by small sub-contracting workshops.[36]

Hopes that the concentration scheme would be the basis for a new system of tripartite industrial reconstruction were soon dashed. The scheme depended on the rationing of raw materials, although, as the Board of Trade noted ruefully, the largest part of the decline of workers in London was in the end achieved 'not by the Ministry of Labour; but by the flying bomb'.[37] Once these controls were withdrawn, labour drifted back to older industrial centres and the demands of fashion-based product markets returned the industry to the seasonal fluctuations that fostered sub-contracting and work-shop production. Surveys of East End clothing manufacturers who had moved from London during the war years found that while they could draw on satisfactory pools of unskilled female labour, they had to rely on wartime regulations to force key skilled workers, especially cutters, to move from the East End. Although employers expressed themselves happy with the move, they recognised that it would be unsustainable in peacetime.[38] This set the tone for the postwar period. The physical devastation of much of the East End meant that there could be no simple return to prewar conditions. Attempts to continue the regulation of the industry and planning, however, collapsed when the coercive powers of wartime controls were removed.

These failures were carried over into the postwar years. Several sophisticated attempts to extend the tripartism of the trade boards to industrial planning – to restructure, increase capital investment and mechanise the clothing trades – were successfully resisted by both employers and unions. The Board of Trade attempted to continue the planning structures set up in the war. Working parties were created for each branch of the clothing trades, the industry was actively involved in the Anglo-American Productivity Committee, and in 1948 a Joint Development Council was established. But participation concealed a reluctance to move to implement reform. A joint committee from the clothing industry visited the United States from October to December 1949 to study methods of raising productivity. The report was favourable to a greater 'Americanisation' of the industry, but underlying this was a dose of cynicism. Throughout the visit, the delegates were reminded that 'continuation of Marshall Aid depends on how many lessons are learned regarding American productivity'. As the report was due to appear just as Congress met to consider the future of United States Marshall Aid to Britain, the drafting committee recorded: 'These points have all been born in mind in writing the report.'[39]

A better test of enthusiasm for industrial reconstruction was the unhappy history of the Clothing Development Council. The most vehement resistance came from the employer side: an extended boycott that not only destroyed the Labour scheme, but blocked three years of Conservative attempts to set up an acceptable alternative. This hostility was not unique to the clothing industry. British management viewed with great suspicion the Attlee government's attempts to improve industrial efficiency. The distinctive feature of the clothing trades, and other manufacturing sectors subject to minimum wage regulation, is that this hostility to state intervention did not extend to opposition to strengthened wages councils.[40]

The regulation of wages and industrial reconstruction again took quite different directions. Employers and unions continued to work willingly within a strengthened tripartite wage regulatory structure – as long as the forms of collective bargaining were observed. At the same time, both sides were suspicious, and the employers openly obstructive, towards any attempt to extend tripartite control from wages and conditions to the organisation of industry. A TUC report noted that the unions were 'scared stiff' of making changes in the uncertain postwar labour market. The strengthened wages councils were seen in a purely industrial relations context. They were not to be a mere 'lifebuoy' for the low paid, but the 'springboard' to improved industrial organisation, an interim step to mature collective bargaining, rather than a permanent industrial structure.[41] The key principle underlying the postwar wages councils enshrined these industrial relations functions. The councils were to set minimum rates in any industry where voluntary joint machinery was likely to break down after the war. Unlike the trade boards, the councils could extend their bargaining powers to the full gamut of industrial relations, covering hours and holidays as well as rates of pay. As Bevin argued to the Cabinet in 1944:

> if we are to avoid a collapse of the wages structure, due to a lack of effective regulation on a voluntary basis, the State must provide a means whereby stabilising wage-fixing machinery can be set-up in appropriate cases to fix up minimum remuneration.[42]

For the unions, strengthened minimum wage regulation remained far more than a measure directed against 'sub-normal wages' but was to 'fore-stall a breakdown in the voluntary machinery'. A TUC study in 1957 found that wage rates had risen faster in wages council industries than under collective bargaining.[43]

This model of wage regulation proved resilient. After 1951, when Conservative governments were elected again, there was no return to 'subsis-tence' concepts. The dominant perception was that the unions benefited more than the employers from the strengthened councils. Employers found co-operation far more difficult than did the unions. An attempt to shadow the TUC Trade Board Advisory Committee with an employer equivalent foundered on the unwillingness of firms covered by minimum wage regula-tion to share information on wage rates. Despite these apparent advantages for the unions, employers were just as keen to preserve the wages councils. The fragmented structure of the industry still played a major part in fostering this acceptance. In 1955 the Wages Councils (Employers) Consultative Council of the Federation of British Industry reported:

> The Federation is strongly of the opinion that, owing to the very large number of small firms in the industry who are not covered by the voluntary machinery, the Wages Councils should be retained to enable it to have the agreed wages and conditions made legally effective and to avoid its members being placed at a disadvantage as compared with non-members.[44]

In the paper-box trade – one of the oldest regulated industries – the employers were vehemently opposed to union sympathies for deregulation as 'many small firms could not be organised by voluntary machinery . . . it would be against the interests of both employers and employees for any change to be made'.[45]

During the 1950s there were a few half-hearted attempts by the ministry to assert its independent role as protector of unorganised workers. A 1953 survey found that of 926 workers' seats on wages councils, all but 60 were the nominees of trade unions – despite the alleged lack of effective organisation in these industries. Proposals that the Ministry of Labour should take more responsibility for the representation of unorganised workers on the wages councils failed. Although the majority of those covered were not trade union members, the ministry reported great difficulties in finding effective representatives from amongst the unorganised. It was far simpler to continue to rely on the unions to provide all of the workers' side representatives. Critics of ministry passivity ended by accepting that 'nothing is to be gained by any action likely to antagonise the unions or bring discord to the Councils'.[46]

CONCLUSIONS

Most discussion of the long British experiment with minimum wage regulation has concentrated on welfare consequences. Postwar writing has often treated the wages councils almost as a redistributive arm of the welfare state. The vehemence of the attack on the remaining wages councils under the Thatcher government, which led to their abolition in 1986, shows that this interpretation was shared by the critics of the welfare state. This identification and evaluation of trade boards and wages councils in the context of the amelioration of low pay, however, deflects attention from the main strengths and weaknesses of these institutions. From the start, there were tensions over the objectives of industrial restructuring, over using minimum wage floors to moralise industrial relations, and over the manner in which these efforts to standardise and modernise have been resisted by the industries concerned.

The implementation of the trade board system followed directions quite different from those which might be anticipated from this model. The first trade boards legislation was one in a series of only partly successful attempts to impose new industrial and employment prototypes on the unstable labour markets of the highly seasonal workshop trades. The interwar and post-second world war periods were marked by conflicts over attempts to impose rival models of industrial organisation, with attempts by the Ministry of Labour and the Board of Trade to impose new forms of regularity and discipline on highly seasonal and fragmented industries. Initially, these attempts met with apparent success: the fragmented interests within each workshop trade provided little focus for resistance. However, as they were implemented, each scheme soon lost sight of its original objectives. Relying on existing power brokers – especially trade unions based on the small minority of highly skilled workers' and employers' associations, each did little to affect the dominance of sub-contracting and fragmented workshop production.

NOTES

1 League of Nations Union, *Towards Industrial Peace: Conference at the London School of Economics, 1–4 February 1927*, P.S. King, London, 1927, p. 18.

2 J.J. Mallon and E.C.P. Lascelles, *Poverty: Yesterday and Today*, Student Christian Movement Press, London, 1930.

3 R. Davidson, 'Social intelligence and the origins of the welfare state', in R. Davidson and P. White, *Information and Government: Studies in the Dynamics of Policymaking*, University of Edinburgh Press, Edinburgh, 1988, pp. 53–5.

4 J. Morris, *Women Workers and the Sweated Trades: The Origins of Minimum Wage Legislation*, Gower, Aldershot, Hants., 1986; J. Schmiechen, *Sweated Industries and Sweated Labor: The London Clothing Trades 1860–1914*, Croom Helm, London, 1984; V. Hart, *Bound by our Constitution: Women Workers and the Minimum Wage*, Princeton University Press, Princeton, NJ, 1994.

5 Hart, *Bound by our Constitution*, p. 61.

6 R. Lowe, *Adjusting to Democracy: The Role of the Ministry of Labour in British Politics 1916–1939*, Oxford University Press, Oxford, 1986, pp. 99–105; Davidson, 'Social intelligence'.

7 N. Whiteside and J. Gillespie, 'Deconstructing unemployment: developments in Britain in the interwar years', *Economic History Review*, vol. XLIV, 1991, pp. 665–82.

8 For a more extended account of these industrial shifts, see J. Gillespie, 'Economic and political change in the East End of London during the 1920s', unpublished PhD thesis, University of Cambridge, 1984.

9 W. Addington Willis, *Trade Boards: A Practical Guide to the Operation of the Trade Boards Act*, HMSO, London, 1920, pp. 98–100. Committee Appointed to Enquire into the Workings and Effects of the Trade Boards Act (Cave Committee), *Minutes of Evidence*, HMSO, London, 1922, L.T. Hobhouse, p. 669, B.M. Power, qq. 12,890, 12,906–10.

10 Public Record Office (PRO) LAB 2/918/TB 251 (1923).

11 PRO LAB 2/899/TBM 115/13, Memo, W. Counsell, 29 June 1922; H. Wolfe, 9 June 1922.

12 D. Sells, *The British Trade Board System*, P.S. King, London, 1923, pp. 40–4.

13 H. Llewellyn Smith (ed.), *The New Survey of London Life and Labour*, P.S. King, London, 1931, vol. 2, p. 253.

14 Select Committee on Homework, *Minutes of Evidence, Parliamentary Papers* (P.P.), 1907, vol. XI, qq. 2,526–7, 2,535.

15 The Sweated Industries Bill; Cabinet Memo, February 1908, *Home Office Papers and Memos 1902–9*, British Library Bp. 2.4. See also H.A. Clegg, A. Fox, and A.F. Thompson, *A History of British Trade Unions since 1889*, Oxford University Press, Oxford, 1964, vol. I, p. 404.

16 R.H. Tawney, *The Establishment of Minimum Rates in the Tailoring Industry under the Trade Boards Act of 1909*, G. Bell, London, 1915, p. 32.

17 PRO LAB 11/223, 'Memo on the extent of trade unionism at the time of the passing of the Trade Boards Act', [October] 1913.

18 W. Rines, 'The passing of the first Tailoring Trade Board', *The Tailor and Cutter*, 30 October 1919; on the machinery of the trade boards, see F.J. Bayliss, *British Wages Councils*, Basil Blackwell, Oxford, 1962, pp. 10–11.

19 Tawney, *Establishment of Minimum Rates*, p. 35.

20 J.J. Mallon, 'Trade boards in the tailoring trade', *The Tailor and Cutter*, 27 May 1920.

21 Memo. of Ministry of Reconstruction and Ministry of Labour, 'Industrial Councils and Trades Boards, P.P., 1918, vol. XX: ii, pp. 690–1.

22 J.J. Mallon, *Trade Boards and Minimum Rates of Wages: A Paper Read Before the Manchester Statistical Society, 15 December 1920* (Manchester, 1920); G. Tuckwell, 'Trade Boards Act at the crossroads: comments on the Report of the Cave Committee', *Labour Magazine*, vol. I, 1922–3, pp. 81–2. In 1919 the Wholesale Tailoring Board set rates for all grades, including cutters: PRO LAB 2/18/TBM 149/1925, 'General Notes on the Tailoring Trade Boards'.

23 PRO LAB 2/637/TBM 106/21, Memorandum of Meeting, 14 April 1921.

24 PRO LAB 2/637/TBM 106/21, Humbert Wolfe, Memos, 22 April 1921, 23 April 1921, letter Wolfe to Secretaries, Readymade and Wholesale Bespoke Tailoring and Costume and Mantle Trades Boards, 10 May 1921.

25 Cave Committee, *Evidence*, David Little, q. 3,830. Formal agreements between the TGWTU and the Wholesale Bespoke Manufacturers included clauses that agreements were to be embodied in the Trade Board's determinations. See Labour Research Department, *Wages and Profits in the Clothing Trade*, Labour White Paper no. 50, Labour Research Department, London, 1933, p. 5; A. Conley, 'Clothing Trades Agreements and Holiday Payments', *London Trade Union Handbook*, London Trades Council, London, 1930, pp. 35–7.

26 University of Warwick Modern Records Centre (MRC) MSS 292/231.1/3 and 1/4, TUC Trade Boards Advisory Committee, 'Inquiry on the Effects of Trades Boards, Summary of Statements of Evidence'; MRC MSS 292/230.15/1, 'Current Trade Board Rates, 1 October 1936'.

27 *Woman Worker*, May 1919.

28 *Observer*, 12 April 1936.

29 PRO LAB 2/1613/ TBIA/2182.

30 See the comments of Andrew Conley, the TGWTU General Secretary and Annie Loughlin, the union's women's organiser, to the Cave Committee of Enquiry, *Evidence*, p. 632; MRC MSS 292/230.6/5, TUC Trades Boards Advisory Committee, Triennial Review, 3 May 1934.

31 MRC MSS 292/231.1/4, TUC Trade Boards Advisory Committee, 'Inquiry on the Effects of Trades Boards, Summary of Statements of Evidence', 15 April 1930.

32 MRC MSS 292/238/6, Secretary, British Furniture Trades Joint Committee to A. Shanley and A. Gossip (union leaders in the upholstery and cabinetmaking trades), 14 January 1938.

33 Royal Commission on the Distribution of the Industrial Population (Barlow Report), Cmd 6153, HMSO, London, 1939–40.

34 PRO BT 64/867, 'Memorandum on Concentration Schemes', [March 1944].

35 MRC MSS 222/CM/1/41/1, Wholesale Clothing Manufacturers Federation to Barlow, 24 February 1943.

36 MRC MSS 222/CM/1/41/1, Minutes of Joint Compensation Committee, 11 December 1942.

37 PRO BT 64/867, J.G.H. Rodgers, 'Concentration of the Clothing Industry', [July 1944].

38 D.L. Munby Papers, Tower Hamlets Library, 7/S614, Interviews for Survey of Industry and Planning in Stepney.

39 MRC MSS 222/CM/1.46, Men's Clothing Productivity Team, meeting 25 January 1950.

40 MRC MSS 222/CM/1/17, WCMF, Meeting with H. Wilson, President, Board of Trade, 13 January 1948; Board of Trade, *Proposals for a Development Council for the Clothing Industry*, HMSO, London, 1949; on the broader political context, see N. Tiratsoo and J. Tomlinson, *Industrial Efficiency and State Intervention: Labour 1939–51*, Routledge, London, 1993, ch. 4.

41 MRC MSS 292/230/3, TUC, Report of Joint Discussion between the General Council Side of the Joint Consultative Committee to the Minister of Labour and the Executive Council of the Trades Boards Advisory Council, 9 June 1944.

42 PRO PREM 4 16/6, Memorandum by Minister for Labour to War Cabinet, 16 November 1944.

43 MRC MSS 292/230.152/1, TUC Economic Committee, Minutes, 12 November 1952; MSS 200 TB/3/3/T2, Wages Councils (Employers) Consultative Committee, 'Wage applications – the Exchange of Information', 12 December 1947; MSS 292/230/3, TUC, Wages Council Advisory Committee, Minutes, 6 November 1957.

44 MRC MSS 200 TB/3/3/T2 Pt 4, Wages Councils (Employers) Consultative Committee, 'Voluntary Negotiations in Industries Covered by Wages Councils', January 1955.

45 Ibid.

46 PRO LAB 11/2817, Memo, W. Iley to C.J. Maston, 26 October 1956, J. McCarthy to W. Smith, 28 April 1955.

14

THE STATE AND THE LABOUR MARKET

Reforming employment in the public sector[1]

Noel Whiteside

INTRODUCTION

The sphere of public sector employment in Britain expanded in the course of the 1940s – thanks to the growth of state intervention, the establishment of a welfare state, the nationalisation programme. By July 1948, well over one-quarter of all civilian employees were employed – directly or indirectly – by the state.[2] At the same time, as other contributors show,[3] government became increasingly involved in the modernisation of industry, the promotion of higher productivity and the rationalisation of work practices. Pressure to rationalise employment was as severe in the state sector as anywhere else; labour shortages and the export drive required the dedication of manpower resources to manufacturing industry. Being under state control, we might expect that public sector employment would respond more readily to official policy. As the following account will show, however, the drive towards modernisation and rationalisation in the public sector met with a mixed reception and produced mixed results; resistance to change was most marked in areas with long-established and deep-rooted working conventions which came within the state's permanent purview after the war.

During the 1940s, the government had become involved in industry to an unprecedented degree: as chief purchaser (and distributor) of essential raw materials and foodstuffs; as chief customer for war goods of all types; as regulator of industrial disputes; as director of manpower through Essential Work Orders (which gave all workers so covered a guaranteed weekly wage); through the joint production committees – notably in munitions and engineering, and through the promotion of national collective bargaining. Wartime regulation served as the precedent for postwar policy, although the range and nature of government's role in industrial relations – particularly the establishment of an official framework for the determination of wages

– was strongly contested in the immediate postwar years.[4] In the event, the principle of voluntarism in industrial relations was retained as part of the foundations of Labour Party policy.[5] The war years had witnessed the creation (or revival) of fifty-six Joint Industrial (Whitley) Councils (JICs); by 1946, 175,000 shop stewards were involved in plant-level bargaining.[6] JICs for civil servants had been created during the first world war. The government was therefore following established precedent in extending the industrial council system to its new employees in the welfare services in the late 1940s. These JICs necessarily required the participation of government departments – as ostensible 'employers' (the Ministry of Health in the case of the National Health Service, the Ministry of Education for teachers, and so on).

There were, however, problems. The model for joint bargaining had been adapted from industry, where basic wage rates permitted the addition of bonus payments to reward extra effort. When productivity became a central issue in the postwar years, this type of wage incentive was not transferable to the service sector. Hence public sector earnings lagged behind private industry, stimulating demands from public sector unions. Further, contrary to appearances, new JIC mechanisms did not permit the central rationalisation of pay, grading and working practices in the public sector. The JICs governing the civil service bargained directly with the Treasury. This department, as both employer and the controller of public finance, could reconcile the potential conflict these two roles involved, setting the demands of the civil service unions into the financial constraints imposed by government expenditure. With welfare state employees, this did not happen; spending departments tended to support their unions against the Treasury. No mechanism existed for overruling a ratified JIC agreement; the Treasury could exert no direct influence to rationalise working practices, systems of grading, levels of pay between different areas of welfare employment. Unlike France, whose Treasury established central control over wages and grading of public sector employees in the immediate aftermath of the war, the British Treasury found itself driven before the wind, with no means to regulate differentials – or to control wage costs.

This chapter will explore these issues through the medium of three case studies, each illustrating the different worlds within which the public sector came to operate in the postwar years: Whitehall and local government; the newly created National Health Service (NHS); and the nationalised coal industry. Each reflects different developments: in direct state employment, in the welfare services and in nationalised industry respectively, as the British economy shifted from recession, through the war, into the postwar era of full employment. The object in each instance is to explore how government sought to standardise and rationalise the use of manpower resources and the structure of employment in areas under its control, the constraints it faced and the outcomes. But first it is necessary to provide an overview of the context within which such initiatives developed, the framework within which state management was located and full employment policy came to have its being.

THE RECONSTRUCTION ECONOMY AND ITS PROBLEMS

The objectives of the postwar Attlee governments, to make the British economy more competitive by rationalising production and raising productivity, had implications for the public as well as the private sector. Numerous official reports offered endless critiques of established production systems and labour management practices, seeking to explain the productivity gap between Britain and the United States. In the autumn of 1948, the Cabinet determined that, in this at least, employment reform and job rationalisation in the nationalised industries should prove exemplary.[7] However, this drive to modernisation and higher productivity took place in an economic situation which deserves passing mention.

The structure and nature of Britain's postwar economic situation – and its long-term consequences – is an established area of contention between economic historians. By the late 1940s, Britain had possibly the largest overseas debt incurred by any nation at any time. A substantial proportion of this debt fell within the sterling area, largely the consequence of British wartime defence expenditure in the Far East. Further, repayments to the United States were to commence two years after the cessation of hostilities. Following the aborted attempt to restore convertibility in 1947 and the reimposition of exchange controls (not totally removed until 1958), the problem of dollar shortages became translated into a problem of raw materials shortages, which threatened to restrict production and recovery. In 1945–6, industry sought to re-equip and modernise, generating an investment boom which contributed directly to the subsequent balance of payments crisis, as raw materials essential for production were imported in large quantities. In the words of Jim Tomlinson:

> The crucial point about constraints on investment in Britain in this period is that the problem was one of foreign exchange, overwhelmingly dollars, and the physical resources, such as steel, that at the margin only dollars could buy. Conversely, investment was not constrained by investment demand nor, crucially, the availability of finance to back that demand.[8]

As international suppliers of industrial equipment not requiring payment in dollars, British manufacturers were cash rich, thanks to full order books in the later 1940s. To solve the problems imposed by raw material shortages and

Britain's overseas debts, to earn dollars became vital; hence the Labour government gave top priority to the export drive following the sterling crisis of 1947.[9] Official controls allocated scarce raw materials with this priority in view, pushing the demands of domestic industry for re-equipment into second place and locating the question of productivity firmly within the context of how to get more output from old plant – which meant emphasis on changes in manpower deployment, manning levels and working practices. As the contribution made by the public sector to immediate industrial exports was viewed as marginal, so re-equipment in that sector was not necessarily given top priority. In this respect at least, British policy differed from the French, where re-equipment of the basic industries formed the main focus for reconstruction,[10] producing the chronic inflation which stimulated opposition from the United States. In Britain, by contrast, protection of sterling remained central to economic policy throughout this period, a political consensus reinforced by the support of the City of London and the Treasury until the late 1960s. Arguably, however, the main British problem was one less of low investment than of poor investment, reflecting the weaknesses in technical training[11] and managerial know-how which permeated the public as well as the private sector during these years – a conclusion with which historians from diverse perspectives seem to agree.[12]

Britain's situation was further complicated by the sterling area – a complex of countries trading in sterling which emerged with the establishment of trade protection barriers during the slump years of the 1930s. This trading bloc used common exchange rates with sterling (and therefore with each other), operating common exchange controls with the rest of the world. All reserves were held in London in sterling – an agreement involving the pooling of foreign exchange earnings. By the postwar period, therefore, these sterling balances were effectively the property of overseas governments and outstripped London's foreign reserves by a factor of around 2.5. Hence confidence in sterling was central to the viability of a substantial portion of world trade (nearly 50 per cent was still in sterling in the early 1950s), not only to financial interests in the City of London itself. The United States exerted pressure on the British government to protect sterling in its efforts to promote multilateral trade in the postwar years. This had a number of consequences. First, the convertibility of reserves into dollars was subject to collective agreement among Commonwealth countries; to allocate all such conversion to Britain's domestic reconstruction was to starve dependent countries like Ghana of desperately needed inward investment. Second, the existence of sterling balances reinforced the export drive – which offered one route through which UK debt to other sterling countries could be paid off. This pressure to relieve debt was also visible in Britain's use of counterpart funds under the Marshall Plan. Counterpart was used to pay off domestic debt; being in sterling, it could not be used to increase investment, which was dollar constrained. In contrast, France had a domestic financing problem that counterpart could help to relieve; hence, in France these funds were applied to internal investment.

The strategy adopted by the postwar Labour government of restraining re-equipment and consumption in favour of the export drive meant that home-produced capital goods were exported rather than used to retool domestic plant. Official production controls in the late 1940s operated to focus vital re-equipment on the export sector; elsewhere, the question of higher productivity focused of necessity on manpower management and working practices – which meant reappraising manning systems, grading and other working conventions. Public sector employment became central to government strategy; ministers wanted the performance here to be exemplary. The boards of nationalised industries had a statutory duty to raise productivity, joint consultative machinery already existed, national organisation was already assured.[13] However, the diversity of employments involved – ranging from Admiralty dockyards and Royal Ordnance Factories through to schools, local government and social security offices – made the imposition of central solutions problematic, not least because departments supervising non-productive employment had most difficulty in ascertaining what 'higher productivity' meant. By examining this issue in three very different contexts, the difficulties encountered by government can be revealed and its inability to achieve its objectives can be explained.

CIVIL SERVICE AND LOCAL GOVERNMENT

The reform of public administration developed in part from the analysis implicit in the Beveridge Report, in part from manpower priorities in years of chronic labour shortage. During the 1940s, the rationalisation of government employment was a question of patriotic principle as well as a means of saving public expenditure. Using a construction of administrative efficiency which emphasised centralisation and economies of scale, reform also focused on central–local relations and the introduction of uniform systems of grading, pay and promotion. Here, where central government objectives were least likely to encounter opposition, we can witness a modernisation of employment which exemplifies the type of structure and uniformity that officials sought to promote elsewhere.

In 1931, Whitehall employed around 340,000 'established' (permanent) civil servants in 100 government departments; no uniform system of grading existed. This central core was supplemented by 159,000 'unestablished' (temporary) staff, largely ex-servicemen.[14] By the early 1950s, the global number of civil servants had expanded to 720,000 (including 165,000 unestablished), thanks to the expansion of statutory responsibilities during the 1940s. During the war, automatic annual increments were introduced,

271

to reward loyalty, experience and seniority. In 1945–6, following recommendations of the Barlow Committee, extensive rationalisation resulted in the standardisation of workloads and grading for all administrative staff; the introduction of a training grade; the establishment of specific grades and career structures for scientific, technical, medical and legal personnel; and the centralisation of recruitment. In the following year, standardisation was extended to executive and clerical workers, and uniform promotion procedures were finalised.[15]

These developments were partly a response to growing recruitment problems. In 1936, nearly 6,700 candidates applied for 1,500 clerical officer vacancies; in 1954, 5,500 candidates applied for 4,300 vacancies. In 1936, over 3,000 acceptable candidates had been turned away; in 1954, only 2,500 were even considered suitable for appointment.[16] The problems of recruiting – and retaining – typists and clerical assistants were even more severe.[17] As labour surplus shifted to labour shortage, the attractions of secure employment (long the hallmark of the civil service) dwindled. Scientifically and technically qualified personnel in particular could gain better paid and more attractive employment elsewhere. The cream of this group stayed within the university system, where their rise to top positions was comparatively unimpeded. The British convention of keeping technical expertise 'on tap, not on top' remained entrenched in the civil service; recruitment to a specialist grade confined the occupant to a career in a separate hierarchy with limited promotion prospects. In spite of repeated postwar protests by the Institute of Professional Civil Servants and the reports of the Advisory Council on Scientific Policy,[18] this situation remained unchanged. A top post was only accessible if the specialist transferred to the general administrative grade. As the pay scales of the most senior scientific officers remained well below that of an Assistant Secretary, the system implicitly down-graded technical, scientific and other professional qualifications, fostering problems of recruitment and staff turnover:

> Such recruitment difficulties as existed were ascribed . . . rather to the national situation than to service conditions and civil service rates of pay were competitive up to Principal Scientific Officer level, though starting pay arrangements were not sufficiently flexible to enable adequate terms to be offered to the very best men [sic].[19]

This attitude, accepting that only the second-rate would enter government service, contrasts with the position in France, where the best qualified were recruited – as state engineers – for the top positions. It also explains some of the poor-quality investment decisions made by the British public sector in the postwar decades.

Labour shortages generated similar problems further down the scale. The 'unestablished' sector did not change much in size over this period, but it certainly changed in composition. In the 1930s, this group was composed largely of ex-servicemen eager to secure an established post because of the job security, promotion prospects and pension this offered. In the 1950s, this group was overwhelmingly made up of female part-time clerical and typing staff, where turnover was high and recruitment problematic. Working hours rose to reach 102 per fortnight during the war, only falling back to their pre-war level (88 per fortnight, but 91 in London) in 1949; lower grades were required to work longer. In 1955, overtime was costing £19.5 million per annum and the civil service staff side unions were still fighting for a five-day week.[20] For young female school-leavers, the main prewar source of recruits, the attractions of job security, paid holidays and official training facilities were outweighed by Saturday morning working, competitive examinations[21] and the restrictions of the departmental typing pool. The civil service made up the slack by recruiting older workers (aged over forty-five), a strategy explaining the falling proportion of successful candidates for clerical grades noted above.

Similar patterns are observable at local government level. An expansion in both statutory duties and numbers employed stimulated similar initiatives to rationalise procedure and the personnel who administered them. In the interwar years, local authority structures and employment practices had remained highly idiosyncratic. Sub-contracting was widespread. Although a 'fair wages' clause for government contracts had been accepted in 1909, Whitehall blocked attempts to make this obligatory in 1925. Hence, while centrally subsidised work – such as local authority housing – apparently respected established wage scales,[22] sub-contracted labour was increasingly used on local non-trading services: sewerage and road maintenance, public garden work, cleaning and laundry work in municipal hospitals and other buildings, lamplighting, navvying, refuse collection, demolition work, street cleansing and so on. This fostered job insecurity and raised the incidence of casualism.[23] In the immediate pre-war period, improving trade allowed the nascent National Union of Public Employees to secure bonus payments for anti-social hours, but full union recognition for local authority workers only appeared in the 1940s. Contrary to more recent policy trends, prewar central government opposed prevailing practices and encouraged the use of direct labour:

> The Department [Ministry of Health] has, for many years, encouraged local authorities to carry out schemes in this way [by direct labour], both for the erection of houses and the construction of roads and sewers, and a long experience indicates that those authorities which rely upon this method can do the work more cheaply and more efficiently than contractors.[24]

The notion that efficiency required direct lines of supervision and a full-time labour force predated the start of the war.

This principle underpinned the reform of local government structures in the late 1940s. Before the war, central regulation of local government employment was minimal. During the war, local statutory obligations increased as staffing levels were reduced; part-time female workers were used to release manpower for other essential services.[25] Thanks to the postwar extension of social welfare, this increased workload proved permanent; a growing proportion of local authority activity was subsidised by central government. As local government finance remained rate-based (and as property values varied in inverse proportion to the local demand for social services), the 1948 Local Government Act amended the old system of block grants to increase Exchequer subsidy to those authorities with rateable values below the national average; this stimulated central interest in local systems of labour management. In February 1949, a Local Authority Manpower Committee was created to standardise administrative practices.[26]

This committee restructured local government along common lines, rationalised central surveillance of local authority activity and standardised central–local communications between different government departments. Up to this point, some local authorities had been structured under service committees – health, housing, education – others (the larger ones) by function – works department, surveyor's department, legal department, clerk's department – with yet others a mixture between the two. Under such circumstances, standardised surveillance by the centre was impossible. In 1949, the Exchequer accepted responsibility for paying a proportion of staff costs on condition that staff complements were centrally vetted and that wages (both contract and direct labour) were in line with scales set by JICs.[27] Central supervision of local housing and health policies was simplified and reduced, with the support of local government.[28] On capital projects, manuals of guidance partly replaced inspection of plans, except in water and sewerage, where technical matters tended to traverse local authority boundaries, demanding active central co-ordination. Efforts to persuade all central government departments to handle similar projects in the same way (such as building schools, health centres, children's homes, roads) met with more limited success. The Ministry of Education insisted on managing its affairs along its own lines. Central government could use financial sanctions to force rationalisation on local authorities; there was less leverage to persuade central government departments to follow suit.

These reforms of public administration centralised authority and created pyramidal structures reminiscent of contemporary American business management. Here, structure predetermines behaviour, in compliance with a prevalent administrative convention which sees the roots of equity in uniformity. The foundations of this change were reinforced by wartime discussions on postwar reconstruction, with their emphasis on scientific administration and clear chains of command. The immediate rationale for much postwar reform was less to secure greater efficiency as such than to promote employee loyalty in a period of chronic labour shortage and to contain overall costs. Hence variation in levels of activity became absorbed through more extensive overtime with less reliance on casual employment: although casual and part-time workers were still used, these were the emergency product of recruitment problems and did not form part of the new strategy. On the contrary, these initiatives aimed to 'modernise' employment in the civil service, to reduce the incidence of casualism, to rationalise grading and pay at all levels, to reinforce career structures for public servants at the lower as well as the upper echelons. At the same time, conventional authority structures were upheld: integration of the professionally qualified remained minimal. In contrast to France, scientific or technical ability was not accepted as a sound basis for administrative judgement in postwar Britain. In the long run, this has probably undermined collective faith in the public sector more than any other factor.

THE NATIONAL HEALTH SERVICE

The NHS was a new sphere of state employment; we might expect a similar drive to create a rationalised, 'modern' labour market. However, this was not the case. Albeit in the service sector of the economy, labour management came closer to the wages council model, using wage-based incentives to meet shortages and promote efficiency.[29] This strategy helped create and perpetuate greater employment diversity than existed before the war.

During the 1930s, payment, grading and terms of employment in such public health services as existed were determined by local tradition and circumstance. The health unions, in their infancy, were unable to generate any national framework for the negotiation of employment contracts and pay scales. The voluntary hospitals were completely self-governing. By and large, here – as in the many municipal institutions and infirmaries – the lower grades were underpaid and overworked. Most hospital workers were residential; their wage rates and hours of work varied widely. Following the transfer of poor-law infirmaries to local authority control in the 1930s, it seems that hospital workers in the public sector began to work under more standardised conditions, at least in the more prosperous areas of the country where institutional health care was rationalised (such as London and Oxford). General practitioners who registered under the National Health Insurance Scheme (which covered blue-collar workers) received a centrally negotiated per capita payment for their insured patients; outside this scheme, doctors and dentists operated fee scales which fitted the local market and reflected their reputations and specialist skills. While the qualifications of most medical professionals were standardised, their remuneration and work practices were not.

The creation of the Emergency Medical Service during the war promoted standardisation of pay and conditions, the updating of training requirements and the introduction of more uniform grading. The Rushcliffe Committee in 1943 established national schemes of pay and conditions for state registered nurses, midwives and health visitors.[30] Following its establishment in 1948, the NHS continued to support this policy of standardisation; several Whitley joint industrial councils were created: for nurses, for engineering and maintenance staffs, for midwives and health visitors, for dentists, and so on.[31] This outward appearance of smooth rationality is, however, somewhat illusory and the service was fraught with internal problems. A State Registered Nurse might be employed in an NHS hospital, as an industrial nurse by the private sector, by the local authority as a school nurse or in a geriatric hospital. If the union could bid one employer up, the rest would be obliged to follow; throughout the postwar years, there was a chronic shortage of nurses. The Treasury was beset with problems in rationalising the pay demands from fast-expanding sectors of welfare employment, all seeking to attract recruits from a finite pool of young female labour. Primary school teaching, health visiting, nursing, social work, midwifery were all expanding under public sector ownership; all guarded their differentials jealously against incursions by their rivals, and in this at least their employers were as keen to maintain the attractions of their sector of the job market as were the unions themselves.[32]

The result was, unsurprisingly, wage drift; from the first (much deserved) pay rise for nurses in 1948, other professional sectors fought to re-establish previous differentials. Nor was this trend confined to female employees. Aneurin Bevan, as Minister of Health, had won the co-operation of the hospital consultants by condoning private pay beds, but this did not overcome the problems of continuing consultant shortages, on the one hand, and administrative shortages, on the other. In an attempt to flush out extra qualified labour reluctant to abandon lucrative private practice, the Ministry of Health devised part-time contracts for hospital consultants, which paid a higher rate *pro rata* than the full-time equivalent. By 1950, the numbers of part-time consultants had risen accordingly (a number of previous full-timers transferred to two part-time contracts at different hospitals). That year, 50 per cent of consultant wages in the NHS was being paid to part-time consultants, who comprised only 30 per cent of the consultants employed in the service.[33] Higher rewards for practising medicine made it very difficult for hospitals to recruit persons with appropriate medical qualifications to work as hospital administrators. Health administration was accordingly graded up. This produced a wage demand for parity from the National Association of Local Government Officers (NALGO) in 1948.[34] Again, in order to recruit dentists into the NHS, a very generous system of pay was introduced under the Spens Report in 1948. Unlike GPs, dentistry rates were based on piecework, dependent on treatments given. Costs swiftly ran out of control as there were no administrators to check the verity of dentists' claims.[35] 'The high cost of the dental service', remarked a civil servant acidly in October 1951, ' is made up very largely of the high costs of dentists.'[36] In turn, high dental remuneration stimulated discontent among GPs; the situation was salvaged only when the introduction of dental charges in 1951 reduced demand – and dental salaries – within reasonable bounds. Much of this, we should recall, was taking place in the context of a wage freeze, which held industrial earnings down between 1948 and 1950. Not surprisingly, discussions on a public sector wages policy were well underway within the Treasury by the summer of 1950.[37]

In this way, collective bargaining managed to diversify forms of employment while stimulating wage drift. The standardisation of work practices was further curtailed by agreements reached on the creation of the NHS that voluntary hospital systems of internal administration would not be changed. Here 'modernisation' of labour management was minimal. The treatment of nursing staff illustrates the point. The old system of residential employment, under strict surveillance, continued – in spite of the opposition from nurses, unions and the Treasury (the last because nurses' homes were both expensive and wasteful of potential hospital space). In a system of administration strongly reminiscent of a convent (from which tradition it was arguably derived), every hour of the nurse's day was accounted for. Allowed no privacy and with her room frequently out of bounds to any friend (male or female), the nurse was taught to regard her employment as one of 'service' and complete obedience to her superiors.[38] As nurses were not paid overtime (while domestic staff were), they were expected to take on domestic cleaning out of hours and at weekends.[39] These conditions, coupled with lower pay for residential staff, accounted for the very high wastage rate among trainee nurses during this period. In the words of their union:

> The morale of staff is low. The most glaring instance of this is seen among State Registered Nurses who are often treated like potentially delinquent children and are yet expected to undertake duties of high responsibility.[40]

To make good the constant nursing shortages, the NHS introduced part-time working, using – as with the consultants – higher *pro rata* pay to attract recruits, particularly married nurses. Part-time nurses could dictate their preferred hours of work, leaving the full-timers with the dirty jobs and the unsocial hours.[41] In geriatric and mental health nursing, where recruitment had been particularly problematic, some hospitals converted nursing work to a daily three- or four-shift basis, using 'part-time' payment schemes to attract trained staff.[42]

Even as the union was negotiating another pay rise for nurses in 1952, the Treasury, in an attempt to halt wage drift in the NHS, demanded a 5 per cent reduction in staff costs.[43] In the early 1950s, with NHS expenditure under strict surveillance, the mental institutions and hospitals for the chronic sick as well as the main general hospitals started to sub-contract more of their cleaning and laundry work in an effort to meet official targets. Service engineering and hospital maintenance were pooled in some large cities. And the incidence of part-time work among female employees – domestics as well as nursing staff – rose between 50 per cent and 70 per cent between 1948 and 1956.[44]

This combination of constrained central management, chronic labour shortages, public expenditure restrictions and national collective bargaining generated increasingly diversified systems of employment. Pay scales were established with external differentials in mind; pleas to manage public service employment along the same lines as private industry, by introducing the concept of productivity, fell on deaf ears. 'Traditionally detached from the life of the community at large', one official investigator concluded in 1948, 'the average hospital has tended to perpetuate ways of life which in the outer world have become obsolescent.'[45] Established medical convention proved immune to arguments demanding scientific analysis, prescription and planning in the construction of health service employment.[46] Hence the system remained internally idiosyncratic. We might also note how sub-contracting and part-time employment, visible from the late 1940s, spread in the early 1950s as the government reduced NHS expenditure – a development indicating that recent employment restructuring in this sector is not as novel as is sometimes supposed.

COAL INDUSTRY AND NATIONALISATION

Industrial relations and employment in the coal industry have been subject to extensive comment and analysis. The outline below necessarily focuses simply on change and continuity in work practices and the ways in which these were understood.

In the interwar years, chronic excess capacity helped generate both cartelisation and the extensive use of short-time working among miners. The 1930 Coal Mines (Reorganisation) Act reinforced the move to cartels by creating regional boards to promote rationalisation of the industry by closing down inefficient pits – apportioning output and protecting prices in the remainder. In the event, while securing the latter objectives, no progress was made on the former and the industry entered the second world war with a large number of unproductive pits still in operation and with worksharing commonplace[47] (although miners' lost time fell from an average of seven weeks per year in 1929 to five weeks in 1937).[48] Most amalgamations during the 1930s involved pits that were already profitable. By 1935, 33 per cent of undertakings employed 1 per cent of miners and 2.5 per cent of undertakings produced 45 per cent of national tonnage.[49] Investment in the industry during the 1930s was minimal – lower than during the previous decade; even the most 'modern' pits required extensive mechanisation.

As in other occupations vital to the war effort, an Essential Work Order gave the miners a minimum weekly wage and 'ring-fenced' employment in the industry; this lasted until 1950. In the face of resistance from the coal owners, the wartime Coal Production Council and Pit Production Committees (both including union representatives) sought to concentrate production. Following its creation in 1947, the National Coal Board continued this drive to rationalisation; the Plan for Coal (1950) generated a new phase in modernisation, determining output, wage scales and manning levels.[50] Throughout the 1940s and the 1950s, the demand for coal soared. And throughout this period, the industry experienced acute problems meeting its production targets.

Official concern centred on absenteeism, which apparently rose from 6.4 per cent in 1938 to 10 per cent in 1941 and to over 15 per cent after the war.[51] It was highest among unmarried face workers and underground workers: particularly among the 'Bevin boys' – conscripts sent down the pits between 1943 and 1947 – who were seen to be the root of the problem. The industry's poor reputation as an employer generated recruitment difficulties in the postwar years; those running the industry agreed that dismissals for poor attendance would only make these difficulties worse. In the context of recurring coal crises – in 1947 and 1951 – the mines became a focal point for official and unofficial inquiry, to establish the causes of the problem and effect a cure.[52]

These causes were perceived as various. As on the docks, traditional methods of raising production invoked higher piecework rates; as on the docks, young fit face workers preferred to clear a huge load in one shift and subsequently take time off than to work at a regular pace. The income tax levels for single men reduced the incentive of extra earnings, while raising the attraction of doing odd jobs away from the pits for 'cash in hand'. The introduction of a 'bonus' shift payment in 1948 in return for regular attendance raised the incidence of 'involuntary' absenteeism (a sick note excused a shift missed during the week). Coal mining virtually manufactured sickness and accidents, and the pressure for higher productivity may well have increased physical risk. However, again the strength of established working practices came through. Short-time working had long been common among face workers; work had been so scarce in the interwar years that three or four shifts in many coalfields constituted a 'good' week.[53] Again, as on the docks, the union tried to impose discipline to break traditional work systems, without much success. The Coal Board had powers to restructure pay and work conditions; it attempted to use these to promote more uniform employment. During the 1950s, the NCB moved to standardise grading by rationalising both job descriptions and day wage payment structures, to enforce national agreements, to make systems of bonus payments uniform: moves made acceptable by upgrading several thousand jobs. This did not help the basic problem. By 1960, the NCB was 'writing in' absenteeism in its coal production targets and making good any deficit by importing from overseas.[54]

While most analyses have focused on factors surrounding the pits to explain the issue of absenteesm, it may be more useful to look at the assumptions constructing 'absenteeism' itself, a perspective pursued in the conclusions below.

CONCLUSIONS

Postwar labour shortages encouraged all employers to secure workers' services on a permanent basis. The 1950s witnessed the spread of private superannuation and a variety of private welfare schemes, designed to discourage worker mobility in a seller's market and to reward loyalty to the firm. However, and contrary to what we might assume, postwar labour shortages and the drive for higher productivity did not generate extensive revision in existing systems of labour deployment. In the public sector, the one exception is the civil service itself, where official interest in minimising manpower working on administrative procedures encouraged the rationalisation of central–local relations and the extension of uniform employment at a time when the civil service was expanding rapidly. The tighter control exercised by the Treasury over the civil service establishment permitted the direct implementation of a rationalisation policy in public administration, but even here progress was curtailed by labour shortages and recruitment problems.

Elsewhere, the impact of reform on public sector employment remained more limited. In major industrial strongholds, memories of mass unemployment helped reinforce traditional work practices in areas where wage bargaining had long reflected the state of conflict between employer and employed. Established forms of labour management in the mines, as elsewhere, had relied on unemployment (or the threat of it) to reinforce work discipline. To look at the same situation another way, work-sharing had been embedded into a common morality in the tight communities surrounding the mines, to counteract employers' strategies while protecting older and more vulnerable workers – keeping in place common defences against the future return of bad times. Here, there was no established convention of the six- (or five-) day working week. Managers in the coal industry sought higher productivity through the traditional incentives of higher piece rates and bonus incentives. Output rose without much 'regularisation' of work; the best-paid workers were the worst 'absentees'. Hence the impact of nationalisation on employment presents a mixed picture; regular employment in the electricity industry and on the railways (where it had long been commonplace) expanded with their transfer to the public sector. Elsewhere, the picture was different.

Even in expanding areas of the new welfare services, employment was far from uniform. As noted in the introduction, according to time-honoured convention, the negotiation of pay and conditions remained the subject of private negotiation between employer and employed, subdivided by trade. Newly established JICs appeared centralised and rational; however, they stimulated wage drift and generated greater employment diversity than had existed before the war. Assumptions of Fordist employment structures penetrating the public sector have to be heavily modified. Closer examination reveals the persistence of diversity, in spite of many official efforts to promote uniformity in the name of modernisation, job security and higher productivity.

If the language used in the 1940s' debates about full employment is examined more closely, the roots of a dichotomy emerge. Beveridge, Cripps and many in the Labour government interpreted full employment as the elimination of waste – the absorption of slack time in productive endeavour, the means to secure higher productivity and economic growth. Advocates of reform repeatedly asserted that, in the context of guaranteed full employment and universal social protection, workers would abandon old defences against the threat of redundancy and would co-operate to ensure Britain's industrial future. Such assumptions ignored the convention that rationalisation of employment was beyond the reach of both state and law, belonging to the private sphere of collective bargaining – even in sectors where the state itself was ostensibly the employer. Further, the reformers assumed that all employment could be rationalised into regular working weeks. They overlooked the possibility that, in some sectors of heavy industry, no one could sustain a six-day week month after month indefinitely – particularly in the absence of re-equipment – even if they wanted to (and many coal face workers evidently did not). The arrival of the concept of 'absenteeism', which recurs repeatedly as a 'problem' in the NCB case study, is premised on assumptions of a working week of five or six days. No evidence suggests that any face worker in a coal mine had ever worked six shifts on a regular basis. The wartime (and postwar) situation was unprecedented. Here, the construction of full employment envisaged by Beveridge and his acolytes was quite alien. Shop-floor support for full employment translated as support for job security: the abolition of the labour market experienced in the 1930s, but not necessarily the restructuring of working practices in ways that might undermine established systems of employment protection and job control.

Hence 'short-time working' (with worker as victim) became translated into 'absenteeism' (with worker as villain) without working practices changing that much (although wage rates certainly did). The newly developed language of 'absenteeism' and 'restrictive practices' described working conventions which – to the scientific eye – impeded production unnecessarily and undermined the productivity drive. Such a perspective was born of the belief that prosperity would be raised and productivity secured through a common rationalisation of employment, as promoted by American economists and industrialists in the postwar years and strongly associated with constructions of 'scientific' management of a Taylorite kind. This language appears predominantly in observations concerning employment made from above and outside industry; it was rarely used by employers themselves – except in situations of industrial conflict, when the union rule book might be enforced more strictly than normal. The notion that work practices were 'restrictive' assumed that uniform systems of production co-ordination, derived from scientific observation, would generate greater prosperity. This language, the assumptions it embodied and the right of outsiders to intervene in industrial questions were contested by both workers and their employers. While some politically motivated trade unionists in engineering, like their French colleagues, welcomed the prospect of state direction and planning, there were many others who would have endorsed Walter Citrine's view that it was the duty of the trade union movement to limit arbitrary actions by the state and to check 'Fascist tendencies'.[55] Such suspicion of state regulation was not uncommon.

Less-politicised resistance to the new norms can also be observed among women workers. The postwar expansion in demand for young, quasi-professional female workers in the service sectors forced their state employers to accommodate their preferences. In this group, above all, the preference for part-time work is very evident, among single and married alike. While acknowledging the difficulties of running a household in 'austerity Britain', the constraints of rationing and queuing were temporary; with their demise, there is no evidence of a sudden conversion by female workers to the merits of full-time work. The high level of demand for female workers in the public sector helped promote the extension of training opportunities and the elimination of the marriage bar; while this was hardly revolutionary, it does place government service in the vanguard of a change in working conventions to accommodate its army of new recruits.

This chapter queries the assumed association between the expansion of public sector employment and the 'modernisation' of the postwar labour market; here as elsewhere, uniformity was elusive. Beveridge's ideas on full employment remained external to the labour market; lacking any path of entry into industrial bargaining – even for state employees – this official project failed. Full employment was characterised by job security, less by rationalisation. The recent genesis of a 'postmodern' labour market is best understood as the consequence of two developments: first, a changing analytical focus – away from the car factories (where, incidentally, short-time working and job insecurity still prevailed in the 1950s) and towards the clothing industries, where Fordism had never prevailed, second, workers' loss of control over their own working lives. In the postwar context, alternative work was available; shop-floor bargaining was recognised, hours and conditions were collectively negotiated. Today, the demise of union protection, high unemployment and the determination of recent governments to return public services to the private sector have reversed the situation. The 'postmodern' labour market appears little more than similarly diversified employment without the safety net of the weekly contract and fall-back wage – the product of a changed political environment at least as much as of changed economic circumstances.

NOTES

1 The author would like to thank other contributors and Jim Tomlinson for comments on an earlier draft of this chapter: the usual reservations apply.
2 Monthly Digest of Statistics, July 1948, Modern Records Centre [MRC] MSS 292 552 32(1), Warwick University.
3 See particularly contributions by N. Tiratsoo, J. Gillespie and J. Zeitlin in this volume.
4 N. Whiteside, 'Creating the welfare state in Britain, 1945–60', *Journal of Social Policy*, vol. 25, January 1996, pp. 83–103.
5 J. Tomlinson, 'A missed opportunity? Labour and the productivity problem, 1945–51', in G. Jones and M.W. Kirby (eds), *Competitiveness and the State*, Manchester University Press, Manchester, 1991. The other principles were the sovereignty of Parliament, the reform of corporate structures and economic management through consensual, tripartite negotiation. See also J. Tomlinson, *Democratic Socialism and Economic Policy*, Cambridge University Press, Cambridge, 1996, concluding chapter.
6 H. Gospel, *Markets, Firms and the Management of Labour in Modern Britain*, Cambridge University Press, Cambridge, 1992, pp. 127–9.
7 Sir Stafford Cripps, address to ministers, Public Record Office (PRO) BT 195/20.
8 J. Tomlinson, unpublished paper.
9 Stafford Cripps, in *The Economist*, 22 January 1949.
10 See M. Margaraiz, Chapter 2 in this volume.
11 See K. Burgess, Chapter 7 in this volume.
12 For example, C. Schenk, *Britain and the Sterling Area*, Routledge, London, 1994, concluding chapter; B. Alford, *Britain and the World Economy*, Longmans, London, 1996, ch. 7; C. Bean and N. Crafts, 'British economic growth since 1945', in N. Crafts and G. Toniolo (eds), *Economic Growth in Europe since 1945*, Cambridge University Press, Cambridge, 1997, ch. 6, esp. p. 161.
13 Cabinet meeting, 1 November 1948, 'Productivity in Socialised Industries', minutes: PRO BT 195/20.
14 Royal Commission on the Civil Service, 1953–5: *Report*, PP XI, 1955–6, Cmd 9613, HMSO, London, pp. 4 and 8.
15 Ibid., pp. 10–11.
16 Draft of Royal Commission report, p. 117: PRO T 182/29.
17 Ibid., pp. 121 and 123.

18 *Fifth Annual Report of the Advisory Council on Scientific Policy* (Cmd 8561), HMSO, London, 1952, para. 27; 1954, para. 56.

19 Royal Commission on the Civil Service, *Report*, p. 130.

20 Ibid., pp. 51–3.

21 Typists were initially recruited as temporaries, competing by examination for permanent posts.

22 According to a survey carried out in 1924: PRO HLG 52/56.

23 National Union of Public Employees (NUPE), Lancashire and Cheshire Whitley Council, minutes of trade union side, 1935–9: MRC MSS 281/6/1/1, 1935–41.

24 Ministry of Health, minute, 31 August 1936: PRO HLG 52/1262.

25 Ministry of Labour and National Service Appointments Department survey, 1943: PRO LAB 8/526.

26 Papers PRO HLG 52/1733.

27 Grant claims and loan sanction procedure subcommittee: note by chairman, 6 November 49: ibid.

28 First Report of the Local Government Manpower Committee, confidential print, PRO T 214/244.

29 See J. Gillespie, Chapter 13 in this volume.

30 Ministry of Health, *Report of Working Party on Recruitment and Training of Nurses*, HMSO, London, 1949; also Confederation of Health Service Employees (COHSE) papers MRC MSS 229/6/c/CO/3/2, MRC; PRO T 214/989.

31 Papers in PRO T 214.

32 For example, the nurses pay dispute, 1948–9: PRO T 214/986.

33 Meeting on Sir Cyril Jones's Report on the National Health Service, Prime Minister's room, 21 July 1950: PRO T 214/110.

34 Papers: PRO T 214/353.

35 Papers: PRO T 214/1006–7.

36 Minute: PRO T 214/1006.

37 'Wages Policy', draft paper from Hall to Bridges, 13 July 1950: PRO T 214/294.

38 J. Cohen, *Minority Report of Working Party on Recruitment and Training of Nurses*, HMSO, London, 1948, Appendix.

39 Nuffield Hospital Trust, *Report on the Work of Nurses in Hospital Wards*, (n.d.? mid-1950s): MRC MSS 229/6/C/CO/3/2.

40 Confederation of Health Service Employees (COHSE), *The Hospital Services* (1946): MRC MSS 229/6/C/CO/3/11.

41 The Ministry of Health offered 12.5 per cent *pro rata* hourly rate above the Rushcliffe scale (plus free food, laundry and uniform) to all nurses working less than a thirty-hour week in February 1947: MRC MSS 229/6/C/CO/13/7.

42 Ibid., for papers of Cheltenham Conference on Gloucestershire scheme, introduced in February 1946.

43 Papers: MRC MSS 229/6/C/CO/3/2.

44 C.Webster, *The Health Services since the War*, vol. 1, HMSO, London, 1988, p. 300.

45 Cohen, *Recruitment and Training of Nurses*, p. 47.

46 Ibid., ch. 5.

47 In 1933, formal worksharing arrangements had been negotiated in Northumberland, Durham, Yorkshire and one pit (Blaenavon) in South Wales. BT Mines Department, memo on worksharing, January 1933, PRO POWE 30/36.
48 Report on the Coal Industry (1943), Nuffield Archive, C 4/46, ch. 1, p. 25.
49 Ibid., p. 42.
50 W. Ashworth, *The History of the British Coal Industry*, vol. 5, Clarendon Press, Oxford, 1986.
51 Cabinet Committee on Voluntary Absenteeism, Report, spring 1950: PRO COAL 26/171.
52 Official files on absenteeism in the 1940s include PRO COAL 26/170–2; POWE 20/79 & 122; CAB 124/706.
53 F. Zweig, *Men in the Pits*, Gollancz, London, 1948, ch. XIV, reports a nineteenth-century study of the Northumberland and Durham coalfield which found a four-day week 'normal'.
54 Ashworth, *British Coal Industry*, 160–205.
55 Address by Norman Citrine (General Secretary of the TUC) to Nuffield Conference, March 1944, p. 24: PRO CAB 124/216.

INDEX

244; and JPCs 67–9; and productivity 105–6; and scientific management 59–60; and strike action 85; and wages (France) 181, (Britain) 261–2, 277–8; and welfare benefits (Britain) 243; *see also* industrial disputes
Trades Union Congress (TUC) 17, 55, 59–60, 105, 256, 257, 259; and youth training 152–3, 154
transport industry (France) 28–9, 33, 36–7, 41, 46, 47, 72
Trevelyan, C. 148
Truck Acts 216
Tuckwell, G. 254

unemployment 17, (Britain) 53, 106, 280, 283, (France): 168–9, 171, 171–2, 172, 175, 193–4; eradication of 194–9; as female 195; financial aid for 199–206; French response to 206–7; and job placement 198–9; juvenile 144–5, 151; notion of 15–16; and private charity/public assistance 199–201; seasonal 205; and second world war 204; and technical progress 197; *see also* contract of employment; employment; full employment; labour market
Unemployment Act (1934) 204, 217
unemployment insurance 193; in Britain 13; compulsory 202–6; in France 15–16; subsidized voluntary 201–2

vectorial auto-regressive (VAR) model 82–4, 91–2
Verret, M. 201
Vichy government 7, 41, 195, 197, 204
Villa, P. 84, 92
Vincent, L.A. 92
vocational education (Britain) 147, 152–3, 154, 156–7; *see also* management; Nancy; technical training
voluntarism 9, 17, 268

wages 13–14, (France): 84, 87, 89, 90, 100, 163, 167–74, 180–1, 187; adjustments to 163, 167–74, 175; area zoning of 172; and bonuses 180; and classification of workers 169, 174; in clothing trade (Britain) 253–9; conditions for (France) 169–70; and cost-of-living element (Britain): 243; in the docks 238, 242, 244; during first world war (France) 180–1; during second world war (Britain) 238; efficiency (France): 89, 90, 100; and family allowances 168; forecast index 170; gendering of 173, 180–1, 183–4; in iron and steel industry (Britain): 235–6, 240, 242, 244; minimum 249, 250, 253, 256–9, 261–3, (France) 180, 196; piecework/hourly rates (Britain) 114, 220, (France) 173, 180; and price rises 170; and productivity (France) 170–1; in public sector (Britain): 268; in shipbuilding 237, 242, 244; and trade boards 253–9; two-tier system 235–6; urban/rural differences (France): 172; variety of 186–7
Wages Act (1986) 250
wages councils (Britain) 18, 261–2
Wages Councils (Employers) Consultative Council 262
Weber, E. 193
Wholesale Mantle and Costume Manufacturers' Federation (WMCMF) 257
Wilson, H. 56
Wolfe, H. 257, 258
women: employment of 14–15, (Britain) 150, 153, 251, 258, 273, 274, 276, 278, 282, (France) 194–5; and wages (France) 173, 180–1, 183–4
Woollard, F. 117
work camps 197
work-study methods 114
worker delegates (France) 179–80, 181, 184